LINCOLN AND HIS PARTY
IN THE SECESSION CRISIS

LINCOLN AND HIS PARTY

IN THE

SECESSION CRISIS

BY

DAVID M. POTTER

NEW HAVEN & LONDON: YALE UNIVERSITY PRESS

20739

CONTENTS

PREFACE TO THE 1942 EDITION

THROUGHOUT the lives of Abraham Lincoln and his Republican associates, there was probably no period so vital as that interval during the winter of 1860–61 when the country wavered between union and disunion and between peace and war. Policies and decisions were far more significant at that time than either before or after.

Despite the importance of this period, there are few aspects of Lincoln's life and of the party's history which have been so neglected by historians in general. Lincoln, personally, from the time of his election until his inauguration, sought to efface himself, and he succeeded to such an extent that even history has not seriously disturbed the oblivion which he invited. The many accounts which treat of this period have been content to recount his comings and goings, and to record his utterances, without evincing any real curiosity as to what intentions and purposes occupied his mind. To say that he intended to maintain the Union is a truism, but it is inconceivable that, as he faced inauguration, his mind stopped short at a determination to maintain the Union. Such determination was the point of departure, not the terminus, of his mental processes. The problem that concerned him was how to maintain the Union. Could he save it without compromise? Could he save it without war? Could he save it by a purely negative policy, and, if not, what positive measures were required?

For a long time after the war no one really cared to know how the Republican leaders viewed the crisis late in 1860 and early in 1861. Northern apologists were content to eulogize Lincoln for striking fearlessly at disunion; Southern critics, meanwhile, castigated him for his policy of coercion. Neither advocates nor detractors were interested in the evidence that Lincoln had neither wished nor foreseen that events would go as they did.

A later generation has sought to do more than merely vindicate or indict. Accordingly, historians of the present century have cultivated a broader point of view which explains the war in terms of underlying sectional differences. At times this emphasis has obscured the great similarity, in many respects, between the Northern and Southern people, and has implicitly corroborated the traditional doctrine of an "irrepressible conflict." Consequently, there is still no account which shows why chronic antagonism became open war at the precise time when it did, or why the similarities of the people of the United States, as Americans, failed to offset their differences, as Northerners and Southerners.

To a reader who is grounded in current interpretations, the basic sectional differences preceding the war are like signposts pointing to the impending conflict. With hindsight to re-enforce this viewpoint, it is difficult to remember that the Republican leaders during the secession crisis were quite habituated to chronic antagonism which had not produced war, and that they still relied upon the centripetal force of Americanism to offset the centrifugal force of sectionalism. Whether irrepressible or not, the conflict did not seem irrepressible—in the sense of belligerency—to the Republican leaders who had coined the phrase. Once the full import of this fact is recognized, the developments of the crisis period assume a different aspect, and a vital question, not previously apparent, is brought to the fore: if Republican leaders did not perceive the imminence of war, what did they conceive the situation to be, and what did they propose to do about it? It is primarily to answer this question that I have written the chapters that follow.

The story is a long one, for the situation was constantly being modified by the development of the crisis, but two constant factors prevailed from the evening of Lincoln's election to the morning of Sumter. There was no time, throughout that period, when the Republican leaders did not look to Southern Unionism as the factor by which they would save the Union without either "appeasing" or coercing the secessionists. Nor was there any occasion during that time when Lincoln failed to exercise a decisive control over his party's policy. Seward was far more active than Lincoln, but the ultimate effect of his exertions was only to modify and elaborate Lincoln's policy. Although unaccustomed to his high position, Lincoln was prepared, from the outset, to assume the dominant rôle in shaping his party's course during the Union's severest crisis.

My acknowledgments are few, but my indebtedness is proportionately deep. The late Ulrich B. Phillips had died before I began this study, but his earlier guidance helped me in a way which only his former students can appreciate. One of those students, Professor Gerald M. Capers, now of Sophie Newcomb College, commands my gratitude for his aid when the book was in a formative stage. After it neared completion, Professor J. G. Randall of the University of Illinois read the entire manuscript. His mastery of the field enabled him to criticize it more effectively, I believe, than anyone else could have. At Yale, Professor Ralph Gabriel has been a helpful advisor and a loyal friend. Some of the most onerous parts of the production have fallen upon Professor Leonard Labaree, who has carried on as editor where he left off as advisor, and has offered unfailing assistance in both capacities.

The staffs of the Library of Congress and of the Yale University Library have given indispensable aid in making the resources of their collections available to me. The library of the Rice Institute has co-operated with me steadily. For memorable kindnesses, I am indebted to Mr. Whitman Davis, Librarian of the University of Mississippi.

Miss Ann Tuck has assisted materially in my efforts to achieve textual accuracy.

During the period of my research, Yale University aided by awarding me the Bulkley Fellowship. In an earlier form, this study was submitted as a doctoral dissertation at Yale. Later, when publication drew near, the Department of History there again provided generous assistance by its decision to include my book with those which are published with the income from the Frederick John Kingsbury Memorial Fund.

I am not sure that I am, myself, aware how much of this book is Elmer Henry Potter's. I am sure that I cannot express that part of which I am aware. Certainly it is true that, without her, there would be no book to follow this preface.

D. M. P.

Houston, Texas
March 1942

PREFACE TO THE 1962 EDITION

THIS new edition of *Lincoln and His Party in the Secession Crisis* follows twenty years after the original publication. It sobers me to realize that this is exactly the same period of time for which Rip Van Winkle was locked in sleep in a ravine in the Catskills. Will my book, after twenty years, look as outmoded among the histories written today, as Rip looked among the villagers of the early republic, and can I safely send it abroad without dressing it in the new garments of a revision?

Certainly, the historical literature on Lincoln and on the precipitation of the Civil War have witnessed even more transformation in twenty years than did Rip's village, where, despite changed appearances, life really remained very much the same. To recognize the extent of this change, it is necessary to remember something of the state of the literature in 1942. At that time the papers of Abraham Lincoln had never been opened to any writers other than the authorized biographers, John G. Nicolay and John Hay, and they were still impounded in the Library of Congress, awaiting the expiration of the twenty-one-year period which Robert Todd Lincoln had provided should elapse after his death before the papers became public (he died in 1926). The only full-scale documented account of Lincoln's presidency was the work of his personal secretaries, the same Nicolay and Hay, who had used the papers and had published their ten volumes in 1890.[1] (In saying this, I omit Sandburg's great epic which made Lincoln's War Years live again, but was hardly a history of his presidency.) The only extensive, detailed history of the crisis period was one published between 1893 and 1906

1. John G. Nicolay and John Hay, *Abraham Lincoln: A History* (10 vols. New York, Century, 1890).

by James Ford Rhodes, a man who had been twelve years old when Lincoln became President.[2] The only book devoted entirely to the policy of Northern leaders during the secession crisis was a study by an attorney in Montgomery, Alabama, who argued that Fort Sumter did not even need relief, and implied that Lincoln's claim to be acting on a letter from Major Anderson, stating the need of relief, was a fabrication, since such a letter did not exist and had probably never existed. In short, Lincoln precipitated the crisis needlessly and on deliberately false grounds.[3]

Since 1942 the flow of literature has been not only profuse but continuous. In 1947 the Lincoln Papers were at last opened to scholars. They have not yielded much data of large importance (Nicolay and Hay had combed them thoroughly), although David C. Mearns has published two volumes of selections from them.[4] The Papers also helped pave the way for a long-awaited scholarly edition

2. James Ford Rhodes, *History of the United States from the Compromise of 1850 to the Final Restoration of Home Rule in the South in 1877* (7 vols. New York, Macmillan, 1893–1906).

3. John Shipley Tilley, *Lincoln Takes Command* (Chapel Hill, University of North Carolina Press, 1941). But when the Lincoln Papers were opened, Anderson's missing letter of February 28, 1861, was found, as I had suggested that it might be (below, pp. 333–35). Also there was a report by Anderson, March 2, 1861, giving an exact inventory of commissary stores, sufficient only for six weeks. The letter alone does not show the shortage adequately without the report, and the reading of the one without the other has caused some confusion. Tilley had failed to distinguish between fresh supplies, which Anderson was permitted to buy in the Charleston market—items such as fresh vegetables—and staples, such as flour, etc., on which the supply was very low. Thus Tilley erred both in saying that there was no shortage of supplies and in suggesting that the Lincoln administration had fabricated this claim of shortage in order to cover up the aggressive nature of its policy at Sumter. Robert Anderson to War Department, February 28, 1861; Anderson, Report of Supplies, March 2, 1861; Joseph Holt, Acting Secretary of War, to Lincoln, March 5, 1861, enclosing Anderson's communications—all in the Lincoln Papers, Vol. 34, Nos. 7528–29; and Vol. 35, Nos. 7677–78 and enclosure 7664, and Nos. 7792–94. Library of Congress.

4. *The Lincoln Papers: The Story of the Collection, with Selections to July 4, 1861* (2 vols. Garden City, Doubleday, 1948).

of Lincoln's writings.[5] Before the Lincoln Papers were opened, J. G. Randall brought out, in 1945, the initial volumes of his history of Lincoln's presidency—the first full-scale scholarly study of this subject, and in 1955 this work was completed in a fourth volume, finished by Richard N. Current after Professor Randall's death.[6] In 1952 the late Benjamin P. Thomas published his one-volume biography, *Abraham Lincoln*, a masterly summary of a vast amount of scholarship.[7] In 1960 Reinhard Luthin added another, more extensive, one-volume treatment, *The Real Abraham Lincoln*.[8] All of these far surpass in scholarship the earlier works, though it is questionable whether anyone has yet sized Lincoln up with more wisdom and perception than Lord Charnwood did in 1916.[9] Meanwhile, an extraordinary profusion of good monographs has dealt with many aspects of Lincoln's career. The ones pertinent to the secession crisis include especially William E. Baringer, *A House Dividing: Lincoln as President Elect*,[10] which, however, did not go beyond the inauguration, and which emphasized the problems of the cabinet rather more than the problems of secession; and William B. Hesseltine, *Lincoln and the War Governors*,[11] which showed how the demands of the governors of the Northern States bore upon Lincoln's policy.

In the broader field of literature on the antecedents of the Civil War, again there has been a sweeping transformation. In 1942 the so-called revisionist view was just beginning to gather momentum. Avery O. Craven published his *Coming of the Civil War* in that year, and fol-

5. Roy P. Basler et al., eds., *The Collected Works of Abraham Lincoln* (8 vols. plus index, New Brunswick, Rutgers University Press, 1953–55).

6. *Lincoln the President* (4 vols. New York, Dodd, Mead, 1945–55).

7. New York, Knopf, 1952.

8. Englewood Cliffs, Prentice-Hall, 1960.

9. Godfrey Rathbone Benson, Lord Charnwood, *Abraham Lincoln* (London, Constable, 1916).

10. Springfield, the Abraham Lincoln Association, 1945.

11. New York, Knopf, 1948.

lowed it with his *Growth of Southern Nationalism, 1848–1861* in 1953 and his *Civil War in the Making, 1815–1860* in 1959.[12] I must return to the question of the relation of my own work to revisionism later in this introduction, but to continue here with this overview of the literature, the basic line of development is that Randall's work, mentioned above, as well as essays by him published in 1940,[13] also became a cornerstone of revisionism, and that Roy F. Nichols' *The Disruption of American Democracy* partook of the revisionist view without fully adopting it.[14] Since then, revisionism has come under fire from Arthur Schlesinger, Jr., Pieter Geyl, Harry V. Jaffa, and others,[15] and a considerable body of critical discussion has accumulated concerning this controversy.[16] While this dispute

12. The first of these books was published by Scribners in New York, the latter two by the Louisiana State University Press in Baton Rouge. Prior to these, Craven had begun to enunciate his views in "Coming of the War between the States: An Interpretation," *Journal of Southern History,* 2 (1936), 303–22, and in *The Repressible Conflict* (Baton Rouge, Louisiana State University Press, 1939).

13. "The Blundering Generation," *Mississippi Valley Historical Review,* 27 (1940), 3–28; "The Civil War Restudied," *Journal of Southern History,* 6 (1940), 439–57.

14. New York, Macmillan, 1948.

15. Schlesinger, "The Causes of the Civil War: A Note on Historical Sentimentalism," *Partisan Review,* 16 (1949), 469–81; Geyl, "The American Civil War and the Problem of Inevitability," translation of part of an article published in Dutch in 1949 in *New England Quarterly,* 24 (1951), 147–68; Jaffa, *Crisis of the House Divided: An Interpretation of the Issues in the Lincoln-Douglas Debates* (New York, Doubleday, 1959).

16. Howard K. Beale, "What Historians Have Said about the Causes of the Civil War," in *Theory and Practice in Historical Study,* Social Science Research Council Bulletin, 54 (New York, 1946), 55–102; Thomas J. Pressly, *Americans Interpret Their Civil War* (Princeton, Princeton University Press, 1954); Thomas N. Bonner, "Civil War Historians and the 'Needless War' Doctrine," *Journal of the History of Ideas,* 17 (1956), 193–216; Richard N. Current, *The Lincoln Nobody Knows* (New York, McGraw-Hill, 1958), chap. 4, "The Man Who Said No"; T. Harry Williams, "Lincoln and the Causes of the Civil War," in O. Fritiof Ander, ed., *Lincoln Images: Augustana College Centennial Essays* (Rock Island, Augustana College Library, 1960), 23–29; Denis W. Brogan, "A Fresh Appraisal of the Civil War," *Harpers Magazine,* 220

was raging, Allan Nevins was moving steadily ahead with a monumental history, which was neither strongly revisionist nor antirevisionist, and which gave us, in place of Rhodes' history, a massive survey of the entire crisis period, from the year 1850, using fully the vast body of information now available. Nevins' two-volume *Ordeal of the Union* came in 1947, followed by two more volumes, *The Emergence of Lincoln*, in 1950, and by a single volume, *The War for the Union: The Improvised War*, in 1959.[17] Since then, David Donald has added a contribution of importance in his *Charles Sumner and the Coming of the Civil War*, and Bruce Catton has given a detailed and illuminating account of the final crisis in his *The Coming Fury*.[18]

While these writers dealt with the question of sectional antagonism in general, others have focused intensively on the Sumter crisis in particular. Kenneth Stampp did this, first in an article, "Lincoln and the Strategy of Defense in the Crisis of 1861," in 1945, and later in a book, *And the War Came: The North and the Secession Crisis, 1860–1861*, in 1950.[19] Richard N. Current also did so, in an unpublished paper delivered at the annual meeting of the American Historical Association in 1955, and in a chapter,

---

(April 1960), 123–44; David M. Potter, "Background of the Civil War," in William H. Cartwright and Richard L. Watson, Jr., eds., *Interpreting and Teaching American History*, 31st yearbook of the National Council for the Social Studies (Washington, 1961), 87–119; Edwin C. Rozwenc, "The Present Crisis in the Historical Explanation of the Causes of the American Civil War," in his book of readings *The Causes of the American Civil War* (Boston, Heath, 1961), 225–30; Don E. Fehrenbacher, *Prelude to Greatness: Lincoln in the 1850's* (Stanford, Stanford University Press, 1962), pp. 165–72.

17. New York, Scribners.

18. Donald, published by Knopf, New York, 1960; Catton, by Doubleday, Garden City, 1961.

19. *Journal of Southern History, 11* (1945), 297–323; and Baton Rouge, Louisiana State University Press, 1950. W. A. Swanberg, *First Blood: The Story of Fort Sumter* (New York, Scribners, 1957), gives an excellent narrative of the Sumter crisis, with many rewarding insights but with almost no attention to the question of Lincoln's policy.

"The Bringer of War," in his *The Lincoln Nobody Knows*, in 1958.[20] David R. Barbee renewed the extreme Southern attacks upon Lincoln as a warmonger in an article, "The Line of Blood—Lincoln and the Coming of the War," in 1957.[21] Other writers have written criticisms, more or less extensive, concerning the views of these writers.

In the light of all this flood of new literature, it might be supposed that there is no longer place for a study of the secession crisis written in 1942. Yet, in another sense, it is surprising how little of the new evidence is really out of line with the evidence available in 1942. There are, to be sure, some changes. For instance, the late Frank Maloy Anderson has demonstrated conclusively, in my opinion, that the *Diary of a Public Man* was, if not a forgery, at least not what it purported to be;[22] and if I were writing now I would not use it as a source, as I did in Chapters 11–13. Major Robert Anderson's letter, telling of the imminent exhaustion of his supplies at Sumter has been found (see note 3, above) in the Lincoln Papers, and I would now cite it directly instead of using elaborate indirect evidence to prove its existence. The papers of Charles Francis Adams have been opened, and I would now use them in my account of developments in the Committee of Thirty-Three, and would not rely so much upon what Henry Adams reported. Yet Martin Duberman's very able biography,[23] based upon the papers, does not appreciably

20. The paper was entitled "Lincoln and Fort Sumter: An Exercise in Semantics and Historiography," delivered at Washington, December 29, 1955; for the book, see note 16, above.

21. *Tennessee Historical Quarterly, 16* (1957), 3–54.

22. *The Mystery of a Public Man: A Historical Detective Story* (Minneapolis, University of Minnesota Press, 1948). I do not mean to imply that Anderson's solution of the authorship of the diary was correct, for this is a much controverted question, but simply that he has shown that the diary was not genuine—it described interviews with Lincoln which could not have taken place at the time described.

23. *Charles Francis Adams, 1807–1886* (Boston, Houghton, Mifflin, 1961), chap. 19, "The Secession Crisis and the Committee of Thirty-Three."

alter the story, and it shows that Henry Adams was remarkably accurate. Two letters have turned up in the Lincoln papers, giving Lincoln's statements in 1863 that he had offered to evacuate Fort Sumter in 1861 if the Virginia Convention would adjourn. But I had already concluded on the basis of testimony by C. S. Morehead and John Hay that Lincoln had made such an offer (below, pp. 352–58). We have some interesting new material on Republican opposition to compromise[24] and some striking additional evidence that many Republicans did not believe that the secession threat was in earnest, and therefore that they did not really face the choice between disunion and war, and I would like to exhibit some of this material; but to do so would be merely to extend my original argument.

Where diverging views have developed on the interpretation of the events of 1861, they have resulted no less from the discovery of new evidence than from the development of conflicting interpretations of evidence which had been known for some time and which I used in my account. On the whole, I would still interpret this evidence today very largely as I did before, and I have therefore decided not to make revisions,[25] which would be rather limited if I did make them, and which would only compel thorough scholars to use both editions in order to find how far I might have altered my original position. I admire the decision of David Riesman and Reuel Denney in their 1953 revision of *The Lonely Crowd* "not . . . to take into account the criticism made of the original work, because we believed it would be more helpful to our readers to be loyal to our original errors than to try to conceal them."

At the same time, however, it would be dated indeed to reissue this book without giving some attention to the

24. Robert Gray Gunderson, *Old Gentlemen's Convention: The Washington Peace Conference of 1861* (Madison, University of Wisconsin Press, 1961).

25. The present edition follows the second printing of the first edition, which differed from the first printing only in the fact that on page 276, footnote 69, I supplied a citation which I had not been able to locate at the time of the first printing, and altered the accompanying explanation.

bearing of the scholarship of the last two decades upon it. For inasmuch as my study dealt with the coming of the Civil War, it was almost by definition controversial, and it touched upon two questions which have been the focus of sharp and extensive dispute. One of these is the question whether the Civil War could have been and should have been avoided. This, of course, is a vast problem, and in its full extent reaches back to the earliest divergence between Northern and Southern societies. In its philosophical aspects, it involves all the great questions of causation, of historical inevitability, and of determinism. Obviously my book, with its sharp focus on the events of a five-month interval, did not attempt to deal either with the broad background of sectional antagonism or with the nature of historical forces. I was working on the immediate circumstances which led to the outbreak of war at a particular time—April 1861—and not on the underlying forces of antagonism which were back of these circumstances. If my narrative helps to explain anything, it helps to explain why war came when it did; it certainly does not explain at all why North and South were antagonistic to one another at this time; nor does it measure the depth of their antagonism. In a sense, therefore, there is hardly occasion for me to discuss whether a result was unavoidable from the operation of forces which I have not examined.[26]

But I did suggest very strongly in Chapter 4 that the Crittenden Resolutions represented a possible basis for

26. This question arose at a session of the American Historical Association at St. Louis on December 29, 1956, at which Lee Benson and Thomas J. Pressly presented a paper on the topic, "Can Differences in Interpretations of the Causes of the American Civil War Be Resolved Objectively?" After analyzing writings on the Civil War by Charles W. Ramsdell, Arthur C. Cole, Louis M. Hacker, Allan Nevins, and myself, Benson and Pressly emphasized that the five authors had not arrived at the same answer. In my comment, I pointed out that the five authors had not been asking the same question. The other four were dealing with various aspects of the long-range antagonisms, while I had taken the antagonisms as given and had asked, "why does a given force (antagonism) take a given form (war) at a given time (April 1861)?"

compromise, and I presented evidence throughout that the Crittenden Plan commanded a great deal of support both in the North and in the South—so much, in fact, that if Lincoln had supported it, it might have been adopted. I still think the evidence is impressive, and I still believe that if Lincoln had supported the Compromise it might have been adopted.

This, of course, means that I believed there was a possible alternative to war in 1861. It does not mean that I regarded the crisis as an artificial one, or the sources of sectional antagonism as being in any sense superficial. It does not mean that I subscribed to the doctrine that conflict was "needless" or "repressible," for, as I asserted (below, p. 105), "the slavery issue was certain to arouse emotions which no compromise could pacify—therefore it was beyond compromise." Yet to say that the fundamental source of friction was bound to cause deep antagonism is not, I think, the same as to say that this antagonism had inevitably to take the form of armed combat, and it is certainly not the same as to say that it had to take the form of armed combat at an exact time—April 1861—no sooner, no later.

The Crittenden Compromise had many of the same qualities and the same limitations as the Compromise of 1850. The chief limitation was that it did not and could not settle the slavery question. But within this limitation, it was perhaps less heavily freighted with bones of potential controversy than the Compromise of 1850. At least, it contained no Fugitive Slave Law, and it did not hold any such built-in ambiguities as later made the formula of popular sovereignty a source of chronic conflict. Perhaps it had almost as much popular backing at the beginning of 1860 as the Compromise of 1850 commanded at the beginning of the earlier year. Perhaps, also, it would have been a stopgap, or, as some would say, a "mere stopgap." The Compromise of 1850 is now widely regarded as such a stopgap; yet there is some question whether it failed in its own provisions or whether it was undone by the repeal of the Missouri Compromise in 1854.

I am very reluctant to dismiss Crittenden's plan as a stopgap so long as we maintain a double standard on the subject of stopgaps. For our evaluation of them depends very much upon whose gaps are being stopped. Thus no *modus vivendi* with the Soviet Union can be much more than a stopgap today, given our basic disagreements with that country. But we would be prone to regard it as most praiseworthy to defer a showdown, even for as much as five years. Our attitude is not unrelated to the fact that this would assure us of five years of immunity from being killed by the Russians. It is quite true, no doubt, that if war had been averted in 1861, it would not have meant a settlement of the issues. It would only have meant an indeterminate interval of immunity from being killed by the Rebs or the Yanks, as the case may be—immunity specifically for those who were killed between 1861 and 1865. Since all of these individuals would be dead by now even if the Rebs or the Yanks had not killed them, we can afford to be very bland about how right it was that the issue was met in 1861, and was not put off. All I suggest is that historians who believe so zealously in the virtue of facing up to issues in the past ought not to believe in the expedients of peace in the present. If an interval of peace, without any fundamental solution of issues, is worth something today, it was worth something in 1861. In 1861, as today, it would be worth a great deal less than a real peace—a real settlement of the basic issues.

Those who despise the advantages of a stopgap peace will point out, of course, that the Civil War did settle the basic issues. It saved the Union, and it freed 4,000,000 slaves. Certainly this is true, and it is important. But it can hardly be said that these immense values were gained at a bargain. For every six slaves who were freed, approximately one soldier was killed; for every ten white Southerners who were held in the Union, one Yank or one Reb died.

A person is entitled to wonder whether the Southerners could not have been held and the slaves could not have been freed at a smaller per-capita cost. Certainly few would have purchased these gains at the time if they had known the price, and the mere fact that it has already been paid is not a reason for historians to let it go without questioning now.

The so-called revisionists, who have been most explicit in questioning the necessity for the war, have stressed certain themes: namely that the Republicans were quite prepared to guarantee the continued existence of slavery in all the slave states, and that the difference between what the Republicans proposed to do about slavery and what the Democrats proposed to do was not worth a war (this is, of course, very different from saying that slavery was not worth a war); that North and South had formed unreal, emotional stereotypes of one another, and that the opposing groups fought against these illusory stereotypes, rather than against one another; and that the war resulted from a breakdown of reason and would not have happened if reason had prevailed. In connection with these themes, they have been severely criticized for their moral indifference concerning slavery; for their failure to perceive that overwrought emotions and exaggerated stereotypes are the reflex rather than the cause of deep antagonisms; and for the fallacy that irrational forces are unreal forces. On all of these counts, it seems to me that revisionism is vulnerable, though it by no means follows that everyone associated with revisionism is open to these criticisms. For myself, to repeat, my study makes no attempt to analyze the long-range history of sectional antagonism, and I do not think that a compromise averting war in 1861 would have solved the basic issues or cleared up the basic problem any more than the Compromise of 1850 did. I certainly do not think the issues or the antagonisms were in any sense unreal, nor of anything less than major importance. If I believe there was an alternative course available in

1861, it is not because I am abstractly converted to the power of rationality but because the concrete evidence seems to me to show that a majority in the South did not want disunion and that a majority in the North did not want to press the question of slavery in the territories. I have discussed this evidence at length in my book, but here let me merely point out that in the election of 1860 the combined vote for Douglas and Bell in the slave states exceeded the vote for Breckinridge, and that the combined vote for Douglas, Bell, and Breckinridge in the states which stayed with the Union exceeded the vote for Lincoln. Over all, Lincoln received almost precisely the same proportion of the popular vote in 1860 that Herbert Hoover received in 1932 (39.9% and 39.6%). The evidence further seems to me to show that the Crittenden proposals commanded so much support in 1861 that if the President-elect had thrown his weight in the balance for them rather than against them, they would have been voted in Congress. If this had occurred, the fire-eating secessionists would still have resisted them bitterly, but again the evidence indicates that the fire-eaters almost failed to carry their program anyway, and if the Crittenden proposals had been thrown into the balance against them, they could hardly have gained the minimum support which they needed and which they only barely gained as it was. The Southern Unionists had beaten them in 1850 and might have done so again.

This, of course, would not have solved the ultimate problem. It would have resulted only in temporary peace. But what peace is more than temporary? Peace is essentially finite and temporal, and can be gained only by installments—not in perpetuity. Our peace with the Soviet Union for some seventeen years now has never appeared more than temporary, and indeed future historians may say that it was not worth our while to preserve such a tenuous peace. If it has any merit, it is only the merit of being better than war, and that is the merit which peace in 1861 might have had.

Along with the debate as to what policy ought to have been adopted in 1861, there is also a disagreement as to what policy actually was adopted, for there has been a spirited dispute concerning the real intent of the Lincoln administration. This brings me to the second controversial aspect of my study. My narrative emphasized the idea that Lincoln wanted peace and believed until the last moment that he might be able to preserve it. Many very able historians, like Bruce Catton, David Donald, and Allan Nevins, hold a similar view, but there are other scholars whose work must be taken very seriously who deny that Lincoln wanted peace or, if not that he wanted it, that he either expected it or thought it practicable to seek.

When I wrote in 1942, the chief exponent of this view was the late Professor Charles W. Ramsdell. Ramsdell, a Texan and a man of Southern sympathies, took a fairly clear-cut position. Lincoln, he said, was in a dilemma from which he perceived that he could escape if the Southerners "could . . . be *induced* [his italics] to attack Sumter." Therefore Lincoln deliberately "maneuvered the Confederates into firing the first shot." He adopted a "stratagem," and when Sumter was fired upon he knew that his "strategy had been completely successful." Ramsdell compared Lincoln's handling of the Sumter situation to Bismarck's handling of the Ems telegram.[27]

27. "Lincoln and Fort Sumter," *Journal of Southern History, 3* (1937), 259–88. Ramsdell placed very heavy reliance upon one piece of evidence, an entry in the diary of Orville H. Browning (see below, p. 372). In view of the extent to which he leaned on this, it is interesting that Maurice G. Baxter, *Orville H. Browning: Lincoln's Friend and Critic* (Bloomington, Indiana University Press, 1957), pp. 127–28, cites evidence that Browning was attributing to Lincoln a policy he had personally wished to see adopted, observes that "men sometimes put their own opinions in the minds of others," and concludes that "one hesitates to accept unreservedly Browning's explanation of Lincoln's action."

Professor J. G. Randall challenged this argument, and my book here challenged it also. My argument against Ramsdell's specific contentions is stated on pages 372–74. In a broader sense, a view contrary to his runs through the entire book, so I will not attempt to summarize it here.

A few years after Ramsdell's paper, Kenneth M. Stampp published another interpretation of Lincoln's policy, which was formulated in his paper entitled "Lincoln and the Strategy of Defense in 1861" and in his book *And the War Came*, both mentioned above. Stampp's argument was a subtle and balanced one, less easy to summarize than Ramsdell's, but he seemed to say first that, without really wanting war, Lincoln *expected* war—he saw it was on the way, and he prepared not to be caught at a disadvantage by its coming; and second, that without actually *inducing* (Ramsdell's word) the Confederates to start a war, Lincoln took a position to which he foresaw the Confederates would react by starting a war. In Stampp's opinion, Lincoln was quite satisfied with the outcome. Both writers spoke of Lincoln's action as a "maneuver," and Stampp spoke distinctly of Lincoln's "coercionist views," and of his policy as one of "casting coercion in the mold of defense." According to Stampp, Lincoln saw the possibilities in the situation where "the Union government could easily pretend to forego aggressive action and simulate a defensive pose." [28]

It would be a neat question to determine wherein Ramsdell and Stampp agreed, and wherein they disagreed. Certainly Ramsdell laid emphasis upon the thought that Lincoln actually desired war, while Stampp stressed the thought that he accepted it as something that could not be averted and must be handled in an advantageous way. Also, Ramsdell pictured him as scheming to provoke the Confederates to attack, while Stampp portrays him rather as taking a position which he shrewdly foresaw that they

28. *And the War Came*, p. 280; *Journal of Southern History, 11* (1945), 304, 307, 308.

would attack. But these differences sometimes blur at the edges, and to some extent both writers are saying the same things: Lincoln concluded that he could only save the Union by means of war; he perceived that it would be greatly to his advantage if the adversary did the first shooting; he therefore worked out a policy at Fort Sumter which he clearly foresaw would result in an initiation of hostilities by the Confederates; his claims of a peaceful intent merely to provision the fort were disingenuous; and when war came, he was well satisfied with the result.

The most substantial difference between Ramsdell and Stampp clearly turns not upon what they think Lincoln was doing but upon how they feel about what they think he was doing. Ramsdell, with his Southern sympathies, was shocked and disapproving. Stampp, on the contrary, with solidly Northern sympathies, says in effect that the War was worth what it cost, that it had to be, and that Lincoln is to be admired for putting his adversaries in the wrong and for facing up to the situation without shirking it.[29]

Professor Stampp is a most resourceful scholar, and so is Richard N. Current, who has to some extent associated himself with Stampp's position.[30] They make an impressive presentation. For instance, Stampp adduces a very strong argument that Lincoln must have known that war was likely to result from sending provisions to Sumter. He knew that the Confederates had fired on the *Star of the West* when it brought provisions; members of the cabinet told him plainly that the sending of provisions would result in war; and, as Current emphasizes, his special emissary to Charleston, Stephen A. Hurlbut, reported to

29. "If that step [the Sumter expedition] precipitated hostilities, one cannot indict Lincoln for taking it unless one challenges the universal standards of 'practical' statesmanship and the whole concept of 'national interest.' This was a thing worth fighting for! If Lincoln was no pacifist, neither were his contemporaries, North and South. Southern leaders must share with him the responsibility for a resort to force. They too preferred war to submission." *And the War Came,* p. 286.

30. See above, notes 16 and 19.

him on March 17 that any attempt to send provisions would result in war.

It is certainly true, as Stampp and Current contend, that Lincoln must have seen the likelihood of war, and that his thought must have reckoned with that contingency. I now believe that I should have recognized this fact more clearly and explicitly than I did, and if I were rewriting my account now, I would do so. But for reasons which I will indicate further on, it seems to me that, whatever other effects his recognition of the increasing likelihood of war may have had upon Lincoln, it did not cause him to deviate a single step from a course of action which can be precisely defined. This course was to avoid any menacing action or any action which might precipitate a clash, just as far as was possible consistently with maintaining the principle of Union. As I have argued at some length (below, pp. 323–29), Lincoln pointedly refrained from the exercise of all the customary forms of federal authority in the seceded states, any of which he would have been perfectly justified in asserting.

Not all of Stampp's and Current's arguments seem to me as convincing as their demonstration that Lincoln must have realized the increasing likelihood of war. For instance, they have made very detailed computations to discredit Lincoln's statement in his message to Congress in July 1861 that he had decided upon sending the final expedition to Fort Sumter only after his attempt to reinforce Fort Pickens had failed. He stated that he had wanted to demonstrate, by the reinforcement of Pickens, "a clear indication of policy," and that if he had been able to do this it would have "better enable[d] the country to accept the evacuation of Fort Sumter as a military necessity." [31] Stampp's analysis emphasizes, quite correctly, that Lincoln had certainly ordered the Sumter expedition prepared before he learned that the reinforcement of Pickens had

31. Lincoln, Message to Congress, July 4, 1861, in Basler, ed., *Works of Lincoln*, *4*, 424.

miscarried. It also emphasizes the even more important points that Lincoln had actually gone to the length of ordering the expedition to move, and of sending word to Major Anderson that it would move. But it is crucial that the evidence still indicates that Lincoln did not inform the Governor of South Carolina that the Sumter expedition would be sent until exactly the time when news reached Washington that the orders of March 11 for the reinforcing of Pickens had not been carried out. This news left Pensacola on April 1 and arrived at Washington on April 6, the same day on which Lincoln's message to the Governor of South Carolina was sent.[32] The labored nature of Stampp's and Current's arguments on this point makes it all the more striking that they have found the essential point unassailable: the one irrevocable step, the message to the Governor, was taken on the very day when news arrived of the failure to reinforce Pickens. The first ships of the Sumter expedition did not leave port until two days later.

The assertions, therefore, that Lincoln's later statement about this matter is "scarcely consistent with the known facts" and that "the President had dealt with Sumter and Pickens as separate problems" seem to me arbitrary and insufficiently proved.[33] Also it seems unsatisfactory to say that Lincoln did not need to wait for news of the reinforcement of Pickens, since he "had no reason to doubt that his order would be executed." [34] In fact, his order instructed Union troops to occupy a position which he knew that Confederate forces might try to prevent them from oc-

32. For the date and circumstances of the arrival of the message from Fort Pickens see *Official Records of the Union and Confederate Navies*, 1st ser. *4* (1896), 110; Howard K. Beale, ed., *Diary of Gideon Welles* (3 vols. New York, Norton, 1960), *1*, 29; and Nevins, *The War for the Union: The Improvised War*, p. 65, note 58. The first ships of the Sumter expedition sailed on April 8. In view of this fact, it seems quite untenable to argue that an irrevocable step had been taken as early as April 4.

33. *And the War Came*, pp. 283, 284.

34. Ibid., p. 283.

cupying, and he had very real reason to await the result with anxiety. And, of course, his order was not executed, though the Fort was later reinforced.

Another case in point is the question of Lincoln's offer to the Virginians to evacuate Fort Sumter if they would adjourn the Virginia Convention. Historians have fallen into an endless dispute over the insoluble question whether Lincoln made such an offer to John B. Baldwin. But this focus upon Baldwin is unfortunate, for the testimony of Governor Morehead of Kentucky and of John Hay, reporting the statement of Lincoln himself, has long given evidence that Lincoln did propose to the Border State men terms on which he would abandon the Fort (see below, pp. 352–58). Since the opening of the Lincoln Papers, new evidence in the form of a letter from George Plumer Smith to John Hay on January 9, 1863, asking Hay to secure Lincoln's confirmation of the fact that Lincoln had told him (Smith) of the offer to Baldwin, and a reply from Hay to Smith on January 10 giving this confirmation, tend to corroborate this further. Professor Stampp deals with this evidence by doubting that Lincoln "seriously expected the Virginians to accept the offer," and Professor Current by saying that "these letters, it seems to me, by no means settle the controversy as to whether Lincoln actually made an offer to give up the fort." [35]

There is certainly a substantial amount of evidence, whether it is conclusive or not, both in general terms and in specific terms, that Lincoln thought, until very late in the crisis, if not until the end, that he could achieve both peace and Union and would not have to choose between them. In this connection it is important to remember how consistently the Republicans had ridiculed all threats of secession, and how much they were the captives of their own mental set when secession came. In the light of this mental set, it is not really necessary to attribute such adroit hidden purposes as Stampp attributes to Lincoln

35. Ibid., p. 275; *The Lincoln Nobody Knows,* p. 297.

in explaining his statement that "there is no crisis but an artificial one." [36]

It is also important to remember that in some respects the secession movement, as of March 1861, had failed and that Seward, at least, regarded it as a failure. Eight slave states were still in the Union; only seven had seceded. The secessionists had been beaten in Virginia, North Carolina, Tennessee, Arkansas, and Missouri, and the efforts to create a united South had divided the South as never before.

Another point which it is essential to keep in view if Lincoln's thinking is to be understood is that the President-elect made all his calculations, until March 5, on the assumption that Major Anderson's position at Fort Sumter was secure and that the existing status could continue for some time without any positive action on the part of the new administration. Not until March 5 did Secretary Holt and General Scott confront him with the news that a decision would have to be made at once either to abandon Fort Sumter or to take positive action for the support of the Fort.

Without being repetitious about evidence which is discussed more fully in the main body of this work, I would argue also that there are several items of evidence which indicate that Lincoln did quite seriously consider the evacuation of Fort Sumter. For instance: the fact that he made overtures to the Virginians about this possibility; the fact that Seward expected evacuation with enough confidence to make promises to the Confederates, based upon the expectation; the fact that Trumbull feared evacuation enough to introduce monitory resolutions in the Senate reminding the new head of the Republican party of his duty "to hold and protect the public property." Could these things have happened if the idea of evacuation had not seemed very much a reality?

The dispute concerning evidence, however, could go on

36. *Journal of Southern History, 11* (1945), 310.

endlessly for two reasons. First, because there were large factors working toward war and large factors working for peace, and both left a substantial residue of evidence. Thus one can marshal extensive material to show the magnitude of the demands upon Lincoln to hold Sumter or the extent of the pressure upon him to evacuate the Fort. Applying this ambivalence to Lincoln's own situation, one can legitimately stress his seeming expectation in March that he would abandon Sumter, or one can with equal validity emphasize the deep reluctance with which he arrived at this expectation. The historian can show that many of Lincoln's contemporaries regarded the first inaugural address as a threat of coercion, or he can show that many others thought it was too mild and was a promise of peace. That this disagreement continues is evident from the fact that, in our own time, Stampp sees it primarily as a statement "in which he [Lincoln] took such enormous pains to absolve himself from the charge of aggression," while Allan Nevins sees it as "one long plea for patience, forebearance, and the avoidance of rash action," and Roy F. Nichols calls it "a stirring plea to avoid hostilities." [37]

A second reason that the review of evidence can never be conclusive is that the dispute turns not only upon what Lincoln did but upon what he thought. In other words, it is a question of motive as well as of action. Motive lies to a considerable extent beyond historical proof, partly because historical judgments must depend upon acts, and the same act may be performed with diverse motives by different persons. Thus a man may perform an act which is honest in its effect because he is an honest man on principle, or because he wants whatever policy will prove most advantageous to him and he believes that honesty is the best policy. This example is not far from the point at issue here, for essentially I am arguing that Lincoln followed a

37. *And the War Came,* p. 203; Nevins, *The War for the Union: The Improvised War,* p. 58; Nichols, *The Stakes of Power, 1845–1877* (New York, Hill and Wang, 1961), p. 94.

peaceable-seeming course because he was a peaceable man who wanted peace and thought he could attain it. Stampp and Current are essentially arguing that he wanted an effective policy, knew that a peaceable-seeming policy would be most effective, and therefore took care to make his policy appear peaceable, though there was a covert element of coercion and of aggressiveness in it. They contend that he did not really mind fighting a war to protect the national interest.

If motive cannot be accurately determined, there will always be room both for the beliefs that Lincoln's purposes were peaceable or, alternatively, that the peaceable appearance of his position cloaked a purpose far from pacific. But if the question of motive must, by its very nature, be forever open to doubt, it becomes doubly important to turn back to the question of actions. At this level, the historian faces a different problem: given Lincoln's determination to save the Union, and given his belief that the loss of Fort Sumter, without being sure of Fort Pickens, would make it impossible to save the Union, could he have followed any more peaceable course than he did? Was there any possible means of holding Sumter that would have been less provocative than informing the Confederates that "an attempt will be made to supply Fort Sumter with provisions only and that if such attempt be not resisted, no effort to throw in men, arms, or ammunition will be made, without further notice or [except] in case of an attack upon the Fort." [38] The existence of such an alternative and the demonstration that Lincoln rejected it is essential to any argument that Lincoln was not following the most peaceable course available to him.

Unless the historians who charge Lincoln with coercive or covertly aggressive policies can name a less provocative course that he might have followed, they are in the curious position of arguing that a man may pursue a course which

38. Orders of Lincoln to Robert S. Chew, April 6, 1861, in Basler, ed., *Works of Lincoln, 4,* 323.

offers the maximum possibility of peace and may at the same time be open to the accusation of scheming to bring about war.

If the very nature of human motivation is such that no one can ever say categorically whether Lincoln's purposes were peaceable, perhaps it is more nearly possible to say categorically whether his course of action was peaceable. Here the crucial fact is that no one who attributes to him a purpose to see that the war got started in a way that would be advantageous to him has yet said what else he could have done that would have been more peaceable than what he did, given his purpose not to abandon the principle of Union.

No doubt he must have recognized that war might ensue; no doubt he must have seen that if it did ensue, it would come in a way disadvantageous to the Confederacy; no doubt he was glad this was true. But when we say this, we are back in the realm of motive again. If we confine ourselves to scrutinizing his overt course, the question persists: what could he have done that would have been more peaceable? Two outstanding scholars have defined this point well. J. G. Randall stated it with superb precision when he wrote: "To say that Lincoln meant that the first shot would be fired by the other side, *if a first shot was fired* [Randall's italics], is by no means the equivalent of saying that he deliberately maneuvered to have the shot fired. This distinction is fundamental." Allan Nevins stated it with wonderful force when he said: " 'In your hands, not mine,' he [Lincoln] had told Southerners, 'lies the issue of peace or war.' The shells that burst over a Federal fort awaiting a victualizing expedition which had orders not to fire unless it was fired upon, gave the answer to that statement." [39]

39. For the Randall quotation see below, p. 374, note 89; Nevins, *The War for the Union: The Improvised War*, p. 74.

Los Altos Hills, California
March 1962

LINCOLN AND HIS PARTY
IN THE SECESSION CRISIS

CHAPTER I

THE SHOPWORN THREAT OF SECESSION

D URING the summer of 1851, in the upcountry of
South Carolina, the obscure editor of a weekly
journal wrote a brief history of the beginning of
the American Civil War. In a statement designed to fix
the blame even as it predicted the event, he declared: "We
will secede. . . . The first assault will be made upon us
by the Federal Government by the act of retaining the
Forts about Charleston. *This will be war.*"[1] This singular
prediction went the way of all rural editorials, and for
almost a decade the forts around Charleston were
neglected, save for the perfunctory attentions of a drowsy
War Department.

But if the warning as to the forts perished, the warning
as to secession did not. Minority groups had already used
the threat of secession, and as time passed it was to become
more and more familiar to a public whose chief diversion
was politics. A series of the most able writers—John Taylor of Caroline, Spencer Roane, John C. Calhoun, Abel P.
Upshur, St. George Tucker[2]—elaborated the doctrines of
state sovereignty in such a form as to make them readily
available for political use; and when passions began to run
high after the war with Mexico, the threat of secession
became a standard minority weapon. If it was not used
in presidential elections, this was only because parties
contrived to straddle the sectional issue and to present
tickets which were not wholly obnoxious to either North or
South.

In 1856, however, sectionalism approached its climax;

1. Camden [S. C.] *Southern Republic,* July 5, 1851, C. A. Price, editor.
From photostat in possession of the late Ulrich B. Phillips.
2. Jesse T. Carpenter, *The South as a Conscious Minority, 1789–1861*
(New York, 1930), pp. 200–213.

for the first time in history, the free states gave a plurality of their popular votes for a candidate who carried scarcely one-tenth of one per cent of the votes in the slave states. In the campaign preceding this result, Republicans assailed slavery as a "relic of barbarism" and pledged themselves to exclude it from all Federal territories. In response to this, Southern Democrats did not hesitate to advance their minority weapon: domination by one section would be met by the secession of the other. On this point, they showed surprising unanimity. Robert Toombs wrote, "The election of Frémont would be the end of the Union, and ought to be."[3] John Slidell, James M. Mason, Henry A. Wise, Andrew P. Butler, and many others were equally unequivocal.[4] It is true that Sam Houston and John Bell repudiated these threats, as did the New Orleans *Picayune* and *Daily Bee*,[5] but still the New York *Times* was able to say, "The Southern press, of every political shade of opinion, with hardly an exception, threatens disunion in the event of defeat in the present contest for the presidency."[6]

Whether these threats were sincere or not, they were found to have excellent persuasive powers. In the North, in fact, the chief Democratic argument was that the maintenance of the Union depended upon Buchanan's election.[7] This reasoning rallied to his cause Rufus Choate[8]

3. Letter of Toombs, July 8, 1856, in New York *Tribune*, Aug. 13, 1856, quoted in James Ford Rhodes, *History of the United States from the Compromise of 1850 to the Final Restoration of Home Rule at the South in 1877* (New York, 1914), II, 204–205.

4. Rhodes, *Hist. of U. S.*, II, 204–206, has an excellent discussion, with full citations. In addition see Loring Moody, *The Destruction of Republicanism the Object of the Rebellion* (Boston, 1863), p. 11; Virginia Mason, *The Public Life and Diplomatic Correspondence of James M. Mason* (Roanoke, 1903), pp. 117–118; Barton H. Wise, *Life of Henry A. Wise of Virginia, 1806–76* (New York, 1899), pp. 209–210.

5. Rhodes, *Hist. of U. S.*, II, 205.

6. New York *Times*, Aug. 29, 1856, quoted by Rhodes, *Hist. of U. S.*, II, 205.

7. Buchanan to Nahum Capen, Aug. 27, 1856, in John Bassett Moore, editor, *The Works of James Buchanan* (Philadelphia, 1908–1911), X, 88.

8. Campaign Pamphlet, "The Old Line Whigs for Buchanan, Letters of Rufus Choate and George T. Curtis of Massachusetts," p. 1.

and many other Whigs, including a son of Henry Clay.[9] These accessions to the Democratic ranks were of vital importance in such hotly contested states as Pennsylvania. When the final returns of November 4 carried Buchanan safely to victory, it must have occurred to even the most abstract of secessionists that the doctrine was far more than a constitutional theory; it was an effective vote-winning formula when used on the stump.

Whether or not Southerners distinguished between the threat of secession as a campaign device and the actual use of secession as a minority safeguard, they invoked it again in 1860, perhaps more freely than ever before. Long use had by now made the doctrine orthodox throughout the South; constant reiteration had enabled every politician to master the theory of secession; and continued practice at sectional debate had made Southern advocates "quick on the draw" with this weapon. Furthermore, John Brown's raid in the autumn of 1859, and the turbulent sessions of an unorganized House of Representatives in the following winter, had kept the disunion issue at white heat. Thus when Lincoln was nominated the secession cry did not have to be revived—it was merely transferred; and the strategy which had halted John Sherman's attempt to become Speaker was now applied to prevent Lincoln from capturing the presidency.

Secession threats had been made freely in 1856, and although the individual utterances of 1860 were scarcely more numerous, they seemed "more grave and sincere."[10] Also, they were issued much earlier, before the campaigning actually began, and thus they took on the status of solemn notices, given deliberately, rather than mere cam-

9. Campaign Pamphlets, "Old Line Whigs for Buchanan and Breckinridge, Hon. James Alfred Pearce and Hon. Thomas G. Pratt to the Whigs of Maryland. Speeches of Hon. J. W. Chrisfield of Maryland and Hon. James B. Clay of Kentucky," pp. 14–15; "Buchanan and Breckinridge, The Democratic Handbook," compiled by Mich. W. Cluskey of Washington City, D. C., pp. 26–27; "The Real Issue, Union or Disunion. Letter of Hon. S[amuel] S. Marshall on the Parties and Politics of the Day," p. 25.

10. Rhodes, *Hist. of U. S.*, II, 487.

paign ruses, resorted to in the heat of partisan combat. Jefferson Davis, a full ten months before the nomination of Lincoln, made his declaration: "For myself, I say, as I said on a former occasion, in the contingency of the election of a President on the platform of Mr. Seward's Rochester Speech,[11] let the Union be dissolved."[12] Robert Toombs, in much more impassioned language, cried: "Freemen of Georgia, redeem your pledge. . . . Your honor is involved; your faith is plighted. I know you feel a stain as a wound; your peace, your social system, your firesides are involved. Never permit this Federal Government to pass into the traitorous hands of the Black Republican party."[13] In addition to these leaders, many lesser lights took up the cry. Clingman from North Carolina, Hammond and Orr from South Carolina, Iverson, as well as Toombs, from Georgia, Moore and Curry of Alabama, Reuben Davis and Governor McRae of Mississippi, and, by plain implication, Slidell of Louisiana, were agreed in considering Republican victory a proper cause for secession.[14] The list might be lengthened indefinitely. Parson Brownlow enumerated twenty-six eminent secessionists;[15] Henry Wilson counted almost as many more.[16] According

11. In this speech, Seward popularized his phrase, "the irrepressible conflict."

12. Speech of Davis, July 6, 1859, in Dunbar Rowland, editor, *Jefferson Davis, Constitutionalist* (Jackson, 1923), IV, 87.

13. Speech of Toombs in the Senate, Jan. 24, 1860, in *Congressional Globe* (hereafter cited as *Cong. Globe*), 36th Cong., 1st sess., appendix, pp. 88–93.

14. See a collection of quotations by Senator Clark of N. H. in *Cong. Globe,* 36th Cong., 1st sess., pp. 840–841. For Hammond and Orr, see Rhodes, *Hist. of U. S.,* II, 490, with citations; for Slidell, address to Fellow-Citizens of Louisiana, Sep. 25, 1860, in New Orleans *Weekly Delta,* Oct. 6, 1860, quoted by James Kimmins Greer, "Louisiana Politics, 1845–61," in *Louisiana Historical Quarterly,* XIII (1930), 479. "Unless some great, and . . . unexpected revolution shall take place in the sentiment of . . . the free States, we can not with safety and honor continue the connection much longer."

15. Speech of Parson Brownlow, Oct., 1860, in William Gannaway Brownlow, *Sketches of the Rise, Progress and Decline of Secession* (Philadelphia, 1862), pp. 200–201.

16. See pamphlet, "Tribune Tract no. 2, Democratic Leaders for Disunion. Speech of Hon. Henry Wilson of Mass., delivered in the Senate . . . Jan. 25, 1860." Also in *Cong. Globe,* 36th Cong., 1st sess., pp. 568–576.

to Dumond, "Every governor but one and virtually every senator and representative in Congress from the seven states of the lower South was on record as favoring secession in the event of Republican victory.[17]

Such unanimity among the politicians was also reflected in the press. The organs of the ultra party, and especially the Charleston *Mercury*, damned the Union unsparingly throughout the campaign. The Richmond *Enquirer* declared that there was no odium in the charge of disunion, if it were made conditional upon the triumph of Republican principles. And the more conservative sheets, while deploring the secession threat, were quick to admit its potency. The Nashville *Patriot* was "clear in the conviction that it [Lincoln's election] will lead to a direct attempt to dissolve the government," and that "war to the knife" would ensue; the Louisville *Journal* likewise foresaw "a settled and widely-extended purpose to break up the Union if a Republican shall be elected to the Presidency." Even when there were no specific warnings, the idea was implicit. Every journal used the same basic argument—namely, that the voters should concentrate on the editor's candidate (be he Bell, Douglas, or Breckinridge) because that candidate alone could offer effective opposition to Lincoln, whose defeat was essential to the safety of the Union. This point was sometimes not emphasized, but always it was implicit as a basic part of the argument. This tendency to assume it as a premise, rather than to defend it as a conclusion, was a more serious evidence of danger than any amount of rant and gesticulation.[18]

17. Dwight Lowell Dumond, *The Secession Movement, 1860–1861* (New York, 1931), p. 99.

18. Dwight Lowell Dumond, editor, *Southern Editorials on Secession* (New York, 1931), contains excellent and extensive specimens of newspaper opinion from Jan., 1860 to May, 1861. My quotations are from the editorials of the Charleston *Mercury*, July 25, 1860 (p. 151); the Richmond *Enquirer*, July 10 (p. 141); the Daily Nashville *Patriot*, July 25, Oct. 13 (pp. 148, 190); and the Louisville *Daily Journal*, Aug. 13 (p. 159). The implicit assumption that Republican victory would cause a crisis is found in the New Orleans *Bee*, Jan. 18; Louisville *Daily Courier*, May 26; Richmond *Semi-Weekly Examiner*, June 1; Columbia *Daily South Carolinian*, Aug. 3; Weekly Montgomery *Confederation*, Aug.

In addition to these warnings from the politicians and the press, there were other and more conclusive proofs that feeling was much deeper than it had been in '56. One of these evidences was the general diffusion of the disunion feeling through the Bell, Douglas and Breckinridge parties in 1860, as compared with its concentration in the Democratic camp four years earlier, when the Fillmore party had been whole-hearted in its Unionism. The Douglas and Bell groups both wished to appear to the nation as thoroughly loyalist, and accordingly they sought to conceal the mental reservations of their Southern adherents. Thus Miles Taylor, manager for Douglas in the South, ventured to use the slogan, "Thank God no disunionist sustains Stephen A. Douglas." For a time this boast held good, although some of the converts to Unionism were suspiciously fresh from the ranks of secession; but at last the Atlanta *Confederacy*, a Douglas paper, spoiled the whole pretense by declaiming its intent to pave Pennsylvania Avenue ten fathoms deep with mangled bodies rather than submit to the inauguration of Lincoln. The Bell element was not embarrassed by any defection as spectacular as this one, but its adherents also expressed a distinct unwillingness to sit down with the Republicans at the head of the table. Benjamin H. Hill, the leading Constitutional Unionist of Georgia, thought that if Lincoln were elected, "the fact will turn out to be . . . that this Government and Black Republicanism cannot live together," and the New Orleans *Crescent* was very explicit in pointing out that its Unionism did not bind it "to . . . submit patiently to every indignity that may be offered."[19] In short, all parties at the South were agreed in either threatening to leave or reserving the right to leave a government administered by Republicans.

Far more ominous than speeches and editorials, how-

17; Augusta *Daily Chronicle and Sentinel,* Oct. 10; Nashville *Union and American,* Oct. 12; New Orleans *Daily True Delta,* Oct. 13; New Orleans *Daily Crescent,* Oct. 13; Augusta *Daily Constitutionalist,* Nov. 3.

19. Dumond, *Secession Movement,* pp. 103–107, with full citations.

ever, was the action of Southern state legislatures. There had been nothing comparable to this in 1856. At that time no effort had been made to devise a program of Southern action except by hot-headed Governor Wise of Virginia, who failed miserably in an attempt to secure an informal conference of state governors.[20] The change in temper by 1860 was indicated by the fact that three of the Southern states took formal legislative measures preparatory to action in the event of a Republican victory. The first of these states, characteristically, was South Carolina. When her legislature met in 1859, Governor Gist, in his message, warned that "The election of a black Republican President will settle the question of our safety in the Union; and although the forms of the Constitution may be complied with, its vital principle will be extinguished, and the South must consent to occupy an inferior and degrading position, or seek new safeguards for her future security."[21] In response to this message the legislature passed resolutions which made John Brown's raid their chief cause of complaint, but which were certainly intended to provide for action in the event of a Republican triumph. By these resolutions, Carolina announced her "deliberate judgment . . . that the slave-holding States should immediately meet together to concert measures for united action," and urged these states to appoint delegates for such a meeting.[22]

Mississippi was the only state which joined in the conference movement. Her legislature seized upon the South Carolina proposal, and by formal resolutions declared the coming election to be the crucial issue. These resolutions of February 10, 1860, asserted that: "the election of a President of the United States by the votes of one section of the Union only, on the ground that there exists an irreconcilable conflict between the two sections . . . and

20. Wise, *Wise*, pp. 209–210.

21. Henry D. Capers, *The Life and Times of C. G. Memminger* (Richmond, 1893), p. 241.

22. Text of resolutions in *ibid.*, pp. 241–242. They passed the General Assembly unanimously on Dec. 22, 1859, *ibid.*, p. 245.

with an avowed purpose of hostility to the institution of slavery . . . would so threaten a destruction of the ends for which the Constitution was formed, as to justify the slaveholding states in taking counsel together for their separate protection and safety; in order to be prepared for such a contingency, Mississippi accepts the invitation of South Carolina . . . to meet in convention, and proposes the first Monday in June, next, and Atlanta, Georgia, as a suitable time and place to meet and counsel together and recommend the action they should take in such an event."[23]

The legislature proceeded to name delegates, but the Atlanta Convention never materialized. This failure was partly, but only partly, due to Unionist opposition. An equally important factor was the hostility of a certain class of secessionists who were sick of all co-operative enterprises. Thus, in Alabama, the plan was rejected not because of any fear of drastic action, but because of an apprehension that the whole thing would end in talk. Alabama meant to act independently of her neighbors, and to that end she also passed resolutions, even more portentous than those of Carolina and Mississippi. There was a grimness in Alabama's almost unanimous resolve, "that upon . . . the election of a President advocating the principles and action of the party in the Northern States, calling itself the Republican party—it shall be the duty of the Governor, and he is hereby required, forthwith, to issue his proclamation calling . . . a convention of the State to consider, determine, and do whatever in the opinion of said convention the rights, interests, and honor of the State of Alabama require to be done for their protection."[24]

Such were the warnings which issued from the South

23. *Laws of the State of Mississippi passed at a Regular Session of the Mississippi Legislature held in the City of Jackson, November, 1859* (Jackson, 1860), p. 566.

24. Clarence Phillips Denman, *The Secession Movement in Alabama* (Montgomery, 1933), pp. 78–79, gives full text. Resolutions passed Senate 28 to 0; House, 75 to 2; approved Feb. 24, 1860.

early in 1860. The public men were of record; the press was incessant in its warnings; every party contained a vigorous element opposed to "submission"; and in three states the legislatures had indicated most unmistakably that they would regard Republican victory as a cause for the most drastic action. One might suppose that these signs and portents would have impressed even the most partisan Republicans.

But the realistic man, sometimes imagined by the historian, is quite as fictitious as his cousin, the economic man of the Benthamites. And though the Republicans were faced with this mass of evidence of impending catastrophe, they were able to ignore the whole thing. The constantly reiterated threats of secession, like the ticking of a familiar clock, had, to all intents and purposes, ceased to be audible to them. They had heard it too often; they had become agitated too many times; and now, at last, their capacity for alarm was exhausted. Time and again, as it seemed to them, they had seen the South stand on the brink of disunion. Once, South Carolina had actually seemed to plunge over the edge; but always the danger had been avoided; and now, at last, blasé Republicans could witness the most convincing display of secession purpose without turning a hair. In short, the law of diminishing returns had set in on threats of secession.

As a matter of campaign technique, the Republicans avoided arguing the disunion issue and treated all threats with ridicule and contempt. The keynote of this policy was expressed in Henry Wilson's supremely scornful remark that the South could not be kicked out of the Union.[25] On this theme, stump speakers and pamphleteers played every possible variation.

When the canvass of 1860 began, Republican campaigners were adept at this trick of laughing the secession threat out of court, for they had already used it to very

25. April 14, 1856, *Cong. Globe,* 34th Cong., 1st sess., appendix, p. 394. "Sir, you cannot kick out of the Union the men who utter these impotent threats."

good effect in the previous campaign. Thus one speaker for Frémont, dramatizing his argument, put this speech into the mouth of Southern Democrats: "Oh, blood and thunder, don't you know we are all cooperative disunionists? Don't you know we are all colonels? If you do [elect Frémont] . . . a whole battalion of colonels will come up to Washington and seize the Federal archives, and seize the Federal Treasury—particularly the Treasury."[26] In a similar vein were the descriptions of secession as a "bugbear cry," a "potent brag,"[27] and the assertion of Hamilton Fish that the "jails and lunatic asylums are of sufficient capacity to accommodate" all disunionists.[28] Especially important for the future were similar opinions of two law partners of Springfield, Illinois. The younger of the pair, William H. Herndon, thought, with specific reference to the Charleston *Mercury*, that "some of the wind needs to be taken out of the bloat."[29] And the senior partner, Abraham Lincoln, said bluntly, "All this talk about dissolution of the Union is humbug, nothing but folly. We do not want to dissolve the Union; you shall not."[30]

Although this attitude did not serve to save Frémont from defeat, it was used again, with increased emphasis, in the contest of 1860, and the Republican press began making light of fears of secession months before the campaign opened.[31] To James Russell Lowell, the threat of

26. Campaign pamphlet, "The Issue and Its Consequences, An Address at Philadelphia by Edwin Troxell Freedley," 1856.

27. Campaign pamphlets: "Plain Reasons for the Great Republican Movement . . . Remarks made at a public meeting at Geneva, N. Y., July 19, 1856, by C[aleb] S[prague] Henry," pp. 18–19; "Letter from Hon. John J. Slingerland," p. 2.

28. Campaign pamphlet, "Frémont the Conservative Candidate. Correspondence between Hon. Hamilton Fish . . . and Hon. James A. Hamilton . . . ," p. 11.

29. Herndon to Trumbull, Feb. 15, 1856, in Albert J. Beveridge, *Abraham Lincoln, 1809–1858* (Boston, 1928), II, 366.

30. Speech at Galena, Ill., Aug. 1 [?], 1856, in John G. Nicolay and John Hay, editors, *Complete Works of Abraham Lincoln* (New York, 1906. Tandy-Thomas edition), II, 295.

31. Lawrence Tyndale Lowery, *Northern Opinion of Approaching*

dissolution was an "old Mumbo-Jumbo";[32] to Greeley, it
was "as audacious a humbug as Mormonism, as preposter-
ous a delusion as Millerism";[33] even to the realistic Thurlow Weed, it was "a game for the Presidency. . . . nothing
but a game. That it will be played desperately we admit,
because southern sportsmen play desperately." In the heat
of the contest, the idea of disunion was scorned in even
more violent language. The *Tribune* declared that, "The
south could no more unite upon a scheme of secession than
a company of lunatics could conspire to break out of
bedlam."[34]

The argument of the press was repeated from the stump
throughout the free states. As Fite says, "Secession was
seldom made an issue . . . by the Republicans; they
ridiculed the Southern braggadocio, joked about it, but
almost never took it up in earnest debate. . . . Up to the
election, a serious Republican argument against disruption can scarcely be found."[35] Seward's speech at Saint
Paul was characteristic of the approach: "the slave power
. . . rails now with a feeble voice, instead of thundering
as it did for twenty or thirty years past. With a feeble
and muttering voice they cry out that they will tear
the Union to pieces. . . . Who's afraid? [Hundreds of
voices responded, 'Nobody.'] Nobody's afraid. Nobody
can be bought."[36] Other leaders of the party took exactly
the same position. "Long John" Wentworth of Chicago
was sure that secession talk was just "the old game of

Secession, October, 1859–November, 1860, in *Smith College Studies in
History,* III (1918), 195–196, gives citations to the New York *Tribune,*
New York *Evening Post,* Pittsburgh *Evening Chronicle,* Newburyport
Herald, and Pottsville [Pa.] *Miners' Journal.*

32. James Russell Lowell, *Political Essays* (Boston, 1904), p. 41.

33. New York *Tribune,* July 11, 1860.

34. For Weed, the Albany *Evening Journal,* Dec. 13, 1859; New York
Tribune, July 28, 1860.

35. Emerson David Fite, *The Presidential Campaign of 1860* (New
York, 1911), pp. 187–188. The writer has inverted a phrase in this quotation.

36. Speech at Saint Paul, Sep. 18, 1860, in George E. Baker, editor,
The Works of William H. Seward (Boston, 1884), IV, 344.

scaring and bullying the North into submission,"[37] and Salmon P. Chase expressed confidence that Republican victory would restore the old days of concord and good will between North and South.[38] The subject lent itself readily to humorous treatment, as that rising young Republican, Carl Schurz, showed in a speech described by the Kentucky *Yeoman:* "There had been two overt attempts [at secession] already, [he said]—one, the secession of the Southern students from the medical school at Philadelphia, which he ridiculed abundantly; the second, upon the election of Speaker Pennington, when the South seceded from Congress, went out, took a drink, and then came back. The third attempt would be, he prophesied, when old Abe would be elected. They would then again secede and this time would take two drinks but come back again."[39] This bantering style was no doubt very effective, and Schurz should have stuck to it, for his efforts at serious treatment were not so happy. At Saint Louis, for instance, he used a particularly unfortunate figure: "By dissolving the Union! This specter has so long haunted the imagination of superstitious people, that it is time at last to anatomize the bloodless body."[40] Schurz, of course, was wrong. It was not yet time, nor was it for Schurz to perform the task; and when Livermore at last anatomized the body in his *Numbers and Losses in the Civil War,* it was shown to be by no means bloodless.

To one looking back at these events, across the years, with Gettysburg and Shiloh lying between, it is scarcely credible that the Republicans should have been so oblivious to the impending tragedy. Inasmuch as they had been

37. New York *Herald,* Aug. 1, 1860, quoted in Fite, *Campaign of 1860,* p. 188.

38. Mary Scrugham, *The Peaceable Americans of 1860–1861,* p. 45, in Columbia University *Studies in History, Economics, and Public Law,* XCVI (1921), no. 3, whole number 219. Paraphrase of New York *Evening Post,* Aug. 25, 1860.

39. The *Yeoman,* of Kentucky, Dec. 15, 1860, quoted in Scrugham, *Peaceable Americans,* p. 46.

40. Speech, Aug. 1, 1860, quoted in Fite, *Campaign of 1860,* p. 264.

first to foresee an "Irrepressible Conflict," it seems implausible that they should have been last to recognize that the conflict was on the eve of materializing. Because they ought to have sensed it, and because it is evident now, one tends to assume that they did sense it, that it was evident then. This, of course, is the fallacy of reading history backward. In the specific case of the Republicans of 1860, this fallacy leads one to believe that they must have known that the crisis was at hand, even if they would not admit their knowledge publicly. In other words, it is easier to believe that their public statements were insincere than that their private perceptions were completely wrong. Accordingly, one writer, who has found it impossible to credit such utter blindness to coming events, suggests that Republican ridicule of secession "doubtless proceeded from a deliberate purpose" to avoid an issue which would tend "to frighten their own supporters, many of whom would consider long before casting a ballot for Lincoln if persuaded that that ballot would hasten secession and civil war."[41]

This observation, if substantiated as a fact, would constitute a major indictment of the Republican party, and would bear directly upon the question of responsibility for the Civil War. For, if it were correct to say that all the ridicule of secession was mere dissembling to prevent timid voters from taking fright, then it would also be correct to argue that the Republicans deliberately led a confiding electorate, without warning, to the brink of war. Carried to a logical end, this would be tantamount to saying that the Republicans valued a partisan triumph above national peace.

Although fallacious, such a view seems highly plausible —even inescapable—if one assumes that the trend of events seemed as clear to the men of 1860 as it did later to historians. It is now clear that the only reliable indices of the future were the warnings of secession which came from Southern politicians, editors, and legislators, with scarcely

41. Fite, *Campaign of 1860,* pp. 187–188.

a distinction of party. The events following secession demonstrated the validity of these indices; but contemporaries did not have the light of secession. All they had was a long, long experience of Southern threats which had never led to action. For thirty years the Republic had flourished and expanded under constant threats of dissolution. Crisis after crisis had been safely passed, and on one occasion South Carolina had submitted to Federal authority after setting it at defiance in the most formal and solemn manner. Disunion had for so long kept the bad company of sheer rhetoric that it was looked upon as a mere stage property of the spellbinder. When it was, at last, introduced into the quadrennial election carnival, its dignity and its potency sank lower still. Thus in 1856, Buchanan wrote: "We have so often cried 'wolf,' that now when the wolf is at the door, it is difficult to make the people believe it."[42] And Schuyler Colfax, in 1859, informed his mother of the further operation of the law of diminishing returns: "We [in the House of Representatives] are still just where we started six months ago, except that our Southern friends have dissolved the Union forty or fifty times since then."[43]

The credit of Northern Democrats and Old Whigs[44] was not sufficient to redeem this depreciated currency of dissolution. Fillmore might declare, in '56, that "if this sectional [Republican] party succeeds, it leads inevitably to the destruction of this beautiful fabric reared by our forefathers";[45] Buchanan might endorse this statement verbatim.[46] And when the election of 1860 came, Douglas

42. Buchanan to Nahum Capen, Aug. 27, 1856, in Moore, ed., *Works of Buchanan*, X, 88.

43. Colfax to his mother, Jan. 15, 1859, in O. J. Hollister, *Life of Schuyler Colfax* (New York, 1886), p. 151.

44. By Old Whigs I mean, approximately, the Americans of 1856 and the Constitutional Unionists of 1860.

45. Speech at Albany, June 26, 1856, in Frank H. Severance, editor, *Millard Fillmore, Addresses, Private Correspondence and Miscellaneous Writings*, II, p. 21, in Buffalo Historical Society, *Publications*, X–XI (1907).

46. Speech at Wheatland, Nov. 6, 1856, in Moore, ed., *Works of Buchanan*, X, 96.

might declare, "I'm no alarmist, but I believe that this country is in more danger now than at any other moment since I have known anything of public life."[47] But to no avail. The Republicans had heard it too often. Too often had they witnessed a scene in which Southerners threatened disunion, while their Northern partisans explained to the onlookers that a victory for their party would prevent any rupture. This little act always ended with Southern disunionists and Northern Union-savers walking off arm in arm, dividing the spoils. It had all the earmarks of a political confidence game, and it is not strange that the Republicans should have felt a growing skepticism of the whole performance.

This skepticism must have been enormously increased by the corresponding skepticism of certain Unionist elements in the South. If the whole thing looked suspicious in itself, it must have seemed much more so when the very neighbors of the fire-eaters sometimes laughed at them. What New Englander could have accepted, at face value, the secession threats of 1860, after reading the following editorial words from the heart of the Cotton Belt after Buchanan carried the election of '56? "As their candidate is elected, we suppose that the disunion party will now doff the lion skin for a time, and be content to plod along like a quiet beast of burden. . . . We shall not probably hear their discordant bray again until there arises a possibility that they may be deprived of their fodder from the public crib."[48] This cynical comment may never have reached Northern eyes, but in that period, when newspapers copied each other freely, similar expressions must certainly have received notice in the North.

But even if they did not, there were other evidences of a lack of unanimity south of the Potomac. For instance, when South Carolina, Alabama, and Mississippi had made their attempt, in the winter of '59–'60, to arrange the

47. George Fort Milton, *The Eve of Conflict, Stephen A. Douglas and the Needless War* (Boston, 1934), p. 496, citing Chicago *Times and Herald*, Oct. 6, 1860.
48. Augusta [Ga.] *Chronicle*, Nov. 12, 1856.

preliminaries of secession, twelve other slave states had conspicuously failed to co-operate.[49] Moreover, the political parties in the South tended to counteract their own warnings of an impending dissolution by the ardor with which each one of them repelled the charge that it, individually, was tainted with disunionism *per se*. The party of Bell was satisfied to have, as its whole platform, "The Constitution and the Union"; the party of Douglas professed to rejoice that no disunionist supported its ticket;[50] and even John C. Breckinridge, the candidate of such fire-eaters as Yancey, declared, "The man does not live who has power to couple my name successfully with the slightest taint of disloyalty to the constitution and the Union."[51] At least one Northern journal was much reassured by these professions, and without distinguishing between secession as a remedy for grievances, real or fancied, and secession *per se*, concluded that there was no great danger so long as all parties avowed "the most peaceful and friendly disposition."[52]

In short, the Republicans remained incredulous of all threats of disunion. They based their skepticism primarily upon a belief that secession was a mere rhetorical weapon, devised to frighten the electorate, but not for a moment seriously intended to be used, except by the most ultra of the fire-eaters. Furthermore, even if they conceded this point and admitted the sincerity of the more outspoken secessionists, they still felt confident that the latent mass of the Southern people were devoted to the Federal government, and that any overt attempt at secession would arouse this large and heretofore inarticulate majority to violent opposition, thus destroying secession by local action, and

49. Above, pp. 7–8. Unfortunately there seems to be no account of the circumstances connected with the lack of success, in these states, of the Southern convention plan, as proposed by South Carolina.

50. Above, p. 6.

51. Speech at Lexington, Sep. [?], 1860, in New York *Herald,* Sep. 6, 1860, quoted in Fite, *Campaign of 1860,* p. 175.

52. New York *Weekly Journal of Commerce,* Sep. 20, 1860, quoted in Lowery, *Northern Opinion of Approaching Secession,* p. 249.

incidentally freeing the Republican party of a very tire-
some incubus.

The surest proof of this Republican incredulity lies in
the fact that it was expressed not only in speeches and
pamphlets and editorials, which are seldom completely
forthright, but also in the private letters with which
Republican leaders unburdened themselves of inner
thoughts, and took counsel of one another unreservedly.
These communications show a complete unconcern with
what was to be the first and greatest Republican problem.
This heedlessness was expressed not so much by belittling
secession, as by ignoring it altogether. For instance, in a
group of more than thirty letters received late in the
campaign by Salmon P. Chase from Republican politicians throughout the North, there was not a single expression of solicitude for the future.[53] Similarly, letters of
Seward and Chase, Grimes, David Davis, Weed, and
Fessenden indicate no fears. Precisely because of this easy
unconcern it is hard to find explicit statements belittling
the dissolution threat; but later comments by Chase and
Seward show expressly that they were not apprehensive
of trouble.[54] The attitude of Carl Schurz is typical. He
ranged over the entire North in a strenuous speaking
tour, deriding the threat of secession, and then, three days
after the election, he discovered, with obvious astonish-
ment, that "The South appears actually to want to kick
over the traces . . ."[55] Schurz was considered one of
the chief intellectual ornaments of his party; and it is
notable that he did not perceive this major implication of
the campaign until three days after it was over. But, even
so, he showed as much insight as another observer, an
eminent realist, in the heart of the South: William T.
Sherman wrote, "Of course no one can guess what the

53. Papers of Salmon P. Chase, Aug. 1–Nov. 7, 1860, in Library of
Congress.   54. See below, pp. 237, 240–245.
    55. Joseph Schafer, editor, *Intimate Letters of Carl Schurz, 1841–69*,
p. 232, in State Historical Society of Wisconsin, *Publications, Collections*,
XXX (1928).

wild unbridled passions of men may do, but I don't believe
that the present excitement in politics is anything more
than the signs of the passage of power from southern
politicians to northern and western politicians."[56] And out
in Springfield, one of America's shrewdest politicians, he
who was to face the crisis and to be apotheosized as a result
of it, likewise failed to perceive that it was coming. On
August 15, 1860, Abraham Lincoln wrote to John B. Fry
that he received from the South many assurances that "in
no probable event will there be any very formidable effort
to break up the Union. The people of the South have too
much of good sense and good temper to attempt the ruin
of the government rather than see it administered as it
was administered by the men who made it. At least, so I
hope and believe."[57]

So, too, Republicans in general hoped and believed
until, and even after, the sixth of November. With little
foresight, but with perfect sincerity, therefore, they were
able to assure voters, later to be conscripted into the army,
that Lincoln's election would bring tranquillity to the
Republic. But their sincerity itself heightened the peril
greatly. For they were riding blindly toward a crisis in
which clear perceptions would be desperately needed.

After the election, the great question was whether they
would recognize the danger in time. Up to this point there
had been justification for their skepticism of secession.
They had taken into account the element of bluff in the
secession party, and the powerful Union sentiment which
prevailed in the South. But they overlooked the fact that
this Unionism was conditional, and that a threat may be
intended as a bluff and still may be fulfilled if the bluff

56. Sherman to his wife, July 10, 1860, in M. A. de Wolfe Howe, editor,
Home Letters of General Sherman (New York, 1909), p. 179.

Note also the later confession of John Bigelow that, while campaigning for Lincoln, "I scoffed at the threats of disunion which reached us
from Charleston and Mississippi. They never cast a shadow on my
brow." *Retrospections of an Active Life* (New York, 1909), I, 290.

57. Lincoln to John B. Fry, Aug. 15, 1860, in Nicolay and Hay, eds.,
Works of Lincoln, VI, 50.

fails. In an effort to simplify the issue for the electorate, and to dissipate fears which they held to be groundless, they consistently denied that the secession threat deserved serious consideration. By these constantly repeated denials of danger they warped their own perspective, and destroyed their own capacity to evaluate the signs of the times. In the period following the election, new evidences of Southern unrest and new responsibilities of victory might well have led them to take a more realistic view. But the impact of events failed to arouse them to an awareness of the danger. At first, they disbelieved that ordinances of secession would be passed; later, when the ordinances were of record, they relied upon the people of the South to repudiate these measures; finally, when the Southern Confederacy was formed, they still clung to the belief that the Unionism of such states as Virginia and Kentucky would induce the Gulf States to return voluntarily to the Union. Throughout the crisis leading to military conflict, this Republican failure to comprehend the reality of secession remained a basic factor. Without recognition of it, Republican policy must be regarded as either vicious or aimless; without reference to it, there can be no thorough understanding of the course of events which led, ultimately, to war.

CHAPTER II

THE IRREPRESSIBLE CONFLICT WITHIN THE REPUBLICAN PARTY

IF the election of Lincoln marked a crisis, real or apparent, for the defeated Southern states, it also marked a crisis for the Republican victors. Ultimately, this crisis united most of the slave states in secession, and nearly all Republicans in a war for the Union. But in its initial effect, it split the South into blocs consisting of seven secessionist and eight Unionist states; and, while thus dividing the South, the same crisis produced divisions in the Republican ranks which very nearly shattered the party in its moment of victory.

To appreciate the effect of the secession movement upon the Republican organization and to understand the disagreement engendered in Republican ranks, it is necessary to recognize that the party which elected Lincoln in 1860 was neither as zealous nor as homogeneous as the crusading band which had sprung up six years before in response to the Kansas-Nebraska Act. Constant accessions during the interval had steadily swelled its ranks, diversified its interests, and diluted its zeal. Great numbers of Old Whigs had sought a Republican refuge at the breakup of their party, and many dissatisfied Democrats had left their organization to join the new group, which for a time indicated its catholicity by styling itself simply the People's Party, or merely the "opposition."

So long as it remained the opposition, it had been able to accommodate its diverse elements with comparative comfort, and to subordinate all internal cross-purposes in a common hostility to the administration. But there were within it such conflicting interests and objectives, such wholly different types of men, that it was certain to face grave dissensions as soon as it assumed administrative responsibility. At the first taste of power, every public man in the party would inevitably seek patronage for his own friends and enactment for his own measures. This problem, of course, was common to all parties; but in the case of the Republicans it was rendered especially grave by two underlying dualisms which might easily evolve into bitter feuds, intense enough to disrupt the whole organization. The first of these was the demarcation between ex-Whigs and ex-Democrats; the second, the antagonism between "practical politicians" and ideologues.

For the moment, converts from all parties had joined in a violent hatred of the Pierce and Buchanan version of Jacksonian Democracy, and all had agreed in repelling what they considered the greedy demands and unfair tactics by which Southern Democrats sought to extend slavery into the territories. But if the Democratic machine should be driven from power and the territorial issue set at rest, there was no real bond, no common interest, to hold the victors together. Rather, there were many old wounds which would be easily re-opened at a distribution of the spoils of victory. For instance, no one who had been a Democrat during the Mexican War was likely to forget the hope of Whiggish Tom Corwin that the enemy would welcome American soldiers "with bloody hands, to hospitable graves." No one, on the other hand, who had believed in the cult of Henry Clay, would fail to remember that Francis P. Blair, Sr., had been a member of the "Kitchen Cabinet" and editor of Jackson's Washington *Globe* when it was making its fiercest attacks upon Clay and his measures. Blair, a man of violent hatreds, was, in turn, unlikely to forgive Thurlow Weed and the New York Whigs for the claptrap which they used in defeating his personal friend, Van Buren, in 1840. Many Whigs in the West distrusted Chase because they believed that he had secured his seat in the Senate by a corrupt bargain; and Chase hated the Whigs even more enduringly because of their accusations.[1] Aside from these particularly spec-

1. J. W. Schuckers, *Life and Public Services of Salmon Portland Chase* (New York, 1874), p. 94.

tacular feuds, there were doubtless hundreds of others, running down into the pettiest phases of local politics, and completely interpenetrating the new party.

In the case of old partisan grudges, of course, experienced politicians could be expected to make allowances for the give and take of party warfare and to recognize the fact that party organization is based upon reciprocal concessions. The bedding habits of politicians are proverbial. Among the Republicans, however, there was another sort of antagonism which would not yield so readily to the cohesive force of public plunder. This division lay between the original crusaders of the party and the later adherents who joined only when they saw that there was a reasonable hope of living by, as well as for, the cause. These two factions felt toward each other the scorn which is always manifest between zealots and opportunists. Their temperamental incompatibility was, in its nature, wholly unrelated to the grudges arising from previous political rivalry. But as it happened, this temperamental difference coincided roughly with the old political alignment, and thus tended to emphasize and perpetuate the dualism of the new organization.

The political and temperamental dualisms coincided for this reason: the Democratic party, almost constantly in control of offices and patronage, lost only those members who were of stout conscience; whereas the Whig party, by its dissolution, thrust into the Republican ranks many office-seekers of no conscience whatever. Democrats who had abandoned their party to support the Wilmot Proviso, to vote for Van Buren in '48, or to repudiate the Kansas-Nebraska Act in '54, were all voluntary exiles from place and power—men who had deliberately joined with a group of despised abolitionists for the sake of righteousness.[2] Because of party pressure, many of them had joined the

2. E.g., John P. Hale, after being expelled from the Democratic party, expressed a desire to have as an epitaph, "He who lies beneath, surrendered office and place and power, rather than bow down and worship slavery." Henry Wilson, *History of the Rise and Fall of the Slave Power in America* (Boston, 1872–1877), I, 627.

persecuted band as early as 1848, thus forming the Free Soil party. The Whigs, on the other hand, had not been subject to such severe party discipline, and had, for the most part, remained safe in their usual fold until the debacle of Scott's candidacy in 1852 warned them of dissolution. When the Kansas-Nebraska Act offered a promising issue, they simply transferred their allegiance. They did this, for the most part, with undisguised caution and with a plain display of enlightened self-interest. They sacrificed nothing, suffered nothing, and did not fall within the period of the martyrs at all. Many of them cared very little about slavery, but were motivated simply by the fact that every politician must have a party.

It was to be expected that there would be a sharp animosity between these "practical politicians" and the zealots who had been the original nucleus of Republicanism. The idealistic founders of the party concentrated, for the most part, on one fixed principle—anti-slavery—which they cherished fiercely with what Sumner considered a "sacred animosity." Convinced of their mission under God, they were intolerant of opposition within or without. It was natural that they were especially hostile to the eleventh-hour laborers who, as they saw it, were about to reap the profit of their endeavors. Sacred principle, they believed, should not be soiled by compromise or expediency, and, in their eyes, moderation of views indicated baseness of principles. Accordingly, they regarded Thurlow Weed as only a spoilsman; Simon Cameron, as a corruptionist; and even Seward himself, despite his appeal to the "higher law," as an opportunist who might temporize and equivocate and yield ground under pressure.[3]

3. "Mr. Seward, adhering to the vacated shell of Whiggery, has stood aside and allowed the great movement of the free states to go forward without a word of bold and hearty encouragement." New York *Tribune,* Nov. 9, 1854, quoted in Frederic Bancroft, *The Life of William H. Seward* (New York, 1900), I, 375. Weed's supporters are described as "the New York banditti," in a letter of Fitz-Henry Warren to James S. Pike, Feb. 25, 1860, in James S. Pike, *First Blows of the Civil War,*

The intransigence of the radicals, on the other hand, excited the impatience of the moderates. Most of them, like Weed, Seward, and Cameron—to use the same examples—had learned by administrative experience that adjustment, concession, and compromise are the essence of government. They were prone to treat absolute principles as a luxury which they could not afford; and it was, in their view, better to sacrifice a part of any program than lose it all. Their political strength derived from the operation of extensive "machine" organizations and, as with all such leaders, their chief public purpose was to secure what would satisfy their constituents without disturbing the *status quo*. Specifically, they desired to reserve the best parts of the territories for Northern free homesteaders, to the exclusion of Southern expansionist slaveholders. To this end, they fought the battle for restriction of slavery and, in so doing, made direct frontal attacks upon the institution itself. But withal, they shunned the violence of abolitionism and sought the substance of victory rather than the literal enforcement of doctrinaire principles. To men with this realistic philosophy, Greeley would obviously seem a faddist, Sumner, a zealot, and such men as Joshua R. Giddings and George W. Julian mere crackpots.[4]

The Ten Years of Preliminary Conflict in the United States from 1850 to 1860 (New York, 1879), p. 497. William Cullen Bryant wrote to John Bigelow from New York, Feb. 20, 1860, "There are bitter execrations of Weed and his friends passing from mouth to mouth among the old radical democrats of the Republican party here. I suppose Weed never behaved worse than now." Bigelow, *Retrospections,* I, 252.

4. "[Greeley's] sympathies with 'Fourierism' have led him into an error, in which he has deeply injured men worthy of all respect and confidence." Letter of Seward, July 12, 1848, in Frederick W. Seward, *Seward at Washington as Senator and Secretary of State. A Memoir of His Life with Selections from His Letters* (New York, 1891), II, 71.

"I have been anxious that you should *comply* a little more than you have done—not by yielding in principle—but by supporting those . . . not so *decided* against slavery as yourself." Chase to Julian, Apr. 9, 1860, in Grace Julian Clarke, *George W. Julian* (Indianapolis, 1923), p. 202–203.

"The intemperate zeal of the Republican leaders is now the only dan-

This deep-seated antagonism was only partly reconciled by the common animosity with which both factions viewed the administration. Aside from this negative bond of union, the chief factor in preventing a rupture was the leadership of William H. Seward. One of Seward's most notable qualities was his genius for disarming hostility, and he exercised this gift strenuously in the maintenance of the most varied friendships. He had successfully charmed even declared enemies,[5] and with his ostensible allies in the new party he took every pains to establish good feeling. Making up in zeal what he had lacked in promptness in coming to the standard, he indulged in extreme anti-slavery utterances by means of which he soon established among the Republicans the same ascendancy which he had enjoyed as a Whig. Even the most radical approved: Sumner wrote to him, "I am so happy that you and I are at last on the same platform"; Cassius Clay assured him, "You'll soon be as much of a fanatic as myself! Good"; even Wendell ·Phillips praised him.[6]

Seward sought in every way to maintain this cordial feeling. He played the host to Sumner; he treated Giddings with marked consideration; he corresponded with such militant abolitionists as Theodore Parker and Gerrit Smith.[7] More than this, he matched their denunciations of slavery almost word for word. Most of all, he always avoided needless friction. Thus, when the nomination of '56 promised to be an empty honor, Seward let it go

ger which threatens defeat to us." Thomas Corwin to Colfax, 1860, in Hollister, *Colfax*, p. 145.

5. See Bancroft, *Seward*, II, 79–85, and [Varina Howell Davis], *Jefferson Davis, Ex-President of the Confederate States of America, A Memoir by his Wife* (New York, 1890), I, 579–583, for his remarkable friendships with Southern political foes.

6. Sumner to Seward, Oct. 15, 1855; C. M. Clay to Seward, Nov. 16, 1855; both in Seward MSS., quoted in Bancroft, *Seward*, I, 394. Speech of Phillips, Dec. 21, 1855, in Wendell Phillips, *Speeches, Lectures, and Letters* (Boston, 1863), p. 232.

7. Seward, *Seward*, II, 250, for his entertainment of Sumner; George W. Julian, *Life of Joshua R. Giddings* (Chicago, 1892), p. 356; Seward to Parker, Dec. [?], 1855, in Seward, *Seward*, II, 262–263; Seward to Smith, Mar. 31, 1858, in Bancroft, *Seward*, II, 87.

uncontested to Frémont.[8] He did this reluctantly, but with a characteristic inclination to let his extremist colleagues do as they pleased when no tangible objective was involved. It was his avowed policy to stay on good terms with every one.

But, by temperament, Seward distrusted these extremists and, with discreet privacy, he began to express this distrust very early in his career as a Republican. In 1855, he wrote to Theodore Parker, complaining of certain New England abolitionists who were accustomed to "censure and cast suspicion on the public laborers . . . who did not at all times and on all occasions, great or small, . . . act with themselves and exactly in their own way." In defense of his own policy against these unreasonable critics, he added: "When I seem unmoved and inactive . . . it is only because I am keeping steadily in view a coming occasion and opportunity to move and act, as I think, more wisely and effectively. . . . my life is chiefly dedicated to the advancement of a reform which I think cannot be hastily or convulsively made."[9] His impatience with the militant group was more concretely expressed when, in predicting the loss of the election of '56, he said: "Rash counsels will probably prevail, and the first assault will be repulsed, not so much because the enemy is strong, but because of the infatuation of the besiegers."[10]

This distrust of fanaticism in politics was as yet concealed behind a personal cordiality and a heartiness in the denunciation of slavery. But if Seward was willing to hide his impatience and to exaggerate his views in order to win party leadership, he was equally willing to moderate and equivocate when it was necessary to act with other parties. This was abundantly clear when, in 1858, he joined with Douglas and Crittenden to defeat the Lecomp-

8. Thurlow Weed Barnes, *Memoir of Thurlow Weed* (Boston, 1884), p. 245 (published as Vol. II of the *Life of Thurlow Weed*); Seward to his wife, June 6, 11, 13, 14, 17, 1856, in Seward, *Seward*, II, 276–278.

9. Seward to Parker, Dec. [?], 1855, in Seward, *Seward*, II, 262–263.

10. Seward to George E. Baker, 1855, in *ibid.*, II, 252.

ton Constitution. To solidify this coalition, Seward took a very friendly tone toward Douglas, and even went so far as to say, "I shall not insist, now, on so radical a measure as the restoration of the Missouri prohibition. . . . Go back only to the ground assumed in 1854, the ground of popular sovereignty. . . . popular sovereignty in Kansas may now be made a fact, and liberty there may be rescued from danger through its free exercise. . . . It is on this ground that I hail the eminent Senator from Illinois and his associates."[11] When Seward spoke of popular sovereignty, he did not mean the doctrine of Douglas. That applied to the organization of territory; Seward had reference to the process of preparation for statehood. But while this position conceded nothing, it revealed much about his approach to political problems. It showed, for instance, that he would indulge in deliberate ambiguity to facilitate cooperation with people who accepted his purposes, but balked at his reasons. It showed also that he did not care about declarations, so long as he achieved results. Call it Popular Sovereignty, or call it the Sacred Principle of Freedom in the Territories—he made no point of it, so long as Kansas came in without slaves. It showed further that he would take allies where he found them. On this occasion he coalesced with Crittenden, a slave-state Senator, and with Douglas, who was the anathema of the Republican party. It was a strange triumvirate, and even stranger was the fact that it would reappear within three years, to champion the cause of peaceable adjustment in the greatest crisis of all.

Aside from the light which the Anti-Lecompton coalition cast upon the character of Seward, it was important because it marked the beginning, or at least the first overt

11. Senate speech, Mar. 3, 1858, in *Cong. Globe,* 35th Cong., 1st sess., pp. 939–945. The radical reaction to this speech was indicated in a note from Chase, Mar. 11, 1858, complimenting Seward but adding, "I regretted the apparent countenance you gave to the idea that the Douglas doctrine of popular sovereignty will do for us to stand upon for the present." Robert B. Warden, *An Account of the Private Life and Public Services of Salmon Portland Chase* (Cincinnati, 1874), p. 343.

evidence, of a conservative trend which was to prevail throughout the remainder of his life and to cause him, a few years later, to stand by Andrew Johnson when most Republicans were shouting for impeachment. Heretofore he had been the phrase-maker and the spearhead of the anti-slavery party; hereafter he increasingly subordinated the slavery issue. It is true that he repeated the old words of fire, but there were no new phrases. It is also true that with characteristic adroitness he kept the friendship of some of the radicals, but only with increasing strain.

After the Lecompton contest, the first evidence of this change in Seward came with the campaign of 1860. In that year, unlike 1856, the auspices pointed to Republican victory. Accordingly, Seward and his silent political partner, Thurlow Weed, entered the contest vigorously, and at the same time that they sought the nomination, they undertook to prepare their party to assume the responsibilities of national administration. To do this, it was necessary to modify the extreme anti-slavery position maintained previously and to substitute for this one issue a balanced, moderate, and constructive program. Such a policy would serve to keep the party together after the slavery issue should be settled, and would establish the organization on a national, rather than a sectional basis.

This new departure was indicated two months before the nomination when, on February 29, 1860, Seward spoke in the Senate. Following upon an extended trip to Europe, it was his first full-dress speech in almost two years. Because of this, and because of the publicity preceding it, it attracted general attention. Everyone knew that a major political development was likely; but no one could have expected such a general change of base as Seward hinted at. His remarks were guarded and tentative, but his silences were revolutionary. The man who had risen to leadership by his "higher law" and "irrepressible conflict" doctrines, who had won the approbation of Sumner, and even of Wendell Phillips, now treated the sectional issue with such delicacy that even the most sensitive of Southerners could scarcely take offense.

In his euphemisms the slave states now became the "capital States," and the free states, "labor States," whose people were "not enemies but friends and brethren of the South." These friends and brethren did not "seek to force, or even to intrude" their system upon the Southern people. And as for the Republican party, it was ready to play a national rôle. Thus far, it had avowed only one policy, namely, the exclusion of slavery from the territories, but Seward did not hesitate to predict that "it will favor the speedy improvement of the public domain by homestead laws, and will encourage mining, manufacture, and internal commerce, with needful connections between the Atlantic and Pacific States. . . . For all the rest, the national emergencies, not individual influences, must determine, as society goes on, the policy and character of the Republican party. Already bearing its part in legislation and in treaties, it feels the necessity of being practical in its care of the national health and life, while it leaves metaphysical speculation to those whose duty it is to cultivate the ennobling science of political philosophy."[12]

This sharp contrast of the "practical" and the "metaphysical" foreshadowed clearly what Seward's policies would be, if, as was generally expected, he should lead his party in the coming election. It was a warning to the doctrinaires of the party to refrain from untimely abstractions.[13] And, as unfolding events were to disclose, it was, in a sense, the keynote speech for the nominating convention

12. *Cong. Globe,* 36th Cong., 1st sess., pp. 910–914.
13. The radicals did not like this speech. Greeley wrote to Pike, Mar. 5, 1860, " 'Capital States' and 'Labor States' is foolish. Slave States and Free States tells the story, and no one can misunderstand it." Pike, *First Blows of the Civil War,* p. 501. George W. Julian "was not enthused by reason of his [Seward's] cold speech in the Senate." Julian to Giddings, May 21, 1860, in Clarke, *Julian,* p. 204. Conservatives, on the other hand, were pleased: Samuel Bowles wrote to Weed, Mar. 5, 1860, "I hear of ultra old Whigs in Boston who say they are ready to take up Mr. Seward upon his recent speech." Barnes, *Weed,* p. 260.

which met in Chicago ten weeks later. Even before Seward spoke, in fact, the conservatives had already won a sharp skirmish with the radicals in the National Committee. This arose in connection with the call for the nominating convention: the radicals wanted to exclude all but orthodox Republicans, while the moderates wished to invite "members of the People's Party of Pennsylvania and of the Opposition Party of New Jersey, and all others who are willing to cooperate." The broad constructionists prevailed, and the diverse elements of opposition were invited.[14]

All this, however, was a mere preliminary to the action of the convention itself. For it inevitably devolved upon this body to draft a new platform which would, of necessity, either repudiate or reaffirm the radicalism of the platform of '56. That document had devoted itself chiefly to such quotations from the Declaration of Independence as would most annoy slave-holders, and to denials that the territories were open to slavery, which was termed a "relic of barbarism." Only by afterthought, apparently, did the platform of '56 endorse a Pacific railroad, river and harbor appropriations, and equality for the foreign born.[15]

The convention of 1860 definitely receded from this ultra position. It adopted a platform which, as compared with the previous one, was milk and water. True, it attacked the Dred Scott decision, denounced the smuggling of slaves, and still denied "the authority of Congress, or a territorial legislature, or of any individuals, to give legal

14. The call for the convention is in the New York *Tribune,* Dec. 23, 1859; Senator Jas. R. Doolittle wrote to his wife, April 4, 1862, "I drew the call for the Chicago convention. . . . I labored as I never labored before to get the discordant elements of the Republican organization so bound together that we could get Pennsylvania and New Jersey into the Chicago Convention. . . . I thought I should not be able to get the radical self-conceited Republicans to consent to invite into the convention any delegate from Pennsylvania or New Jersey and without them we might as well have had no Convention at all." In Doolittle MSS., Wis. Hist. Soc., quoted by James Lee Sellers, "The Make-up of the Early Republican Party," in Illinois State Historical Society, *Transactions,* 1930, pp. 46–47.

15. *Proceedings of the First Three Republican National Conventions of 1856, 1860, and 1864, etc.* (Minneapolis, 1893), pp. 43–45.

existence to Slavery in any territory of the United States."[16] But in contrast to the platform of Frémont, which had placed almost complete reliance upon the slavery issue, it diversified by endorsing a tariff for protection and a Homestead Act—two measures which were desired by innumerable voters. The allusion to slavery as a relic of barbarism was omitted; John Brown's raid was described as a "lawless invasion . . . among the gravest of crimes"; and "the maintenance inviolate of . . . the right of each state to order and control its own domestic institutions" was recognized as "essential to that balance of powers on which the perfection and endurance of our political fabric depends."[17] In an effort to moderate even further, the platform committee proposed to omit the words of the Declaration of Independence which had been incorporated in '56, and the convention sustained the proposal; but to this, old Joshua Giddings objected violently, and expressed his dissent by seceding from the convention. Since the death of John Quincy Adams, Giddings had been the Grand Old Man of the anti-slavery cause. Rather than alienate him, therefore, the convention rescinded its action. In this the Seward men, eager for harmony, were instrumental.[18] They were still on good terms with the radicals, still known as "Irrepressibles," and they had no idea of sacrificing their support from the left wing. But in all this, they had none of the crusading, almost theocratic leanings of the idealists with whom they still allied. In many ways they presented a sharp contrast to these sternly pious souls: "The New Yorkers here are of a class unknown to Western Republican politicians. They can drink as much whiskey, swear as loud and long, sing as bad

16. *Ibid.,* pp. 131–133. This phrase is virtually identical with the one used in '56.

17. *Ibid.,* pp. 131–133.

18. *Ibid.,* pp. 133–137, 140–142; Julian, *Giddings,* pp. 371–374; M[urat] Halstead, *Caucuses of 1860. A History of the National Political Conventions of the Current Presidential Campaign, etc.* (Columbus, 1860), pp. 135–138, 140.

songs, and 'get up and howl' as ferociously as any crowd of Democrats you ever heard, or heard of. They are opposed, as they say, 'to being too d——d virtuous.' . . . They slap each other on the back with the emphasis of delight when they meet, and rip out 'How *are* you?' with a 'How are you hoss?' style, that would do honor to Old Kaintuck on a bust. At night, those of them who are not engaged at caucusing, are doing that which ill-tutored youths call 'raising h——l generally.' "[19]

Thus far, the new moderation preached by Seward had carried everything before it. According to all logic, it was now due to sweep him into the nomination, and perhaps into the White House. But instead, it defeated him, or at least contributed to his defeat. The reason for this was that all good Republicans had sniffed victory in the air, and all of them knew that it depended upon Pennsylvania, New Jersey, and Indiana—the states which had defeated Frémont four years previously. These states were, to a certain extent, border states, containing a large body of moderates who opposed the Democracy, but opposed even more the agitation of slavery. To insure victory, it was vital to conciliate these moderates by a show of conservatism. All but the blindest radicals could see this; consequently, conservatism was accepted on every hand with a zeal as extreme as it was temporary. The Blairs, with their own unique and erratic ultraism, proposed to nominate an out-and-out Whig, Edward Bates, and actually secured for him a ponderable block of votes in the convention.[20] Many others could not reconcile themselves to

19. Halstead, *Caucuses of 1860*, p. 140.
20. William Ernest Smith, *The Francis Preston Blair Family in Politics* (New York, 1933), I, 461–469, for a full account. The Bates movement was supported by Horace Greeley and was described by Israel Washburn as "deep, widely extended and formidable." Greeley to Colfax, Feb. 3, 1860, in Greeley-Colfax MSS., quoted in *ibid.*, I, 464; Addison G. Proctor, *Lincoln and the Convention of 1860* (Chicago, 1918), pp. 9–10; Washburn to Pike, Jan. 31, 1860, in Pike, *First Blows of the Civil War*, p. 483.
The Blairs had previously suggested the even more conservative Crittenden for the nomination. F. P. Blair, Sr., to Crittenden, Feb. 16,

Bates, but, like Fitz-Henry Warren, would accept almost anyone else: "I am for the man who can carry Pennsylvania, New Jersey, and Indiana, with this reservation, that I will not go into cemetery or catacomb; the candidate must be alive, and able to walk, at least from parlor to dining room."[21]

What was required was not conservatism in essence, but rather the appearance of conservatism. To fulfill this requirement, the recent moderate speech of Seward did not at all suffice. It was too new to have produced any deep impression on the public mind, and too late to efface from conservative memories the radical speeches of Seward's Republican novitiate. These speeches had established him as the foremost political leader of the anti-slavery cause, and this reputation, acquired over a period of six years, was not to be discarded overnight. Availability was the touchstone of the moment, and where this was the criterion, Seward was badly handicapped. He was an enemy of the Masons, a foe of the Nativists, a "rawhead and bloody to the South,"[22] and therefore frightful to all those who were timid on the slavery issue. With the Pennsylvania, New Jersey, and Indiana delegations all vowing that he could not carry their states,[23] even his friends were reluctant to insist upon him.

Meanwhile the opportunists were effecting a last-minute concentration upon Abraham Lincoln. Unlike Bates, Lincoln was a sound Republican; unlike Seward, he was acceptable to the moderates in Pennsylvania and along the Ohio. By nominating Bates, the party would have surrendered to the Whiggish moderates; by nominating Lin-

1860, in Mrs. Chapman Coleman, *The Life of John J. Crittenden with Selections from his Correspondence and Speeches* (Philadelphia, 1871), II, 186.

21. Warren to Pike, Feb. 2, 1860, in Pike, *First Blows of the Civil War*, p. 484.

22. Montgomery Blair to Welles, Oct. 17, 1870, Dec. 12, 1873, in Blair MSS., quoted in Smith, *Blair Family in Politics*, I, 477.

23. Proctor, *Lincoln and the Convention of 1860*, p. 13; Halstead, *Caucuses of 1860*, pp. 142–144.

coln, it might capture them. Lincoln fitted the exigencies of the moment perfectly. He was morally opposed to slavery at all, and actively opposed to its extension. But he had never alarmed the moderates as Seward had. He had stuck to the Whig organization long after Seward left it; and though he had talked of a house divided against itself, he had never used phrases so direct and unequivocal as "the irrepressible conflict." As for the "higher law" of Seward, Lincoln repudiated it explicitly.[24] Lincoln, by reason of his great debates, was associated primarily with the territorial question; Seward, despite his recent drift toward the right, was associated with the slavery question *per se.* Therefore it was a clear gain for conservatism when the party chose Lincoln as its nominee.[25]

This conservative note continued to dominate throughout the campaign. When Charles Sumner disregarded the new policy in his violent speech on the "Barbarism of Slavery," he was swiftly ordered to get back in line. The leading Republican papers received his outburst with marked coolness;[26] a committee called on him and suggested very pointedly that he confine himself, for a time, to the transaction of senatorial business; so firm was this

24. A few days before the nomination, Lincoln wrote, "I agree with Seward in his 'Irrepressible Conflict,' but I do not endorse his 'Higher Law' doctrine." William H. Herndon and Jesse W. Weik, *Abraham Lincoln, the True Story of a Great Life* (Chicago, 1888), p. 462.

25. "Fortunately, he [Lincoln] will not be thrown upon an extreme party for support. The conservative interest nominated him and that also will elect him." Campaign pamphlet, "Speech of Hon. Thomas Ewing at Chillicothe, Ohio, before a Republican Mass Meeting, September 29, 1860."

The New Orleans *Bee,* May 21, 1860, recognized that the platform and the nomination at Chicago both had the effect of "moderating the frantic zeal of faction," that Seward was defeated by the conservative element, and that Lincoln belonged to the moderate wing of the party. Dumond, ed., *Southern Editorials on Secession,* pp. 103–105.

"Lincoln was selected on account of his *location* . . . It is also true that some of the Doughfaces seemed to think him more popular because his anti-slavery sentiments have been less prominent." Giddings to Julian, May 25, 1860, in Clarke, *Julian,* p. 206.

26. Extensive press comments in Charles Sumner, *Complete Works* (Statesman ed., Boston, 1900), VI, 241–258.

disapproval, that he wrote to some friends, "I see clearly that there is an effort to disown me in the Republican party, and to *read me out*."[27]

But all this trend toward the right was accomplished not so much by the ascendancy of the conservatives as by the complaisance of the radicals. Seward was rejected as too extreme, not by the moderates, but by men who were personally more radical than he was. Having sought to identify himself completely with Republican principles, he was now repudiated by Republicans precisely because of his success in that endeavor. Having paid lip-service to ultraism, he was rejected by the ultras as they paid lip-service to moderation.

The nomination of Lincoln, then, was primarily a bid for support outside the party, but viewed in another phase, it was a postponement of the internal contest for party control. This practice of deferring the struggle for party command until the common enemy has been vanquished is a familiar political maneuver. To accomplish it, it is necessary only to select a nominee whose qualities give both factions hope of controlling him. Lincoln fulfilled this requirement admirably. He was nominated to attract conservative votes, and this would bind him to the conservatives; but he was supported by certain radicals, and this would draw him toward them. His personal antecedents were entirely Whiggish, but he was a close friend of Lyman Trumbull, and a beneficiary of the support of the Democratic Blairs, who threw their strength to him after the Bates candidacy was exhausted. His own record was conservative, but his law partner and intimate, "Billy" Herndon, was an ardent abolitionist. His nomination was a defeat for Seward, but it was not precisely a victory for Seward's foes, for they had supported Bates, and accepted Lincoln only as a second choice.

27. Sumner to S. G. Howe, E. L. Pierce, *et al.*, June, 1860, in Sumner MSS., quoted by Laura A. White, "Charles Sumner and the Crisis of 1860–61," in Avery Craven, editor, *Essays in Honor of William E. Dodd by his Former Students* (Chicago, 1935), p. 140.

Consequently no one knew to which side the nominee would lean, and every one hoped to gain his ear. There was the usual rush to pay court to him, and those who had opposed him most bitterly in the convention were first to bend the knee. Thus Thurlow Weed, who had wept in chagrin at the nomination, visited Springfield almost at once. Constantly the candidate was besieged by visitors, and as the preliminary elections indicated more and more certainly that the party would control the presidency, attention shifted to the struggle to determine who should control the party.[28]

After the sixth of November, this attention was redoubled, and from then until the fourth of March the factional rivalry within the party and the ebb and flow of individual influences became topics of national importance. Even after the secession crisis developed in all its overpowering gravity, the conflict between radicals and conservatives[29] continued to preoccupy. Apparently no one felt any certainty as to Lincoln's views, and each wing was afraid that he would join the most extreme element in the rival faction. Thus, the friends of Chase, Wade, Sumner, and the radicals were afraid that the old Henry Clay men of the Border, the so-called "fossil Whigs," might dominate. There were three men of this class whom they especially dreaded. One was John Bell of Tennessee, who

28. Chase MSS., Aug. 1–Nov. 7, contain thirty-odd letters which generally assumed that Lincoln would be elected and were not apprehensive about anything except the possibility that the conservatives might control him.

Thurlow Weed, *Autobiography* (Boston, 1883), p. 602 (edited by his daughter, Harriet A. Weed, published as Vol. I of *The Life of Thurlow Weed*); Barnes, *Weed*, p. 271; John G. Nicolay and John Hay, *Abraham Lincoln, A History* (New York, 1890), II, 286; J. G. Holland, *The Life of Abraham Lincoln* (Springfield, 1866), p. 232.

29. These designations were in general use. E.g., "Of all the Radicals, old 'Rough and Ready' Wade would suit me best." Colfax to Samuel Bowles, Mar., 1860, in Hollister, *Colfax*, p. 144; "You need not fear that Lincoln will fall into the keeping of Corwin, Schenck, Ewing, and other old conservatives. . . . His main dependence will be on the radical element." William M. Green, quoting Joseph Medill of the Chicago *Tribune*, to Chase, Nov. 26, 1860, in Chase MSS.

was expected to have influence with Lincoln despite the fact that he had been an opposing candidate in the election. Another was Thomas Ewing, a veteran Whig of Ohio, who, in the campaign, had supported Lincoln but not the Republican ticket. In fact, he had rejoiced openly in the belief that the admission of Kansas would end the slavery contest, and that the "Republican party cannot possibly maintain itself as a general Anti-Slavery party."[30] A third Old Whig, one who now gave his allegiance to the Republican party, but who cherished a violent and unconcealed contempt for the negrophiles, was Thomas Corwin of Ohio.[31]

Throughout the Border states, the small minority of militant Republicans feared that the fruits of victory would be spent not to reward them, but to appease and win over their opponents. In Kentucky, the followers of Cassius Clay suspected that Crittenden and the old Know-Nothing clique were scheming to get control of the patronage of the state.[32] In Virginia, the Republicans of the mountain region dreaded a possible alliance between the incoming administration and men like John Minor Botts,

30. Campaign pamphlet, "Speech of Hon. Thomas Ewing, Sep. 29, 1860."

31. Corwin's relations with the friends of the Negro race may be imagined from an incident described by him in a letter to James A. Pearce, May 16, 1856: "A Yankee lawyer came into my sanctum yesterday, his eyes bloodshot and shooting out of their sockets half an inch, the cold sweat dropping from his for[e]head and nose, ejaculating broken execrations upon the Supreme Court, because he said they had recently decided . . . that a nabob from K[en]t[uck]y could pick up . . . his negroes and bring them over into our *religious* and *free* State, and keep them here during hot months of Summer, provided he could prove he came to be cured of a bilious cholic! He demanded of me what I thought of this enormity. After a moment's reflection, I told him I hoped they would come in winter, as in that case the smell would be more agreeable to our free and evangelical nostrils. My interrogator opened his eyes until they resembled two dogwood bushes in bloom, swelled out his cheeks, snorted like a horse who sees fox-fire in the night and bolted out . . . with a stride that would have done credit to Gilpin's Horse." Bernard C. Steiner, editor, "Some Letters from Correspondence of James Alfred Pearce," in *Maryland Historical Magazine,* XVI (1921), 166–167.

32. R. Murdy, Frankfort, Ky., Nov. 15, 1860, to Chase, in Chase MSS.

who had supported Bell during the campaign. One Republican, embittered by this prospect, wrote, "We cannot believe that the Republican party will really confess itself so much sectionalized as to fear to recognize its own friends outside of the free states."[33] Perhaps the most savage feelings of all were aroused in Maryland, where the outright Republicans, led by the Blairs, competed with the powerful "plug-ugly" machine of Henry Winter Davis, which had supported Constitutional Unionism while taking care not to close the door against preferment under Lincoln. Both the Blairs and Davis were finished politicians; both knew all the tricks and dodges; and the rivalry between them was sharp. A Baltimore editor who had suffered at the hands of Davis wrote, "now that victory perches on the Republican banners, are we to have a Republican administration . . . ? A conspiracy is on foot to prevent it. Ewing, Bates, Winter Davis, Corwin, J. M. Botts, W. C. Rives, Winthrop, *et id omne genus*, are in it. . . . Our Winter Davis was fatal to the Republican vote of M[arylan]d. . . . The Republicans of M[arylan]d protest against a hybrid administration. They look for an *in* and *in* and *out* and *out* Republican government. Shall we have it? I believe it. I hope it. I look for it."[34] This writer expressed a prevailing sentiment in his fear of the conservatives, but not in his expectation of an outright Republican administration. John Sherman reported a general foreboding that Lincoln would "surround himself with old men and thus adopt a timid, vacillating policy."[35] Dread, rather than hope, was the mood of the radicals. For instance, one of them, writing to Chase, expected Corwin to dominate; another feared Bell and Corwin; still another, Ewing, Corwin, and Benjamin Stanton; a fourth

33. Alfred Caldwell, Wheeling, Va., Mar. 27, 1861, to Chase, in Chase MSS.; John Minor Botts, *The Great Rebellion, Its Secret History, Rise,· Progress, and Disastrous Failure* (New York, 1866), p. 127.
34. W[orthington] G. Snethen to Chase, Nov. 14, 1860, in Chase MSS.
35. John Sherman to F. P. Blair, Jr., Feb. 9, 1861, in Blair Family MSS. in Library of Congress.

likewise feared Corwin and Ewing, and added to the list Robert Schenck.[36] Fitz-Henry Warren was troubled by the possibility that Lincoln might fill his cabinet with such men as Corwin, Schuyler Colfax, who had supported Douglas against Lincoln in '58, and Alexander Pennington, whom the Republicans had reluctantly accepted as Speaker of the House when they could not elect Sherman.[37]

It was perfectly clear that the Democrats had lost the election, but there was still grave doubt as to who had won it. The radicals hoped for the fruits of victory, but they were more than a little afraid that all their efforts had gone to reestablish Whiggery. To these crusaders, it was a bitter thought that perhaps they had overthrown one set of time-servers only to set up another.

However, their apprehension was tempered by a basic regard for Lincoln. Giddings wrote that he would trust Lincoln on slavery, as readily as he would trust Chase or Seward; and Chase thought that Lincoln would not disappoint the true Republicans. "He may not be so radical as some would wish," wrote Chase, "but he . . . will never surrender our principles. . . ."[38] More than this, current rumor at times gave them hope of enjoying the especial favor of the president-elect. A persisting report indicated that Sumner would be Secretary of State; this fiction continued, somehow, to circulate even after knowledge of the selection of Seward became widespread.[39] Other early predictions awarded dominant influence to various radicals,

36. Letters to Chase from C. F. Cleveland, ex-gov. of Conn., Nov. 12, 1860 (Bell and Corwin); J. C. Brand, Nov. 13 (Ewing, Corwin, Stanton); Wm. M. Green, Nov. 26 (Corwin, Ewing, Schenck); Wm. D. Bickham, Dec. 4 (Corwin); O. W. Nixon, Nov. 13; J. H. Purdy, Nov. 26; George G. Fogg, later Senator from N. H., Nov. 25; Edward D. Mansfield, Nov. 26; all in Chase MSS.

37. Warren to Pike, Dec. 16, 1860, in Pike, *First Blows of The Civil War,* p. 526.

38. Giddings to Julian, May 25, 1860; Chase to Julian, Dec. 15, 1860; both in Clarke, *Julian,* pp. 206–208.

39. Anon., "Diary of a Public Man," entry for Feb. 28, 1861, in *North American Review,* CXXIX (Aug.–Nov., 1879), 268.

and these forecasts seemed justified when the first publicly announced cabinet selection was that of Edward Bates.[40] Bates was personally Whiggish but this seemed of little significance in comparison with his position as a protege of the Blair family. Rumor constantly asserted that David Wilmot and John C. Frémont[41] would also be included among Lincoln's advisers. Frémont was even more a creature of the Blairs than was Bates; and as for Wilmot, his name was a symbol of Free-Soil Democracy. With these reports issuing from Springfield, the New York *Herald* seemed justified in supposing that "the old free soil Democratic element of the Republican party are to have the front seats in the new tabernacle. But," it inquired, "are the old line whigs . . . going to submit to play second fiddle . . . ?" It did not think they would, and it concluded that there was "an irrepressible conflict in the Republican party."[42]

To the participants in the political maneuvering of the moment, the friction within the party seemed most serious as it related to party control and appointments to office. But, from a broader viewpoint, the chief importance of the growing rift lay in its relation to the situation in the South. This was true in a double sense: first, if the South should defer immediate action and await developments, there were strong evidences that the Republican moderates might force an unexpectedly mild course upon their party; second, if the South should embark upon a program of secession, such a step would tend further to divide the ideologues and the opportunists of the Republican party, as they respectively turned to coercion or to compromise as their means of preserving the Union.

40. Lincoln to Bates, Dec. 18, 1860, authorized the announcement. Nicolay and Hay, eds., *Works of Lincoln,* VI, 83. The announcement was made in the *Missouri Democrat,* Dec. 21, according to a dispatch in the New York *Tribune,* Dec. 22.

41. New York *Herald,* Dec. 20, 25, 27, 1860; Jan. 1, 1861; Allan Nevins, *Frémont, Pathmarker of the West* (New York, 1939), pp. 470–471.

42. New York *Herald,* Dec. 27, 1860.

First, the likelihood of the Republicans adopting a moderate program was already indicated by a distinct trend toward conservatism within the party. Over a period of years the accessions from the Whig party had undermined the control of the evangelical Democrats. The triumph of the Whigs' mild policy had been foreshadowed by Seward's speech of February, 1860; it had been indicated by the broad terms of the call for a National Convention, and accomplished by the platform which that convention adopted. The new departure was fixed almost beyond recall when an Old Whig, a cautious politician, Abraham Lincoln, was nominated, out of deference to moderate sentiment in certain states. There was no categorical proof that this trend would continue, but it was not likely that a party whose moral principles were severely shaken by a mere glimpse of worldly power would prove very quixotic in the actual possession of authority. Nor was it likely that Abraham Lincoln, nominated and elected because he could carry certain non-Republican elements, would be unduly zealous in precipitating the "irrepressible conflict."

From the standpoint of the South, therefore, there were advantages to be gained by letting matters take their course. With the Republican party already torn by dissension and tending toward conservatism, there was good reason to await the time when the assumption of responsibility would further widen the rift, and the charm of office would further dilute the idealism of the victors. In short, the South might have gained much by allowing the Republicans enough rope.

It is a fact of capital importance that the South collectively had lost its capacity to analyze the situation coolly and to perceive the potential advantages of a waiting game. If Southern public men had retained enough detachment of mind to weigh the factors involved, they might well have chosen not to inaugurate the program of secession. But the South, in general, attempted no analysis; it preferred an emotional stereotype which pictured Lincoln and all his supporters as negrophiles of such extreme fanaticism that they had chosen a mulatto, Hannibal Hamlin, for the Vice-presidency.[43] Men who would believe this were, of course, too distraught to observe that many abolitionists distrusted Lincoln, and that Wendell Phillips denounced him as the "Slave-hound of Illinois."[44] In the angry mood that followed years of sectional agitation, the South could not distinguish degrees of hostility to slavery, nor could it coolly play a cynical game of delay. A wave of secession, consequently, swept across the lower South, and the possibility of the Republican party turning moderate was never fully tested. For practical purposes, therefore, the pertinent question was not how the Republican situation would influence the action of the South, but how the action of the South would affect the stability of the Republican party.

Here was involved the second major aspect in which Republican discord held significance—that is, in the liability of the factions of the party to be further estranged as they failed to agree upon a response to secession. For if they lacked unanimity in other matters, there was certainly no prospect that they would agree on how to save the Union. Again, one must recall the diversity of their background. On one hand were those who had been Whigs. Men of this class adhered to the Henry Clay tradition of compromise. Forty years earlier they had averted a sectional crisis by establishing the 36° 30′ line as the division between slavery and freedom in the territories; and in

43. The New Orleans *Crescent,* Nov. 12, 1860, described Lincoln as "a thorough radical Abolitionist, without exception or qualification." Dumond, ed., *Southern Editorials on Secession,* p. 231. For the Hamlin matter, see Laura A. White, *Robert Barnwell Rhett, Father of Secession* (New York, 1931), p. 169, and Charles Eugene Hamlin, *The Life and Times of Hannibal Hamlin* (Cambridge, 1899), pp. 223–224 and 354–356.

44. The *Liberator,* XXX, 99 (June 22, 1860), quoted by [W. P. Garrison], *William Lloyd Garrison, 1805–1879, The Story of his Life Told by his Children* (New York, 1885-1889), III, 503. The *Liberator* of Nov. 23, 1860, carried a letter which declared that Lincoln's election placed the anti-slavery cause in "a new, a critical, and a trying position; demanding additional vigilance, inflexible steadfastness . . . and unrelaxed energy." *Ibid.,* IV, 1.

later decades they had endowed this Missouri Compromise with a sacrosanct quality, as if it were part of the Constitution. In the Nullification Crisis, they had voted for the compromise tariff as a means of appeasing the open defiance of South Carolina. In 1850, they had again stood with their "Great Pacificator" in enacting an omnibus compromise. In another crisis, greater than any preceding, there could be little doubt that men whose political lives had fallen into such a pattern, would again be responsive to the idea of a compromise settlement.

Acting with this Whiggish element, in nominal association, was the old Free-Soil Democratic group. Members of this faction had consistently opposed concessions to the South. As far back as the crisis of 1832, Francis P. Blair, Sr., had endorsed the fighting language of Jackson's Nullification Proclamation. After the Mexican War, proponents of a "firm" policy had fought for the Wilmot Proviso and had organized the Free-Soil Party to prevent any further territorial compromise. Men of this type had, naturally, opposed the compromise of 1850, and had stigmatized everyone who supported it. For more than a decade they had consistently maintained an attitude of militant hostility to slave-holders. In the approaching crisis, such a faction could not possibly accept any sort of compromise settlement without doing violence to their entire political record.

On the face of it, therefore, the Republican party consisted of two factions which had never concurred in their approach to the sectional problem. So sharply did they differ upon the merit of compromise, that they would probably never have been united in one party if the Kansas-Nebraska Act, with its repeal of the Missouri settlement, had not offended adherents of compromise and driven them into a coalition with the extremists.

This coalition faced its supreme test after the election of Lincoln. If, in the secession crisis, yielding opportunists and inflexible ideologues should fail to reach agreement, their whole program was likely to shatter in the moment of its inauguration. If, on the contrary, the coalition should survive, the future of the Republic depended upon the contest for power within the party. Let the Old Whig element gain control of the administration, and compromise would certainly become the response to secession. Let the true Free-Soilers seize the controls, and a policy of coercion was indicated. Neither moderates nor extremists in November, 1860, anticipated the full implications, but ultimately there evolved from this situation the alternatives of peace and war.

CHAPTER III

CERTAIN REPUBLICANS DISCOVER A NEW CRISIS AND AN OLD COMPROMISE

IN 1860 the presidential electors of South Carolina were not chosen by popular vote but were still named by the legislature, which customarily met in brief special session for this purpose and adjourned as soon as electors were designated. But the legislative body which met on November 5, 1860, did not follow the usual procedure. After appointing electors who were instructed to vote for Breckinridge and Lane, it waited ominously to see what the popular vote would produce, and when the election of Lincoln followed, it turned at once to the question of calling a state convention for the purpose of immediate secession.[1] A few proponents of joint or cooperative action by the states, as opposed to separate state action, offered brief, half-hearted opposition to such haste, but they quickly bowed to the popular pressure and joined with the majority, on November 10, in passing unanimously a bill providing for a convention of the people of South Carolina, to be elected on December 6 and to meet on December 17. In celebration of this act, Charleston proceeded to hold high carnival with wine flowing, palmetto flags flying, and hot-heads reveling in martial display. Barnwell Rhett rejoiced that "The tea has been thrown overboard—the revolution of 1860 has been initiated."[2]

Carolina had been preparing for this form of tea party off and on for thirty years; she had refrained from giving it only because no one else would attend. But the revo-

1. This purpose was explicitly stated in the message of Gov. Gist, Nov. 5, recommending that the legislature remain in session to call a convention if Lincoln should win the election.
2. Rhodes, *Hist. of U. S.*, III, 114–125.

lution of 1860 was now truly begun; and at last the lower South showed itself ready to follow Carolina's lead. Eight days after the Palmetto State called a convention, Georgia's legislature took the same momentous step; within eleven days more, Florida and Mississippi also summoned their people to meet in sovereign conventions; Alabama had already instructed her governor, in the previous winter, to call a convention in the event of Republican victory. He was still awaiting the formal electoral vote, but his state, too, was avowedly ready to invoke its ultimate powers.[3]

Three weeks and two days after the election of Lincoln, every state of the deep South except Louisiana had initiated the process of secession. From the low country of Carolina to the banks of the Mississippi, from the Appalachians to Key West, the states were going methodically about the business of breaking up the Federal Union.

For the Republicans, this marked an hour of decision. The swift-moving developments of the last weeks of 1860 challenged them to recognize at once the proportions of the movement which they confronted, and to determine upon their response to measures of disunion.

With a few individual exceptions, the members of the Republican party failed to meet this challenge. During the critical secession winter, the Republican majority in the House of Representatives failed to agree upon any

3. Dumond, *Secession Movement,* p. 148, tabulates the preliminaries:

	Legislative act calling a convention	Election of convention	Meeting of convention
Alabama	Feb. 24, '60	Dec. 24, '60	Jan. 7, '61
South Carolina	Nov. 10, '60	Dec. 6, '60	Dec. 17, '60
Georgia	Nov. 18, '60	Jan. 2, '61	Jan. 16, '61
Florida	Nov. 28, '60	Dec. 18, '60	Jan. 3, '61
Mississippi	Nov. 29, '60	Dec. 20, '60	Jan. 7, '61
Texas	(Dec. 3, '60)	Jan. 8, '61	Jan. 28, '61
Louisiana	Dec. 11, '60	Jan. 7, '61	Jan. 23, '61

In Texas the call for the convention was irregular, the legislature not being in session.

basic measure either to strengthen the power of the Federal Government or to conciliate the South; Republican editors, adopting no uniform policy, expressed their individual preferences for compromise, coercion, or peaceable separation; and the policy of the incoming administration remained an enigma. In Republican quarters, little effort was made either to avert or to prepare for the impending conflict.

In seeking an explanation of the unrealistic response of the Republicans, due weight should be given to their tendency, as politicians, to avoid commitments, and also to the paralyzing effect of dissension within the party. Apart from these factors, however, the greatest obstacle to effective action by the Republicans lay in their continued incredulity of secession itself, and their acceptance of certain corollary ideas which derived logically from that incredulity.

One such attitude was a fixed and indiscriminate hostility to all compromise and all compromisers. Republicans who believed that the disunion threat was not sincere, but was designed only to procure concessions, could see no reason, of course, for surrendering any part of their position. Thinking as they did that secession was designed only to frighten cowards and time-servers, it was quite natural for them to reverse the direction of their reasoning, and to suppose that only cowards and time-servers were frightened. With all the thoroughness of doctrinaires, the Republicans applied this interpretation to the events of history as well as the problems of the day, and found the national annals one long shameful record of concession after concession to the insatiable Slavocracy. The annexation of Texas, the Mexican War, the Fugitive Slave Act of 1850, the Kansas-Nebraska Act, all were designed to buy off the South. As these concessions demonstrated the nuisance value of secession, threats of disunion increased until finally there was no election too trivial and no issue too petty to evoke the thunders of secession. This view galled the Republicans the more bitterly because they re-

garded all of the compromise measures as unnecessary—
mere cringing, gratuitous submissions to empty threat
and deliberate bluster.[4] Never but once had the Southern
threat been challenged, and on that occasion, when Jackson toasted the Federal Union and sponsored the Force
Bill, South Carolina came tamely to heel. From that one
episode, Republicans drew a parallel, and inferred that
secessionism would have collapsed at any time when confronted by firm resistance.[5]

While this attitude of mind prevailed, the "Union-
savers" could expect nothing but scorn. If less malicious
in intent than the secessionists, they were held to be
equally as dangerous in effect, and even more contemptible,
because of their supposed cowardice. In the forthright
words of Thaddeus Stevens: "I do not blame the gentlemen from the South . . . for the language of intimidation, for using this threat of rending God's creation from
the turret to the foundation. All this is right in them, for

4. In the Senate, Mar. 3, 1854, William P. Fessenden said, "Gentlemen have talked here of a dissolution of the Union. We have heard
that threat until we are fatigued with the sound. We consider it now,
let me say, as mere *brutum fulmen,* noise and nothing else. It produces
not the slightest impression upon the thinking portion of the public.
You laugh at it yourselves."
Sen. Butler: "Who laugh?" [Laughter.]
Fessenden: "You at the South. You do not carry it seriously into private conversation." *Cong. Globe,* 33rd Cong., 1st sess., appendix, p. 323.
5. "To those who remember the nullification disturbance of 1832, these
inflammatory appeals seem comparatively tame and pointless." New
York *Tribune,* Nov. 12, 1860.
If South Carolina should "undertake to repeat in 1861 the tantrums of
1833," she would be "treated as she was then—kindly but firmly." *Ibid.,*
July 25, 1860.
"The manner in which that incipient rebellion [the South Carolina
Nullification] was snuffed out, encouraged many of us, who were old
enough to have remembered it, to believe with Mr. Seward that these
demonstrations of discontent in the South would also, in a few weeks
or months after the installation of a Free Soil President, end, like
their predecessor, in smoke." Bigelow, *Retrospections,* I, 296.
John Minor Botts wrote to a secessionist editor, Nov. 27, 1860, that
South Carolina "may even declare herself out of the Union. She did so
by *ordinance* in *convention* in 1833, but still the Union was not rent
asunder, nor will it be now, as I think." Botts, *Great Rebellion,* pp.
230–239.

they have tried it fifty times, and fifty times they have found weak and recreant tremblers in the North who have been affected by it, and who have acted from those intimidations."[6]

No less orthodox, no less able than Stevens as a spokesman of Republicanism, was Senator Henry Wilson of Massachusetts. And he, like the Pennsylvanian, had more contempt for Northern Union-savers than for Southern fire-eaters. In his view, the "DISUNION FARCE" existed only because Southern political adventurers knew how effectively it served to "startle and appal [sic] the timid, make the servility of the servile still more abject, [and] rouse the selfish instincts of . . . nerveless conservatism."[7]

Up to the time of Lincoln's election, these sentiments were reiterated. Greeley's *Tribune* denounced as "simpletons" those who gave heed to the warnings of "Southern braggarts" and "Northern demagogues."[8] Seward hammered the same point vigorously in his campaign speeches, especially at Saint Paul, where he rejoiced that, "for the first time in the history of the republic, the slave power has not even the ability to terrify or alarm the freeman so as to make him submit, or even to compromise. . . . I do not believe there has been one day from 1787 until now when slavery had any power in the government, except what it derived from buying up men of weak virtue, little principle and great cupidity, and terrifying men of weak nerves in the free states."[9]

In contrast with these abusive phrases, the words of Abraham Lincoln were restrained and dispassionate, but no less strong in meaning. It was characteristic of him that he refrained from all personal allusion to the men who favored compromise, but that he renounced compro-

6. Speech in House, Dec. 6, 1859, *Cong. Globe,* 36th Cong., 1st sess., part I, p. 24.

7. In Senate, Jan. 25, 1860. *Ibid.,* p. 572.

8. New York *Tribune,* July 11, 1860.

9. Speech at Saint Paul, Sep. 18, 1860, in Baker, ed. *Works of Seward,* IV, 344-345.

mise itself unconditionally, and in language of such quality
as to carry by implication utter condemnation of all who
were associated with it. Without abuse, without stridency,
but with carefully weighed words, Lincoln stated his rejection of compromise in his uniquely important speech
at the Cooper Institute: "Can we . . . allow it [slavery]
to spread into the national Territories . . . ? If our sense
of duty forbids this, then let us stand by our duty fearlessly and effectively. Let us be diverted by none of those
sophistical contrivances . . . such as groping for some
middle ground between the right and the wrong: vain as
the search for a man who should be neither a living man
nor a dead man . . . such as Union appeals beseeching
true Union men to yield to Disunionists, reversing the di-
vine rule, and calling, not the sinners, but the righteous
to repentance. . . . Neither let us be slandered from our
duty by false accusations against us, nor frightened from
it by menaces of destruction to the government, nor of
dungeons to ourselves. Let us have faith that right makes
might, and in that faith let us to the end dare to do our
duty as we understand it."[10]

Six days later, in a speech at Hartford, Lincoln repeated this declaration of policy; and twice thereafter,
at Norwich and New Haven, he reaffirmed his position
in substantially the same language.[11]

In the light of all these expressions, a faithful Republican could scarcely dally with the idea of compromise without peril to his political soul. The platform said that secession was treason, from which he might infer that compromise was a compact with traitors. Mr. Greeley said that
the compromisers were simpletons; Mr. Seward said that
they were men of weak virtue or weak nerves; Mr. Lincoln
indicated that they were persons who permitted themselves
to be slandered or frightened into desertion of duty. True,

10. Speech in New York, Feb. 27, 1860, in Nicolay and Hay, eds.,
Works of Lincoln, V, 327.
11. Speeches of Lincoln, Feb. 27 through Mar. 6, 1860, in *ibid.,* V,
327–371.

Lincoln did not employ such hearty abuse as Thad Stevens and Henry Wilson dealt in, but even in his measured words, "right" and "the righteous," "faith" and "duty," on the one hand, were opposed by "sinners" who used "sophistical contrivances, false accusations, and menaces of destruction" in a cause of "wrong," as incompatible with the cause of right as is life with death.

By the year 1860, these attitudes had taken root so firmly as to be virtually a part of the Republican creed. In this creed the threat of secession was regarded as a sham and an instrument of extortion. Those who heeded it were mere gulls and victims. And any material concession in the face of such a threat was thrice shameful as a desertion of principle, a submission to menace, and a credence of fraud. Holding these beliefs, few Republicans could be expected, in November, 1860, to consider the question of compromise entirely on its merits. Exigency must press and pride be mortified before any of them could accept a policy so long despised and so explicitly condemned.

In the sequence of corollaries which followed from incredulity of secession, still another must be noted. This was an attitude of readiness, on the part of some Republicans, to make verbal renunciation of force as a means of maintaining the Union. As this idea expressed itself, it took the deceptive form of suggestions for peaceable separation. Historians dealing with it in this form have usually interpreted it as a pacifistic revulsion from the prospect of bloodshed. Such an interpretation probably has some validity, but much of the evidence points to a far more subtle motivation. The later unwillingness of any of the "separationists" to separate suggests that many of them had never intended to permit a dissolution of the Union, but had offered their proposal in the confident assurance that the South would reject it. Furthermore, the promptness with which some of them dropped the voluntary separation plan as soon as the possibility of compromise had been eliminated, seems to indicate that aversion to compromise rather than aversion to war would have induced a preference for disunion, if anything would have. In short, the long-standing Republican disbelief of secession led partisans to believe that coercion would not be necessary, and could be safely abjured. At the same time, the long-standing Republican hostility to compromise led them to emphasize their antipathy by declaring that even the most obnoxious alternative—disunion—would be preferable.[12]

Ultimately, this "peaceable separation" policy came to nought, and historians have tended to pass over it casually. But in the initial burst of secession excitement, there were Republican editors in plenty who wrote as if they were becoming reconciled to a voluntary dissolution. During November and early December, every great city of the North had at least one Republican newspaper which voiced this attitude. In Boston, the *Advertiser* advocated dissolution as an alternative to bloodshed. In New York, the *World* maintained the same position less consistently, and the *Times*, under Henry J. Raymond, assumed a similar attitude for a brief period, but soon fell to denouncing its own abandoned policy as "the most mischievous nonsense," inasmuch as South Carolina would "be compelled to yield."[13] Meanwhile, Greeley's *Tribune* expressed an unwillingness to live in "a Republic whereof one section is pinned to the residue by bayonets." In the same editorial it declared, "If the Cotton States shall become satisfied that they can do better out of the Union than in it, we insist on letting them go in peace."[14] The objectives of the *Tribune* were, in fact, much more complex than this statement indicated, and the qualifying phrases went far to nullify the entire declaration. But public attention fixed upon the phrase "go in peace," and the *Tribune* took rank

12. For a more extensive discussion of the complex motives and the underlying significance of the peaceable secession movement, insofar as it was exemplified by the New York *Tribune,* see David M. Potter, "Horace Greeley and Peaceable Secession," in *Journal of Southern History* (May, 1941), VII, 145–159.

13. See footnote 16, below.

14. New York *Tribune,* Nov. 9, 1860.

as the foremost defender of peaceable separation. This distinction might better have been accorded to the Philadelphia *Daily News* which declared, some weeks before the election, that dissolution would be preferable to war.[15] The Republican journals of Cincinnati likewise seemed little disposed toward combat, for the *Press* and the *Daily Commercial* consistently opposed coercion until the end of the year, while the *Daily Gazette* alternated between demands that the South strive for dissolution "in a constitutional way" and that the laws against treason be invoked. The most influential paper in Indiana was the Indianapolis *Daily Journal*, and it asserted categorically that South Carolina ought to be permitted to leave the Union, whether her complaints seemed valid or not. In Illinois, the Chicago *Tribune*, already powerful, was less pacific in its tone, but it definitely flirted with the proposal of peaceful dissolution. In the wake of these journalistic leviathans, numbers of smaller dailies, weeklies, and semi-weeklies followed. Altogether, there appeared to be a large body of Republicans who were reconciled to disunion.[16]

In fact, however, the proposal of voluntary separation was never intended as an affirmative policy. In its origin, it was partly a negative expression of hostility to union-through-compromise, and partly a nominal abandonment of force in a situation where few could conceive that the

15. Philadelphia *Daily News*, Aug. 20, 1860, cited in Lowery, *Northern Opinion of Approaching Secession*, p. 248.

16. Howard Cecil Perkins, editor, *Northern Editorials on Secession* (New York, 1942), I, 332–379, contains a section on "Peaceable Separation," with the texts of twenty editorials. Perkins' admirable collection appeared in print too late to be fully utilized in this study. Prior to publishing his *Northern Editorials*, however, Dr. Perkins wrote a Ph.D. dissertation (Yale) on "The Northern Press on Approaching Civil War," and to this he generously allowed me access. In his thesis, the following citations are relevant: Boston *Advertiser*, Nov. 12, 1860 (p. 130); New York *World*, Feb. 15, 1861 (p. 129); New York *Times* (p. 37 and p. 129); Cincinnati *Press*, Nov. 13 (p. 119); Cincinnati *Daily Commercial*, Dec. 13 (p. 117); Cincinnati *Daily Gazette*, Jan. 10 (p. 70, and for coercionist editorial Dec. 26, same page); Indianapolis *Daily Journal*, Dec. 7 (p. 44); Chicago *Tribune*, Dec. 13 (p. 101). In a similar vein were editorials of Republican organs in Springfield, Mass., New Haven, Conn., Akron and Columbus, O., Lafayette and Logansport, Ind., and other places (pp. 112, 128–132).

disunion movement might be formidable enough to require force.

As regards the connection between complaisance toward disunion and opposition to compromise, it is very suggestive to note that the most violent enemies of slavery were also the promptest advocates of voluntary dissolution. William Lloyd Garrison declared publicly that "all Union-saving efforts are simply idiotic," and privately, "I fervently trust this pro-slavery Union is broken beyond the possibility of restoration by Northern compromises."[17] On this topic, as on others, Garrison outdid everyone in the extremism of his speech, but many other opponents of slavery shared his feeling. This was especially true in the abolitionist intellectual circles of Massachusetts, where E. Rockwood Hoar, Charles Eliot Norton, Samuel Gridley Howe, James Freeman Clarke, Rev. John Pierpont, and Henry W. Longfellow all seem to have entertained the idea of peaceable dissolution. Charles Sumner apparently took a similar view, though political exigencies inhibited him from stating it openly.[18] Other notables who viewed disunion with complacency were Henry Ward Beecher[19] and John Greenleaf Whittier, whose sonnet, "A Thought for the Hour" suggested a policy:

Pity, forgive, but urge them back no more
Who, drunk with passion, flaunt disunion's rag . . .[20]

17. *The Liberator,* Jan. 4, 1861, and Garrison to Oliver Johnson, Jan. 19, 1861, in [W. P. Garrison], *Garrison,* IV, 3.

18. For Longfellow, see Samuel Longfellow, editor, *Life of Henry Wadsworth Longfellow, With Extracts from his Journals and Correspondence* (Boston, 1891), II, 409; for Howe, Clarke, and Pierpont, see Edward L. Pierce, *Memoir and Letters of Charles Sumner* (Boston, 1893), IV, 5; for Sumner, see White, "Charles Sumner and the Crisis," in *Essays in Honor of . . . Dodd,* pp. 131–193; for Hoar and Norton, see *ibid.,* p. 150. Miss White also regards James Russell Lowell as a potential separationist because he wrote, "If the Republicans stand firm, we shall be saved, even at the cost of disunion." But in the same letter he rejoiced that Massachusetts was about to "be instantly put on a war footing." This is a good example of the prevalent equivocation, which made it possible to classify men either as coercionists or as separationists. Charles Eliot Norton, editor, *Letters of James Russell Lowell* (New York, 1894), I, 308.

19. Address of Beecher, Nov. 27, in New York *Tribune,* Nov. 30, 1860.

20. John Greenleaf Whittier, *Writings* (Riverside ed., Boston, 1888–

Further evidence that ostensible willingness to separate was, essentially, reluctance to compromise, appears from the later conduct of those who had advocated peaceable secession. For, as the prospect of compromise faded and the prospect of war grew imminent, the Unionism of the abolitionists and their sympathizers grew militant. Garrison gloried in a war against slavery in which the issue of Union was only a "verbal and technical" *casus belli*;[21] Greeley's *Tribune* urged the Federal armies prematurely "Forward to Richmond!"[22] From this, one may fairly infer that the Northern publicists who, for a brief time, bespoke the cause of voluntary dissolution, advocated it only as an alternative to compromise and not as a principle of action. When the choice lay between dissolution and war, all accepted armed conflict; some welcomed it.

A second factor which led Northern leaders to speak of dissolution with such misleading glibness was their continued belief that the South would not put them to the test. Mistaking the secession movement for a mere angry ebullition, they cheerfully supposed that patience and tact alone would suffice to mollify it. From this standpoint, it appeared to them that threats of coercion would only serve to inflame the Southern temper, "fire the Southern heart," and strengthen the Southern radicals; whereas a show of acquiescence might allay the Southern fear of aggression, remind the South of the fellowship that had existed in the Union, and give Southern Unionists an opportunity to rally their forces. Inasmuch as the South was almost unanimous in upholding the theoretical right of secession, it obviously behooved the friends of Union to avoid offering challenge on a point so tender. That they were aware of this aspect of the matter, and had for some years been aware of it, is evident from the language of the *Tribune* as early as 1854: "Instead of bolting the door in alarm, and calling for help to guard it, in case the

1889), III, 218–219. This poem was dated Jan. 16, 1861, and published in *The Liberator,* Feb. 8, 1861.

21. *The Liberator,* May 20, 1861, as quoted by [W. P. Garrison], *Garrison,* IV, 23.

22. New York *Tribune,* June 26, 1861, and thereafter.

South should hereafter threaten to walk out of the Union, we would hold it politely open and suggest to the departing the policy of minding his eye and buttoning his coat well under his chin preparatory to facing the rough weather outside. And this, we insist, is the true mode of reducing his paroxysms and causing him to desist from such raw-headed demonstrations in [the] future."[23]

A program such as this one, proposing nothing more than the use of tactful language and the avoidance of threats, was clearly based on a belief that secession would, if let alone, subside of itself. Greeley continued to believe this and, when the crisis came, he emphatically rejected all compulsory devices for saving the Union, because he emphatically believed that the South would need no compulsion. Perhaps he acted upon this view of things without fully analyzing his own motives, and, therefore, without deliberate dissembling. But it is significant that, in the pages of the *Tribune*, proffers of voluntary disunion are frequently paralleled by assurances that no such offer would be accepted. Thus, at the very time when the *Tribune* was asserting a qualified willingness to dissolve the Union, it was also assuring its readers that "we are convinced that the agitation raised in the South will gradually and surely subside into peace."[24] In the eyes of the *Tribune*, the secessionist newspapers were "silly, gasconading journals,"[25] and South Carolina, it was predicted, would shrink from the "solitary plunge."[26] On November 20, Greeley's paper expressed the opinion that "the great majority" of Southerners did not mean to dissolve the Union. "They simply mean to bully the Free States into concessions."[27]

Without denying a modicum of confused sincerity to the movement for peaceable separation, it is possible, then, to say with some degree of assurance that the spokesmen of the movement were motivated chiefly by an ulterior

23. New York *Tribune*, May 2, 1854.
24. *Ibid.*, Nov. 9, 1860.
25. *Ibid.*, Nov. 8, 1860.
26. *Ibid.*, Nov. 15, 1860.   27. *Ibid.*, Nov. 20, 1860.

purpose to soothe the anger of the South and the alarm of the North, thus preventing rash action by one and panicky concession by the other. To achieve these ends, disingenuous proposals of separation were made in the false expectation that fulfillment would never be demanded. Viewed in this connection, the significance of the peaceable secession movement is a curious one. The go-in-peace program probably never achieved a place in the realm of practicable solutions. It was, in this sense, largely illusory. But, like other illusions, it bore great importance. For it constantly obscured the clarity of the true alternatives—compromise or war. Whenever compromise was urged as the unpleasant alternative, but still the only alternative, to arms and blood, opponents could reply that it were better to separate than to concede. This reply blunted the argument for compromise and deflected it from its mark. It concealed the imminence of the crisis, and dissuaded a bewildered people from choosing between two repugnant courses. They chose neither, and to make no choice was to choose war. This was the chief significance of the ambiguous and hollow talk of peaceable secession. The fictitious go-in-peace alternative continued to obscure the situation until the occasion for compromise had passed and war remained as the only means by which the Union could be maintained.

Despite Republican indifference to the secession crisis and Republican hostility to the practice of compromise, events were soon to force the question of compromise upon the party. For there existed, outside of party ranks, a tradition of compromise, deep-rooted and powerful. Coeval in origin with the Constitution itself, this policy of compromise had been used to heal every major sectional dispute in the history of the Republic. It reconciled the claims of a slaveholding South and a non-slaveholding North as to the representation of slaves in 1787; it drew the line 36° 30′ between these same forces when they contested for control of the Louisiana Territory in 1820;

it prevented the collision of Nullification Ordinance and Force Bill in 1833; and it adjusted the conflicting claims which racked the country in 1850. For every compromise adopted dozens of others had been proposed, and plans of adjustment sprang up, as if by reflex action, from every violent agitation.

This tradition of compromise was especially powerful in the Border states. There it commanded the primary allegiance of almost all politicians, whatever their party labels might be. The old followers of Henry Clay made conciliation their paramount policy, and it would not be too much to say that they constituted a distinct compromise party. When this party proposed John Bell for the presidency in 1860, with no platform save "the Constitution and the Union," it was with no purpose to shirk the issues of the day, but to stress the complete subordination of these issues to a single-minded policy of saving the Union. Compared with this great objective, all other issues were of negligible importance and would be settled in any way which gave promise of maintaining the Federal relationship.

For the six years prior to Lincoln's election, however, the compromise party had been forced to forego efforts for definitive compromise. The violent antagonism between the sections made legislative agreement virtually impossible. The South brandished the Dred Scott decision and resolved to open all territories to slavery, while Northern majorities supported the Republicans in their policy of complete exclusion. As time passed, the assault on Sumner, Bleeding Kansas, the Lecompton contest, the literary incendiarism of Hinton Helper and Mrs. Stowe, and the raid at Harpers Ferry intensified sectional discord and destroyed every possibility of reconciling divergent sectional policies.

In these circumstances, it was fruitless to propose legislative compromise and none was seriously attempted. But this does not mean that the spirit of compromise had withered under the cross-fire between North and South. It

means, rather, that as the conciliators despaired of negotiating an agreement they labored instead to banish the
slavery question from Congress, and to elect moderate
men to public office. To denationalize the slavery issue,
they proposed to leave each territory free to choose for
itself, or, as they expressed it, to exercise the right of
"popular sovereignty." While thus excluding the slavery
issue from the legislative branch of government, they also
strove to exclude sectionalism from the executive branch
by securing the election to the presidency of men who
commanded appreciable support in every part of the country. Thus, many Whigs in 1856 deserted their own candidate, Fillmore, and supported the Democrat, Buchanan,
solely for the purpose of defeating Frémont and averting
the crisis which his election would have caused.[28] Similarly,
the moderates of 1860 gave strenuous support to the campaigns of Bell and Douglas. This *ad hominem* method succeeded, for a time, in forestalling the crisis, and it may
well be that the defeat of Frémont had averted a sectional
conflict quite as effectively as any of the Clay compromises.
But peace maintained on such a basis was little more than
an armed truce, for the Union became, in effect, a federal-
ization of two divergent sections under an executive acceptable to both. Should this precarious executive ambi-
dexterity be disturbed, the Union itself would be jeopardized.

The election of Lincoln produced exactly this effect.
There were some who hoped to temporize a little longer,
reminding the South that she still held a veto in the Senate,
and urging that Lincoln be trusted until he should commit
an "overt act." But the election itself was overt enough
to unloose the fire-eaters, and South Carolina's haste imposed upon the moderates the task of improvising at once
a compromise more extensive than any that had been

28. The campaign literature of the election of 1856 contained long lists
of Whigs who entered the Democratic ranks in order to secure the election of a moderate. For titles of relevant campaign pamphlets, see
above, p. 2, note 8, and p. 3, note 9.

formulated in the previous six decades. Yet hopeless as this seemed, it was made easier, paradoxically, by the same factor which made it necessary—that is, by the very imminence of the crisis. As disunion loomed up, nationalistic pride could be expected to assert itself, and in many cases to override partisan zeal and sectional principles. It was the task of the moderates, therefore, to sponsor measures to evoke the full tide of Union sentiment, while arousing sectional bias as little as possible.

It was their task, more particularly, to win some degree of Republican support. For the Republican party was in every sense at the center of the problem. The crisis was precipitated by Republican victory, and secession resulted from fear of Republican aggressions. Fear thus excited could be allayed, if at all, by none but the Republicans who had aroused it; concessions in the moment of victory could be given by none but the Republicans who had won it; promises of forbearance in the administration could be fulfilled only by the Republicans who would control it; and proposed compromises could be enacted into law or embedded in the Constitution only by legislative majorities which were Republican in the Federal House of Representatives, and in both houses of fourteen of the eighteen free state legislatures.[29] In short, the future lay with the Republicans, and without their active support compromise would be impossible. No proposal of adjustment could have any efficacy except insofar as it secured Republican endorsement.

Despite the importance of Republican approbation as a prerequisite to the success of any compromise scheme, it is not of record that anyone waited to consult Republican wishes. Instead, men of good will in astonishing numbers began, immediately after Lincoln's election, to flood the country with formulas for healing all sectional dissen-

29. New York *Herald,* Nov. 25, 1860, contains data on state legislatures, showing Republican majorities in both houses of all free state legislatures except those of California, Oregon, New Jersey, and Rhode Island.

sion. These proposals achieved infinite variety. Some were brief and simple, others lengthy and involved; some realistic, others visionary; some superficial, others drastic and far-reaching. During the autumn and winter months of 1860–1861, an untold number of such plans appeared. Most of them gained little currency, but a few received the concentrated attention of the entire country.[30]

In this multiplicity of proposals, it is impossible to assign priority to any one. But it is certain that the first preceded Lincoln's election, for there were reports in Baltimore before November 2 that leading men of the Bell and Breckinridge factions had agreed to urge the withdrawal of the Gulf states from the Union and the subsequent meeting of all the states in a constitutional convention.[31] This may have been intended to bring maximum pressure upon the North, in a genuine effort to revitalize the Union; again, it may have been designed as a soporific to lull Southern Unionists into secession. Secession first, negotiation afterward, is a rather questionable manner of compromising, but on its face, at least, the Baltimore proposal looked to the ultimate perpetuation of Federal union.

An important variation on this plan emanated from Unionists of Richmond within four days after Lincoln's election. This scheme definitely excluded any hasty resort to secession, and yet, at the same time, showed a proper appreciation of the depth of Southern feeling, and of the necessity of substantial concessions if the South were to be appeased. The Richmond plan provided for a convention of the Southern states to formulate Southern demands, while maintaining their place in the Union. After

30. A great variety of compromise proposals is to be found in the files of the New York *Herald* and New York *Times* throughout the crisis. Correspondents of Franklin Pierce and of Martin Van Buren were also prolific of plans which are preserved in the letter files of the recipients, now in the Library of Congress. The papers of John J. Crittenden, also in the Library of Congress, teem with compromise suggestions by correspondents throughout the country.

31. New York *Herald*, Nov. 5 (Baltimore, Nov. 2), 1860. Also Nov. 9. In connection with this, see New York *Times*, Nov. 15, account of a speech by Mayor Swann of Baltimore urging a national convention.

the minimum Southern demands were thus determined, they were to be presented to a national constitutional convention which would, presumably, ratify them as amendments.[32]

This proposal was sponsored by Unionists at Richmond. Their plan showed, in dramatic fashion, how rapid had been the growth of ultraism in the months preceding, for in the previous winter South Carolina and Mississippi had begged Virginia to join in a convention, and had been repulsed by the conservatives. Within a year, these same conservatives took up the rejected program only to find that its former champions had advanced to a far more extreme position.[33]

As compared with the Baltimore and Richmond proposals, however, there were numerous advantages to be secured by holding a convention under the terms of the Constitution, which specifies (Article Five) that Congress may, by a two-thirds vote in both houses, call a convention to propose amendments to the Constitution, subject to ratification by the requisite number of states. Such a convention would have enjoyed an impressive Constitutional sanction to which the conventions proposed in Baltimore and Richmond would have had no claim. Certainly, also, it would have commanded great public respect. It is not strange, therefore, that, within a week after the election, Washington gossiped of a constitutional convention which would be recommended to Congress by President Buchanan in his annual message.[34]

None of these conventions ever materialized, and none of their proponents ever produced any convincing evi-

32. New York *Herald*, Nov. 11 (Richmond, Nov. 10), 1860. Also Nov. 14, 18.

33. Another type of convention, proposed as early as December 4, was that of the Border states, both Northern and Southern. This proposal was predicated on the theory that the thoroughgoing Unionists of these states might act as intermediaries between New England and the deep South, and might even exert pressure upon the extremists of these sections. New York *Times*, Dec. 10 (Louisville, Dec. 4), 1860.

34. New York *Herald*, Nov. 11 (Washington, Nov. 10), 1860.

dence that they would be able to discover a basis for compromise, if convened. They won no favor with the Republicans, and were, therefore, not practicable. But the proposal of such meetings did indicate that certain minds turned back to the compromise tradition almost in the moment of Lincoln's election. As increasing numbers of people joined in this discussion of compromise, it became progressively more difficult for the Republicans to ignore the question themselves.

For several days after the election, however, the Republicans appeared completely oblivious to the crisis. They continued to insist, as they had so long insisted, that there was no cause for concern, no crisis which needed to be averted, no antagonisms which required adjustment. Three days after South Carolina called her convention, the New York *Times* reported that "disunion sentiment is rapidly losing ground in the South" and commented editorially: "There seems to be a great panic about disunion. We cannot, for the life of us, see the least foundation for it. Our Southern brethren talk loudly about secession,—but they have done little else for the last ten years. . . ."[35]

For some time thereafter, the *Times* avoided any direct admission of the existence of a crisis, and even carried occasional dispatches which minimized the danger of secession.[36] But on November 14 it published an editorial which indicated a sudden sense of the gravity of affairs. This editorial was one of the first compromise proposals —if not the very first—to issue from the Republican camp. It was not sweeping, nor, in the outcome, important, but it was the first outstanding evidence of conciliatory spirit in the Republican ranks, and it came from a leading Republican organ. Less brilliantly edited and less widely read than the *Tribune*, the *Times* was nevertheless a powerful journal. It followed a steadier course than Greeley's paper, and it derived strength from the fact that its words

35. New York *Times,* Nov. 13, 1860.
36. *Ibid.,* Dec. 8 (Washington, Dec. 7), 1860.

were often inspired by William H. Seward. In Henry J. Raymond, it possessed one of the foremost editors of the century.

This periodical broached the ticklish question of secession on November 14, in a long editorial on the Fugitive Slave Law. Recognizing that the South was entitled to property protection, and justified in complaining of the obstacles which were placed in the way of enforcement, this editorial at the same time insisted that Northern aversion to man-hunting could not be ignored. Yet was there no way, the *Times* queried, to protect the slaveholder from loss without violating the moral sentiment of the North? "There is one plan . . . ," it replied. "It is simply to provide by law for paying to the slaveholders the value of their fugitive slaves, instead of restoring them." Pursuing this idea, the *Times* estimated in detail that the cost would be about $1,000,000 per annum—a cheap price if it would end wrangling on this subject. The editorial did not speak of danger to the Union, nor of the necessity of conciliating the South. But it concluded by suggesting that the proposed measure would demonstrate "a spirit of compromise and conciliation which, at the present moment, would be of incalculable value to the cause of Union."[37]

In these words, the *Times* signified its awareness of the crisis. In the same words, it renounced the Republican policy of ignoring all Southern threats. The fugitive slave proposal was supported by the *Times* for several weeks in subsequent editorials, and it furnished material for a lively skirmish with the *News*, the *Herald*, and the *Journal of Commerce*, and with papers outside of New York. But it never received serious consideration; it was unsatisfactory to the South because, through taxation, it would have caused the slaveowners to pay part of the compensation for their own slaves, and because it only touched one minor issue among a host of causes of sectional dis-

37. New York *Times*, Nov. 14, 1860.

cord. But it did have significance as a first sign of Republican anxiety, a first impulse in the direction of conciliation. The Baltimore *Exchange* was quick to see in this editorial a plain manifestation that "the *Times* begins to feel that a dangerous crisis in National affairs has at length been reached."[38]

As a straw in the wind, the *Times* pronouncement was notable; as a proposed basis of compromise it was not. No conceivable settlement of the fugitive-slave question could have conciliated the sections, so long as other issues remained unsettled. For there still remained questions of slavery in the District of Columbia, slavery in the Federal forts and arsenals of the South, the transportation of slaves in free states, the interstate slave trade, and even the African slave trade. Most of all, there remained, towering above these minor issues, the problem of the status of slavery in the territories. For the whole slavery contest had centered upon the status of the Federal territories. The territorial question had first been raised when a real empire was at stake, and it had continued to dominate political thought even after the issue was limited, in its application, to areas where slavery was already barred by physical environment. But thus reduced to an abstraction, devoid of tangible significance, it retained such emotional potency as a symbol that it remained the point of focus of all the political, economic, and social antagonism of the two sections. The history of the slavery contest was a record of paroxysms arising from territorial rivalry, and of lulls following upon territorial compromise. So invariable was this recurrence that a cycle of slavery agitation had been defined. This cycle always began with the acquisition or opening of new territory. Such an event proved the signal for a conflict between slavery expansionists and exclu-

38. For repetitions of the proposal to pay indemnity for fugitive slaves, see *ibid.*, Nov. 17, 27, Dec. 3.

For attacks on this proposal on ground that slaveholders would be, indirectly, paying a part of their own indemnity, see *ibid.*, Nov. 17, quoting Baltimore *Exchange.* For opposition of New York *News,* New York *Herald,* and New York *Journal of Commerce,* see *Times,* Nov. 16.

sionists. As the violence of their contest increased so far
as to threaten the security of the country, moderates and
Unionists became alarmed and intervened to impose some
sort of territorial adjustment, whereupon the excitement
diminished and the country lapsed into a period of relative quiet.

This had first occurred in 1820, when Missouri's application for statehood precipitated a struggle to exclude
slavery throughout the region of the Louisiana Purchase.
This flare-up was settled by the first Missouri Compromise, which admitted slavery below, and excluded it above,
the parallel 36° 30′, and gave to this imaginary line a political significance far exceeding that of any natural land-
mark in America. After that, the question did not again
present itself in acute form until the acquisition of clear
title to Oregon and the conquest of the Southwest reopened
the territorial question on a grand scale.[39] On this occasion,
the congressional battle lasted for more than four years,
and the moderates were taxed to the utmost to devise a
compromise formula.[40] Quite naturally, they sought again
to apply the compromise line which had proved so satisfactory in 1820, and the Senate actually voted, 33 to 21,
to extend the Missouri line to the Pacific.[41] In the House,

39. While the annexation of Texas and other events had kept the
slavery issue alive, they had not presented any questions of territorial
status, and they had not culminated in a crisis.

40. The contest began on Aug. 8, 1846, with the introduction of the
Wilmot Proviso by the exclusionists. The extensionists replied on Feb.
19, 1847, with a set of resolutions by Calhoun, denying the authority
of Congress to restrict slavery in the territories. These opposing forces
continued to struggle with each other until the passage of Clay's compromise measures. The last of these passed on Sep. 9, 1850.

41. No sooner was the Wilmot Proviso introduced into the House,
Aug. 8, 1846, than William W. Wick, of Ind., proposed a measure to
extend the Missouri Compromise line. This motion was rejected by a
vote of 54 to 89, without a roll call. *Cong. Globe*, 29th Cong., 1st sess.,
p. 1217.

Two years later, in the Senate, Stephen A. Douglas proposed, as a
modification of another bill, an amendment to extend the Missouri
Compromise line. This measure passed, Aug. 10, 1848, by a vote of
33 to 21. Northern senators opposed the measure, and none supported
it except Douglas of Ill., Bright and Hannegan of Ind., Cameron and

however, Northern members offered virtually unanimous opposition, and the measure was defeated by a vote of 82 to 121.[42] The Senate thereupon receded,[43] and agitation continued until Henry Clay succeeded in pushing through a piecemeal compromise which admitted California as a free state and organized the territories of Utah and New Mexico without restrictions on slavery. Once more, harmony was restored. It was disturbed again, in 1854, not by the acquisition of new territory, but by the reopening of the slave question in the Louisiana Purchase Area. As part of a plan for organizing the territories of Kansas and Nebraska, Stephen A. Douglas proposed the repeal of the Missouri Compromise and carried his measure against bitter opposition.[44] From the hour of its passage, a renewed territorial question produced violent sectional antagonism, and, on this occasion, the moderates were helpless. The Republicans anathematized Douglas, but

Sturgeon of Pa., Dickinson of N. Y., and Fitzgerald of Mich. Slave state senators were solidly in favor of the measure, and none voted against it. Calhoun of S. C. and Westcott of Fla. regarded the measure as unconstitutional, but voted for it as the alternative to the section to be amended, which they also regarded as unconstitutional. They later registered their constitutional objections by voting against the bill into which the amendment had been inserted. *Cong. Globe,* 30th Cong., 1st sess., p. 1061.

42. *Ibid.,* p. 1062–1063, Aug. 11, 1848. Division as follows:

	yeas	nays
Free states	3	119
Slave states	79	2
	82	121

43. The vote to recede was 29 to 25. All free state senators affirmative, all slave state senators negative, except Benton of Mo., Houston of Tex., and Spruance of Del., who were affirmative. Aug. 12, 1848. *Ibid.,* p. 1078.

44. The division on the Kansas-Nebraska Act follows (*ibid.,* 33rd Cong., 1st sess., pp. 532, 1254. The votes were taken on Mar. 3, and May 22, 1854.):

	Senate		House	
	Yeas	Nays	Yeas	Nays
Free states	14	12	44	91
Slave states	23	2	69	9
	37	14	113	100

at the same time they refused to restore the compromise which they cursed him for undoing. In 1856, efforts to revise the 36° 30′ line failed miserably.[45]

Thus the Missouri Compromise line appeared to have been renounced by both sides, even before the Dred Scott decision. That ruling struck a posthumous blow at it by declaring it unconstitutional. The old compact went under a legal cloud and for four years it appeared to be an utterly dead issue. Yet even at its lowest ebb it was still a talisman which had stilled one sectional storm, which, being violated, had precipitated another, and which had been regarded as sacrosanct for a generation. With such a tradition behind it, it could not entirely lose its magic. Inevitably, therefore, in any great national crisis, despairing Unionists would turn once more to the remedy which had, at one time, given peace to the Republic. Further, it was inevitable that the acuteness of the danger would rally many supporters who normally spurned such moderation. Thus the logic of events in 1860 promised that the moderates would once again seek a territorial adjustment, and that, in all probability, their middle ground would be traversed by the line 36° 30′.

It is not strange, therefore, that, within two weeks after Lincoln's election, the Missouri Compromise was once again the subject of gossip in Washington, where its revival was vaguely assigned to the sponsorship of "leading men."[46]

The whole thing was still in the stage of mere rumor, however, when it suddenly received endorsement from a source so high that it promptly assumed major signifi-

45. On motion of Representative George G. Dunn of Ind., that the Missouri Compromise ought to be restored, the House voted, Jan. 26, 1856, in the affirmative, 101 to 100. On June 30, Representative Dunn secured the passage of an amendment to a substitute, by which amendment the repeal of the Missouri Compromise was repealed. This carried by a vote of 109 to 102, but the substitute to which it had been attached was then rejected by a vote of 2 to 210. This vote shows quite clearly that the Northern members were glad to berate the repeal but unwilling to undo it. *Cong. Globe,* 34th Cong., 1st sess., pp. 301, 1513, 1515, and appendix, pp. 957–960.

46. New York *Times,* Nov. 19 (Washington, Nov. 18), 1860.

cance, and so purely Republican that it automatically acquired some prospect of success. This support came unexpectedly from Thurlow Weed, through his Albany *Evening Journal*. The fame of Weed has grown shadowy in the twentieth century, but to his contemporaries he was a great power, if not a great man. Awe-inspired politicians knew him as America's most formidable political boss. Thurlow Weed was a man who, when asked if he knew a certain senator, could snort, "Know him! I created him." Weed had been a maker of presidents—both Harrison and Taylor owed their elections largely to him. Furthermore, he was the political partner, and even the *alter ego*, of William H. Seward. Seward owed his senatorship, his political independence, and his freedom from routine political cares entirely to Weed's painstaking political guardianship. Weed, therefore, shared Seward's prestige, as Seward shared Weed's power, and each exercised the full strength of their partnership. In addition to the prestige which he drew from this political combination, Weed also possessed great influence as a spokesman of the propertied interests of New York City—the commercial powers which constituted the Wall Street of his day. Therefore, when he spoke, it was not as an Albany editor to his townsfolk, but as one of the most powerful figures in the Republican party.

As a Republican leader, Weed had shown characteristic partisan scorn of the secession threat.[47] He had evinced a Jacksonian dogmatism in asserting that the Union "must and shall be preserved,"[48] and a readiness to threaten hanging as his remedy for disunion.[49] At the same time, his skepticism of the whole movement led him, as late as

47. See above, p. 11.
48. Albany *Evening Journal*, Dec. 6, 1859, as cited in Lowery, *Northern Opinion of Approaching Secession*, p. 197. Note, however, that the *Journal* was not altogether consistent in this matter, and on Dec. 3, 1859, it had remarked that "When a Republican President is elected those who *wish to go out of the Union can do so.*"
49. Albany *Evening Journal*, Nov. 2, 1860. "The fire-eaters say that they will dissolve the Union if Lincoln is elected; and that they will 'laugh to scorn' all the efforts he may make to prevent them. If they 'laugh,' it will be because they are ticklish about the neck."

November 10, 1860, to burlesque disunion in a mock-heroic account of the secession of Coney Island, where local patriots were represented as swearing that, "The sons of Coney Island will stand upon their arms, and vindicate in blood, if they must, their natural and constitutional rights."[50]

But on November 13, while still disavowing any Republican responsibility for the crisis, he announced that he had instituted "a rigid personal inquiry into our own course and conduct toward the South."[51] At the time, and for ten days thereafter, he found nothing to repent except the endorsement, two years before, of Helper's *Impending Crisis*, but on November 22 he admitted that the Union sentiment in the South had been overawed, and that it needed encouragement from friends of Union elsewhere.[52]

By this time, Weed's serious tone and his anxiety to be fair showed that the crisis had impressed him deeply. He had made no positive overtures to the South, but his whole attitude suggested that he refrained not because of unwillingness to make offers, but because of uncertainty as to how they would be received.[53] South Carolina was so evidently unwilling to negotiate that friendly gestures in her direction were bootless. But so soon as Union sentiment in the South should express itself, Weed stood ready to encourage it.[54]

50. *Ibid.*, Nov. 10, 1860.   51. *Ibid.*, Nov. 12, 1860.
52. *Ibid.*, Nov. 22, 1860.

53. "The persons in whose minds treason lurks do not want anything said or done for the Union. They are against it for the reasons which nothing . . . will change. . . . South Carolina has been surly, sore-headed, and mutinous for more than thirty years. . . . Mr. Lincoln could neither say nor do anything that would change the design or appease the indignation of the disunionists. His more patriotic and generous avowals would be followed by perversions and ridicule. He would be taunted with cowardice and pusillanimity in the Organs and by the Orators of disunion." *Ibid.*, Nov. 12, 1860.

54. "Under these elements of disunion there is . . . an intelligent and earnest but overawed Union sentiment—a sentiment strong enough, if developed, to resist and thwart disunion. But that sentiment needs encouragement either from the General Government or from the friends of the Union in other States." *Ibid.*, Nov. 22, 1860.

In this receptive attitude, he very quickly found the expression of Union sentiment which he was seeking. He learned that resolutions had been introduced into the Georgia legislature demanding the repeal of Personal Liberty Laws and the enactment of laws to protect slavery in the territories, as conditions precedent to Georgia's remaining in the Union. Taking these resolutions as a text, he redeemed his two-day-old promise to encourage Unionism in the South, and, by a startling editorial on November 24, he brought the question of territorial compromise into the open and set most of the Republican press in an uproar.

"Here," he said, alluding to the proposal from Georgia, "is something tangible. It suggests a basis on which negotiations can be inaugurated. South Carolina goes ahead without 'rhyme or reason.' There it is not disunion for cause but disunion *per se*."

Continuing in a rather mild vein, he observed that he would be hopeful of a solution if the sectional issue were approached in a spirit of good will. Turning then to the fugitive-slave problem, he suggested that the existing law —"a law repugnant to manhood and honor"—might be replaced by an enactment arming "the Federal authorities with all needful powers," and providing that counties where fugitives were rescued from officers by violence should be "liable for the value of the slaves so rescued."

Thus far Weed had merely offered a variation on the *Times* proposal, and, ignoring the basic territorial issue, had dallied with non-essentials. But, in a final dramatically abrupt paragraph, he came to the crux of the crisis: "And in regard to the other vexed question, viz: the right of going into the Territories with slaves, why not restore the Missouri Compromise Line? That secured to the South all Territory adapted by Soil and Climate to its 'peculiar institution.' "[55]

That was all. The proposal was not elaborated, nor was it mentioned in any way for several days following. One

55. *Ibid.*, Nov. 24, 1860.

feels that Weed wrote this passage and withdrew forthwith into his cyclone cellar. In a single sentence, he had
renounced the platform of his party, flouted the policies
of all his associates, and abandoned a position which he
had held for years. Having packed so sweeping a proposal
into so brief a statement, he might well retire to await the
reaction to his words.

All in all, the reaction was sharply adverse. The greatest
potential force in Weed's pronouncement lay in its possible
effect upon his fellow-Republicans, and, among these, it
failed decisively. There were a few notable exceptions, but
the mass of the party responded with disfavor, if not with
anger. Greeley's *Tribune* flew promptly into opposition,[56]
and Preston King, Seward's colleague in the Senate, wrote
dramatically: "Dear Weed,—It cannot be done. You must
abandon your position. . . . You and Seward should be
among the foremost to brandish the lance and shout for
war."[57] Weed replied with restraint and good sense,[58] but
without effect, for he soon found that Republican opponents of compromise refused to be persuaded. Nowhere
except in the financial district of New York City did his
proposal elicit very much support.[59] From August Belmont, A. T. Stewart, and other capitalists in that quarter,
he received commendatory letters, but the general trend
of public opinion was so adverse that an Albany observer
reported that "no influential man agreed with Mr. Weed's
view and . . . it had no support in the rural districts."[60]

If there be any doubt as to the reaction of the inarticulate public, there can be none as to that of the Republican
press. It condemned Weed's proposal unequivocally. Almost at once the Rochester *Democrat* and the Syracuse
Journal expressed their disapproval, and, within four days
after making his proposal, Weed virtually conceded that

56. New York *Tribune,* Nov. 27, 1860.
57. King to Weed, Dec. 7, 1860, in Barnes, *Weed,* p. 309.
58. Weed to King, Dec. 10, 1860, in *ibid.,* p. 309.
59. Below, p. 116.
60. George E. Baker to Charles Sumner, Dec. 3, 1860, in Pierce,
Sumner, IV, 6.

the public reaction was negative. He spoke editorially of "our dissenting friends . . . who mistrust our judgment," expressed his consciousness of the "feebleness of a single voice in such a tempest," admitted his foreknowledge that the proposal would prove "distasteful" to "our most valued friends," and carefully avowed that "we think and speak only for ourself."[61] A little more than two weeks later, the trend of opinion had become so clear that Weed made no pretense of having any appreciable amount of support. On December 17, he admitted quite frankly that "With two or three exceptions the suggestions of the *Evening Journal* . . . have elicited from the Republican press in this and other states responses [that there must be] . . . no more compromises, no backing down. . . . That our views encounter the 'vigorous resistance' of our political friends causes less of surprise than of regret. . . . The prevalent sentiment . . . rejects all compromises."[62]

Republican coldness to Weed was clearly evident, and was reported, gleefully, no doubt, by the New York *Herald*, which observed on December 6 that Weed's position was execrated by all his fellow-Republican editors except Raymond of the *Times*;[63] a few days later it recorded an effort by irate Republicans to punish Weed by depriving him of the printing patronage of the state.[64]

Even the New York *Times*, though it was friendly to Weed,[65] admitted that he had been roughly handled. It went further than the other papers, however, to offer an explanation for the attitude of those who rebuked him. "The *Evening Journal* has incurred a good deal of cen-

61. Albany *Evening Journal*, Nov. 30, 1860.
62. *Ibid.*, Dec. 16, 1860.
63. New York *Herald*, Dec. 6, 1860. On the same day, the *Herald's* Springfield correspondent remarked that Wall Street influenced Weed, and added, "Would that he could see the negative interest with which his *Journal* is daily read by the future dispenser of what he yearns for most."
64. New York *Herald*, Dec. 14, 1860.
65. Albany *Evening Journal*, Nov. 27, 1860, quotes the *Times*, in an editorial which seemed almost to endorse the 36° 30' proposal.

sure from an influential section of the Republican Party, for its offers of concession. That was to have been expected, simply because the mass of the people do not realize, as thoroughly as the veteran Editor . . . , the absolute necessity of such concessions, to the safety of the country and the success of the Republican Administration. As we have more than once remarked, the people in the interior do not believe that there is danger of disunion. . . . Naturally enough, therefore, they resent the suggestion that they are to make sacrifices or concessions . . . for the sake of averting an imaginary danger. . . . The relative wisdom of their course turns on the question whether the danger is imaginary."[66]

The *Times* wrote a month and a day subsequent to Lincoln's election. During that interval, Republican organs, with the exception of the *Times* and the *Evening Journal*, had evinced little readiness to regard the danger otherwise than as imaginary. The tone of the Republican press had indicated a bellicose spirit in some quarters, a fatuous tendency to toy with the fictitious alternative of voluntary separation in others, a serious effort to grasp the problem and achieve a solution in almost none. Meanwhile, party leaders had maintained a discreet silence, which left the whole question in a preliminary stage.

The politicians maintained silence because they were awaiting the meeting of Congress. For them, the third of December would bring the second session of the Thirty-Sixth Congress. On that day, public opinion would turn from the scattered, preliminary newspaper discussion to concentrate upon the arena where policy is translated into law. From that day, Republican senators and representatives would face the question whether to discount the danger, as did a majority of their partisans, or to heed the warnings of the small but able minority of which Raymond and Weed were the first spokesmen.

66. New York *Times,* Dec. 7, 1860.

CHAPTER IV

INTERREGNUM IN THE REPUBLICAN PARTY

CONGRESS met on December 3, 1860. Lincoln's election was not yet a month past, but events were moving rapidly. Five Southern states had already called conventions, with secession in prospect, and in two other states proclamations had been issued convening the legislatures in special session.[1] Major Anderson had written from Charleston that additional forces would be necessary to maintain control of the harbor there. All these developments had been publicized to the fullest. Southern political leaders united their voices in a universal chorus of threat or warning that secession was imminent. These outcries, as always, were echoed by Democratic speakers and writers in the North.

The din of secession had never been louder; furthermore, the material evidences of secession had never been more tangible. What had long found expression only in the realm of elocution, now manifested itself in terms of special legislative sessions, of state conventions, of financial derangements, of economic boycotts, and of military preparations by Southern states.

The concrete impact of these developments had, for the first time, made the secession threat seem real to two of the foremost Republican publicists. It had convinced Henry J. Raymond that "it is idle to deny that the secession movement is assuming formidable proportions . . .

---

1. Bills providing for state conventions passed the legislatures of Alabama, Feb. 24 (authorizing the governor to call a convention if a Republican should be elected); South Carolina, Nov. 10; Georgia, Nov. 18; Florida, Nov. 28; and Mississippi, Nov. 29. An extra-legal call for a convention was issued in Texas, Dec. 3. Special sessions of the legislature were called in Virginia, Nov. 15, and in Louisiana, Nov. 19. The governors' proclamations appear in the New York *Herald*, Nov. 18 and 30,

the movement is too deliberate not to be serious"; [2] and
it had sobered Thurlow Weed from his parodies on the
secession of Coney Island to the point of declaring, as an
"earnest admonition," that "There is imminent danger of
the dissolution of the Union."[3]

Thus the developments of an interval of less than a
month had shaken the dogma of incredulity in two minds,
at least. But these were minds superbly informed and
singularly free from preconception and wishful thinking.
Other minds, less informed or more indoctrinated, were not
so quick to sense the crisis. Not only in the Republican
party, but throughout the North in general, the public
was very slow to perceive that the Southern movement was
more than another episode in the sham battle of party
warfare. The observation of Henry Adams affords striking illustration of this fact. "At the beginning of December," he declared, "the country was in a condition of utter
disorganization. A new question had been sprung upon it
before men had had time to discover where they stood, or
what the danger really was, or indeed whether any real
danger in fact existed. In the extreme North the belief
was general that the whole trouble was only sheer panic,
which would be short-lived as it was violent. . . . In the
middle states, however, there was great alarm."[4]

Other witnesses, who surpassed Adams in age and experience, agreed with him in his observation. Henry J.
Raymond, whom Adams admired as a "man of the world,"
reiterated in the New York *Times*, early in December, a
conviction that he had already "more than once remarked," namely, that "the people in the interior do not
believe that there is danger of disunion."[5] To the same
effect, Amos A. Lawrence, a distinguished Bostonian, be-

2. New York *Times,* Nov. 19, 1860.

3. Albany *Evening Journal,* Nov. 30, 1860.

4. Henry Adams, "The Great Secession Winter of 1860–61," in Massachusetts Historical Society *Proceedings,* XLIII (1910), 660. Although
not published until 1910, this account was written by Adams prior to
May 1, 1861.

5. New York *Times,* Dec. 7, 1860.

lieved late in December that "nine out of ten of our people would laugh if told that blood must be shed."[6] Later in the winter, a resident of New York gained the impression, which he recorded years after, that, "While war was much talked of at this time, there were not many who really believed that it was coming."[7] In Washington, Senator Seward's son, Frederick, found that thinking tended to follow the usual partisan channels, and that there was a general inclination to view the crisis as a "political flurry."[8] To much the same effect, Gideon Welles observed that "Neither party appeared to be apprehensive of, or to realize the gathering storm. There was a general belief, indulged in by most persons, that an adjustment would in some way be brought about, without any resort to extreme measures."[9] All in all, much evidence exists to controvert the dictum of a later historian that "a disposition to look matters squarely in the face prevailed."[10]

Of all the doubters who declined to look matters squarely in the face, the Republicans were the most obdurate. By long mental conditioning, they had learned to discount all evidences of Southern discontent, and now eminent Republican leaders—as well as members of the rank and file—seemed unresponsive to the events of secession. Copious proof of this reaction is offered by the testimony of their opponents and their sympathizers, as well as by their own subjective statements.

This Republican shortcoming evoked annoyed comment from the New York *Herald*, which found that its daily warnings of danger fell on deaf ears. As early as November 14, the *Herald* had reported that there was not a man south of the Mason-Dixon line who doubted the inevita-

6. Lawrence to John J. Crittenden, Dec. 29, 1860, in Coleman, *Crittenden*, II, 240.

7. William Dudley Foulke, *Life of Oliver P. Morton, Including his Important Speeches* (Indianapolis, 1899), I, 104.

8. Seward, *Seward*, II, 490.

9. John T. Morse, Jr., editor, *Diary of Gideon Welles, Secretary of the Navy under Lincoln and Johnson* (Boston, 1911), I, 10.

10. Rhodes, *Hist. of U. S.*, III, 139.

bility of secession.[11] But Republican leaders remained heedless, and, at the opening of Congress, the *Herald* lamented that, "Strange as it may seem, they [the Republican leaders] affect to believe that the South is not in earnest, and that the storm will blow over."[12]

One must allow for a certain bias in the *Herald*, and its word alone would carry little weight. But Republican authorities offered testimony which substantiated the observation of Bennett's paper. Henry Adams wrote at the time that many Republican congressmen "underrated the danger," and he later described himself as having been "ignorant and helpless" when he went to Washington in December, 1860, but "the knowledge possessed by everybody about him was hardly greater than his own."[13] The New York *Times* observed that "The mass of the party do not realize . . . the absolute necessity of . . . concessions to the safety of the country."[14] Even more explicitly, William H. Seward wrote from Washington, to his family, on December 1: "The Republicans who come here are ignorant of the real design or danger."[15]

Senator Fessenden could well have been one of those described by Seward. For it was at this time that he recorded his opinion that "much of the noise is got up for effect in the hope that the North will be frightened and the Republicans induced to falter and thus lose the confidence of the people. . . ."[16] Fessenden came from Maine, and his judgment suffered because of his remoteness from the South. But proximity alone conferred no immunity to

11. New York *Herald*, Nov. 16 (Richmond, Nov. 11), 1860. "There is not . . . at this moment a man south of Mason and Dixon's line, uncontrolled by the influence of some prospective gain at the hands of Lincoln, who is not convinced that the secession of three or more Southern States is inevitable. Not one."

12. *Ibid.*, Dec. 4, 1860.

13. Henry Adams, "Secession Winter," in Mass. Hist. Soc., *Proc.*, XLIII, 668; Henry Adams, *The Education of Henry Adams, An Autobiography* (Boston, 1918), p. 99.

14. New York *Times*, Dec. 7, 1860.

15. Seward, *Seward*, II, 478.

16. Letter of Fessenden, Dec. [?], 1860 [?], in Francis Fessenden, *Life and Public Services of William Pitt Fessenden* (Boston, 1907), I, 116.

error, for Edward Bates of Missouri, soon to enter Lincoln's cabinet, held an equally distorted view of the Southern upheaval. "The news from *the South*, as to secession," he noted in his diary, "does not improve. . . . Still I think that (except with a few demented fanatics) it is all brag and bluster, hoping thus to make a better compromise with the timid patriotism of their opponents."[17]

From Maine to Missouri, Republicans both prominent and obscure seemed oblivious to the dangers of secession. None, however, appear to have developed as high a degree of nonchalance as some of the Ohioans who wrote to Salmon P. Chase. One of these declared that he did "not heed the fiery resolves that come from the Cotton States— they are but the bubbling over of disappointed ambition and will soon cease or be put down by the sober second thought of the people of that region without any help from the North." Another spoke of the secession movement as "the present flurry in S[outh] Carolina." Still a third carried the theory of bluff and bluster to its logical conclusion: "I am inclined to think that it will be better for the Republican party, *in the end*, to have the Disunion movement go just as far as its leaders dare go. We have been frightened too long with this bug-bear, and I know of no way of convincing our political old ladies of its entire harmlessness, so good, as that of letting it swell to the most alarming dimensions it can attain before it collapses. Anything therefore which would give the fire-eaters an excuse for concluding this act of their farce without coming to the real dénouement would be unfortunate. We want the thing played entirely through. Nothing less will develope [*sic*] that healthy sentiment at the South which is necessary for the ultimate triumph of Republican principles."[18]

17. Howard K. Beale, editor, *The Diary of Edward Bates, 1859–1866*, Nov. 22, 1860, p. 157, in American Historical Association, *Annual Report, 1930*, IV.

18. Letters to Chase from, respectively, T. R. Stanley, McArthur, O., Nov. 13, 1860; James T. Worthington, Chillicothe, O., Nov. 22; and Luther B. Bruen, Dayton, O., Nov. 13; in Chase MSS.

Of all the evidences of Republican short-sightedness that have survived, however, probably none is more emphatic than a statement in the autobiography of the younger Charles Francis Adams. Adams was twenty-five in the summer of 1860. During that summer he went on a speaking tour in the West with his father and William H. Seward. Throughout the trip, he lived intimately with men who ranked at the head of the party. Recalling this experience later, he felt that he and everyone else had failed to perceive what ought to have been evident: "We all dwelt in a fool's Paradise. It is a source of amazement now to realize our own short-sightedness; for, however much people may since have educated themselves to believe that they foresaw everything, and looked for exactly what afterwards took place, it is all pure self-deception—cases of wisdom after the event. We were, all around, of an average blindness. I know it was so in the case of Seward and my father; as it was absolutely so in that of Sumner. We knew nothing of the South, had no realizing sense of the intensity of feeling which there prevailed; we fully believed it would all end in gasconade."[19]

Aside from the handicap of misconceiving the importance of the secession movement, the Republicans were also placed at a great disadvantage by their lack of experience as a majority party and their lack of a leader to chart their course for them. The crisis overtook them before they could remedy these defects. It demanded that they produce a formula to save the Union, and made this demand at a time when they had never even borne the responsibility of appointing a postmaster. They were as yet a minority party, not destined to assume office for three months to come. They had never been anything other than a minority party, skilled in opposition tactics, steeped in opposition psychology, unused to responsibility, unaccustomed to the formulation of policy. Unprepared

19. Charles Francis Adams, Jr., *Charles Francis Adams, 1835–1915, An Autobiography* (Boston, 1916), pp. 69–70.

as they were to cope with a crisis, they clung to their nominal position as a minority group and shrank from taking affirmative action. Yet the future belonged to them; they alone could pledge it; and consequently they alone could wield the initiative.

This handicap might have been overcome by clear-cut and decisive leadership. But in the moment when an unexpected crisis and unfamiliar responsibility fell simultaneously upon Republican congressmen, they found themselves with no unquestioned leader. Abraham Lincoln was, of course, the elected chief, but he had been silent for more than half a year. Mr. Lincoln was, in the eyes of many, simply an ex-congressman from Illinois, now President-elect, because he had once trapped Stephen A. Douglas in a dilemma, and because Horace Greeley held a grudge against Seward. Leading politicians were maneuvering for ascendancy over Lincoln as if they expected a regency. Certainly they gave no sincere allegiance to the unknown quantity from Springfield, and if anyone held the position of leadership it was Lincoln's rival, William H. Seward.

Seward had been the leader of the Republican party, and especially of the Republicans in Congress, for nearly six years. He held this pre-eminence by qualities which peculiarly fitted him for a position of influence in a parliamentary body. Though he lacked the erudition and grandiose pedantry of Charles Sumner, he was probably the most intelligent member on the Republican side of the Senate. Keen insight, balanced judgment, and a capacity for thinking in broad terms characterized his mind. Moreover, his intellect was free from the rigid moral dogmatism which hardened the mental arteries of many anti-slavery men. Because of this, he was quick to sense the trend of events and to alter his own course according to circumstances. This quality may be regarded as tactical skill or as conscienceless opportunism, but it made him, in either case, a dangerous antagonist, for he strove only for objectives which he might hope to win. The moral grandeur of "lost causes" held little appeal for him. Consequently he became a superb politician, a master of artifice, equivocation, and silence. His lack of moral fervor made it possible for him to maintain an astonishing diversity of friends—ranging from Jefferson Davis to Theodore Parker. And, when applied to himself, his detachment of mind left him free from senatorial pomposity. This did not mean that he lacked self-confidence; on the contrary, he sometimes magnified his own rôle. But the cynical vein in his nature took an introspective turn, and left him without any touch of the *ex cathedra* attitude.

In spite of these qualities, Seward was sometimes led into error by his excessive optimism and his tendency to view matters in the large, thus ignoring immediate difficulties. But all in all, he was a man of unusually sound judgment, and of unusual fitness for leadership.

Seward, more than anyone else, held the center of attention when Congress met. Lincoln, who might have received greater public notice, was clinging scrupulously to his position as a private citizen, not yet formally elected, much less inducted, as President. With Lincoln silent in Springfield, the public gaze turned upon Seward, the leader in Congress, and, as rumor had it, the next Secretary of State.[20]

Had Seward been prepared to act vigorously at this juncture, he might have exerted an enormous influence. Certainly he would have had all the advantage which a decisive man always enjoys in dealing with those who are bewildered. But he was, himself, inhibited at this critical moment by his reticence in assuming leadership so soon after his defeat for the nomination, by his underestimate of the crisis, and by his anxiety not to take any step that would impair his prospective influence with the new administration.

Seward's chagrin at the nomination of Lincoln had been

20. Lincoln alluded to such rumors in his letter to Seward, Dec. 8, offering him the Department of State. Nicolay and Hay, eds., *Works of Lincoln*, VI, 76.

deep, and for a time he was "content to quit with the political world, when it proposes to quit with me."[21] It cost him a great psychological effort to face his senatorial associates after his defeat, and for a time he seemed eager to escape every responsibility and every act which would require him to assume a position of leadership.[22] This heartsickness found expression in a letter to Mrs. Seward: "I have not shrunk from any fiery trial prepared for me by the enemies of my cause. But I shall not hold myself bound to try, a second time, the magnanimity of its friends."[23] During the campaign, Seward imposed upon himself the discipline of a speaking tour, and as time healed his wounds, he recovered his zest for politics. But as late as November 18, he declared, "I am without schemes, or plans, hopes, desires, or fears for the future that need trouble anybody, so far as I am concerned."[24] While this mood endured, Republican senators could not look to their New York colleague for his customary leadership.

Even if Seward had retained his usual brisk initiative in political matters, however, it is unlikely that he could have offered effective guidance to his party. For he showed, at this time, little apprehension of trouble ahead; and whatever desire he felt to placate the South was overshadowed by his anxiety to avoid any commitment at that time. His chief reaction to Weed's editorial was, in fact, a feeling of purely personal annoyance that his name would be linked with the proposal, as he foresaw that it would. The lifelong collaboration of the two men, in fact, justified the public in supposing that Weed's editorial was a feeler or

21. Seward to Weed, June 26, 1860, in Seward, *Seward,* II, 459.
22. Seward wrote to his wife, May 30, 1860, "The journey [from Auburn] and the reappearance at Washington in the character of a leader deposed by my own party, in the hour of organization for decisive battle, thank God, are past—and so the last of the humiliations has been endured." On June 13, he wrote wearily of "the Senate treadmill," but professed to be "cheerful, however, in the thought, that responsibility has passed away from me, and that the shadow of it grows shorter every day." *Ibid.,* 454, 458.
23. Seward to his wife, May 30, 1860. *Ibid.,* 456.
24. Seward to Weed, Nov. 18, 1860. *Ibid.,* 478.

"trial balloon" to test opinion, a mere foreshadowing of Seward's course in Congress. Seward anticipated that his name would become involved, and when he set out for Washington on November 28, he appears to have been more disturbed by the Albany *Evening Journal* than by the ferment south of the Potomac.

He arrived in New York City that night; stopped at the Astor House; met Weed, and talked with him until one o'clock, though he intended to rise at five to resume his journey. One is tempted to imagine the interview, with Weed defending his policy and emphasizing the crisis, with Seward urging the inexpediency of assuming a position at that time; but all that can be reconstructed now is the fact that Weed promised to make a statement freeing Seward from all connection with his proposal.[25] He fulfilled this promise on November 30, in a long, dignified, and rather sad editorial in which he twice asserted that "we speak only for ourself."[26]

Despite these belated efforts on the part of Weed, Seward's worst expectations were fulfilled. At best, he would have had difficulty in getting clear of the *Evening Journal* proposal, and in this case the task was made more difficult, so Seward believed, by the deliberate misrepresentations which emanated from the unfriendly *Tribune* office. There certain Republican congressmen visited while *en route* to Washington, and there Charles A. Dana assured them that the voice was the voice of Seward, even though the hand was the hand of Weed—that Weed had merely penned the editorials, while Seward had actively inspired them because he " 'wanted to make a great compromise like Clay and Webster.' "[27] The congressmen repeated Dana's gossip in Washington, as they were doubtless expected to do, and the rumor quickly spread

25. Account of this meeting and statement of Weed's promise appear in letters of Seward to his family, Nov. 30 [?] and Dec. 2, 1860, in Seward, *Seward,* II, 478, 479. The New York *Tribune,* Nov. 29, 1860, reported Seward's presence at the Astor House.

26. Albany *Evening Journal,* Nov. 30, 1860.

27. Seward to Weed, Dec. 3, 1860, in Barnes, *Weed,* p. 308.

over the capital, where it was, ironically, picked up by the *Tribune's* correspondent, who reported that "Mr. Seward is expected to make an important speech on the condition of the country, soon after the delivery of the [President's] Message, and to take the *role* of pacificator."[28] On the same day, the *Herald* also learned from Washington that "It is reported that Senator Seward will take the earliest opportunity to introduce in the Senate a bill restoring the Missouri Compromise line, extending it to the Pacific. . . ."[29]

As a result of these dispatches, Seward's efforts to avoid being identified with Weed's policy failed completely. While the *Tribune* hinted that the policies of Weed "gain interest from the fact that he sustains relations of peculiar intimacy with Mr. Seward,"[30] a group of Republican senators called Seward into caucus to pose embarrassed questions as to whether he had inspired the proposals of Weed and Raymond. Seward answered coolly —and evasively—that "they would know what I think and what I propose when I do myself; and as for influencing those . . . editors . . . they would find them as independent as the Senate itself, and more potential."[31] But, less debonairly, he wrote to his wife, "Mr. Weed's articles have brought perplexities about me which he, with all his astuteness, did not foresee."[32] Apparently the senatorial inquisition had convinced him that the rumor was doing him injury, and that a public denial was necessary. Almost certainly he authorized a statement which appeared in the *Tribune* on December 5: "Mr. Seward will make no speech immediately, and will submit no proposition. All rumors to the contrary are entirely unfounded. He is in no manner or form responsible for the various suggestions recently put forward in various newspapers, which have been supposed to reflect his views, and was not consulted

28. New York *Tribune,* Dec. 3, 1860.
29. New York *Herald,* Dec. 3, 1860.
30. New York *Tribune,* Dec. 3, 1860.
31. Seward to Weed, Dec. 3, 1860, in Barnes, *Weed,* p. 308.
32. Seward to his wife, Dec. 4, 1860, in Seward, *Seward,* II, 480.

concerning, or in any way privy to, their publication. His policy is to watch the development of events, and to direct them wisely at the proper time for peace and the preservation of the Union."[33]

It is worthy of note that, in issuing his denial, Seward did not express any opposition to compromise. In all probability, he did not feel any, for it appears that, at a later time, when he was assured of an offer of the State Department, he shared in a renewal of the *Evening Journal's* compromise proposal.[34] But until he received the anticipated offer of a cabinet post, he did not wish to take any position which would offend the President-elect. Moreover, it seems likely that he had not, at this time, formed any such decisive opinions as were manifested by Weed. He had, in fact, scarcely begun to evaluate the crisis. He already anticipated that no compromise amendment could command the requisite majorities in Congress, and that five Southern states would pass ordinances of secession.[35] But he contemplated these prospects with extraordinary coolness. On the day that he issued his denial to the press, he remarked that he had at last thrown all the dogs off his track, and then he turned to the completion of a brief which he had been preparing for use in a case before the Supreme Court. Having put the finishing touches on it, he began, on the same day, "at a very distant point, to study the great political crisis."[36]

The session was two days old; South Carolina's convention was scheduled to meet within two weeks. And at this point Seward leisurely wound up his unfinished business and began to speculate on the more recondite aspects of secession. It ill became him to write that "The Republi-

33. New York *Tribune,* Dec. 5 (Washington, Dec. 4), 1860.
34. See below, pp. 165–166.
35. Seward to Weed, Dec. 2, 1860, in Seward, *Seward,* II, 479. "No amendment that can be proposed, and would be satisfactory, can get two-thirds of both Houses; although just such amendments might pass three-fourths of the States." Seward predicted the secession of South Carolina, Florida, Mississippi, Alabama, and Georgia, in this letter.
36. Seward to his wife, Dec. 5, 1860, in *ibid.,* 480.

cans who come here are ignorant of the real . . . danger."[37] At the moment when leadership was most needed, Mr. Seward put his feet, figuratively, on his desk and lapsed into philosophy.

Seward's disavowal of the Weed proposals and his negative attitude in general left the Republicans a bewildered and leaderless crew. Perhaps no major party group has ever begun a congressional session amid such perplexities. They gathered to find the capital in a buzz of activity.[38] Southern congressmen were reported in conference endlessly, but no one knew the conclusions of their discussions.[39] The Democrats of the Northwest were said to be taking counsel of one another, but to what effect was not known.[40] The men of the Border states were brimming over with compromises, but what these would embrace and whether they would be acceptable to either side, remained a mystery.[41] To the Republican in the ranks, even the activity of his own leaders must have been a puzzle, for he heard it constantly asserted that Seward favored a territorial compromise. He could read in the papers that Republican leaders and Southern leaders had held conversations giving "a strong prospect of a satisfactory settlement of the difficulties on a permanent basis,"[42] or even that "it is understood that the Republican members are a unit in favor of compromise."[43] Next day, if he still thought the newspapers worth while, he could learn, on

37. See above, p. 78.
38. Seward to Weed, Dec. 3, 1860, in Barnes, *Weed*, p. 308. Hereafter, where Nov., Dec., Jan., Feb., Mar., and Apr. are cited without year, 1860 will be understood for Nov. and Dec., and 1861 for Jan., Feb., Mar., and Apr.
39. New York *Herald*, Dec. 3, reported such a caucus, and the New York *Tribune*, Dec. 10, reported two others.
40. New York *Herald*, Dec. 3.
41. Compromise activities of Gov. Letcher of Va., and of George D. Prentice and Vice-president Breckinridge of Ky. were reported in the New York *Times*, Dec. 1, 6, 7, 10; of Senator Crittenden, in *ibid.*, Dec. 3.
42. *Ibid.*, Dec. 3 (Washington, Dec. 2).
43. New York *Times*, Dec. 4 (Washington, Dec. 3).

the contrary, that "the consultations among the republicans result in the almost unanimous conclusion that they will offer no compromise."[44]

If, at this point, he cursed all reporters and sought out Seward, to learn his party's policy from his party leader, he found a man who appeared "as chipper as a lark and swore by yea and by nay that everything was going on admirably,"[45] a man who would "talk very little, and nothing in detail," a man who would advise, as a line of action, nothing but silence—"respectful and fraternal" silence.[46]

Thus the twenty-six Republican senators and one hundred and fourteen Republican representatives assembled in Congress on December 3 without a policy. They had agreed on nothing except the expediency of practicing "reticence and kindness,"[47] because they did not wish to play into the hands of "the madcaps of the South [who] want to be inflamed." Inasmuch as they had formulated only this passive and negative policy, the initiative of action was thrown upon other groups.

Amid this welter of confusion, Congress at last convened. The proceedings began, as always, with a joint session of the two houses, at which members listened, with rather more curiosity than respect, to the President's message.[48] This document mitigated no one's bewilderment, for in it Buchanan set forth his belief that the states could not legally secede, but that the Federal government could not legally restrain them; in it he also recommended that Congress call a constitutional convention, for the purpose of framing amendments to recognize expressly the institution of slavery in states which wanted it, and in all of the common territories, and to insure the restoration

44. New York *Herald*, Dec. 4 (Washington, Dec. 3).
45. Henry Adams to C. F. Adams, Jr., Dec. 9, in Worthington C. Ford, editor, *Letters of Henry Adams, 1858–1891* (Boston, 1930), p. 63.
46. Seward to his family, Dec. 1, 2, in Seward, *Seward,* II, 478, 479.
47. Seward wrote to his wife, Dec. 7, "Our Senators agree with me to practice reticence and kindness." *Ibid.,* II, 480.
48. Letter of Henry Adams, Dec. 4, in the Boston *Advertiser,* Dec. 7.

of fugitive slaves.[49] It is safe to assume that not one Republican dallied for even an instant with the idea of extending slavery to all the territories, and not one Democrat supposed such an extension to be possible. Thus, in a sense, Buchanan dealt in fantasies; no effort was made in Congress to implement his proposals, and it remained for the legislators to devise their own measures.

In both houses of Congress, the problems of the secession movement were referred to special committees. It is characteristic, however, that the Senate deliberated for nearly two weeks before setting up the Committee of Thirteen, while the House authorized the appointment of a committee immediately after the reading of Buchanan's message. The initiative in this matter came from Representative Alexander Boteler of Virginia, who offered a motion "that so much of the President's message as relates to the present perilous condition of the country, be referred to a special committee of one from each State." The motion was put to a vote without being debated, and was carried, 145 to 38.[50]

Inasmuch as the motion for a committee passed without discussion, the significance of its passage was not entirely clear. But Alexander Boteler, with his Virginia residence and Whiggish affiliations, clearly intended that the committee should seek a basis of negotiation with the

49. Buchanan's message is in *Cong. Globe,* 36th Cong., 2nd sess., appendix, pp. 1–7. Hereafter, when the *Cong. Globe* is cited without indication as to the number of the Congress and the session, the 36th Congress, 2nd session, is indicated.

50. *Ibid.,* p. 6. It is worthy of note that Representative John Cochrane, Democrat, of New York, had also made plans to move for the appointment of a committee of 33. These plans were ready the Sunday before the opening of the session, and Cochrane actually rose to offer a motion for his committee, but yielded to Boteler. New York *Herald,* Dec. 3, 5. It was later reported that Boteler had made his motion at the instance of a member of the Republican party. He formally denied this, on Jan. 10, asserting that he had consulted only Southern members of both the Democratic and American parties (he was an American), and that Representatives Winslow of N. C., John Cochrane of N. Y., and Maynard of Tenn. had prepared similar resolutions which they yielded in order that he might present his. *Ibid.,* p. 316.

South; and the large majority which his measure commanded might be regarded as an evidence of a wide-spread desire for conciliation. Under analysis, however, the vote reveals two factors which gave no promise of harmony. One of these was the extent to which members from the seceding states refused to vote. There were twenty-two congressmen present from the states which had called conventions,[51] and of this number sixteen declined voting on the ground that their secession policy was determined, and not subject to negotiation. Six others voted for the committee, but if the sixteen represented Southern opinion, secession was inevitable.[52] The other factor was the concentration of the negative vote entirely within the Republican ranks. Not a single Democrat voted against the committee, and indeed the Republicans favored it by a vote of 62 to 38,[53] but still it was notable that a substantial proportion of the Republican membership seemed hostile not only to specific concessions, but even to conciliation as such.

On the day following, Speaker Pennington, after much anxious consideration,[54] named the committee, which soon became known, from the number of its members, as the

51. Ala., Fla., Ga., Miss., and S. C. had 26 Representatives, but Crawford of Ga., and Barksdale, Lamar, and McRae of Miss. had not yet arrived in Washington. *Journal of the House of Representatives,* 36th Cong., 2nd sess., pp. 38, 77. Hereafter, when *House Journal* is cited without indication as to the number of the Congress and the session, the 36th Congress, 2nd session, is indicated.

52. Pugh and Clopton of Ala., Gartrell and Jones of Ga., Hawkins of Fla., and Singleton of Miss. (all as individuals); and McQueen, Miles, Keitt, Bonham, Ashmore, and Boyce of S. C. (as a group, speaking through Miles) stated their refusal to vote inasmuch as secession was predetermined. Curry and Moore of Ala., Underwood and Jackson of Ga., refrained from voting, without explanation. Houston and Cobb of Ala., Love, Hardeman, and J. Hill of Ga., and R. Davis of Miss., voted for the committee. *Cong. Globe,* pp. 6–7; *House Journal,* pp. 36–37.

53. My analysis of this vote, and all subsequent analyses, are compiled from roll calls in the *House Journal* and the *Senate Journal.* In determining party affiliation, I have accepted the classification of members as given in the *Tribune Almanac for 1861.*

54. Henry Adams to C. F. Adams, Jr., Dec. 29, in Ford, ed., *Henry Adams Letters, 1858–1891,* p. 74.

Committee of Thirty-three. Although Northern Democrats protested that they were not represented,[55] and the New York *Herald* complained that appointments were partisan,[56] it appears to have been a well-balanced committee. Sixteen of its members were Republicans; fourteen were Democrats; and three were of that Southern group of ex-Whigs and ex-nativists called South Americans. Four of the Republicans had opposed the committee by voting against it, and two of the Democrats had repudiated it even more completely by refusing to vote at all; but, with these exceptions, Speaker Pennington's appointees were apparently prepared faithfully to seek an adjustment of sectional antagonisms.[57] The most eminent members of the committee were chairman Thomas Corwin, a veteran Whig and Republican of Ohio, who hated Democrats and abolitionists; Henry Winter Davis, gilded aristocrat and political boss of Baltimore; and Charles Fran-

55. Democrats Vallandigham and McClernand protested thus on Dec. 10, but Sickles of N. Y., also Democratic, defended the appointments. *Cong. Globe,* pp. 38–40.

56. New York *Herald,* Dec. 7, 1860.

57. The membership of the House Committee of Thirty-three follows: twelve Republicans who had voted for the committee—Thomas Corwin of O., Charles Francis Adams of Mass., James Humphrey of N. Y., James H. Campbell of Pa., Orris S. Ferry of Conn., Christopher Robinson of R. I., John L. N. Stratton of N. J., Justin S. Morrill of Vt., W. McKee Dunn of Ind., William Kellogg of Ill., Samuel R. Curtis of Ia., and William Windom of Minn.; four Republicans who had voted against the committee—Mason Tappan of N. H., Freeman Morse of Me., C. C. Washburn of Wis., and William A. Howard of Mich. (only in Michigan had the whole delegation voted against the committee, and so, in three cases, Pennington voluntarily appointed men who had voted against it); three South Americans, who had voted for the committee—Thomas A. R. Nelson of Tenn., Francis M. Bristow of Ky., and H. Winter Davis of Md.; twelve Democrats who had not opposed the committee—John S. Millson of Va., Warren Winslow of N. C., Peter E. Love of Ga., M. G. Whiteley of Del., Miles Taylor of La., Reuben Davis of Miss., George S. Houston of Ala., John S. Phelps of Mo., Albert Rust of Ark., Andrew J. Hamilton of Tex., John C. Burch of Cal., and Lansing Stout of Ore. (all of these voted for the committee except Taylor and Hamilton, absent as shown in *House Journal,* pp. 38, 51); and two Democrats who had refused to vote—George S. Hawkins of Fla. and William W. Boyce of S. C. (Florida and South Carolina delegations had solidly refused to vote, so, in these cases, Speaker Pennington had no option).

cis Adams, long a leader of the anti-slavery cause. Corwin and Adams were Republicans; Davis was classified as a South American.

Having appointed its committee, the House, with unaccustomed restraint, refrained from any protracted discussion of the sectional issue. Only in a few minor episodes did the conflict prove itself "irrepressible." On one occasion, George S. Hawkins of Florida and William W. Boyce of South Carolina created a lively scene by demanding to be excused from service on the committee, which Hawkins described as a "Trojan Horse."[58] A few days later, much time was consumed in voting on various declaratory resolutions designed to reveal the true sentiment of Congress.[59] For the most part, however, the problems of the immediate crisis were left to the Committee of Thirty-three, and the House held aloof. Whenever any member wished to propose compromise measures, he introduced them into the House with the understanding that they would be referred to the committee. One day especially, December 12, was specifically set aside for the introduction of such resolutions, and on that day alone, more than a score of compromise proposals were introduced. None of these ever emerged from "the coffin of the Committee of Thirty-three," but though unproductive of result, they did reflect the attitudes of individual congressmen and, especially, of individual Republicans.

Ever since Thurlow Weed's proposals had been so violently rebuffed, no Republican of any consequence had ventured to propose concessions to the South. Among the numerous conciliatory resolutions of December 12, however, there were three by Republicans. One of these, by David Kilgore of Indiana, took its cue from the New York *Times*, and proposed that the Federal government pay compensation to the owners of fugitive slaves.[60] An-

58. In House, Dec. 6, 10, 11. *Cong. Globe*, pp. 22–23, 35–41, 59–62. The New York *Tribune*, Dec. 10, reported that the secession group had held a caucus to bring pressure on cotton-state representatives not to serve.
59. Proceedings of Dec. 17 and 18. *Cong. Globe*, pp. 108–125.
60. *Ibid.*, p. 78.

other resolution, far more sweeping in content, was that of Eli Thayer of Massachusetts, who proposed to take the territorial question out of national politics by applying the formula of popular sovereignty.[61] Thayer had first been attracted to this highly unorthodox doctrine through a connection with the Emigrant Aid movement, which had convinced him that a program of organized Western colonization would enable the settlers themselves to outlaw slavery in the territories, thus rendering congressional prohibition unnecessary.[62] While remaining an abolitionist, a friend of John Brown, and a zealous Republican in his objectives, he adopted for tactical reasons, therefore, the heresies of Stephen A. Douglas. This irregularity led Thayer's party, in the November elections, to choose a new congressman in his place. He had already been repudiated, therefore, before Congress met. But as a possible means for conciliating the South without losing the territories, his doctrine assumed new importance, and it was not finally eliminated from consideration until Lincoln pronounced against it.[63]

Thayer and Kilgore were both "lame ducks"; more zealous Republicans had already been selected to supersede them; and for this reason their proposals were hardly representative of their party. But another resolution introduced on December 12 came from a ranking party leader—John Sherman. At the first session of the Congress then sitting, he had been, for eight weeks, the candidate of the Republicans for the speakership. Yet Sherman now presented compromise measures which were, in effect, if not in principle, almost as drastic as Thayer's. For Sherman proposed to cut the Gordian knot by an astonishingly simple device. His resolution avowed a purpose "to

61. *Ibid.*, pp. 76–77.

62. Thayer had supported the same plan previously. See his speech of May 11, 1860, advocating it, in *ibid.*, 36th Cong., 1st sess., pp. 2073–2077. For Thayer's connection with the Emigrant Aid movement, see Ralph Volney Harlow, "The Rise and Fall of the Kansas Aid Movement," in *American Historical Review* (Oct., 1935), XLI, 1–25.

63. See below, pp. 157–158.

avoid all further controversies in regard to the several Territories of the United States," and proposed to instruct the Committee of Thirty-three to "divide said Territories into States of convenient size, with a view to their prompt admission into the Union on an equal footing with the other States."[64]

The problem, as Sherman must have seen it, was this: the South would not submit to the exclusion of slavery from the territories; the Republican party was pledged to precisely this exclusion; neither side would yield. As long as any regions with a territorial form of government existed, therefore, there was an "irrepressible conflict." But if there were no regions with a territorial form of government, no issue would exist. Let all the territories be admitted to statehood with appropriate labels, and the question which had wracked the country for the previous six years would be reduced to abstraction. Such a course would leave the South free to indulge the folly of carrying slaves into the uncongenial Southwest. Inevitable failure lay at the end of this course. Meanwhile, the free-state representatives would avoid any Federal sanction of slavery and would retain an unimpaired and robust sense of rectitude.

Sherman's proposal was in a sense superficial, for it simply proposed to confer a new status—statehood—upon the unsettled areas in which the effort to extend slavery would continue as before. But in another sense it was inspired, for it recognized the importance, in politics, of the distinction-without-a-difference. In its actual effect, it would have produced the same result as Thayer's plan. The two coincided in proposing that the elected representatives of the inhabitants should decide whether or not they would have slavery, but Thayer had no more imagination than to call these representatives a territorial legislature, while Sherman, with a touch of genius, would call them a state legislature instead. Although meaningless as a concession by the North and valueless as an advan-

64. *Cong. Globe*, pp. 77–78.

tage to the South, this measure, if adopted in time, might have inhibited theory-ridden politicians from resorting to realistic disunion and waging realistic war.

A few days later, Sherman published a letter in which he renewed his proposal for the admission of the territories to statehood. This letter was widely circulated, and, as Sherman believed, "generally . . . approved in the North,"[65] but his position naturally did not meet with the favor of the sterner sort of anti-slavery men, and Henry Adams wrote angrily, "All the mean material we've got is coming out now. Sherman . . . has flattened out."[66] There was irony in the fact that another month would find Charles Francis Adams supporting a plan almost identical with Sherman's.[67] For the moment, however, Republican leaders proved unresponsive, and his proposal was permitted to lapse.

The resolutions of Kilgore, Thayer, and Sherman are of interest because they indicate an early desire, among a few Republicans, to effect a compromise. As issues of the day, however, they are negligible. The authors of the proposals did not even make speeches in behalf of their resolutions, and the House ignored them. The only sustained discussion of the crisis, and of possible remedies, meanwhile took place in the sessions of the Committee of Thirty-three. This body did not meet for a week after its appointment, but, beginning on December 11, it began to hold sessions of several hours duration every day.[68] The

65. Sherman to a Philadelphia committee, Dec. 22; Sherman's comment on the way in which this letter was received appears in a letter to W. T. Sherman, Jan. 6. Both in Rachel Sherman Thorndike, editor, *The Sherman Letters, Correspondence between General and Senator Sherman from 1837 to 1891* (New York, 1894), pp. 92–104.

66. Adams to C. F. Adams, Jr., Dec. 13. I have transposed the words of the latter sentence. Ford, ed., *Henry Adams Letters, 1858–1891*, p. 64.

67. See below, pp. 293–294.

68. *Journal of the Committee of Thirty-three,* in *Report of the Select Committee of Thirty-three on the Disturbed Condition of the Country,* in *Reports of Committees of the House of Representatives,* 36th Cong., 2nd sess., Vol. I, No. 31, shows meetings on 13 days in December, including and after Dec. 11. It does not record the duration of meetings, but

members indulged in full-dress speeches, just as they would in the House itself, and on occasion they fell back into the old recriminating style of sectional debate, but on the whole their proceedings began in a more desultory and more amiable vein than the public proceedings of the House.[69] Furthermore, it soon became evident that a conciliatory tone was growing in the Republican portion of the committee; the spirit of compromise, which had previously manifested itself only in isolated individuals of the Republican group, now began to make appreciable inroads. The strength of this trend appeared in a very striking fashion at the third meeting of the committee.

The date was December 13. Everyone knew that, within a fortnight, South Carolina's convention would meet, and Florida, Mississippi, and Alabama would elect conventions to act on the secession question. No one could fail to see that, if conciliation were to be attempted, it must be attempted at once. Under these circumstances, General Albert Rust, committee member from Arkansas, introduced a resolution that "the existing discontents among the southern people . . . are not without cause, and that such just concessions and additional and more specific and effectual guarantees . . . as will or *should* allay them, are indispensable to the perpetuation of the Union." In presenting his resolution, Rust appears to have remarked that "it was necessary to adopt it in order to arrest secession."[70] Some Southerners interpreted this statement as an avowal of an opportunistic purpose to halt the secession movement by a mere rhetorical expression of good intent, without tangible concessions, and Mississippi's Reuben Davis condemned it as an effort to delude Southerners with false hopes. Northern members, on the other hand,

the New York *Herald* of Dec. 13, 14, 15, 18, and 19, reported meetings on Dec. 12 (4 hrs.), 13 ("nearly all day"), 14 (4 hrs.), 17 (4 hrs.), and 18 (3 hrs.).

69. New York *Herald*, Dec. 13, account of committee proceedings on Dec. 12.

70. Resolution in *Journal of Committee of 33*, p. 7. Remark attributed to Rust by Reuben Davis, *Recollections of Mississippi and Mississippians* (Boston, 1899), p. 399.

from motives either sincere or ulterior, were prone to accept it. However, they could not bring themselves to affirm that the discontent of the South was justified, and therefore McKee Dunn, a Republican of Indiana, proposed to substitute a resolution that "whether the discontents and hostility [of the South] are without just cause or not, any reasonable, proper, and constitutional remedies, and additional and more specific and effectual guarantees of their peculiar rights and interests as recognized by the Constitution, necessary to preserve the peace of the country and the perpetuation of the Union, should be promptly and cheerfully granted." The Dunn resolution, if less explicit than Rust's in admitting the justice of Southern complaints, was more explicit in stating that they should be satisfied. It was, in fact, so favorable to the South that Rust withdrew his own resolution in favor of it. This was too much for the more stalwart Republicans and they made spirited efforts to prevent the resolution from coming to a vote. A milder substitute measure was offered by Justin Morrill of Vermont, for the purpose of displacing the Dunn resolution, and nine Republicans voted for it for this purpose, though they would probably not have supported it on the final question of adoption. But with seven other Republicans voting against them, their efforts failed, with the result that the Dunn resolution was brought promptly to a vote. On the roll call, the Republicans divided evenly; eight voted against the measure; eight others, joining with fourteen non-Republicans, voted for it, and thus secured its adoption by a vote of 22 to 8.[71] The more zealous Republicans, therefore, found themselves not only defeated, but also divided, as their party colleagues voted to assure the South of "additional and more specific and effectual guarantees."[72]

71. Republicans voted on the Dunn resolution thus: aye, Campbell, Corwin, Curtis, Dunn, Howard, Kellogg, Stratton, Windom; nay, Adams, Ferry, Humphrey, Morrill, Morse, Robinson, Tappan, Washburn. On the Morrill substitute, the votes were exactly reversed, except in the case of Corwin, who voted aye on both roll calls.

72. For proceedings of committee on Dec. 13, see *Journal of the Committee of 33*, pp. 5–8.

What impulses motivated the Republicans who supported the Dunn resolution, it is difficult to say. Their action may have resulted from a wholly sincere desire to extend full justice to the South. On the other hand, they may have acted in bad faith, as Reuben Davis accused them of doing,[73] promising concessions with no intent to fulfill the promise, but simply to dissuade Southerners from taking the measures they considered necessary to their security.

If Republicans were sincere in endorsing the principle of compromise, the response of Southern congressmen must be counted as a heavy blow against the cause of conciliation. For, on the night following the passage of the Dunn resolution, thirty Southern senators and representatives issued to their constituents a manifesto: "The argument is exhausted. All hope of relief in the Union through the agencies of committees, Congressional legislation, or constitutional amendments is extinguished, and we trust the South will not be deceived by appearances or the pretense of new guarantees."[74]

This manifesto may have reflected a sincere, and even a justified, distrust by Southerners of Republican motives. It may, on the other hand, have reflected an attitude of hostility toward any form of compromise because of an unconditional preference for secession. Whatever impelled it, its issuance signified that the cause of compromise faced many obstacles, and that powerful forces, in the South as well as the North, were prepared to resist a peaceable adjustment of sectional issues.

Despite the sharp rebuff contained in the Southern manifesto, the Committee of Thirty-three continued its activities, and some of the Republican members made active efforts to formulate "reasonable, proper, and constitutional" remedies. Orris S. Ferry of Connecticut offered a resolution to give greater force to the Constitution's provision that "The citizens of each state shall be

73. Davis, *Recollections*, pp. 396–400.
74. Text of manifesto in Nicolay and Hay, *Lincoln*, II, 436.

entitled to all privileges and immunities of citizens in the
several states."[75] This proposal was rather Delphic in
phraseology, but to Southerners, constantly asserting
their right to carry property (in slaves) to the territories,
it could have but one meaning, and that a pleasant one.
Another resolution of less equivocal nature was that of
James Humphrey of New York, who wanted Congress to
implement the fugitive slave clause of the Constitution by
penalizing any county where a fugitive should be rescued
from law officers "by force or riot."[76] On this same subject
of fugitive slaves, Thomas Corwin also submitted resolutions looking to an adjustment.[77] Still another resolution
from the Republican group came from William Kellogg
of Illinois, who seems to have been influenced by the ideas
of Eli Thayer. He wanted to establish territorial governments for all the unorganized area of the United States,
and to endow the territorial legislatures with "authority
over all subjects not inconsistent with the Constitution of
the United States."[78] Kellogg and Corwin, in fact, appear
to have been particularly active in the cause of good will.
On December 13 and 14, respectively, they made long,
conciliatory speeches in the committee, and it was reported
that they both tried to reassure Southern members as
to Lincoln's conservative attitude. Kellogg, a personal
acquaintance of the President-elect, spoke with authority
on Lincoln's position, and he was questioned freely by the
committee.[79] Freeman Morse of Maine and Samuel R.
Curtis of Iowa were also reported to have spoken in a
conciliatory vein.[80]

The extent and the limitations of Republican concession
were indicated fairly clearly, at last, on December 17 and
18, when the committee voted on questions relating to the
Personal Liberty laws and to the old matter of Federal

75. Dec. 17, in *Journal of Committee of 33*, p. 11.
76. Dec. 17, in *ibid.*, p. 11.
77. Dec. 18, in *ibid.*, p. 12.
78. Dec. 17, in *ibid.*, p. 10.
79. Speeches reported in New York *Herald*, Dec. 14 and 15.
80. Speeches made on Dec. 12, reported in *ibid.*, Dec. 13.

recognition of slavery in the territories. On December 13, Henry Winter Davis had introduced resolutions by which Congress would urge the states to repeal any statutes which tended to interfere with the capture of fugitive slaves.[81] This was taken up five days later, and passed without a record vote in the committee.[82] According to current report, only two members had voted against it.[83] In the matter of fugitive slaves, therefore, it appeared that the Republicans wished to give the South complete satisfaction. They showed no impulse to dodge this issue. On the day previous, however, they displayed unanimous reluctance on the territorial question. This topic had preceded all others in the committee, for the first resolutions introduced were those of Thomas A. R. Nelson of Tennessee, to divide the territory once more on the line 36° 30′.[84] Despite their priority, these resolutions were neglected until December 17, when their author moved to take them up. On this motion, every Republican voted in the negative, and every other member present, except Henry Winter Davis, voted in the affirmative, and it failed, 14 to 17.[85] The Nelson resolution was, therefore, not brought to a formal vote, but this preliminary test of strength, together with the vote on the proposals of Henry Winter Davis, showed with reasonable accuracy the position of the Republican members. All but a corporal's guard were willing to offer concessions to the South in the matter of fugitive slaves, and, by implication, in other matters; but they unanimously adhered to their determination not to permit slavery in Federal territories.

By the time that South Carolina passed her Ordinance of Secession, there was still no comprehensive plan of adjustment, either completed or in preparation, in the lower house; in the sense of final accomplishment, nothing

81. *Journal of Committee of 33*, pp. 5–6.
82. *Ibid.*, pp. 11–12.
83. New York *Herald*, Dec. 19.
84. Resolutions introduced Dec. 12, *Journal of Committee of 33*, pp. 3–4.
85. *Ibid.*, pp. 9–10.

had been done. Yet in a very brief interval of time, the long-standing Republican disregard of Southern protests had broken down in a dozen places. In the House itself, there were the resolutions of Kilgore, Thayer, and Sherman. In the Committee of Thirty-three, there were more resolutions, by Ferry, Humphrey, Corwin, and Kellogg; there were conciliatory speeches by Morse and Curtis; on a formal resolution, half of the Republican committee members signified a willingness to offer the South "additional and more specific and effectual guarantees"; and as an evidence of good faith, all but two would urge the repeal of Personal Liberty laws. Never before had the Republicans spoken in such placating tones.

These developments were not without significance as indications of a trend. They reflected a new attitude on the part of many members of the Republican group, and they betokened a drift toward compromise which, if it persisted, might achieve vast importance. But it must be admitted that none of the developments in the House were important except as signs of the times. Of all the measures proposed, not one was enhanced by the support of a great name, nor magnified by a thorough campaign of publicity, nor even bolstered by skillful management in Congress itself. More than that, it is likely that none of them was drawn with any reference to the primary question whether its terms would appease the South. Most of the proposals were haphazard gestures of leaderless men. In the absence of leadership, there was no prospect that the conciliatory impulses of individuals would be translated into terms of a great compromise in the House.

The House of Representatives preceded the Senate in giving its attention to compromise. But it remained for the upper house, moving unhurriedly, to produce the first mature and comprehensive plan of adjustment. The champion of this plan, and, indeed, of the whole program of conciliation, was the senior senator from Kentucky, John J. Crittenden. Both by locale and by tradition, Crittenden was fitted to assume this leadership. As a Kentuckian, he was peculiarly qualified to understand both the intensity of Southern excitement, which Northerners could not grasp, and the essential sanity and moderation of the Republicans, which were not appreciated in the lower South. For Kentucky, with its own minority of rampant secessionists, and its Republican neighbors across the Ohio, was in position to observe how acute, and how unnecessary, the secession crisis was.[86] As an old-line Henry Clay Whig, moreover, Crittenden was uniquely eligible to lead the compromise movement. The practice of compromise had attained its ultimate expression and its traditional form in the career of Clay, and Crittenden had been one of the most devoted of Clay's followers. Born during the sessions of the Constitutional Convention, he loved the Republic with a sentiment peculiar to those who had known it in its heroic age. This loyalty had merged readily into a loyalty to Clay, and for a quarter of a century Crittenden had never deviated from his support of the "Pacificator" except to support Zachary Taylor for the Presidency in 1848. Even then, he refused a cabinet position out of respect for Clay's wounded feelings. In a distinguished career, he had twice been a member of the cabinet, and had shared in some of the leading political movements of his time. But, in this, his seventy-third year, the greatest effort of his life still lay before him. For Crittenden took up his political heritage from Clay amid such

86. A correspondent of Senator Crittenden wrote: "Kentucky is now an epitome of the Union. There are three parties struggling in her bosom. There is along her Southern border, with a smart sprinkle of the same type scattered abroad, a party who would drive the State into cecession [sic] tomorrow. There is another faction, for the most part found along the Ohio[,] who would surrender all rights under the Constitution . . . to hang the gallant old commonwealth to the yankee states. . . . Then there is a third party—the great, sound, conservative, central heart of the Commonwealth, who are for the Union[,] the Constitution, the whole flag, every stripe and every star in its place. This party will struggle to the last for the Union as it was." Thomas W. Riley, Kimbo Hill, Ky., Feb. 8, 1861 [incorrectly dated and calendared 1860], to Crittenden, in Crittenden MSS.

a tempest as Clay had never witnessed. Five states were in
process of secession and every indication promised that
Crittenden would survive the Union which he had preceded
into the world. The only hope of peaceful union lay in the
possibility of a comprehensive settlement dealing fully and
finally with all the points of sectional controversy.

With the expectation that he would assume the leadership of a movement for reconciliation, public attention
quickly focused upon Crittenden. Even before the opening of Congress, he was being publicized as the author of
a compromise proposal, and from the beginning of the
session he was constantly in the news. One report pictured
him in conference with Stephen A. Douglas, who was still
a powerful, and always a resourceful, man. Another
credited him with plans to discover the precise terms on
which the South would abandon secession—a species of
information essential to compromise, yet one which other
conciliators apparently made no effort to secure. His plan,
as reported, was to arrange a caucus of Southern senators,
who would state the terms on which their section would
adhere to the Union, and to follow this with a caucus of
Northern members, who would consider the possibility of
negotiating on the Southern terms.[87] A day later, Senator
Crittenden was reported to have forestalled a caucus of all
Union men, for fear ill-feeling might be generated.[88] Soon
after, rumor was sending him south as an official emissary
of Kentucky to plead for delay in South Carolina.[89] Before
this fiction was cold, Crittenden was again in the news as
one of the leaders at an informal senatorial conference
where revival and extension of the Missouri line was proposed.[90] And, on the very next day, he was named as one

87. All these reports in New York *Herald,* Dec. 3 (Washington,
Dec. 2).

88. *Ibid.,* Dec. 4 (Washington, Dec. 3).

89. New York *Times,* Dec. 6.

90. New York *Tribune,* Dec. 8 (Washington, Dec. 7). In this dispatch
the name Fessenden was used where Crittenden was intended, but the
error was noted in the *Tribune* of Dec. 10.

of the champions of union at a caucus of Southern senators.[91]

Despite all this publicity, Crittenden's actual conduct on the floor of the Senate was notably unobtrusive. His whole policy was to negotiate privately, to work quietly, and, as far as possible, to avoid the irritations that arise from public debate. During the first two weeks of the session, he took the floor only twice, and occupied it for not more than fifteen minutes altogether. Once he rebuked Clingman of North Carolina for a particularly angry speech, and pled for calm consideration of future remedies, rather than constant detailing of past wrongs. Later, he rose to caution against the dangers of premature discussion and to express the hope that the Senate would remain calm until specific measures should be presented to it, instead of working itself into a passion of recrimination during hasty and aimless debate.[92] But for the most part he practiced his precept of maintaining tranquillity by silence, and he even refrained, until December 18, from presenting his compromise resolutions.

Crittenden's delay was a consequence of the tardiness of the Senate in appointing a special committee to deal with the question of compromise. As early as December 6, Senator Lazarus W. Powell, also of Kentucky, had, pursuant to previous notice, offered a resolution to refer "so much of the President's message as relates to the present . . . distracted condition of the country, and the grievances between the slaveholding and the non-slaveholding States . . . to a special committee of thirteen members."[93] The House had passed a comparable resolution in half an hour, but in the Senate a desultory, and at times acrimonious, debate ran on for nearly two weeks before senators saw fit to authorize the appointment of a committee. Then,

91. This conference of Dec. 8 was reported in *ibid.*, Dec. 10 (Washington, Dec. 9).
92. Remarks in Senate, Dec. 4, 10, in *Cong. Globe*, pp. 5, 32.
93. *Ibid.*, p. 19.

on December 18, they approved the resolution without a record vote.[94]

Not until the adoption of this measure did Crittenden make public the compromise resolutions which he had prepared.[95] Now, however, he introduced them forthwith. They were referred, of course, to the newly authorized committee, but he took occasion to explain them to the Senate.[96]

The Crittenden resolutions were evidently drawn with care. They were predicated upon a recognition of the important distinction between the slavery issue as such, and the issue of the impingement of Federal jurisdiction upon slavery. The slavery issue itself was, of course, certain to arouse emotions which no compromise could pacify—therefore it was beyond compromise. But the Federal government came into contact with slavery only in a tangential way, as, for instance, when slavery extended into places not under state jurisdiction, such as territories, the District of Columbia, and forts and arsenals, or when it became involved in such Federal spheres as that of interstate commerce. To remove the question of slavery from the realm of Federal activities, therefore, it was only necessary to deal with it in these specific and limited aspects. Such a policy would not solve the social and economic problems of sectionalism, but it would remove the points at issue, upon which sectional antagonism exercised itself. As a result, sectional rancor might be expected to abate for want of objectives for which to wage the contest. Superficial as this concept might appear philosophically, it had the merit of recognizing that minor frictions and petty "incidents" frequently

94. *Ibid.,* p. 117. The resolution had been modified, with the consent of Senator Powell, on Dec. 10. *Ibid.,* p. 28.

95. However, the New York *Tribune* learned of Crittenden's plan and published a complete summary of his proposals on Dec. 11.

96. The resolutions and accompanying speech appear in *Cong. Globe,* pp. 112–114.

cause collision and convert animosity, which might otherwise remain latent, into open war.

Acting on this concept, the Kentucky Senator methodically sought out all the points where Federal intervention in connection with slavery might be invoked, and where, therefore, Federal policy might become the subject of agitation. Having segregated these potential issues, Crittenden proposed the adoption of a definitive policy to apply to each, in order to preclude future contest.

In a few minor cases these policies were to be established by congressional sanction alone. Thus the resolutions provided for statutory correction of certain highly obnoxious features of the Fugitive Slave Law.[97] They also contained resolutions placing Congress on record in favor of the "faithful . . . execution" of this modified law, the repeal by the states of their Personal Liberty laws, and the maintenance and thorough enforcement of the prohibition upon the African slave trade.

On these minor aspects of the slavery controversy, statutory action was sufficient. But where more important aspects were concerned, the success of compromise depended less upon its comprehensiveness than upon its

97. The existing law provided a larger fee for commissioners when the alleged slave was delivered to the claimant than when he was set free. Crittenden did not regard this as unjust. "The reason for this," he said, "is very obvious. In the case he [the commissioner] delivers the servant to his claimant, he is required to draw out a lengthy certificate, stating the principal and substantial grounds on which his decision rests, and to return him either to the marshal or to the claimant to remove him to the State from which he escaped. It was for that reason that a larger fee was given to the commissioner, where he had the largest service to perform. But, sir, the act being viewed unfavorably and with great prejudice, in a certain portion of our country, this was regarded as very obnoxious, because it seemed to give an inducement to the commissioner to return the slave to the master, as he thereby obtained the larger fee of ten dollars instead of the smaller one of five dollars." (In Senate, Dec. 18, *Cong. Globe*, p. 112.) But because of the intensity of feeling on the subject, Crittenden proposed, in his resolutions, to make the fee the same regardless of the decision. He also included provision to limit the right of any citizen to summon the *posse comitatus* to aid in enforcing a warrant for the arrest of a fugitive.

permanence. Statutory settlements could never be effective in withdrawing sectional issues from the legislative arena, for the edict of one Congress could be undone by another. The discord between the sections arose no less from their failure to agree than from their lack of faith in the maintenance of the agreement. The Republicans still considered the Kansas-Nebraska Act an evidence of Southern bad faith, while the South felt that Republican disregard of the Dred Scott decision indicated a purpose to destroy Constitutional bulwarks as soon as Northern predominance was great enough. Recognizing, therefore, the importance of making his settlement permanent, Crittenden proposed to render his compromise irrevocable by embodying the major part of it in a series of unalterable Constitutional amendments—amendments which "no future amendment of the Constitution shall affect."[98] This would calm Southern fears, for it would give to the institution of slavery full protection against the people, the state legislatures, and the congressmen of the North—no matter how great their political preponderance might become. And, at the same time, it would discourage Northern agitation by making it as futile as baying the moon.

Six such amendments were proposed, to embrace every phase of the slavery controversy. Of these, the first may be passed over for the moment. The second denied Congress any power to abolish slavery on government property, such as forts and arsenals, in states which permitted slavery. The third denied Congress the power to abolish slavery in the District of Columbia unless it should be abolished in both Virginia and Maryland, and not then unless the inhabitants should consent, the owners be in-

98. The idea that certain provisions of the Constitution may be exempted from liability to amendment is sustained by the Constitution, Article V. This sets forth the process which shall make amendments valid, "Provided that no Amendment which may be made prior to the Year One thousand eight hundred and eight shall in any Manner affect the first and fourth Clauses in the Ninth Section of the first Article; and that no State, without its Consent, shall be deprived of its equal Suffrage in the Senate."

demnified, and the officials of the government be exempted so that they could bring their slaves with them. The fourth took from Congress the power to hinder the transportation of slaves from one slave state or territory to another. The fifth imposed upon Congress the duty of providing compensation for the owners in cases where recovery of fugitive slaves was prevented by violence, or intimidation, or rescue by force, and empowered the Department of Justice to sue the county where such violence occurred; the county, in turn, could sue the individuals engaged in such lawless activity. And, in addition to all these, which were designed rather to preclude future strife than to heal existing dissension, the first amendment sought to end the territorial quarrel forever by providing that "in all the territory of the United States now held, or hereafter acquired, situate north of latitude thirty-six degrees and thirty minutes, slavery or involuntary servitude, except as a punishment for crime, is prohibited while such territory shall remain under territorial government. In all the territory south of said line of latitude, slavery of the African race is hereby recognized as existing, and shall not be interfered with by Congress, but shall be protected as property by all the departments of the territorial government during its continuance [as a territory]." All these provisions were irrevocably sealed by the sixth proposed amendment, which would render the whole settlement perpetual by exempting the slavery clauses from the process of amendment. Not only were the five proposed amendments thus secured, but it was further added that no future amendment should ever alter the provision by which three-fifths of all slaves were counted as population for purposes of apportionment; none should ever abridge the constitutional right to recover fugitive slaves; and none should ever give Congress power to encroach upon slavery in the states.

Judged upon its fitness as an instrument for effecting its purpose—that is, for removing the slavery issue from the realm of Federal activity—the Crittenden plan was outstanding. For affording the South security in a minority status it was no less so. The South declared itself ready to secede, because an anti-slavery majority in the North and an anti-slavery administration in Washington threatened the security of the Southern institution. Crittenden proposed to offer the South protection by giving to slavery a permanent constitutional status beyond the reach of any administration, however hostile, or any popular majority, however large. Under this arrangement, the South could rely implicitly upon the maintenance of a representative system in which three-fifths of the slaves would be counted for purposes of apportionment. It could rely upon the return of all fugitive slaves, or indemnification in default of return. Likewise, it could rely upon an unhampered continuation of the interstate slave trade, and, most important, it could expect slavery to remain free from any external threat, not only in the slave states themselves (including Federal property therein), but also in the District of Columbia and in all existing or prospective territory, be it New Mexico or Nicaragua, south of the line 36° 30'.

Obviously, the plan had both limitations and defects. It ignored the ethical problem of slavery, and therefore offended those who regarded the moral issue as primary. It ignored the democratic principle and the principle of change, by providing for Constitutional controls that would be beyond the reach of any future majority. It achieved completeness at the cost of planting slavery in hypothetical future territory, as well as in the existing territory south of 36° 30'. In this respect it was far more than a mere revival of the Missouri Compromise line, and it might be regarded as an incentive to filibustering, to which Southerners were already prone.[99] But, with these

99. Senator James W. Grimes wrote to Gov. Samuel Kirkwood of Ia., on Jan. 28, decrying the prevailing conception that the Crittenden Compromise is "simply a reestablishment of the Missouri Compromise line." As he saw it, "The sum and substance of the whole matter is, that we are asked, for the sake of peace, to surrender all our cherished ideas on the subject of slavery, and agree, in effect, to provide a slave

failings, it was characterized by several merits which no other compromise proposal possessed in such high degree. More than any other, it was comprehensive, cutting off not only the existing, but also the potential sectional issues. Similarly, it was final; it was designed to establish a condition of permanent peace, rather than of truce, which would be jeopardized by every congressional election. Finally, it was potentially acceptable, for it contained terms which might actually cause the South to abandon secession in favor of security within the Union. In this respect, the Crittenden plan was unlike many other proposals, which were never designed to win Southern confidence, but were intended only to save face, to shift blame, or to cloud the issue.

These Crittenden proposals were the most important measure that came before the Senate Committee of Thirteen. The committee was appointed by Vice-president Breckinridge on December 20, the day of South Carolina's secession, and it met for the first time on the day of its appointment.[100]

The caliber of the committee was high, and its personnel was representative. The cotton states could scarcely at any time have put forward two more able men than Robert Toombs and Jefferson Davis. The Border states received three appointments in which distribution was sacrificed for ability: Robert M. T. Hunter, later Secretary of State in the Confederacy; Lazarus W. Powell of Kentucky, mover of the committee; and John J. Crittenden, made up the middle group. This left eight appointments for the North. Three of these went to Democrats. Fore-

---

code for the Territories south of 36° 30′ and for the Mexican provinces, as soon as they shall be brought within our jurisdiction. It is demanded of us that we shall consent to change the Constitution into a genuine pro-slavery instrument. . . ." William Salter, *Life of James W. Grimes* (New York, 1876), pp. 133–134.

100. *Cong. Globe*, p. 158; *Journal of the Committee of Thirteen*, p. 1, in *Report of the Select Committee of Thirteen on the Disturbed Condition of the Country*, in *Reports of Committees of the Senate*, 36th Cong., 2nd sess., Vol. I, No. 288.

most of these was Stephen A. Douglas, who completely overshadowed William Bigler of Pennsylvania and Henry M. Rice of Minnesota. Five other Northern members were Republicans. This group was headed, very appropriately, by William H. Seward. Only one New Englander, Jacob Collamer of Vermont, was included; he was representative —quiet, thorough, earnest, and relatively moderate. The truly intransigent bloc in the party had its spokesman in Ben Wade of Ohio, well known for his willingness to answer with a squirrel rifle for his intemperate remarks. Less picturesque, but scarcely less irreconcilable, was James W. Grimes of Iowa. And, finally, ranged not quite so surely on the stalwart side, stood James R. Doolittle of Wisconsin.

All in all, it was an able body of men—far more commanding than the House committee; nearly half of its members were of the first rank of talent. Such a committee might well have commanded notice even with less momentous duties. But now public attention focused upon it with extraordinary intentness. The myriad of plans hastily concocted during the previous month now went into limbo. The devotees of compromise, hitherto leaderless, had found their program and their leader.

CHAPTER V

CONSERVATIVE PRESSURE DEMORALIZES
THE REPUBLICAN RANKS

AS LATE as November, Republican rejection of any territorial compromise seemed perfectly certain. Before the meeting of Congress confusion prevailed, and no strong impulse in favor of concession was evident. The vigorous negative reaction to Weed's proposals indicated a steadfast adherence to the Chicago Platform. But, in the weeks after Congress met, a marked trend toward moderation set in. As the crisis developed, pressure from the conciliatory groups began to grow strong. As the weight of this pressure accumulated, the Republicans found increasing difficulty in holding their ranks firm.

A primary source of weakness in the Republican position, and one which greatly increased the party's vulnerability, was the fact that, although victorious, the Republicans remained a minority group. In all of American history, no President has ever been elected with so small a percentage of the popular vote as Lincoln received in 1860. His vote amounted to 39.9 per cent of the total cast. Thus, his actual strength was not only less than that of any other man who has won the presidency, but it was less than that of most of the major candidates who have failed to win it. When Lincoln ran again, in 1864, McClellan received 44.9 per cent of the vote, and was defeated. And in the campaigns of the ensuing forty years, there was never a time when the defeated candidate could not claim a larger share of public support than Lincoln received in 1860. Not until Parker lost to Roosevelt in 1904, did any major candidate command less strength in losing than Lincoln had commanded in winning.

This minority status inevitably impaired Republican capacity to resist pressure. A clear majority would have armed the party with a "mandate from the people," strengthening their public prestige as well as their moral assurance, and bestowing upon them the ultimate sanction of a democracy. But, lacking this sanction, Lincoln and his party were subjected to an unremitting barrage of demands, especially from Northern Democrats, that they subordinate their minority wishes to the popular desire to conciliate the South. Beginning on November 8, the New York *Herald* took up this cry, and played every variation as the mood suggested. On some days it demanded that Mr. Lincoln release his electors, and relinquish his claim on the presidency;[1] in more reasonable moments, it simply demanded from him a statement with which to reassure the South;[2] again, it demanded conciliatory measures from Seward and the Republicans in Congress,[3] or from the governors of important Northern states.[4] And whether exhorting governors, congressmen, or President-elect, the *Herald* reminded them at regular intervals that they had no majority.

The *Herald*, however, not content merely to emphasize that the 1,865,000 Republican voters were, as a class, in the minority, was also impelled to analyze these voters to show that not all of them were slavery exclusionists. Many had voted as they did to secure a tariff, or to get a homestead, or to rebuke the corruption of the Democratic machine. They had certainly not intended to pursue the anti-slavery cause into the cannon's mouth, and many had never become wholehearted Republicans. According to the *Herald's* plausible estimate, 900,000 of these voters had been conservative Whigs, followers of compromising Henry Clay only a few years before, and another 315,000 were squeamish Democrats who could not stomach the

1. New York *Herald,* Nov. 17, 1860.
2. *Ibid.,* Nov. 8, and almost daily thereafter.
3. *Ibid.,* Dec. 26.
4. *Ibid.,* Dec. 26.

doings of the machine.[5] Half of the Whigs and all of the Democrats, reckoned the *Herald*, were indifferent or hostile to the Chicago Platform. This would leave barely 1,000,000 voters, or less than one-fourth of the electorate, who had voted for the exclusion of slavery, and even these could not be supposed to have any notion of the consequences of their action.[6] Implicitly, the *Herald* posed the question: Was this vote in any sense a mandate to reject compromise and to embark on a program which might result in war? To this query, it responded with a thumping negative.

While the accuracy of the *Herald's* figures may be questioned, the validity of the basic argument is hard to challenge. If the majority against Lincoln was 3 to 2, the majority against the Republican program of slavery exclusion must have been even heavier. Because of this pronounced lack of majority support, the Republicans were at a moral disadvantage in maintaining their program, and they were perhaps more susceptible than they would admit to demands that they abandon their partisan platform.

The pressure of the majority could not have been entirely without effect, but it appears that the Republicans were more influenced by a much weaker group—that is, by the Unionists in the Border states. Where the Douglas-Breckinridge-Bell majority peremptorily de-

5. August Belmont, writing to John Forsyth, Nov. 22, remarked that the South regarded the result of the election as "convincing proof of an overwhelming anti-slavery feeling at the North." He believed, however, that the result of the election was "mainly owing to other causes. The country at large had become disgusted with the misrule of Mr. Buchanan and the corruption which disgraced his administration. The Democratic party was made answerable for his misdeeds, and a change was ardently desired by thousands of conservative men out of politics." *Letters, Speeches, and Addresses of August Belmont* (Privately printed, 1890), pp. 23–24.

Horatio Seymour wrote to John J. Crittenden, Jan. 18, that thousands who were not Republicans had voted for Lincoln, in order to avoid voting for Lane on the Breckinridge and Lane ticket. This statement may be regarded with skepticism. Coleman, *Crittenden*, II, 254–255.

6. New York *Herald*, Dec. 19.

manded that Republicans repudiate their platform, the Border Unionists only pleaded for some show of good will, as a sign which they might show to their people. Of the two approaches, the latter was more persuasive by far. Some of the men involved—like John Minor Botts of Virginia, John Gilmer of North Carolina, and Emerson Etheridge of Tennessee, presented the affecting spectacle of men incurring social ostracism and personal danger in the cause of Union, and crying desperately to Northern Unionists for aid. Thus, to the annual New England dinner held in New York on December 23, John Minor Botts wrote that a compromise would save every state but South Carolina, and begged that it might be forthcoming.[7]

One could hardly be unmoved by their situation, and it is evident that not only Thurlow Weed,[8] Hamilton Fish,[9] and other moderates, but also the more irreconcilable Republicans, felt keenly their responsibility to the Border Unionists. Governor Morgan of New York, for instance, was, on one occasion, denouncing compromise as a surrender to South Carolina, when someone reminded him of "our Union loving Sisters, Virginia, Kentucky, Tennessee, and Maryland." At once he took a more patient tone, and remarked that the North would cooperate with them in any reasonable settlement.[10] Somewhat later, Senator Fessenden explained privately that he was refraining from a speech against compromise because "some noble fellows, such as Etheridge and Winter Davis, beg so hard for aid that it is difficult to refuse them the benefit of *silence*

7. Letter of Botts, in New York *Herald,* Dec. 24.
8. Weed wrote on Jan. 9, "We have urged and do urge that the position of Union men in Southern States should be considered. . . . The Union men of southern states . . . amidst the pitiless peltings of the disunion storm, sought like the dove sent out from the ark, a dry spot on which to set their feet." Barnes, *Weed,* pp. 315–316.
9. Fish wrote, "I think concessions should be offered (and honest and *substantial* concessions, too) to secure Virginia and other Border States, and to strengthen the hands of Union men, South." Fish to W. S. Thayer, Dec. 15, in Allan Nevins, *Hamilton Fish, The Inner History of the Grant Administration* (New York, 1936), p. 80.
10. James B. Murray to Crittenden, Dec. 22, in Crittenden MSS. Murray was describing his own interview with Morgan.

where we can give nothing more."[11] And, during February, Salmon P. Chase wrote, "Half a dozen of the border state gentlemen have been in our room tonight: Etheridge and Stokes of Tennessee, Adams and Bristow of Kentucky, Gilmer of North Carolina, and others. I really sympathize with them."[12]

But all the popular pressure from Northern Democrats and sentimental pressure from Border Unionists were easy to resist in comparison with the influence exerted by the capitalists of the day. Zachariah Chandler showed insight when he complained that, "From the days of Carthage to those of James Buchanan the great mercantile centres have been peaceable—ever ready . . . to *buy* immunity but not to fight for it."[13] For the wealth of the country consistently and emphatically advocated some sort of concession.[14] It was Wall Street, according to the *Herald*, which had induced Thurlow Weed to flout his party and propose territorial compromise.[15]

Because of the very nature of the capitalist system, Northern financiers were, from the outset, eager for tranquillity and for "business as usual." Because of their deep-seated respect for property rights, moreover, they were unsympathetic toward abolitionist attacks upon property in Negroes. These basic impulses would probably have

11. Fessenden to his family, Feb. 10, 1861, in Fessenden, *Fessenden*, I, 122.

12. Chase to a friend, Feb. 9, 1861, in Barnes, *Weed*, p. 329. These expressions by Chase and Fessenden came later than the period which I am discussing in the context, but it seems valid to incorporate them as evidences of Northern reaction to Border pleas.

13. Chandler to Lyman Trumbull, Nov. 17, in Trumbull MSS. in Library of Congress.

14. For a full and able exposition of the attitude of New York capitalists throughout the period of crisis, see Philip S. Foner, *Business and Slavery, The New York Merchants and the Irrepressible Conflict* (Chapel Hill, 1941), especially pp. 169–322.

15. New York *Herald*, Dec. 6. In this matter, it is pertinent to note that August Belmont was in communication with Weed, encouraging him in his compromise policy. See letter of Belmont to Weed, Dec. 19, in Belmont, *Letters*, p. 35. For a full discussion of the extent to which New York merchants supported Weed, see Foner, *Business and Slavery*, pp. 235–237.

predisposed them in favor of compromise, even if they had possessed no monetary stake in the Southern economy. But their anxiety for compromise was much accentuated by their deep involvement in Southern commerce and finance. The port of New York had, for some decades, derived a large share of its prosperity from its dominant position in the cotton carrying trade.[16] This commercial relationship had, in turn, led to the development of an extensive credit system, and it was estimated that Northern capitalists had extended credit to the South to the amount of $150,000,000 or $200,000,000,[17] which would be irrecoverable in the event of war. To one observer, the position of New York as broker of Southern cotton made that city seem "a prolongation of the South,"[18] and there were those who believed that, deprived of Southern trade, the metropolis would be ruined[19] and would sink to be "no more than a fishing village."[20] Although these statements were exaggerated, it was true that five cotton states provided the metropolis with at least $200,000,000 worth of business yearly.[21] Even the city of Boston found annually in the South a market for goods worth $60,000,000, according to the estimate of the Boston *Post*, which argued, therefore, that one section could not "live and flourish without the other."[22]

16. For the Northern merchant-capitalist stake in the Southern economy, see Foner, *Business and Slavery*, pp. 1–14; Robert Greenhalgh Albion, *The Rise of New York Port (1815–1860)* (New York, 1939), pp. 95–121.

17. The New York Chamber of Commerce estimated this debt at $200,000,000; Foner, *Business and Slavery*, p. 218. Emerson David Fite, *Social and Industrial Conditions in the North during the Civil War* (New York, 1910), p. 108, estimates $300,000,000.

18. Agénor de Gasparin, *The Uprising of a Great People*, pp. 76–77, 162, as cited in Arthur C. Cole, *The Irrepressible Conflict, 1850–1865*, p. 279.

19. [Catherine C. Hopley], *Life in the South from the Commencement of the War, by a Blockaded British Subject* (London, 1863), I, 140.

20. Newark *Mercury*, Feb. 11, as cited in Cole, *Irrepressible Conflict*, p. 279.

21. Foner, *Business and Slavery*, p. 7.

22. Boston *Post*, Dec. 21, 1859, as cited in Cole, *Irrepressible Conflict*, p. 279.

Because of these economic factors, New York City had always been hostile to the Republicans and their program. The metropolis had given tangible evidence of this attitude in the November election, when it cast 62 per cent of its votes for Lincoln's opponents.[23] The Republicans were at no loss to explain this defeat, but promptly attributed it to the "very general enlistment of the Mercantile and Capitalist classes in the Fusion cause."[24] The New York *Tribune* complained of the "intensity and unanimity of commercial furor" which was manifested in "shrieks of apprehension that the Union was about to be dissolved in case of Lincoln's election."[25]

This "commercial furor" was not merely alarmism. Much of the distress arose from conditions which manifested themselves immediately upon Lincoln's election, and most of the apprehension was justified, for the crisis imperiled, and for a time impaired, the financial prosperity of the country. Alexander T. Stewart, whose dry goods business had brought him perhaps the largest fortune in America, wrote to Thurlow Weed: "The refusal at Washington to concede costs us millions daily."[26] George Livermore assured Charles Sumner that "It is an awful time for merchants,—worse than in 1857; and if there is not some speedy relief, more than half the best concerns in the country will be ruined."[27]

23. The returns for the New York City area were:

	Lincoln	Fusion
Kings	15,883	20,583
Queens	3,749	4,392
New York	33,290	62,293
	52,922	87,268

Extracted from *Tribune Almanac* for 1861, p. 41. For an account of the exertions of the New York merchants in achieving this result, see Foner, *Business and Slavery*, pp. 169–207.

24. New York *Tribune*, Nov. 8.

25. *Ibid.*

26. Stewart to Weed, Feb. 20, in Barnes, *Weed*, p. 318.

27. Livermore to Sumner, Dec. 12, in Pierce, *Sumner*, IV, 2. D. D. T. Marshall wrote to Salmon P. Chase, Nov. 13, that "The Secession howl attracts no attention here except among stock jobbers and Southern traders[.] To them, things look blue."

During November and early December, this dire prediction seemed well on the way to fulfillment. The election of Lincoln was promptly followed by two panics on the New York Stock Exchange. The banks were in serious trouble, as was indicated by the suspension of specie payment in Charleston, Washington, Baltimore, and Philadelphia, and the issuance of clearing house certificates by the banks of New York. Unhappy creditors awaited Southern repudiation of debts at any moment, and it soon developed that they were not indulging groundless apprehension, for the repudiation ensued quickly, and business failures followed in such numbers that the total for 1861 exceeded that for the panic year of 1857.[28] The North averted a major economic collapse only because of purely fortuitous crop failures in Europe which caused a heavy demand for American grain, and thus offset the forces which were leading toward a depression.[29]

In these premises, the men of property were fearful of crisis, friendly to the South, and anxious for compromise. As a group, therefore, they responded enthusiastically to the Crittenden proposals. Without attempting to enumer-

28. For evidence of the financial distress, see Foner, *Business and Slavery*, pp. 208–223, 259–260. Also, see Rhodes, *Hist. of U. S.*, III, 172, note 1; Fite, *Social . . . Conditions in North During Civil War*, pp. 105–108; Cole, *Irrepressible Conflict*, pp. 282–283.

29. Charles A. Davis wrote to Crittenden, Jan. 21: "in November . . . there was every reason to suppose that the *then* impending evil could scarcely fail to make 'mince meat' of every commercial and trading interest in all this quarter. That such has not been the case may be attributed to two leading causes: 1st, The continued demand for bread stuffs (food of all kinds) in Europe, which of course has been a great boon to North and West—and 2nd, the vast increase of the *consumption* of cotton everywhere, coupled *just now* with a fear in Europe that our present crop, and especially the next, may be obstructed in its production by political embroilments reaching the *labor* of producing. Hence good prices, and hence comes gold to us, and the balance of trade is in our favor yet . . . and hence *secession* thus far has not worked the evil that was deprecated three months ago. Had these causes (especially demand for food ahead) not existed . . . there would have been such a *financial smash up* in this whole country, that no one could now calculate the extent of it." Crittenden MSS.

ate all of the major capitalists who sympathized with these measures, it is impressive to list those who sent the Kentucky Senator written assurance of their support. Among his approving correspondents were: Jay Gould, who assured Crittenden that "a great majority in Pennsylvania" favored his compromise; Daniel Lord, eminent insurance lawyer, who wrote repeatedly of his activities in circulating memorials and petitions in support of compromise; James William Beekman and James DePeyster Ogden, heirs to the wealth and prestige of old New York families; Anthony B. Allen, one of America's leading manufacturers of farm machinery; John Brodhead, president of the Camden and Atlantic Railroad; Charles Augustus Davis, another frequent correspondent, and owner of a fortune accumulated in the iron trade; Edwin Croswell, who had become affluent as a public printer and as a member of the "Albany Regency," and who had then gone into business in New York; Amos Adams Lawrence, of Boston, an opulent cotton manufacturer and large scale philanthropist; and August Belmont, who engaged in banking with all the financial prestige appropriate to one affiliated with the Rothschilds.[30]

As late as December 15, the Northern capitalists had made very little effort in behalf of conciliation, except to address individual appeals to extremists of both sections. When writing to Southern correspondents, they usually sought to emphasize that the ascendancy of the Republicans was only transitory, that the Northern majority was not hostile to the South nor to slavery, and that the force of anti-slavery was losing its effectiveness within the Republican ranks.[31]

30. Letters to Crittenden from Gould, Jan. 4, 1861 [incorrectly dated and calendared, "1860," in the printed calendar of Crittenden MSS.]; Lord, Dec. 22, 29, Jan. 26; Beekman, Jan. 24; Ogden, Jan. 29; Allen, Jan. 19; Brodhead, Jan. 4; Davis, Dec. 31, Jan. 7, 21, 28, Feb. 14; Croswell, Dec. 24; Lawrence, Jan. 22; Belmont, Dec. 26 [also in Belmont, *Letters,* p. 41]. All in Crittenden MSS. See also Davis to Winfield Scott, Dec. 26, in *ibid.*

31. Belmont to John Forsyth of Ala., Nov. 22, Dec. 19; to Herschel V. Johnson of Ga., Nov. 22, Dec. 30; to John C. Bradley of Ala., Nov. 28;

But appeals to the South were incidental. Businessmen tended to admit that Southern grievances were justified, and that continued forbearance could not be expected of the South unless concessions were granted. To secure concessions, therefore, they must seek to influence the Republicans, and to influence the Republicans they must organize. A recognition of this fact led these men and many like them to rally to the cause of compromise and to work to mobilize public opinion and confront the Republicans with that mobilization. They held conferences to elaborate their strategy; they wrote letters extensively; they drew up and circulated memorials or petitions, to which they secured more than one hundred thousand signatures; they organized great mass meetings in New York and Philadelphia; and they sent delegations to Washington to exert their influence directly.

One of the first steps in this program of organization took place in mid-December, when a number of outstanding capitalists, including William B. Astor and William H. Aspinwall, made arrangements and issued a call for a "private" meeting of a large number of merchants, with a view to adopting resolutions expressive of their feeling. This meeting took place on December 15 at the offices of Richard Lathers at 33 Pine St., and was known thereafter as the Pine Street Meeting. More than two thousand merchants attended. Charles O'Conor presided, and a number of speeches were made. Some speakers berated the secessionists and some the Republicans, but the consensus was expressed by a speech of Hiram Ketchum, and by an address and resolutions which were adopted: if the South

to William Martin of S. C., Nov. 30. Belmont, *Letters,* pp. 24–29, 36–39.

See also letters of William H. Livingston and Co. of New York to Henrey and Co. of Charleston, and James A. Hamilton to Thomas C. Pinckney, quoted in Foner, *Business and Slavery,* p. 226.

In an address to the people of the South, adopted at the Pine Street meeting (below, p. 176–177), it was argued that the anti-Republicans had gained 22 seats in the recently elected House of Representatives, that the Republican party was splitting apart, and that "Anti-slavery-ism has constituted but one of various political elements combined in that 'Republicanism' which has elected Mr. Lincoln." Foner, *Business and Slavery,* p. 229.

would refrain from rash action, Northern conservatives would combine with moderate Republicans to secure the recognition of the right to carry slavery into the territories, and the redress of Southern grievances. A delegation was even appointed to visit the Southern States and present this assurance.[32]

The Pine Street meeting marked the beginning of vigorous activities. During the ensuing weeks of December and January, the capitalists exerted themselves in various ways. Among their earliest endeavors was the arranging of mass meetings, which were held in nearly all the large cities of the North, and at which great numbers of people were present. Philadelphia held one of the greatest on December 13.[33] Boston was the scene of a large gathering when conservative forces broke up a meeting in honor of the memory of John Brown, and improvised a counter-meeting of their own.[34] But the most spectacular of these great public demonstrations was probably that held at the Cooper Union on ·January 28. This assemblage was originally planned for January 22, but the control of the committee on arrangements fell into the hands of out-and-out secessionists. The committee, therefore, had to be "reconstructed," and a delay was necessary. But when the meeting did assemble, with Crittenden's friend, James DePeyster Ogden, in the chair, a huge crowd was in attendance. Eminent speakers, representing both parties, presented arguments in favor of compromise, and commissioners were appointed to go to the seceding states to seek a basis for conciliation.[35]

But mass meetings were, at best, only an indirect way

32. Best account of the Pine Street meeting is in Foner, *Business and Slavery,* pp. 227–232; see also Rhodes, *Hist. of U. S.,* III, 173–174. The New York *Herald,* Dec. 16, contains an account.

33. Rhodes, *Hist. of U. S.,* III, 173.

34. *Ibid.*

35. Appleton Oaksmith to Crittenden, Jan. 19; Jas. DePeyster Ogden to Crittenden, Jan. 29; in Crittenden MSS. DeAlva Stanwood Alexander, *Political History of the State of New York* (New York, 1906), II, 351–352.

of exercising suasion upon Congress. Another and a more direct form was that of petition. From the outset of their activity, the mercantile-capitalist group relied heavily on this device, and the accumulation of signatures appears as one of their most constant enterprises. As early as December 19, August Belmont wrote: "A very strong memorial, to be signed by all the leading men of both parties who are for the maintenance of the Union, is now preparing and will be forthwith sent to Washington."[36]

Some of these petitions, like the one mentioned by Belmont, circulated only among special groups of outstanding men. A striking example of this type of resolution was produced on January 18 by a body of New York merchants, meeting in the Chamber of Commerce, and adopting unanimously a memorial to Congress urging the acceptance of the Crittenden Compromise.[37] Another such resolution, with an even more limited group of subscribers, was one supported by a number of railway presidents who met in Washington in January. These magnates, too, sent a memorial to Congress, implementing their recommendations with the assertion that they represented $300,000,000.[38]

The most publicized petitions, however, were those intended to demonstrate that the public at large favored compromise. To adduce proof of this, countless petitions were launched. In New York, "a number of gentlemen of our best sort, including some leading Republicans," drafted a memorial on December 28 and planned to print and circulate it before the new year came in.[39] By January 11, a correspondent of Crittenden assured him that these memorials were then in circulation, and were meeting with prompt and almost universal response.[40] Two weeks later, Daniel Lord, who had pushed the enterprise from the

36. Belmont to William Sprague, Dec. 19, in Belmont, *Letters,* pp. 34–35.
37. Alexander, *Polit. Hist. of N. Y.,* II, 349–350.
38. Speech of Crittenden, Feb. 9, in *Cong. Globe,* p. 822.
39. Daniel Lord to Crittenden, Dec. 29, in Crittenden MSS.
40. Simeon Baldwin to Crittenden, Jan. 11, in *ibid.*

beginning, reported that the memorial, "very numerously signed," would be brought to Washington on January 29 by a "very large and respectable committee" of New Yorkers.[41] The memorial was indeed "numerously signed"; it contained 38,000 names, and was brought to Washington ceremoniously by a committee of outstanding merchants. These gentlemen entrusted their document to Senator Seward. One cannot believe that he derived any pleasure from this guardianship, but he presented the petition to Congress, and accompanied the presentation by a speech in which he stated that 63,000 signatures had been collected altogether, many having been presented previously. He was careful to state that he could not promise to support the petition, but he freely admitted that it was "a fair exponent of . . . the whole commercial interest of the United States," and that, "in any other part of the world, such a communication would command obedience."[42]

While these activities were in progress in New York, similar exertions were being made in Boston. There the leadership in circulating petitions fell to Crittenden's friend Amos A. Lawrence, a wealthy textile industrialist. His group thought it best to offer two forms of petitions: one for Republicans, and therefore phrased in rather general terms, urging the maintenance of harmony; the other, more specific in its approval of the Crittenden plan.[43] The first of these two forms was circulated in Boston, and appears to have received about 14,000 signatures, which is an astonishingly high total for a city with only 19,000 voters.[44] Meanwhile, the second petition, endorsing the Crittenden compromise by name, was circulated hastily through 182 Massachusetts communities, where, in a very limited time, it gathered 22,313 signa-

41. Lord to Crittenden, Jan. 26, in *ibid.*
42. In Senate, Jan. 31. *Cong. Globe,* p. 657.
43. Lawrence to Crittenden, Jan. 22, in Crittenden MSS.
44. *Ibid.;* speech of Crittenden in Senate, Feb. 12, *Cong. Globe,* p. 862.

tures.[45] Those signatures which had been collected were presented to the Senate by Crittenden on February 12.

Sheafs of petitions and resolutions of mass meetings served excellently as silent witnesses, to Congress, of a strong demand for compromise. But such documents were passive, and Northern merchants wanted more than merely passive appeals. Accordingly, throughout the crisis they sent numerous delegations to Washington, to labor personally with recalcitrant congressmen. Without attempting to record all of these missions, it may suffice to note that several important ones visited Washington during January. Early in the month, a party of leading Republicans, including A. A. Low, Hamilton Fish, Moses H. Grinnell, and J. C. Green, went from New York to the capital. At about the same time, a delegation of non-Republicans made a similar trip. These delegates accomplished little, but their failure, instead of discouraging the business men, merely provoked them to a greater effort. On January 29, accordingly, a delegation of leading merchants arrived at Washington by special train. In this party were A. A. Low, Peter Cooper, William H. Aspinwall, William E. Dodge, Thomas Phelps, Wilson G. Hunt, A. R. Wetmore, and James Gallatin. They brought with them the huge petition, already mentioned, which Seward presented to the Senate. But their activity by no means ceased with the fulfillment of this mission. On the day after witnessing the presentation of their memorial, the merchants met in conference with the congressmen of the Border states. At this meeting, the visitors found the atmosphere rather chilly, until they pointed out that it lay within their collective power to prevent a government loan from being subscribed, whereupon they found the Border statesmen more cordial. But the most important meeting by far was a dinner at Willard's, tendered by the

45. An undated, unsigned memorandum concerning this petition may be found in the Crittenden MSS., Vol. 24, numbered 4901a. See also speech of Crittenden, Feb. 12, in *Cong. Globe,* p. 862.

visitors to the Republican members of Congress. About seventy of the one hundred and forty Republican members attended. At this affair, A. A. Low and William E. Dodge spoke for the merchants, admitting that they had encountered little success in their conciliatory mission, but insisting that they would not despair, and appealing for the abandonment of the Chicago Platform: "Shall we . . . stand upon a platform made some time ago in view of facts which then existed, and which have ceased to exist now; or shall we be willing to . . . yield some fair concession, without any sacrifice of principle?"[46]

In response to this query, it is a notable fact that a number of Republicans replied with brief speeches in favor of compromise. Senators Simon Cameron of Pennsylvania and Lafayette S. Foster of Connecticut, as well as Representatives John Sherman of Ohio, Elbridge G. Spaulding of New York, John T. Nixon of New Jersey, James T. Hale of Pennsylvania, W. McKee Dunn of Indiana, and Samuel Curtis of Iowa were among this number. The merchants believed that most of their seventy guests shared in these compromise sentiments. They did not deceive themselves, however, as to the continuing opposition of the absentees.[47]

If by these varied activities the merchants gained less support than they hoped for among the Republicans in Congress, they at least gained enough to excite newspaper comment[48] and to cause grave concern to staunch Republicans. Senator Fessenden confided that, "My great anxiety is lest the spirit of trade in our large Northern cities should so operate as to frighten our people."[49]

46. Foner, *Business and Slavery*, pp. 248–258, gives full accounts of the activities of these delegations, and especially of the dinner at Willard's, which was written up fully only in the Philadelphia *Press*, Feb. 4.

47. Foner, *Business and Slavery*, pp. 257–258.

48. "There is a great pressure here from the business and high social circles of all our great cities for a compromise." New York *Tribune*, Feb. 3 (Washington dispatch).

49. Fessenden to his family, Feb. [?], 1861, in Fessenden, *Fessenden*, I, 124.

Charles Sumner complained openly in the Senate that the merchants of New York and Boston wanted him, and the men of his type, "to surrender our principles."[50] Even before these two took alarm, Zachariah Chandler had written to Lyman Trumbull of his anxiety: "The mercantile world is in a ferment, even some good reliable Republicans are alarmed and wish something done. Now I have no fear that the senseless Southern howl will affect Mr. Lincoln in the least, but I do fear that this Republican alarm may extend even to Springfield."[51]

Chandler's apprehensions were justified. A few days later, Henry Villard wrote from the Illinois capital that every day brought letters and personal appeals to Lincoln to adopt a conciliatory policy, in order to soothe the South. Even Republicans joined in this plea, and among the most anxious were the men of wealth: "But a few steps from his reception room, the leading financiers of the State were assembled for many days to counsel and devise the best means of averting the commercial crisis. . . . Telegraphic dispatches conveying the troubles and anxieties of Eastern financial commercial centers, constantly flashed upon him."[52]

With all this storm of pressure which beat upon the Republican party, it is natural that lines began to waver. For a minority party which knew itself to be a minority party, the force of demands from the divided majority in opposition, from the pitifully sincere Border Unionists, and from the importunate financiers, must have seemed almost irresistible. Perhaps the remarkable thing is that the Republican lines did not buckle completely.

But though they showed resistance, they did not remain intact. Even before the opening of Congress, signs of

50. Speech in Senate, Feb. 12, in *Cong. Globe,* p. 863.
51. Chandler to Trumbull, Nov. 17, in Trumbull MSS. Meanwhile, Senator Trumbull himself experienced some pressure from the commercial classes of Chicago. Horace White, *The Life of Lyman Trumbull* (Boston, 1913), p. 117.
52. New York *Herald,* Nov. 26 (Springfield, Nov. 22).

defection were evident. Thurlow Weed's unexpected endorsement of a renewal of the Missouri Compromise constituted, by itself, a serious breach in the Republican solidarity. Faithful partisans received it with a volley of abuse which purported to show unanimity of disapproval. But, in spite of the outcry, there were indications that other Republicans of the first rank shared Weed's desire for conciliation, though they hesitated to concede so much or to express themselves so freely. Thus the New York *Times* was less bold than the *Evening Journal* in the remedies which it proposed, but Henry J. Raymond had committed himself, no less than Weed, to the desirability of concessions to the South. Meanwhile, James Watson Webb, editor of the New York *Courier and Enquirer*, had acted with characteristic verve, endorsing Weed's position and sending a copy of his endorsement to every member of Congress.[53]

Thus the ranks were perceptibly shaken even before Congress assembled. The New York *Herald* professed to believe that "There is a strong prospect of a satisfactory settlement of the difficulties on a permanent basis."[54] This observation was predicated upon the erroneous assumption that Seward would take up the cause of compromise, and therefore it seems less valid than the simultaneous observation of Seward himself that "the Republican party today is as uncompromising as the Secessionists in South Carolina." But, he added, "A month hence each may come to think that moderation is wiser."[55] In this anticipation, Seward mistook the Carolinians, who developed no tendency toward moderation, but he correctly gauged the direction of thought among his fellow-Republicans, who·showed an increasing willingness to scuttle the Chicago Platform.

Indications of this attitude began to appear during the first week of the session. On December 9, the *Herald* again asserted that peaceful solutions were imminent, or, as it said, "better things will occur within a fortnight than the

53. Seward to Weed, Dec. 3, in Barnes, *Weed,* p. 308.
54. New York *Herald,* Dec. 3.
55. Seward to Weed, Dec. 3, in Barnes, *Weed,* p. 308.

most ultra of either side anticipate."[56] On this occasion, Republican evidence did not contradict the *Herald,* but, rather, corroborated it. For Henry Adams, whose home was an informal Republican headquarters, noted on the same day the first signs of Republican defection in the Senate. The two Rhode Island senators, he said, were "both very fishy and weak-kneed."[57]

The next four days witnessed a further development of conciliatory spirit, to such a point that the guardians of the Chicago Platform were badly discouraged. Senator James Dixon of Connecticut showed something of the new tone when he expressed, on the Senate floor, a readiness to make any reasonable and honest sacrifice to preserve the Union. He proposed to give the South all the rights which it could properly claim under the Constitution, and although he took care to assert a consistent adherence to principle, he repudiated the idea of an irrepressible conflict. His hostility to the doctrinaires of both sections found emphatic expression in a closing assertion that "if the question of slavery shall destroy our Union, it will not be because it could not be satisfactorily and rightfully adjusted, but because the statesmen of the day are incompetent to the task."[58] Meanwhile, John Sherman was trying to prove himself not incompetent to the task by formulating his scheme to end the territorial controversy by admitting the entire territorial area to statehood.[59]

On the day following Sherman's new departure, the Republicans in the House Committee of Thirty-three made their first collective move toward conciliation. With the secession of South Carolina only a week in the offing, the committee began to hold prolonged meetings, and to give other evidences of concern. William Kellogg of Illinois, a personal friend of Abraham Lincoln, and, accordingly, a man of influence, made a notably conserva-

56. New York *Herald,* Dec. 9, 1860.
57. Adams to C. F. Adams, Jr., Dec. 9, in Ford, ed., *Henry Adams Letters, 1858–1891,* p. 63. The Rhode Island senators were Henry B. Anthony and James F. Simmons, both Republicans.
58. Speech in Senate, Dec. 10, in *Cong. Globe,* pp. 32–33.
59. Above, pp. 93–95.

tive speech in the committee, defending Lincoln against the charge of abolitionism, and saying that all proper concessions to the South would be made. This pronouncement was, if anything, more advanced than Dixon's speech or Sherman's resolutions, and it derived additional importance from the possibility that Lincoln might have inspired it.[60] Forthwith, the committee proceeded to act, and half of the Republican members joined the Democrats and Americans in a resolution endorsing the "prompt and cheerful" grant of constitutional remedies and specific guarantees to mollify Southern discontent "whether such discontent and hostility are without just cause or not."[61]

To militant Republicans, it looked as though the old story was to be re-enacted. Frightened liberals would forsake their principles to allay Southern hostility, whether justified or not. At the Adams house, dejection prevailed, and Henry wrote to his brother a melancholy account of the course of events. "All the mean material we've got is coming out now," he reported. "Dixon of Connecticut flattened out, and so has Sherman; so will Anthony,[62] Foster,[63] Collamer,[64] I believe, and a heap in the lower House. The Thirty-Three committee is sitting now every day and all day, and they'll be reporting some damned nonsense or other soon. Today we were all waiting for our good father before dinner, when in he popped in a state of considerable friction and reported that his committee had sprung a resolution on them yielding everything, which had passed in spite of him with only eight negatives;[65] New England, New York, and Wisconsin. . . . It embroils things badly and will inevitably break the Republican line."[66]

60. Committee proceedings of Dec. 14, reported in New York *Herald,* New York *Tribune,* Dec. 15.
61. See above, p. 97.
62. Henry B. Anthony, Senator from R. I.
63. Lafayette S. Foster, Senator from Conn.
64. Jacob Collamer, Senator from Vt.
65. This, of course, was the Dunn resolution. See above, p. 97.
66. Henry Adams to C. F. Adams, Jr., Dec. 13, in Ford, ed., *Henry Adams Letters, 1858–1891,* pp. 64–65.

Of course, Henry Adams was unseasoned, and perhaps impressionable and easily alarmed. But it is also true that he was in intimate political communion with his father and with Seward, and their outlook was apparently not such as to temper his pessimism. Near the end of the letter quoted above, he returned to a supremely dismal statement of the condition of his party: "I'm afraid . . . I only speak exact truth when I tell you to prepare yourself for a complete disorganization of our party. If the South show any liberal spirit, the reaction will sweep us out dreadfully and thin our ranks to a skeleton. . . . How many there will be faithful unto the end, I cannot say, but I fear me much, not a third of the House."

Nor was Adams' grimness the mere manifestation of a transient mood. Five days later, he lamented that "our men hardly dare say they'll take the prize they've won." Then, with something of the acrimony of his grandfather, he proceeded to particularize on the weak places of Republican morale. Representative Rice of Massachusetts was held firm, he said, only by "some pretty tight screws on him." Pennsylvania seemed to him to show "some sound principle in the western counties," but Philadelphia was "all about our ears," and the state as a whole was "rotten to the core." "Ohio is not all she should be, and Indiana is all she should not be, just as that mean state always was." He found Illinois "tolerably well," and Wisconsin earned his approbation as "a new Vermont," but there was "too low a tone everywhere."[67]

The Republicans avoided publicizing their misgivings, and Henry Adams was restrained from expressing publicly the concern which he had revealed to his brother.[68]

67. Adams to C. F. Adams, Jr., Dec. 18, in *ibid.,* p. 66.

68. At this time, Adams was writing occasional letters for the Boston *Advertiser,* and it appears that he wrote one about Dec. 14 which was not published. This is evident from his letters to C. F. Adams, Jr., on Dec. 13 and 20. In the first of these he states his intention of writing a letter to appear on Monday, Dec. 17. In the second, he writes, "As to last Monday's letter, which has not appeared [and which never did appear], I am not sorry for it, as it was written when everything looked

Because of the general concealment of all such qualms, it is now difficult to find evidences of the demoralization in the Republican ranks. But the surviving indications suffice to show that it was widespread and increasing. The party which drafted the Chicago Platform and achieved the election of Lincoln was, in fact, an unstable minority coalition of true anti-slavery radicals and of opportunist groups which were essentially moderate. Promptly after its victory, this imperfect coalition was subjected to enormous pressure,[69] not only by the threat of secession, but by the entreaties of the Border Unionists, by the united force of the Northern conservative majority, and by the demands of the masters of finance. At the same time, public reaction moved toward compromise, and vast numbers of Republicans who had cast ballots for Lincoln and free territory in November, signed petitions for Crittenden and territorial compromise in the month following.[70] Under this impact, the Republican Congressmen, never oblivious to the tenor of opinion, began to temper their zeal. Certain isolated ones—at first confirmed heretics like Eli Thayer, or lame ducks, like David Kilgore; later, representative men like John Sherman and James Dixon—began cautiously to cast about for a basis for compromise. This movement remained subterranean, but gained momentum and adherents until it was strong enough to induce half of the Republican members of the Committee of Thirty-three to declare themselves in favor of "constitutional remedies" and "specific guarantees" for the South.

As yet no general action of significance had taken place. Many Republicans, like Sumner and Fessenden, adhered to their policies as if there were no crisis. Some of

fishy. You can tell Hale [editor of the *Advertiser*] this, and mark me what he says or looks, for I do much mistrust me that he suppressed that letter." *Ibid.,* pp. 65, 68.

69. John A. Gurley, irreconcilable Republican representative from Ohio, spoke of the fact that "Weed and others brought every influence to bear to break us down and make our men surrender." Gurley to Salmon P. Chase, Jan. 24, in Chase MSS.

70. Below, pp. 190–192.

them would have held steadfast to this attitude regardless of consequences, and Adams was unduly glum when he predicted that two-thirds of his party in the House would go with the tide. But he was right that the tide was ebbing, for in December the Republicans exhibited a temper so conciliatory as to have been unimaginable in November. The effect of such movements is usually cumulative, and there was no saying how rapidly this temper would spread. The individual congressman was ill fortified to resist all the pressure upon him, and he was especially ill prepared to resist it alone. The Chicago Platform was not without value in his eyes, but it was, after all, only a campaign document, and the campaign was over. In the absence of a re-statement of policy, or an assumption of responsibility by a leader, he would hesitate to assume the responsibility of defeating compromise. He had waited five weeks for such leadership, and it had not been forthcoming. As time passed, he found his constituents more clamorous for compromise, and his colleagues more receptive to it. In these premises, he must inevitably view it with increasing complaisance.

But whether most Republican congressmen would soon have accepted compromise must remain in the realm of speculation. For the growing tendency was not permitted to continue uninterrupted. From the first appointment of the Committee of Thirty-three, the President-elect had followed its proceedings apprehensively.[71] It is evident that his apprehension increased with the unfolding of events. In consequence he abandoned his policy of remaining inactive until his inauguration, and quietly but effectively he brought the vast weight of his influence to bear. Assuming a momentous responsibility, he intervened to arrest the growing sentiment for compromise among the Republicans in Congress.

71. New York *Herald,* Dec. 15 (Springfield, Dec. 10).

CHAPTER VI
LINCOLN'S PERILOUS SILENCE

AMONG the distinctive features of the American governmental system, one of the best known is that anachronistic arrangement which, until 1937, permitted the President and the members of Congress to continue in service for four months after their successors were chosen. The curious status of the "lame duck" congressman, and the impotence of executives like Herbert Hoover or James Buchanan in the last winter of their administrations, are familiar topics. But there is another aspect of the same situation which is equally striking, though less familiar. This aspect concerns officers-elect, who were placed in the anomalous position of incurring fierce publicity and wielding vast influence, weeks before they assumed the powers of office.

Throughout American history, this anomaly was never so vividly illustrated as during the four months when Abraham Lincoln waited in Springfield for the Buchanan administration to expire. Nominally, Lincoln was simply a private citizen of Illinois, the senior partner in the law firm of Lincoln and Herndon. Potentially, he had been chosen to the highest office in the nation. His contemporaries did not know that the future would reveal him as "the War President," and "the Emancipator," but his importance, if not his greatness, was understood. From the moment of his nomination, Springfield had become a political Mecca, and even before the Committee of Notification sipped lemonade in Mrs. Lincoln's meagerly furnished parlor, politicians had come to seek her husband's favor.

Lincoln might have expected a swarm of political mendicants in any case, but the unique element of his position lay in the fact that, from the moment of his election, he was held responsible for the secession movement, and was constantly importuned to move to allay the outburst with which the lower South had responded to his triumph. From all sides came demands for a statement, a program, a letter, a gesture, a list of appointments, to indicate the moderation of his policy and purpose.

These demands derived especial point from the fact that Lincoln had waged one of the most laconic campaigns in history. In fact, he had probably indulged himself in public utterance less than any other aspirant to the Presidency except, perhaps, Zachary Taylor. Until Lincoln went to New York to speak at the Cooper Institute in February, 1860, he had never made a significant speech in the East; and, after that trip, he did not speak significantly again until he stood on the east portico of the Capitol and delivered his First Inaugural Address.

Thus, for nearly a year, when his ways were least known and his attitude was of greatest import, Lincoln remained silent. Not one campaign speech did he make; not one public letter did he write, save to acknowledge his nomination in a statement and a letter which together contain less than three hundred words. In these lapses from silence, he affirmed that the Chicago Platform "meets my approval, and it shall be my care not to violate it or disregard it in any part." He acknowledged, also, his "due regard . . . to the rights of all the States and Territories and people of the nation" and "to the inviolability of the Constitution."[1] But beyond this, he said not one word to reaffirm, much less to elaborate, his position.

This unusual silence derived not so much from native taciturnity, as from Lincoln's firm conviction that sectional antagonism fed upon discussion of sectional issues, and especially upon misconstruction of what had been said. He suspected his Democratic antagonists of seeking to bully him into a modification of the Chicago Platform, or to goad him into an injudicious statement which might

1. Letter of acceptance, to George Ashmun and the Republican National Convention, May 23, 1860, in Nicolay and Hay, eds., *Works of Lincoln*, VI, 14–15.

be used against him.[2] In consequence, he deliberately adopted a policy of silence. This policy found expression in his abstention from public utterance, and again in his refusal to answer the interrogations of persons who wrote to him. He avowed this policy frankly, making it the theme of a form letter which went forth to all who sought to draw him out. This letter, sent over the signature of his secretary, explained that Mr. Lincoln received many such inquiries as to his position, and that he also received many other communications beseeching him "to write nothing whatever upon any point of political doctrine." The letter asserted that "his positions were well known when he was nominated, and that he must not now embarrass the canvass by undertaking to shift or modify them." Thus implicitly declining to furnish the desired statement, the letter closed with an expression of regret that it was impossible to oblige everyone.[3]

Occasionally, when the caliber of the correspondent or the circumstances of the case forbade the use of his form letter, Lincoln wrote an individual reply, but he made these exceptions only to defend his silence more effectively, and never to deviate from it.[4] On occasion, he made reference to his earlier utterances, which, he steadily maintained, were self-explanatory. Thus, to two seekers for a gloss upon the House Divided Speech, he wrote, "Look

2. Lincoln wrote to George Denison Prentice, Oct. 29, 1860: "If I . . . abstain [from issuing a statement], it will be because of apprehension that it would do harm. For the good men of the South—and I regard the majority of them as such—I have no objection to repeat seventy and seven times. But I have bad men to deal with, both North and South; men who are eager for something new upon which to base new misrepresentations; men who would like to frighten me, or at least to fix upon me the character of timidity and cowardice. . . . I intend keeping my eye upon these gentlemen, and to not unnecessarily put any weapons in their hands." Nicolay and Hay, eds., *Works of Lincoln*, VI, 66–68.

3. Letter in *ibid.*, VI, 22–23.

4. Such letters were written to William S. Speer, Oct. 23; George Denison Prentice, Oct. 29; Truman Smith, Nov. 10; N. P. Paschall, Nov. 16; and Henry J. Raymond, Nov. 28. *Ibid.*, VI, 63–74.

over it carefully, and conclude I meant all I said, and did not mean any thing I did not say, and you will have my meaning."[5]

The pressure upon Lincoln for a statement may have seemed heavy during the campaign, but it was slight compared to that which developed after his election. So soon as it appeared that he would be in position to execute his policies, the lower South looked to secession, without waiting to be certain what his policies were. This, of course, created a furor, and in the North it led to frantic appeals for some sort of declaration to quiet Southern fears.

Characteristically importunate was the New York *Herald*, which reported a few days before the election that Lincoln was said to have a letter already prepared to be published as soon as his election was assured.[6] When this fabulous letter failed to materialize, the *Herald* began to demand one. Two days after the election, it urged, in an editorial, that Lincoln ought to make a statement affirming his support of the Fugitive Slave Law and his readiness to subordinate the interests of his party to those of his country.[7] The same idea received editorial repetition on the day following, and frequently thereafter. Always the *Herald* emphasized the gravity of Lincoln's responsibility —the enormous power which he could exert for good or evil: "There is only one man in the United States who has it in his power to restore the country to its former happy and prosperous condition, and that man is the President elect. . . . He can be either Catiline or Cincinnatus. . . . If Mr. Lincoln will speak out in a manner calculated to reassure the conservative masses of all the States, the present cloud will pass away like a summer shower. . . ."[8]

The pressure was so heavy that, to one staunch Republi-

5. Lincoln to O. P. Hall and I. H. Fullininder, Feb. 14, in Gilbert Tracy, editor, *Uncollected Letters of Abraham Lincoln* (Boston, 1917), pp. 132–133.
6. New York *Herald*, Nov. 2.
7. *Ibid.*, Nov. 8.
8. *Ibid.*, Dec. 15.

can, it seemed as if "the 'real tug' of the war" had just begun, because of "the tremendous effort . . . in every
quarter by the 'nominal republicans' to draw Lincoln's
fire and, by getting from him a premature announcement
of the policy of his administration, to weaken the moral
force of our triumph."[9]

Without agreeing as to the purpose of those who sought
"to draw Lincoln's fire," one may safely accept the statement that their effort was "in every quarter." From New
Orleans, the sister of Salmon P. Chase wrote to him, pictur-
ing the boundless gratitude of his countrymen if he would
only "Make Lincoln write a manifesto to the *country*."[10]
From Kentucky, another writer thought that the adoption
by Lincoln of a "truly national and constitutional programme" would render the country "ultimately, safe."[11]
From the neighboring state of Tennessee, another Unionist wrote to Crittenden that Lincoln "has but to speak.
. . . He has the power, to save his country. . . ."[12] From
the East came a chorus of demands, from the Democrats,
from the powerful commercial interests, and sometimes
from Republicans, one of whom was the eminent Henry J.
Raymond.[13] And in Springfield, where all these plaints
converged, the correspondent of the New York *Herald*
reported that "every mail brought him [Lincoln] written,
and every hour, verbal entreaties to abandon his perilous
silence . . . and pour the oil of conciliatory, conservative
assurances upon the turbulent waves of Southern excitement. Even among his own political adherents many
Union-loving men exhorted him to yield."[14]

9. Luther B. Bruen, Dayton, O., Nov. 13, to Chase, in Chase MSS.

10. Mrs. R. L. Hunt to Chase, Nov. 23, in *ibid.*

11. George B. Robertson to Crittenden, Dec. 16, in Coleman, *Crittenden,* II, 222.

12. Simon Bradford, Memphis, Feb. 21, to Crittenden, in Crittenden
MSS.

13. Nicolay and Hay, *Lincoln,* III, 279–282.

14. New York *Herald,* Nov. 26 (Springfield, Nov. 22). Henry Villard
was the *Herald's* correspondent at this time, and his dispatches are
invaluable on the subject of Lincoln as President-elect. A regrettably
small selection from these dispatches appears in Harold G. and Oswald

The President-elect was not wholly impervious to these importunities, but so far as he yielded at all, he yielded very little and very slowly. The demands upon him not only required a complete reversal of his own policy, but they also ran counter to the wishes of many of his most ardent followers. For the more radical Republicans were in complete sympathy with his policy of silence, and they were hostile to any step suggestive of compromise, or even of moderation. Their attitude is typified by certain correspondents of Salmon P. Chase, who hoped that Lincoln would preserve his silence. They felt that the issuance of an address by him would be a "weak and foolish . . . thing," and one of them hoped that "he will not open his mouth, save only to eat, until March 4th." To the same writer, Lincoln's position seemed "like that of a pillar upon which rests a mighty superstructure. This strength is in his uprightness—his *perpendicularity*. Let him bend or incline a hair's breadth and he is irretrievably gone."[15] This sentiment was widespread. Seward's colleague, Senator Preston King, wrote to John Bigelow exulting that Lincoln would make no declaration, while William Cullen Bryant, it appears, wrote directly to Lincoln urging him to adhere to his silence.[16] Even the Albany *Evening Journal* had condemned "those who ask Mr. Lincoln to say or do something," for taking "counsel of their fears rather than their judgment,"[17] and though Thurlow Weed later changed his policy, he could not recall his words.

Garrison Villard, editors, *Lincoln on the Eve of '61, A Journalist's Story by Henry Villard* (New York, 1941). For Villard's later reminiscences of his association with Lincoln, see *Memoirs of Henry Villard, Journalist and Financier, 1835-1900* (Boston, 1904), I, 140–161.

15. Letters to Chase from Edw. D. Mansfield, Morrow, O., Nov. 26; Luther B. Bruen, Dayton, O., Nov. 13; R. V. Marsh, Brandon, Vt., Nov. 7; George A. Nourse, St. Paul, Minn., Nov. 17; in Chase MSS.

16. Preston King to Bigelow, Nov. 12, in Bigelow, *Retrospections*, I, 316. The letter of Bryant is mentioned in King's letter.

17. Albany *Evening Journal*, Nov. 12. The same editorial also declares that any aid which a statement would afford to Southern Unionists would be neutralized by perversions of the statement, taunts of cowardice and pusillanimity, attribution of unworthy motives, and contumely and jeers generally.

So long as Republican party feeling ran in these channels, Lincoln did not lack support for his policy, and he maintained it with some determination. He made "frequent and unmistakable declarations to visitors as to his unwillingness to define his executive intentions . . . previous to the 4th of March,"[18] and he was quoted as saying that the South had "eyes but does not see, and ears but does not hear," from which premise he concluded that a statement would have no effect.[19] It is not strange that he should have felt so, when reports from various parts of the South asserted that no offer to negotiate could halt the progress of secession.[20]

Despite all the pressure which was brought to bear upon him, Lincoln held true to his determination to issue no public statement until he should take office as President. But, while he maintained the substance of his policy, it is clear that he began to sense the extreme anxiety with which Southerners anticipated a hostile administration. As a result of this, he was moved, within two weeks after his election, to call upon his friend Lyman Trumbull to act as his spokesman. An occasion offered itself readily, for Lincoln and Trumbull were engaged to attend a meeting in Springfield on November 20, at which Trumbull would speak, while Lincoln would merely be introduced to the audience. However, the presence of Lincoln on the platform would give a certain authority to anything which Trumbull might say concerning Lincoln's policies. Recognizing this aspect of the matter, Lincoln resolved to make use of the opportunity, and, accordingly, he prepared a two-hundred word passage which was incorporated bodily in Trumbull's speech.

At the beginning of this statement, the President-elect attempted to reassure slaveholders as to the safety of

18. New York *Herald*, Nov. 26 (Springfield, Nov. 22).
19. *Ibid.*, Dec. 15 (Springfield, Dec. 11).
20. Dispatch from Richmond, Nov. 10, in New York *Herald*, Nov. 13; statement in a Charleston paper, cited by Arthur C. Cole, "Lincoln's Election an Immediate Menace to Slavery in the States?" in *American Historical Review*, XXXVI (July, 1931), 744.

their property. To this end, he verbally endowed Senator Trumbull with "entire confidence" that "each and all of the States will be left in as complete control of their own affairs respectively, and at as perfect liberty to . . . employ, their own means of protecting property, and preserving peace and order within their respective limits, as they have ever been under any administration."

Although this statement, with its neglect of the territorial question, could not, by itself, have won Southern confidence, it might have assumed great importance if it had marked a dawning recognition, by Lincoln, of the Southern crisis. In its first phrases, it suggested such an awareness, but as the statement continued Lincoln revealed for the first time his complete and tragic failure to understand the temper of the South. The memorandum prepared for Senator Trumbull continued by asserting that it was "extremely fortunate for the peace of the whole country" that Republican respect for the rights of the states should now "be brought to a practical test." Secessionists, *per se*, it asserted, "are now in hot haste to get out of the Union, precisely because they perceive they can not, much longer, maintain apprehension among the Southern people that their homes, . . . and lives, are to be endangered. . . . With such [the secessionists] 'Now or Never' is the maxim." Then, with consummate folly Lincoln added, "I am rather glad of this military preparation in the South. It will enable the people the more easily to suppress any uprisings there, which their [i.e., the secessionists'] misrepresentations of purposes may have encouraged."[21] Thus the President-elect recorded a delusion to which he clung throughout the crisis. That is, he looked upon the secessionists not as leaders of a force with which he would have to deal, but as a losing minority group, faced with repudiation by the Unionist majority, and pushing their policy frantically, just as a speculator plunges most reck-

21. Memorandum prepared by Lincoln for Trumbull to insert in a speech at Springfield, Nov. 20, in Tracy, ed., *Uncollected Lincoln Letters*, p. 168.

lessly when he faces bankruptcy. In a word, Lincoln believed, if his words represent him accurately, that the secession movement would be suppressed within the South, and that no sort of blandishments by the Federal Government were necessary.

This vital misconception, which reappeared later, will require more extended examination. Meanwhile, the speech at Springfield produced certain immediate consequences. From the time of its delivery, Trumbull's address was more or less openly recognized as a statement of Lincoln's policies.[22] Therefore, it received extensive publicity and evoked widespread response. Altogether, this response was of a sort to deter Lincoln from further revelations of his policy. Southern critics denounced the speech as evasive and altogether unsatisfactory;[23] the Washington *Post* treated it as a declaration of hostility toward the South. At the opposite extreme, the Boston *Courier* appealed to Northern excitability with the alarming contention that the speech foreshadowed an abandonment of Republican doctrine,[24] and sentiment in Springfield was pessimistic. It was felt that the experiment had failed to mitigate Southern unrest.[25] After this one venture in the direction of a public statement, therefore, Lincoln said no more publicly, on the platform or in the press, in person or by proxy, until he left Springfield to assume the presidency.

For a time after the Trumbull episode, Lincoln still hoped to win the confidence of Southern Unionists, and though he made no appeal to them *en masse*, he did com-

22. New York *Herald,* Nov. 21 (Springfield, Nov. 20), described this speech under a headline, "SEMI-OFFICIAL EXPOSITION OF THE VIEWS AND POLICY OF THE PRESIDENT-ELECT." In the text of the dispatch, Trumbull's address was described as "a reflex of the views of Mr. Lincoln." *Ibid.,* Nov. 26, (Springfield, Nov. 22), spoke of the "explicit proclamation of his [Lincoln's] programme through the medium of Senator Trumbull's speech. . . ."

23. *Ibid.,* Nov. 22.

24. Press attitude discussed in letter of Lincoln to Henry J. Raymond, Nov. 28, in Nicolay and Hay, eds., *Works of Lincoln,* VI, 74–75.

25. New York *Herald,* Dec. 6 (Springfield dispatch).

municate with several leaders outstanding among them. Probably he gave Cassius M. Clay, of Kentucky, some indication of his good will toward the South,[26] and it is certain that he corresponded with John A. Gilmer of North Carolina and Alexander H. Stephens of Georgia, who were leading exponents of Unionism in their respective states. In Gilmer's case, it was the Southerner who opened the correspondence, asking Lincoln's opinion on several points connected with the slavery issue, and adding the oft-expressed hope that "a clear and definite exposition of your views on the questions mentioned may go far to quiet, if not satisfy, all reasonable minds," since it would show that "there is much more misunderstanding than difference."[27] To this Lincoln replied with evident reluctance, reciting at length that his views were already available in published speeches and in the Chicago Platform. So long as the South ignored these statements, he doubted that "any additional production of mine would meet a better fate." He did not wish to "appear as if I repented for the crime of having been elected, and was anxious to apologize and beg forgiveness." But, despite these misgivings, he answered Gilmer in detail, stating that he was not disposed to attack the existence of slavery in the District of Columbia, nor the slave traffic between states, nor did he mean to give all Federal patronage in the South to Republicans. He believed the territorial question was the only issue between himself and the people of the South. While he did not directly appeal for Gilmer's co-operation, the entire tone of his letter suggested his friendly feeling toward Southern Unionists.[28]

Evidently Lincoln hesitated to answer Gilmer, for he

26. Cassius M. Clay, *The Life of Cassius Marcellus Clay, Memoirs, Writings, and Speeches* (Cincinnati, 1886), I, 272–278. Clay asserted that Lincoln authorized him to make promises of the pacific intent of the incoming administration, but the accuracy of this claim is open to question, in view of Clay's tendency to exaggerate and distort facts.

27. Gilmer to Lincoln, Dec. 10, in Nicolay and Hay, *Lincoln*, III, 284.

28. Lincoln to Gilmer, Dec. 15, in Nicolay and Hay, eds., *Works of Lincoln*, VI, 79.

did not send his reply until he had secured Edward Bates' approval of it,[29] and then, instead of sending it direct to Gilmer, he sent it to Thomas Corwin (who had sent Gilmer's letter to him), "to be delivered or not as he thought prudent."[30] But, in the correspondence with Stephens, it was Lincoln himself who made the overture. Stephens was an old friend of his; they had been Whigs together in Congress, and Lincoln liked and respected the little Georgian. Therefore he responded with especial zest when reports came from the South that Stephens had defended the cause of Union with great warmth and ability before the Georgia legislature on November 14. Lincoln probably did not fully grasp the distinction between the Unionism of Stephens and the Unionism of the North. One regarded secession as ill-advised, but legitimate; the other regarded it as treasonable. But whether he had analyzed it or not, Lincoln felt responsive to Stephens' sentimental Unionism, and, on November 30, he sent the Georgian a note asking for a copy of the speech of November 14. Complying on December 14, Stephens took occasion to remark upon the great responsibility resting upon Lincoln. These preliminaries apparently inspired Lincoln's confidence, and he, in turn, replied, on December 22, with a letter endorsed "for your own eye only." Behind this request for secrecy, he asked if the people of the South really feared Republican interference with slavery. "If they do," he added, "I wish to assure you, as once a friend, and still, I hope, not an enemy, that there is no cause for such fears." Then he added, less hopefully, "I suppose, however, this does not meet the case. You think slavery is right and ought to be extended, while we think it is wrong, and ought to be restricted. That, I suppose, is the rub." To this, Stephens retorted spiritedly. The South did think slavery right; the South distrusted any party which made an issue of slavery; and Stephens would regard a Union perpetuated by force

29. Beale, ed., *Bates Diary*, Dec. 16, p. 167.
30. Lincoln to Trumbull, Dec. 17, in Tracy, ed., *Uncollected Lincoln Letters*, p. 171.

as "nothing short of a consolidated despotism." The letter was distinctly instructive as to the Southern viewpoint, but it was not conducive to further correspondence. Lincoln did not answer it, and, from that time forward, he abandoned any attempt to reassure the South privately, as he had already abandoned public reassurance.[31]

Lincoln's extreme reluctance to give any assurance was fully illustrated when Duff Green[32] visited Springfield late in December. Green came as a messenger from President Buchanan, who wanted Lincoln to visit Washington and use his personal influence in effecting an adjustment. If Lincoln would not consent to such vigorous action, Green hoped at least to secure an endorsement of the Crittenden Compromise, and, to this end, he carried with him a copy of the Crittenden resolutions. The President-elect read over this document, and expressed an opinion: he believed that the proposals, if adopted, would quiet agitation for a time, but that the whole controversy would be renewed by filibustering in Mexico, and by Southern demands for the annexation of Mexican territory. Despite this adverse opinion, Green requested from Lincoln a letter which might be used to allay Southern apprehensions. Lincoln did not refuse point-blank to make a statement. In fact, Green understood him to promise one, and was bitter when it did not materialize.[33]

Green did not know it, but Lincoln actually prepared a letter, beginning abruptly, "I do not desire any amend-

31. The entire Lincoln-Stephens correspondence (Lincoln to Stephens, Nov. 30; Stephens to Lincoln, Dec. 14; Lincoln to Stephens, Dec. 22; Stephens to Lincoln, Dec. 30) is given in Alexander H. Stephens, *A Constitutional View of the Late War Between the States* (Philadelphia, 1868–1870), II, 266–270.

Lincoln was also reported to have written to Jefferson Davis. New York *Herald,* Dec. 9; the report was denied, *ibid.,* Dec. 15 (Springfield dispatch).

32. Duff Green, 1791–1875, journalist, industrialist, member of Jackson's "Kitchen Cabinet," later follower of Calhoun.

33. This interview took place on Dec. 28. Green to Buchanan, Dec. 28, in George Ticknor Curtis, *Life of James Buchanan* (New York, 1883), II, 426; Green to Jefferson Davis, May 26, 1863, quoted in Nicolay and Hay, *Lincoln,* III, 286.

ment of the Constitution," but continuing with an observation that the question of amendment ought to be settled by the whole people, and with a declaration that the right of the states to regulate their domestic institutions must be maintained inviolate. This letter really conceded nothing, and its statement of the right of the states to regulate slavery was copied from the Chicago Platform; but Lincoln treated it as though it were a vital modification of his position. He submitted it to Lyman Trumbull and his "discreet friends," to be approved before it should be delivered; and, in addition, he specified that it should be published only if six Gulf state senators should recommend to their people a suspension of the secession movement.[34]

The letter was never delivered, which was probably fortunate, for it could only have irritated the Southerners. They resented Lincoln's silence; they would have bitterly resented his implication that they might be stupid enough to suspend the secession movement in return for a reiteration of the Chicago Platform.

Entirely apart from the proposals that Lincoln reassure the South by private communication or public statement, there was a widespread desire for him to indicate his good will by giving to the South representation in his cabinet. This proposal found support even among the more zealous Republicans. The New York *Times* endorsed the idea soon after the election, and continued, after Lincoln took office, to suggest that Federal patronage ought to be used to encourage Unionism among Southerners.[35] Hannibal Hamlin urged the matter upon Lincoln personally, in an interview on November 22, and renewed the suggestion in subsequent letters.[36] Thurlow Weed applied his influence in the same cause in an important interview at Springfield

34. Lincoln to Green, Dec. 28, was enclosed in a letter to Trumbull, Dec. 28, both in Nicolay and Hay, eds., *Works of Lincoln*, VI, 87–89.

35. New York *Times*, Nov. 12, Mar. 21.

36. Account of interview, Nov. 22, and letters, Hamlin to Lincoln, Dec. 4, Dec. 24, in Hamlin, *Hamlin*, pp. 369, 371, 373.

on December 20.[37] Seward, acting as usual in harmony with Weed, also besought the inclusion of a Southerner in the cabinet;[38] and other Eastern Republicans expressed the same desire.[39]

On one occasion, Lincoln repelled this suggestion brusquely. A certain friend of Senator Crittenden had been sent to urge the President-elect to form a cabinet of three Southern Unionists and four moderate Republicans. Perhaps Lincoln was offended by the large proportion of Southerners, perhaps by a concealed motive to secure office for Border politicians. Whatever the cause of his irritation, he retorted, "Does any man think that I will take to my bosom an enemy?"[40] But, usually, he treated such proposals with pessimistic tolerance. He recognized that the South was too large a section to be excluded from a place in the administration, and therefore he prepared to invite a Southerner into the cabinet.[41] But he did not entertain the hope that such a gesture would mitigate the crisis, nor did he have much confidence that any representative Southerner would accept a place among his counselors. His pessimism manifested itself in an editorial which he wrote for the Illinois *Journal* on December 12. Alluding to the "supposed purpose . . . of Mr. Lincoln to call into his cabinet two or three Southern gentlemen," the editorial wished to know: "First. Is it known that any such gentleman of character would accept a place in the cabinet? Second. If yea, on what terms does he surrender to Mr. Lincoln, or Mr. Lincoln to him, on the political

37. Weed's account of this interview in his *Autobiography,* pp. 606–614. Leonard Swett's eye-witness account, in Barnes, *Weed,* pp. 293–294.

38. Two letters of Seward to Lincoln, one before Dec. 28, one on that day (the former mentioned, the latter quoted), in Seward, *Seward,* II, 487.

39. On Dec. 31, Lincoln showed Bates a number of letters to this effect. Bates, *Diary,* p. 171.

40. George B. Robertson to Crittenden, Dec. 16, in Coleman, *Crittenden,* II, 222. Robertson refers to the envoy to Springfield as "B," who is unidentified.

41. Herndon and Weik, *Lincoln,* p. 473; Ward H. Lamon, *The Life of Abraham Lincoln from his Birth to his Inauguration as President* (Boston, 1872), p. 457, quoting David Davis.

differences between them; or do they enter upon the administration in open opposition to each other?"[42] While Lincoln harbored these skeptical views, he received a visit from Thurlow Weed who, refusing to be deterred by the editorial, urged that two Southerners be included in the cabinet. Lincoln promptly retorted with a question as to whether such men could be trusted to adhere to the administration if their states should secede. Weed brashly offered to vouch for some of them, and Lincoln said, "Well, let us have the names of your white crows."[43]

There were crows in flocks, named by Weed and, at various times, by other Republicans. Whether they were white or not was another question, but more than a score of Southerners were proposed for Lincoln's consideration. Even before the election, rumor had it that Crittenden might be offered the portfolio of State,[44] and, at the same time, other reports named William Cabell Rives, ex-Senator from Virginia, as Lincoln's choice for the State Department.[45] These names, however, were soon crowded out of the reckoning by a swarm of others. From Virginia, John Minor Botts was repeatedly mentioned,[46] and Robert E. Scott—an able, but much less well known figure

42. Nicolay and Hay, eds., *Works of Lincoln,* VI, 78. The New York *Herald,* Dec. 17 (Springfield, Dec. 12) suggested that this editorial was intended to feel out public sentiment on the question, but the cogency of Lincoln's language argues against such a view.

43. Account of interview in Weed, *Autobiography,* pp. 606–614.

44. New York *Herald,* Nov. 2.

45. William Cabell Rives, 1793–1868, Representative from Va., 1823–29; Senator from Va., 1832–34, 1836–39, 1841–45; U. S. Minister to France, 1829–32, 1849–53; member, Provisional Confederate Congress; representative, Second Confederate Congress.

Report in New York *Herald,* Nov. 2; Rives denied correspondence with Lincoln, *ibid.,* Nov. 3; report repeated, *ibid.,* Nov. 5.

46. John Minor Botts, 1802–1869, Representative from Va., 1839–43, 1847–49; Unionist throughout the Civil War.

Botts was one of the "white crows" offered by Weed to Lincoln, Weed, *Autobiography,* p. 606. Lincoln seems to have regarded him as acceptable, Herndon and Weik, *Lincoln,* p. 473. The New York *Times,* Nov. 12, found him suitable, and, on Nov. 14, reported betting odds of 2 to 1 that he would be offered a post. The New York *Herald,* Dec. 21, reported from Springfield, Dec. 20, that his name was being urged, and, on Dec. 24, that he was still a possibility, though not a likely one.

—was also counted among those whose names might be sent to the Senate.[47] From Tennessee, a full half-dozen individuals were suggested. The most eminent of the group was John Bell,[48] but much speculation centered upon three congressmen—Horace Maynard,[49] Thomas A. R. Nelson,[50] and Emerson Etheridge[51]—and two ex-congressmen —Meredith P. Gentry[52] and Balie Peyton.[53]

47. Robert E. Scott, leader of the Whigs in the Virginia House of Delegates, and of the moderates in the Virginia Convention of 1861. See Henry T. Shanks, *The Secession Movement in Virginia, 1847–1861* (Richmond, 1934), *passim*.

Scott was suggested by Seward in a special note to Lincoln on Dec. 28 (Seward, *Seward,* II, 487). By Jan. 15, Seward thought Scott had been terrified into dropping the subject, which, apparently, Seward had broached to him (Seward to Lincoln, Jan. 15, in Nicolay and Hay, *Lincoln,* III, 364), but he interviewed Scott afterward, and found him "a fit and creditable representative" of the South (Seward to Lincoln, Jan. 27, in *ibid.,* III, 365–366). In Springfield, his name was associated with the Interior Department (dispatch of Dec. 4, in New York *Herald,* Dec. 9), but later he was proposed for the Navy (*ibid.,* Jan. 6); meanwhile, his star was reported to have waned (*ibid.,* Dec. 24, from Springfield, Dec. 19).

48. Bell was mentioned as a possible appointee in the New York *Times,* Nov. 12, but he published a letter (text in *ibid.,* Dec. 12) by which he was said to have eliminated himself. New York *Herald,* Dec. 17, 24 (Springfield, Dec. 19).

49. Horace Maynard, 1814–1882, Representative from Tenn., 1857–63, 1866–75; Postmaster-general, 1880–81.

Herndon and Weik, *Lincoln,* p. 473, names Maynard as one of the individuals whom Lincoln considered acceptable.

50. Thomas A. R. Nelson, 1812–1873, Representative from Tenn., 1859–61.

On Dec. 31, Lincoln showed Bates letters recommending various Southerners, of whom Bates remembered Nelson as one. Beale, ed., *Bates Diary,* p. 171.

51. Emerson Etheridge, 1819–1902, Representative from Tenn., 1853–57, 1859–61; Clerk of House of Representatives, 1861–63; an especially able Unionist.

Hamlin told Lincoln of Etheridge's merits both personally, Nov. 22, and by letter, Dec. 24 (Hamlin, *Hamlin,* pp. 369–373). The New York *Times,* Nov. 12, declared him eligible, and the New York *Herald,* Dec. 15 (Springfield, Dec. 11), said that he was being considered.

52. Meredith Poindexter Gentry, 1809–1866, Representative from Tenn., 1839–43, 1845–53; member, First Confederate Congress.

Gentry was suggested by Seward (Seward to Lincoln, Jan. 8, in Seward, *Seward,* II, 493), but he found little favor with Lincoln, who felt that he did not have "a living position in the South" (Lincoln to Seward, Jan. 12, in Nicolay and Hay, *Lincoln,* III, 364).

In the lower South, prospective cabinet members were not so numerous, but a few were in evidence. From Georgia, Alexander H. Stephens seemed an eligible candidate until he eliminated himself by his correspondence with Lincoln.[54] From Louisiana, Randall Hunt,[55] a brother-in-law of Salmon P. Chase, was suggested by Seward, who was scouting with more enthusiasm than discrimination. From Mississippi, Judge William L. Sharkey[56] was mentioned, because of his slashing attacks upon the secessionists.

But the states of the upper South were richest in candidates, and, at the same time, were apparently more devoted to the Union. It was from these states, therefore, that Lincoln made his selections. Twice he extended offers —to a Kentuckian and to a North Carolinian—and when these overtures were rejected, he filled the posts from the two other Border states of Missouri and Maryland.

The very first offer of a cabinet post went, it appears, to a Kentuckian. The recipient was not Crittenden, as rumor reported, nor Cassius M. Clay, though his perfervid memory afterward invented an offer of the portfolio of War,[57] but a Democrat, who had served in the cabinet of

53. Balie Peyton, 1803–1878, Representative from Tenn., 1833–1837; candidate for elector on the Bell-Everett ticket, 1860.

Peyton was endorsed by Weed, who misspelled his name (Weed, *Autobiography,* p. 606), but appears not to have found favor with Lincoln.

54. Lamon, *Lincoln,* p. 457, and Herndon and Weik, *Lincoln,* p. 473, both indicate that Stephens remained on the list of possible appointees, but this could hardly be true after his letter of Dec. 30 (above, p. 145).

55. Seward suggested Hunt in a letter to Lincoln, Dec. 25 (Nicolay and Hay, *Lincoln,* III, 362), and he later consulted John A. Gilmer on the subject (Seward to Lincoln, Jan. 8, in Seward, *Seward,* II, 493).

56. William Lewis Sharkey, 1798–1873, Chief Justice of the Mississippi Court of Errors and Appeals, 1832–51, had declared he would not participate in any secession which did not include the Border states. See P. L. Rainwater, *Mississippi, Storm Center of Secession, 1856–1861* (Baton Rouge, 1938), p. 176.

The New York *Herald,* Dec. 24 (Springfield, Dec. 19), mentioned Sharkey's eligibility as remaining when certain others were eliminated.

57. Cassius Marcellus Clay, 1810–1903, eminent Kentucky abolitionist, politician, controversialist, and brawler. See E. Merton Coulter's sketch in the *Dictionary of American Biography.*

Clay's *Life of Cassius M. Clay,* pp. 250, 303, asserts that a letter from

Franklin Pierce. This was James Guthrie,[58] who had been Secretary of the Treasury and president of the Louisville and Nashville Railroad. This able, conservative, and rather elderly Kentuckian was recommended to Lincoln by Hannibal Hamlin, on November 22, when the two men were together in Chicago.[59] Lincoln may have been considering Guthrie already. If not, he acted with rare impulsiveness, for he moved at once to invite the Kentuckian into his cabinet. Not wishing to commit himself in writing until he knew more of Guthrie's attitude, he asked Joshua Speed to go to Kentucky with authority "to act in feeling [Guthrie] out" and to offer him a cabinet post. The details of Speed's mission are not known, but it appears that he saw Guthrie, found him a loyal Unionist, and tendered the appointment. The Kentuckian offered his age and physical infirmity as an excuse for declining, and lived to serve as United States Senator for three years after Lincoln's death.[60] Thus failed the first attempt to bring the South into the cabinet.

In January, Lincoln was again disappointed in his efforts to secure a representative of the South. North Carolina offered a number of eligible Old Whigs, chief of whom were ex-Senator William A. Graham,[61] ex-Congressman

Lincoln, offering him the Secretaryship of War, was in the possession of the Kentucky State Historical Society. However, the Society has no such letter at present, and there is no evidence that it ever had. It is at least suspicious that Clay omitted the text of this letter, when publishing in full many less important documents. Letter of Mrs. Jouett Taylor Cannon, Secretary of the Society, to the author, Nov. 12, 1941.

58. James Guthrie, 1792–1869, railway magnate, Secretary of the Treasury, 1853--57, Senator from Kentucky, 1865–68.

59. Hamlin, *Hamlin*, p. 369.

60. Herndon and Weik, *Lincoln*, p. 477, and Lamon, *Lincoln*, pp. 457, 462, agree that, while in Chicago, Lincoln authorized Speed to offer Guthrie a place in the cabinet. Herndon and Weik say the War Department was specified; Lamon says the Treasury. Herndon and Weik alone have the account of the offer being made, and of Guthrie's refusal.

61. William A. Graham, 1804–1875, Senator from N. C., 1840–43; Governor of N. C., 1845–49; Secretary of the Navy, 1850–52; Senator, Second Confederate Congress.

Graham was recommended in letters to Lincoln (Beale, ed., *Bates*

Kenneth Rayner,[62] and Congressman John A. Gilmer.[63] Of this group, Gilmer was the strongest, both because of his active political position, and because he was favored by Hamlin, Weed, and Seward.[64] Hamlin proposed his name when he met Lincoln in Chicago on November 22, and it is likely that Lincoln was more favorably inclined toward him after their exchange of letters early in December. After these rather favorable preliminaries, the matter was brought to a head when Weed came to Springfield on December 20. The New Yorker argued warmly that a Tennesseean or a North Carolinian should be brought into the cabinet. Lincoln retorted that this might lead to a very unhappy situation if North Carolina and Tennessee should secede. But David Davis and Leonard Swett agreed with Weed. All three of them fell to urging Lincoln, and he finally consented to communicate with Gilmer with a view to offering him a cabinet post.[65] Weed was commissioned to act as an intermediary; but it is not clear precisely how much authority was delegated to him. It appears, however, that he was made the bearer of a letter in which Lincoln set forth his views on certain issues, for Gilmer's consideration, and invited him, if he endorsed these views, to enter the cabinet. But apparently the letter also left the way open for negotiation, for it included an invitation for Gilmer to come to Springfield for a personal discussion, and one gathers that it also left the way open for conversations between Weed and Gilmer.[66]

Diary, Dec. 31, p. 171), and was later mentioned in the New York Herald, Jan. 6, as a possible Secretary of the Interior.

62. Kenneth Rayner, 1808–1884, Representative from N. C., 1839–45. Hamlin (Hamlin, Hamlin, p. 369) and Seward (Seward to Lincoln, Dec. 25, in Nicolay and Hay, Lincoln, III, 362) endorsed Rayner.

63. John A. Gilmer, 1805–1868, Representative from N. C., 1857–61; Representative, Second Confederate Congress.

64. Hamlin suggested him on Nov. 22 (Hamlin, Hamlin, p. 369), Weed, on Dec. 20 (Weed, Autobiography, p. 606), and Seward, on Dec. 25 (Seward to Lincoln, Dec. 25, in Nicolay and Hay, Lincoln, III, 362).

65. Weed, Autobiography, p. 611.

66. Accounts of Weed's part in the Gilmer affair vary. Weed himself says (Autobiography, pp. 611, 614) that he was made the bearer of an open letter stating Lincoln's views and inviting Gilmer to enter the

After this abrupt launching, the Gilmer matter proceeded very slowly. Weed saw Gilmer,[67] gave him Lincoln's letter, and talked with him freely. Gilmer seemed to approve Lincoln's views, but he insisted on consulting his Southern colleagues before committing himself.[68] This delay was followed by a series of other delays, until the project simply expired. Weed attempted to see Gilmer again, but failed, and, leaving Washington, turned the matter over to Seward.[69] Meanwhile, in reply to Lincoln's impatient inquiries, Seward reported, on January 4, that Gilmer was considering the matter, and offering to find some other Southerner more eligible than himself.[70] Five days later, Gilmer was still waiting for advice which he had sought from friends in North Carolina.[71] As late as the middle of January, Lincoln and Seward continued to hope for a favorable reply;[72] but these hopes were dashed when Gilmer wrote to Lincoln declining to come to Springfield.[73] As events developed, the last public service of John A. Gilmer was rendered not as a cabinet officer of the Federal government, but as a congressman of the Confederacy. Thus, again, Lincoln was frustrated in his effort to secure a recognized Southerner for his cabinet.

As a consequence of these failures, the cabinet in its completed form consisted entirely of Republicans, and of

cabinet if he endorsed these views. He adds that he discussed the matter with Gilmer freely. Leonard Swett simply indicated that Weed was commissioned to consult Gilmer as to his views on the Union (Barnes, *Weed,* p. 294). Lamon asserts flatly that Weed was commissioned to offer a cabinet post to "Gilmore" [*sic*] of North Carolina (Lamon, *Lincoln,* p. 457). A letter of Lincoln to Seward, Jan. 3, shows that Lincoln requested that Gilmer come to Springfield for an interview (Nicolay and Hay, *Lincoln,* III, 363).

67. New York *Herald,* Jan. 7 (Washington, Jan. 6), reported the presence of Weed in Washington.

68. Weed, *Autobiography,* p. 614.

69. Weed to Seward, Jan. 9, and Weed to Seward, undated, in Bancroft, *Seward,* II, 29, 30.

70. Seward to Lincoln, Jan. 4, in Nicolay and Hay, *Lincoln,* III, 363.

71. Seward to Lincoln, Jan. 8, in *ibid.,* III, 363–364.

72. Lincoln to Seward, Jan. 12; Seward to Lincoln, Jan. 15; in *ibid.,* III, 364.

73. Gilmer to Lincoln, Jan. 29, cited in *ibid.,* III, 364.

men who lacked position in the South. Technically, two of
the secretaries were Southerners—at least they were residents of slave states. The first of these, Edward Bates of
Missouri, received and accepted an offer of the Attorney
Generalship on December 15, and the arrangement was
announced on December 21.[74] The second, Montgomery
Blair, was not sure of his nomination as Postmaster
General until it went to the Senate, for this post, the last
to be filled, was the object of bitter contest between the
Democratic and Whig factions, who made the rivalry between Blair and his fellow Marylander, Henry Winter
Davis, a sort of test of their respective strength. But
neither Bates nor Blair had any standing in the South.
Bates was so strongly identified with the Republican party
that he had been a prominent contender for the Presidential nomination; and the Blair family had joined the
Republican ranks even before Lincoln himself. Lincoln
apparently hoped that the South would think itself represented by his Missourian and his Marylander.[75] But if
the South experienced any reaction, it was one of indigna-

74. Lincoln's communication with Bates, Bates' visit to Springfield,
and the offer and acceptance of the Attorney Generalship, are recorded
in Beale, ed., *Bates Diary,* Dec. 16, p. 164. The public announcement appeared in the Saint Louis *Democrat,* Dec. 21, copied in the New York
Tribune, Dec. 22.

In these cabinet negotiations, Lincoln showed a quality not far short
of duplicity. In his interview with Weed, on Dec. 20, he left Weed
with the impression that he was still in doubt about Bates (Weed,
Autobiography, p. 611), although the arrangement with Bates was already completed. Yet he treated Bates with equal insincerity, on Dec.
15, leading him to believe that no offer had been made to Seward (Bates,
Diary, p. 164), when, in fact, on Dec. 8, he had offered Seward the
Department of State (Lincoln to Seward, Dec. 8, in Nicolay and Hay,
Lincoln, III, 349).

75. Weed, *Autobiography,* p. 608, represents Lincoln as considering
that Blair was the representative of a slave state, and that Bates "not
only resides in a slave State, but . . . is emphatically a representative
man." Again, Lincoln's attitude toward a Marylander, as a Southerner,
was evidenced by his remark that Gilmer was "only better than Winter
Davis in that he is farther South" (Lincoln to Seward, Jan. 12, 1861, in
Nicolay and Hay, *Lincoln,* III, 364).

tion that men who were widely regarded as renegades should be elevated to power as the representatives of a section whose cause they had deserted.[76]

Thus nothing came of the hopes that Lincoln might establish a rapprochement with the South. A public affirmation of moderate policies might have abated the haste of the secessionists; the inclusion of typical Southern men in the new administration might have served the same purpose. But Lincoln's own resolution and the failure of Lyman Trumbull's speech defeated the one, while the reticence of Guthrie and Gilmer and men of their type defeated the other. In the final analysis, therefore, negation was the result, and while it cannot be said that Lincoln had no policy with reference to the South, it is quite accurate to say that the result was the same as if he had had none.

But in another direction his policy was producing momentous results. While the newspapers were engaged in reporting excitement in Congress, plaguing the President-elect for a public statement, and speculating on what influences would control the new administration, Lincoln moved unnoticed to prevent the compromise movement from making further inroads upon his party.

76. George B. Robertson wrote to Crittenden, Dec. 16, deploring the possibility that Lincoln might appoint Cassius Clay and Edward Bates to his cabinet, as representatives of the South: "We would all prefer a northern cabinet. . . . Kentucky would feel insulted at having forced on her as *her organ* a *citizen* over whom she would even prefer *Seward*." Coleman, *Crittenden*, II, 222.

CHAPTER VII

LINCOLN MARSHALS HIS PARTY
AGAINST COMPROMISE

DESPITE his reluctance to make a public statement of his policy, and, especially, of his moderate intentions toward the South, Lincoln was by no means committed to a policy of inactivity during his period as President-elect. He sought diligently to keep himself informed of the course of events, and his vigorous, though unpublicized, activities suffice to show that he was not acquiring this knowledge merely for purposes of future reference. He is known to have studied financial conditions, to have scrutinized the attitude of the press, and to have given attention to other problems;[1] but of all the subjects of his concern, none preoccupied him more than the attitude of members of his party in Congress. On this topic, he gathered information from a number of sources. In addition to the full but unreliable dispatches in the press, and the full but unrevealing speeches in the *Globe*, he drew upon the reports of a number of congressmen. In the Senate, Hannibal Hamlin, William H. Seward, and, most of all, Lyman Trumbull, wrote to him fairly often.[2] In the House, his correspondents included John A. Gurley and Thomas Corwin of Ohio, and Elihu B. Washburne and William Kellogg of Illinois.[3] These writers

1. New York *Herald*, Dec. 9 (Springfield dispatch) speaks of Lincoln's concern with financial matters; Lincoln to Raymond, Nov. 28, in Nicolay and Hay, eds., *Works of Lincoln*, VI, 74–75, shows his familiarity with press opinion.
    2. Letters to Lincoln from Hamlin, Dec. 4, 24, in Hamlin, *Hamlin*, pp. 371, 373; from Seward, Dec. 16, 25, 26, 28, 29, in Nicolay and Hay, *Lincoln*, III, 261–265, 362; from Trumbull, Dec. 2, 4, in *ibid.*, III, 252–254; to Trumbull, Dec. 10, 17, 21, 28, in Tracy, ed., *Uncollected Lincoln Letters*, pp. 171–173.
    3. Nicolay and Hay, *Lincoln*, III, indicates letters from Gurley, Dec. 3 (p. 254); from Corwin, Dec. 10 (p. 255); from Washburne, before Dec. 13 (p. 259), Dec. 17 (p. 250); from Kellogg, before Dec. 11 (pp. 258–259).

supplied him with valuable interpretations of the shifting moods and subterranean trends that were at work in Washington, and it appears that some of them, very early in the session, warned him of the growing tendency to accept a compromise. It is known that he became apprehensive as soon as he learned of the Republican share in the establishment of the Committee of Thirty-three.[4]

In the light of these warnings and this information, Lincoln determined very early upon an unobtrusive but vital step. He decided to interpose his influence with Republican members to arrest the compromise movement. This significant decision was reached even before the resolutions of Kilgore, Thayer, and Sherman had been introduced in the House, and before the Dunn Resolution had passed in the Committee of Thirty-three. Accordingly, at the very first of the session, Lincoln, with all his influence as President-elect, assumed the initiative in defeating compromise.

Probably the first overt manifestation of Lincoln's new policy is to be found in a letter of December 10, to his close friend Lyman Trumbull. It is not certain whether Trumbull applied for advice, or whether Lincoln offered it on his own initiative, but even if it were true that his advice had been solicited, the tone of Lincoln's letter shows that he was not hesitant in assuming leadership. He began this letter abruptly: "Let there be no compromise on the question of extending slavery. If there be, all our labor is lost, and, ere long, must be done again. The dangerous ground—that into which some of our friends have a hankering to run—is Pop[ular] Sov[ereignty]. Have none of it. Stand firm. The tug has to come, and better now than at any time hereafter."[5]

4. Lyman Trumbull to Lincoln, Dec. 4, remarked that the Republicans had no compromises to make, and that "it is impolitic even to discuss making them . . . I was a little surprised that the House voted to raise a committee on the state of the Union." *Ibid.*, III, 254. The New York *Herald*, Dec. 15 (Springfield, Dec. 10), declared that the formation of the committee worried Lincoln.

5. Lincoln to Trumbull, Dec. 10, in Tracy, ed., *Uncollected Lincoln Letters*, p. 171.

Having once taken the step of intervention in this congressional matter, Lincoln followed up his first note by striking two more blows against compromise in the House of Representatives. William Kellogg and Elihu B. Washburne, who were members of the Illinois delegation in the House, both wrote to Lincoln, evidently requesting his counsel,[6] and thus enabling him to advise them without seeming officious. He replied to Kellogg on the day after his note to Trumbull, and the language of this second note closely paralleled that of the first. Beginning, "Entertain no proposition for a compromise in regard to the extension of slavery," he reiterated his conviction that a compromise would leave all the labor of the Republicans to be done over again, his fear that the doctrine of popular sovereignty might mislead some of his party, and his readiness to face "the tug" at once, rather than later.[7] After a lapse of two more days, a letter from Washburne gave him occasion to repeat essentially the same precepts and the same warnings. This time, he cautioned against the Missouri line, as well as the popular sovereignty formula; once more, he asserted that a territorial compromise would leave the whole contest to be waged over again; and he closed by exhorting Washburne to "hold firm, as with a chain of steel."[8] Thus, for a third time in four days, the

6. Nicolay and Hay, *Lincoln,* III, 258–259, show that Kellogg solicited Lincoln's advice. The language of Lincoln's letter to Washburne, Dec. 13, shows that it was a reply. Nicolay and Hay, eds., *Works of Lincoln,* VI, 78.

7. The full text of Lincoln's note to Kellogg, Dec. 11, follows: "Entertain no proposition for a compromise in regard to the extension of slavery. The instant you do they have us under again: all our labor is lost, and sooner or later must be done over. Douglas is sure to be again trying to bring in his 'popular sovereignty.' Have none of it. The tug has to come, and better now than later. You know I think the fugitive slave clause of the Constitution ought to be enforced—to put it in its mildest form, ought not to be resisted." Nicolay and Hay, eds., *Works of Lincoln,* VI, 77.

8. The full text of Lincoln's note to Washburne, Dec. 13, follows: "Yours of the 10th is received. Prevent, as far as possible, any of our friends from demoralizing themselves and our cause by entertaining propositions for compromise of any sort on 'slavery extension.' There is no possible compromise upon it but which puts us under again, and

President-elect wrote to congressmen of his party, urging them to resist all compromise on the territorial question.

For a time, Lincoln expressed his emphatic views only in private communications to personal friends. But, as time passed, he became less reticent and resorted increasingly to more public expressions. This tendency became evident when, on December 17, he sent a message to Thurlow Weed to be transmitted to a conference of Republican governors who were planning to meet in New York. "Should the . . . Governors . . . seem desirous to know my views . . . ," wrote Lincoln, "tell them you judge from my speeches that I will be inflexible on the territorial question; that I probably think either the Missouri line extended, or Douglas's and Eli Thayer's popular sovereignty, would lose us everything we gain by the election; that filibustering for all South of us and making slave States of it would follow, in spite of us, in either case; also that I probably think all opposition, real and apparent, to the fugitive-slave clause of the Constitution ought to be withdrawn."[9]

In this statement, Lincoln still showed a notable degree of reticence in expressing his views. He still stated his opinion only to a semi-private group, and he placed his words in the mouth of a spokesman. But, within a few days more, he completed the transition, and permitted the issuance of a public statement which was clearly authorized. This pronouncement appeared in the New York *Tribune* of December 22: "We are enabled to state in the most positive terms," it said, "that Mr. Lincoln is utterly opposed to any concession or compromise that shall yield one iota of the position occupied by the Republican Party on the subject of slavery in the territories, and that he stands

leaves all our work to do over again. Whether it be a Missouri Line or Eli Thayer's popular sovereignty, it is all the same. Let either be done, and immediately filibustering and extending slavery recommences. On that point hold firm, as with a chain of steel." *Ibid.*, VI, 78.

9. Lincoln to Weed, Dec. 17, in *ibid.*, VI, 82.

now, as he stood on May last, when he accepted the nomination for the Presidency, square upon the Chicago platform."[10]

After this announcement in the *Tribune*, no one could fail to understand that Lincoln was unalterably opposed to territorial compromise.[11] The firmness of his personal conviction emerged as distinctly as words could state it. As an expression of his personal views, therefore, Lincoln's warnings against territorial concession were pointed and effective; but as bases for affirmative action, or as instruments of party leadership, they had marked deficiencies. They were wholly negative, indicating what course the Republican party should eschew, but giving no intimation as to what course it should follow. Moreover, they were poorly adapted to exercise leadership over a large group, for they were addressed, almost confidentially, to individuals, and these individuals lacked the pre-eminence that would have enabled them to marshal the support of their fellow-Republicans.

In this first phase, therefore, Lincoln's intervention was negative and casual. As his attitude was discussed in the cloakrooms of Congress, it probably carried appreciable weight, but this was because of the great influence of his

10. New York *Tribune*, Dec. 22.

11. Twice more, Lincoln is known to have put into writing his opposition to territorial compromise.

He wrote to Lyman Trumbull, Dec. 17, "If any of our friends do prove false, and fix up a compromise on the territorial question, I am for fighting again—that is all." Tracy, ed., *Uncollected Lincoln Letters*, p. 171.

He wrote to Representative James T. Hale of Pa., Jan. 11, "We have just carried an election on principles fairly stated to the people. Now we are told in advance the Government shall be broken up unless we surrender to those we have beaten, before we take the offices. In this they are either attempting to play upon us or they are in dead earnest. Either way, if we surrender, it is the end of us and of the government. They will repeat the experiment upon us *ad libitum*. A year will not pass till we shall have to take Cuba as a condition upon which they will stay in the Union. They now have the Constitution under which we have lived over seventy years, and acts of Congress of their own framing, with no prospect of their being changed; and they can never have a more shallow pretext for breaking up the government, or extorting a compromise, than now." Nicolay and Hay, eds., *Works of Lincoln*, VI, 93.

position and not because his intervention was skillfully directed. Comparing his problem with that of a military leader, one might say that Lincoln was in the position of an absent commander, trying to direct his force by means of orders to individual soldiers on the field of action. What he needed was a deputy leader on the battlefield—a man in accord with his general views, capable of commanding the support of the group, and competent to execute his policies.

Lincoln found his deputy in William H. Seward. In point of leadership and ability, Seward was the obvious choice from the beginning; in the matter of his willingness to take orders, his suitability was highly questionable. But the President-elect refused to be deterred by the possibility that Seward might accept subordination with ill grace, and, on December 8, he invited his recent rival to serve as Secretary of State in his cabinet.

Just why he waited until December 8 is itself a question of some interest. It was not because other candidates were under consideration, for, as he told Seward, "it has been my purpose, from the day of the nomination . . . to assign you, by your leave, this place in the administration," and only a deference for "proper caution," he added, had caused him to delay so long.[12] The term "proper caution" can mean almost anything. But, reviewing the circumstances, one recalls that the first days of December had produced many reports that Seward favored territorial compromise. These reports flourished undenied until December 5, when Seward issued, in the *Tribune*, a blanket repudiation of all the compromise schemes whose paternity was attributed to him.[13] Three days later, Lincoln wrote to offer him the State Department. It may well be that

12. Lincoln to Seward, Dec. 8, in *ibid.*, VI, 76–77.
13. See above, pp. 85–86. Lyman Trumbull had sent Lincoln an implied warning against Seward, in a letter of Dec. 4, in which he declared, "The impression with all, unless there be one exception, is, that Republicans have no concessions to make." Nicolay and Hay, *Lincoln*, III, 354. The "one exception" was, almost certainly, Seward.

Lincoln's "proper caution" was his anxiety to be assured that his intended Secretary would not align himself with the forces of compromise.

Even after this exercise of caution, the President-elect apparently did not act without some hesitation. Inasmuch as he scarcely knew Seward,[14] he did not fully trust his own judgment, and he therefore refrained from sending his offer directly to the New Yorker, but enclosed it, instead, in a letter to Hannibal Hamlin. Hamlin was requested to "Consult with Judge Trumbull; and if you and he see no reason to the contrary, deliver the letter to Governor Seward at once. If you see reason to the contrary, write me at once."[15]

Hamlin and Trumbull, no doubt, discussed the matter. It appears that they then made an attempt, through Preston King, to learn how Seward would receive the offer.[16] But this attempt to procure an acceptance before delivering the invitation failed, and, on December 13, they transmitted to Seward two notes from Lincoln. One of these contained the formal statement: "With your permission, I shall at the proper time nominate you to the Senate for confirmation as Secretary of State for the United States."[17] The other, longer and more personal, denied rumors then current that Lincoln would offer the

14. The only meeting of the two men had occurred during the campaign of 1860, when Seward, on a speaking tour, passed through Springfield. Seward did not get off his train, and Lincoln came on board to meet him during the train's brief stop. Charles Francis Adams, Jr., *Autobiography,* pp. 63–64.

15. Lincoln to Hamlin, Dec. 8, in Nicolay and Hay, eds., *Works of Lincoln,* VI, 75–76.

16. Nicolay and Hay, *Lincoln,* III, 350, asserts that the invitation was delivered at once. But Preston King told John Bigelow, in August, 1861, that Hamlin, acting for Lincoln, had asked him to feel out what Seward's attitude would be toward an offer of the State Department, and that he "ventured a little in the direction of the President's wishes," but met with no success, and told Hamlin that Lincoln had better ask Seward directly. About a fortnight later, Seward told King that he had promised to accept the appointment. Bigelow, *Retrospections,* I, 365–366.

17. Lincoln to Seward, Dec. 8, in Nicolay and Hay, eds., *Works of Lincoln,* VI, 76.

State Department to Seward as a complimentary gesture, with the expectation that it would be refused. "On the contrary," Lincoln assured him, "I now offer you the place in the hope that you will accept it, and with the belief that your position in the public eye, your integrity, ability, learning, and great experience all combine to render it an appointment preeminently fit to be made."[18]

Despite the cordiality of Lincoln's language, the offer of the State Department presented Seward with a serious dilemma. It invited him to identify himself with an incoming administration, without telling him what the policy of that administration would be or what share of control he would exercise in determining its policies. If Lincoln were as weak as people supposed, the invitation might foreshadow Seward's primacy in the new régime. But if the new President should possess unexpected firmness of purpose, then advancement to the cabinet would mean, for Seward, loss of his political independence and of his senatorial leadership. To refuse, therefore, would jeopardize his chance of dominating the new administration; to accept might reduce him to the rôle of agent for a policy which he did not approve. In these premises, Seward desired nothing so much as to learn what the character of the new administration would be.

In his perplexity, Seward wanted time for deliberation, wanted also to discuss the problem with Weed. Instead of accepting Lincoln's offer forthwith, therefore, he responded, on December 13, with a letter in which he set forth his doubts rather frankly. After indicating his full appreciation of the distinction which Lincoln proposed to confer upon him, he spoke of his uncertainty as to whether he was temperamentally qualified for the post, and his more serious concern as to "the very anomalous condition of public affairs." "I wish, indeed," he added, "that a conference with you upon them were possible. But I do not see how it could prudently be held under existing cir-

18. Lincoln to Seward, Dec. 8, in Nicolay and Hay, eds., *Works of Lincoln,* VI, 76–77.

cumstances." In view of these perplexities, he felt the
need of "a little time to consider," and indicated that he
would, "with your leave, reflect upon it a few days, and
then give you my definite answer."[19]

Then, writing on the same day, and somewhat more im-
pulsively, he broke the news to Weed: the long awaited
offer had arrived at last. "I have now the occasion for
consulting you that you have expected."[20] That was on
Thursday; on the next day, apparently, Seward left
Washington, and on Saturday and Sunday, December 15
and 16, he was in Albany with Weed.[21] Probably he went
with no purpose except to discuss his problem with his
trusted associate. But when he arrived there, he learned of
a new factor which entirely altered the aspect of matters:
Lincoln had invited Weed to come to Springfield for a
conference.[22]

This invitation opened new vistas for Seward. He had
wished for a conference with Lincoln, and had despaired
of having one. But his relationship with Weed was so close
that a conference between Lincoln and Weed seemed an
acceptable equivalent for a meeting between Lincoln and
Seward. Whether the conference had been initiated by
Lincoln for purposes of consulting Weed, or whether Weed
had maneuvered for the invitation from Lincoln in order
to discuss political appointments,[23] the meeting of the two
might now be used to enable Seward to learn the views of
the President-elect. With tactful management, Weed
might even bring Lincoln implicitly to accept his and

19. Seward to Lincoln, Dec. 13, in Nicolay and Hay, *Lincoln,* III, 350.

20. Seward to Weed, Dec. 13, in Seward, *Seward,* II, 481.

21. *Ibid.* II, 481–482.

22. Letters of Leonard Swett and David Davis, both on Dec. 10, extended the invitation in Lincoln's name. Letters in Barnes, *Weed,* pp.
293, 301–302.

23. The phrasing of the invitations which Swett and Davis extended
in Lincoln's name, implies but does not prove that Weed had broached
the question of an interview.

But if Weed did initiate this trip, he did so before the State Department was offered to Seward. Swett and Davis invited him to Springfield, Dec. 10; not until Dec. 13 did Seward write him of the offer.

Seward's policies as a basis for Seward's entering the cabinet. Some such possibilities as these must have passed through Seward's mind as he wrote to Lincoln again, to say that he had gone to his home in Auburn and would remain there until Weed's return from Springfield.[24]

What were the policies for which Weed and Seward hoped to secure Lincoln's endorsement? To this involved question, the records supply no direct answer. But a partial, oblique response may lie in the editorial which appeared in Weed's *Evening Journal* on the Monday (December 17) following Seward's and Weed's week-end conference. This editorial renewed the proposal for a revival and extension of the Missouri line as a basis for compromise,[25] and it said nothing which Weed had not said before. But the occasion for repeating the proposal was palpably so inopportune, that it seems fair to believe that the two New Yorkers had very compelling reasons for reopening the question at this time. Less than two weeks had elapsed since Seward had scotched the rumor of his identification with Weed's policy.[26] He was certainly not so naïve as to be blind to the fact that a reaffirmation of the policy, immediately after his conference with Weed, would revive the rumor in full vigor.[27] Nor was Weed so indiffer-

24. Seward to Lincoln, Dec. 16, in Nicolay and Hay, *Lincoln*, III, 261. "Mr. Weed finding it not inconvenient to go West, I have had some conversation with him concerning the condition and the prospect of public affairs, and he will be able to inform you of my present unsettled view of the subject upon which you so kindly wrote me a few days ago. I shall remain at home until his return, and shall then in further conference with him have the advantage of a knowledge of the effect of public events certain to occur this week."

25. Albany *Evening Journal*, Dec. 17, copied by New York *Herald*, Dec. 19.

26. See above, pp. 85–86.

27. The rumor of Seward's authorship was promptly revived. The New York *Tribune*, Dec. 19, said, "The [Albany] *Atlas and Argus* also intimates that Mr. Seward was consulted in devising the new compromise." See Rhodes, *Hist. of U. S.*, III, 159.

Again, Seward's connection with the editorial policy of the *Evening Journal* was emphatically denied. *Ibid.* Rhodes shows that the *Evening Journal*, Dec. 19, issued a denial in its own name, and copied a denial from the Auburn *Advertiser* of Dec. 18. According to the *Evening*

ent to Seward's wishes as to embroil him against his will. Yet the renewal of the Missouri Compromise was urged again in the columns of the *Evening Journal*. It is difficult to avoid the impression that this singular piece of journalism, coming immediately after Seward's and Weed's discussion, and immediately before Weed's trip to Springfield, was somehow designed to clarify matters with Lincoln, or, perhaps, to urge their policy upon him.[28]

If Seward had opposed territorial compromise, it is almost inconceivable that the *Evening Journal* would have run counter to him at such a crucial time. If he had approved of it with real crusading zeal, he might have declared openly in favor of it, thus jeopardizing his influence with the new administration. But if he favored it with the balanced judgment which was characteristic of him, he might well have endorsed it privately, as a device to press Lincoln as far as possible; and, at the same time, might have disavowed it publicly, in order to be free to adopt some attainable objective, if Lincoln's opposition should render this one unattainable. Seward's motives were too deep to permit of dogmatic interpretation, but it seems altogether likely that he hoped for Weed to return from Springfield with Lincoln's endorsement of a policy of territorial compromise.[29]

As matters developed, however, Weed gained very little from the trip except a better understanding of the President-elect. He consulted with Lincoln for two days, December 19 and 20,[30] largely on the question of cabinet

Journal, Weed originally intended to include in his editorial a statement that he spoke "for himself only," but omitted this passage because it seemed ostentatious. This indicates that Weed, himself, foresaw that Seward's name would again become involved.

28. New York *Herald,* Dec. 6 (Springfield dispatch) had already reported that Lincoln disliked Weed's policy. "Would that he [Weed] could see the negative interest with which his *Journal* is daily read by the future dispenser of what he yearns for most."

29. Seward probably did not, at this time, know of Lincoln's private letters against compromise. The first of these had been written to Trumbull on Dec. 10; Seward had left Washington on Dec. 14.

30. Lincoln wrote to Trumbull, Dec. 21, "Weed was with me nearly all day yesterday, and left last night. . . ." Tracy, ed., *Uncollected Lin-*

appointments. During the interview, however, the *Evening Journal* of December 17 arrived (one can hardly believe this was unforeseen by Weed), and its editorial served to turn the discussion to the question of compromise. Lincoln elicited from Weed an admission that his views were not endorsed by the majority of eastern Republicans, and then indicated, with polite indirection, that he, too, disapproved. He felt that Weed had aimed at "friend and foe alike," and would do "some good or much mischief." To these strictures, Weed's reply, as he afterward remembered it, was an argument that a compromise probably would not be arranged in any case, but that the gesture of offering one was necessary in order to unite the North for the impending conflict. But Lincoln, still unimpressed, remarked that he hoped Weed's apprehensions of war were unfounded, and returned to a discussion of patronage.[31] When he again raised the subject, it was not to criticize Weed's policy, but to offer one of his own.

This statement of policy was in the form of three short resolutions which Weed was requested to take to Washington, where Lincoln desired that Trumbull and Hamlin should consider them, and that Seward should introduce them in the Senate.[32] These resolutions are brief enough to quote in full:

"Resolved: That the fugitive slave clause of the Con-

coln Letters, p. 172. Weed, in his *Autobiography,* p. 611, said that the visit lasted two days. Swett, also present, said "several days." Barnes, *Weed,* p. 293.

31. Account of interview in Weed, *Autobiography,* pp. 603–614. New York *Herald,* Dec. 25 (Springfield, Dec. 20), reported that Weed had been with Lincoln from 9 A. M. to 5 P. M., and that Weed had been compelled to modify his compromise plan after a careful overhauling of it.

32. Lincoln wrote to Trumbull, Dec. 21, "Weed . . . left last night with three short resolutions which I drew up, and which, or the substance of which, I think, would do much good if introduced and unanimously supported by our friends. They do not touch the territorial question. Mr. Weed goes to Washington with them; and says that he will first of all confer with you and Mr. Hamlin. I think it would be best for Mr. Seward to introduce them and Mr. Weed will let him know that I think so. Show this to Mr. Hamlin, but beyond him do not let my name be known in the matter." Tracy, ed., *Uncollected Lincoln Letters,* p. 172.

stitution ought to be enforced by a law of Congress, with efficient provisions for that object, not obliging private persons to assist in its execution, but punishing all who resist it, and with the usual safeguards to liberty, securing freemen against being surrendered as slaves—

"That all state laws, if there be such, really or apparently, in conflict with such law of Congress, ought to be repealed; and no opposition to the execution of such law of Congress ought to be made—

"That the Federal Union must be preserved."[33]

33. These resolutions are almost certainly the ones drawn on Dec. 20 by Lincoln, but the identity is not altogether beyond question. Hay and Rhodes believed that Lincoln's memorandum was lost (Rhodes, *Hist. of U. S.*, III, 162), and they knew of it only through a letter of Seward to Lincoln, Dec. 26, in which he stated that Weed had sent him Lincoln's "written proposition." Seward, *Seward*, II, 484–485. But Bancroft found, in the Seward MSS., an unsigned, undated paper, in the handwriting of Lincoln, containing simply the three resolutions quoted in the text. Bancroft, *Seward*, II, 10. He assumed that this was the "lost" memorandum. His assumption is supported by the fact that the resolutions contain certain features known to have characterized Lincoln's resolutions: (1) Seward's letter to Lincoln, Dec. 26, said, "your written suggestion . . . would divide our friends . . . a portion being unwilling to give up their old opinion, that the duty of executing the constitutional provisions, concerning fugitives from service, belongs to the States, and not at all to Congress." This indicates that Lincoln had endorsed Congressional enforcement of the fugitive slave clause; and that is the essence of the first resolution in the paper found by Bancroft. (2) Bancroft's paper contained three resolutions. Since he published it, a letter of Lincoln (quoted in footnote 32), saying that he had drawn up "three short resolutions" which were to be carried east by Weed, has appeared. Lincoln to Trumbull, Dec. 21, in Tracy, ed., *Uncollected Lincoln Letters*, p. 172.

On the other hand, certain factors tend to cast some faint doubt on Bancroft's assumption: (1) It is conceivable that Lincoln prepared two sets of resolutions, for we find that Weed twice sent to Seward resolutions drawn by Lincoln. In Seward's letter to Lincoln, Dec. 26, he acknowledged having received Lincoln's "written propositions" from Weed that day. Yet, on Jan. 9, Weed wrote to Seward (Bancroft, *Seward*, II, 29), "I enclose Mr. Lincoln's propositions, in the hope that you substantially accept his views on the two kindred questions." However, Weed visited Washington between Dec. 26 and Jan. 9, and it may be that he received back the resolutions from Seward and later sent them to him again. (2) The resolutions in the paper found by Bancroft do not correspond with certain resolutions which Seward told Lincoln (letter of Dec. 26) he introduced "to çover the ground of the suggestion made by you, through Mr. Weed, as I understood it [verbally]." For a

That was all. There was no proposal to guarantee the security of slavery in the states; there was no word of commendation for any of the numerous plans of compromise pending before Congress; and, most significant of all, territorial compromise was silently rejected.

Lincoln made Weed the bearer of these resolutions, but he made Seward the agent for them. Weed was requested to take the resolutions with him to Washington, to reveal them to Trumbull and Hamlin, and to inform Seward that Lincoln desired him to introduce them in the Senate.[34] Lincoln also made Weed the bearer of a verbal request that Seward write to him from time to time, informing him of the state of affairs in Washington.[35]

When Weed took the eastbound train from Springfield, his was a less cheerful prospect than when he started west. He had begun the trip with the intent to win Lincoln's endorsement for territorial compromise, and with some prospect of securing, for Seward and himself, control over the new administration. He returned, if he was wise, with the consolation of being one of the first to learn that Mr. Lincoln intended to be President in fact as well as in name. He returned, moreover, with a commission for Seward to sponsor a stated program, and to report at frequent intervals—a commission which Seward could not accept without becoming Lincoln's mere agent, and which he could not reject without jeopardizing his paramount influence in the new administration.

Weed left Springfield on the night of December 20,[36] and, after more than a day's travel alone, met Seward on the train at Syracuse. They traveled together as far as Albany, and, while they rode, Seward heard Weed's story. Weed told of Lincoln's three resolutions, but he did not

full discussion of the discrepancy between these two sets of resolutions, see below, pp. 174–176.

34. Lincoln to Trumbull, Dec. 21, in Tracy, ed., *Uncollected Lincoln Letters*, p. 172.

35. Seward to Lincoln, Dec. 26, in Seward, *Seward*, II, 484.

36. Lincoln to Trumbull, Dec. 21, in Tracy, ed., *Uncollected Lincoln Letters*, p. 172.

show the written copy to Seward; or, if he did, Seward later found it convenient to pretend that he had not done so.[37] But certainly Weed did not fail to convey the one significant point: that Lincoln remained adamant in his opposition to territorial compromise. What comments were exchanged on that trip from Syracuse to Albany is not recorded, but it is scarcely too much to say that, somewhere along the route, the active leadership of the Republican party passed from Seward to Lincoln, and the cause of territorial compromise received a blow from which there was no recovery. These changes found their first confirmation within a week, as Seward agreed to accept the portfolio of State,[38] and as he cast his vote against the Crittenden Compromise.

Seward, meeting Weed aboard train at Syracuse, did so no less because of his eagerness to learn the results of the Springfield conference, than because developments in Washington required his prompt return to the Senate. He had been away during ten of the most eventful days of the crisis. On December 18, the Senate voted to establish the Committee of Thirteen.[39] Two days later, Seward was appointed as one of the five Republican members of that committee;[40] on the same day, South Carolina adopted her Ordinance of Secession. On December 21, the committee held a session at which there was a rather free and informal interchange of opinion among the members,[41] and Senator Wade spoke in opposition to compromise.[42] Then, on December 22, when Seward was just leaving

37. Seward to Lincoln, Dec. 26, in Seward, *Seward*, II, 484, tells of the railway journey from Syracuse to Albany, and says, "He [Weed] gave me, verbally, the substance of the suggestion you prepared for the consideration of the Republican members; but not the written proposition. This morning, I received the latter from him."

38. Seward to Lincoln, Dec. 28, in *ibid.*, II, 487.

39. *Cong. Globe,* p. 117.

40. *Ibid.,* p. 158.

41. Rhodes, *Hist. of U. S.,* III, 152, citing Associated Press dispatch, Dec. 21. *Journal of Committee of 13,* p. 2.

42. New York *Tribune,* Dec. 22.

Auburn, the committee sat for seven hours,[43] and acted with a promptness extremely embarrassing to the Republican members, who were reluctant to proceed at all without Seward.[44] At the outset, the committee adopted a rule that no motion could be carried except by dual majorities of the Republicans on the committee and of the other members as well.[45] That is, any measure to be reported to the Senate must be adopted by a majority containing at least three Republicans and five other members. This rule was adopted for the very sound reason that no measure of compromise, and certainly no Constitutional amendment, could be finally adopted unless it were supported by a large section of the Republican party. There was clearly nothing to be gained by letting the Democrats on the committee report out some measure which the Republicans were certain to defeat; from the standpoint of the South, there was even something to be lost by it, for if compromise negotiations should be protracted, and should then break down, the golden opportunity for launching the secession program without Federal interference would have passed.

As soon as this question of procedure was settled, Senator Crittenden brought forward the same compromise measures which he had already introduced in the Senate. The committee discussed these proposals freely. Crittenden, of course, defended them, and Douglas and Bigler supported him zealously. The Southern Democrats—Hunter, Toombs, and Davis—assented more grudgingly, and indicated that they would not vote for the measure unless the Republicans should endorse it in good faith. But this prospect was blasted by the unanimous refusal of the Republicans to endorse it at all.[46] This clash of views produced a spirited but good-tempered discussion in

43. New York *Herald*, Dec. 23, described it as a 6½ hour session; New York *Tribune*, Dec. 24, 7 hour.

44. New York *Herald*, Dec. 23.

45. *Journal of Committee of 13*, p. 2.

46. Account of meeting in New York *Tribune*, Dec. 24 (Associated Press, Dec. 22).

which every member participated.[47] Following the discussion, a vote was proposed, and, probably because of the acuteness of the crisis, the proposal met with favor. The Republicans, unwilling to act without Seward, urged a delay until he should return. Others demanded to know how much longer he would be absent. But since the Republicans could give no answer to this query, it was decided to vote forthwith.[48]

Here the strength of territorial compromise was tested by vote for the first time. The test confirmed what the discussion had foreshadowed: on the vital first resolution of the Crittenden proposals—the resolution to revive and extend the Missouri Compromise line—all the Border state senators (Crittenden, Powell, and Hunter) voted in the affirmative. But the four Republicans (Collamer, Grimes, Doolittle, and Wade) voted solidly in the negative, and, because they did so, the Southern Democrats (Davis and Toombs) also voted against the resolution.[49] Although the non-Republican group favored the resolution, 6 to 2, the vote of the Republican section stood 4 to 0 in opposition. Under the rule, therefore, the resolution was defeated.[50]

That was on Saturday (December 22). On Sunday evening, Seward left New York City on the sleeping car, and on Monday morning he arrived at the capital, to find his Republican colleagues on the committee awaiting him. He met with them that morning, and with the full committee later that day.[51] Wade, Collamer, Grimes, and Doolittle were, no doubt, gladder than usual to see their colleague. Whether Seward professed to represent Lincoln or not, they could be quite sure that he knew Lincoln's wishes. If he supported their action in the committee, it meant that Lincoln, too, would support them,

47. New York *Tribune,* Dec. 24 (Washington, Dec. 23).

48. New York *Herald,* Dec. 23; Rhodes, *Hist. of U. S.,* III, 164.

49. For discussion of the reasons for the vote of Davis and Toombs, see below, pp. 204–206.

50. *Journal of Committee of 13,* Dec. 22, p. 5.

51. Seward to his family, Dec. 24, and to Lincoln, Dec. 26, in Seward, *Seward,* II, 483–484.

and that they could stand by their position. If he did not, it meant that the party was in chaos.

They did not remain long in suspense. On the day of his return, Seward asked permission of the Committee of Thirteen to record his vote on the questions on which action had already been taken. Consent being granted, he voted, as all the Republicans had done, against every important feature of the Crittenden Compromise, including, of course, the territorial line.[52] At the same session, he introduced a set of three resolutions, which were drawn either by him or by Senators Collamer and Grimes, and which had received the approval of all the Republican members of the committee.[53] These resolutions were phrased to express the will of Congress, first, that the Constitution should never be so altered as to permit congressional interference with slavery; second, that the Fugitive Slave Law should be amended by granting the right of jury trial to the person claimed as a fugitive; and third, that the states be requested to repeal any Personal Liberty Laws remaining on their statutes.[54] Two days

52. *Journal of Committee of 13,* p. 8.

53. Seward wrote Lincoln, Dec. 26 (Seward, *Seward,* II, 484), "I met . . . my Republican associates on the Committee of Thirteen. . . . With the unanimous consent of our section, I offered three propositions which seemed to me to cover the ground of the suggestion made by you, through Mr. Weed, as I understood it."

The fact that Seward introduced these resolutions, and the implication that they were modeled upon Lincoln's proposals, create a presumption that he wrote them. However, they did not follow Lincoln's policy closely enough to suggest dependence, and the New York *Tribune,* Dec. 25 (Washington, Dec. 24), stated that they were drawn by Grimes and Collamer.

54. The exact text of the resolutions follows:

"Resolved, that no amendment shall be made to the Constitution which will authorize or give to Congress any power to abolish or interfere in any State, with the domestic institutions thereof, including that of persons held to service or labor by the laws of such state.

"That the Fugitive Slave Law of 1850 shall be so amended as to secure to the alleged fugitive a trial by jury.

"That the legislatures of the several states shall be respectfully requested to review all their legislation affecting the right of persons recently resident in other states, and to repeal or modify all such acts as may contravene the Provisions of the Constitution of the United States, or any laws made in pursuance thereof." *Journal of Committee of 13,* p. 10–11.

later, at another meeting with his associates, Seward suggested a fourth resolution, to which they agreed,[55] and it, too, was introduced into the Committee of Thirteen. This proposal affirmed that Congress ought to pass a law to punish invasions, or plots for invasions, of one state from another, as the John Brown raid.[56]

So far as the Senate and the Committee of Thirteen were concerned, these four resolutions constituted the entire reply of the Republicans to the threat of secession. Other resolutions were considered, but none were supported by the Republican group. Even when Thurlow Weed belatedly sent the Lincoln memorandum to Seward, and the Republican members of the committee met with Trumbull and Fessenden to consider it, they decided not to alter their position to accord with it.[57]

When Lincoln's proposals are considered in detail, it is evident that Seward and the Republican committee members did not act in very literal conformity with his wishes. Lincoln had expressed a desire that no one save Seward, Trumbull, and Hamlin should know of the resolutions which he had drawn, but, despite his request, they were shown also to Fessenden and the Republican members of the Committee of Thirteen.[58] Also, the content of these

55. Seward to Lincoln, Dec. 26, in Seward, *Seward,* II, 484.

56. The text of the resolution follows:

"Resolved that, under the fourth section of the fourth article of the Constitution, Congress should pass an efficient law for the punishment of all persons engaged in the armed invasion of any state from another by combinations of individuals, and punishing all persons in complicity therewith, on trial and conviction in the State and District where their acts of complicity were committed, in the Federal Courts." *Journal of Committee of 13,* p. 13.

57. Seward to Lincoln, Dec. 26, in Seward, *Seward,* II, 484-485.

58. Lincoln to Trumbull, Dec. 21, in Tracy, ed., *Uncollected Lincoln Letters,* p. 172, expressed a wish that no one save Seward, Trumbull, and Hamlin should know of Lincoln's resolutions. However, Lincoln failed to make this clear to Weed, or Weed failed to make it clear to Seward, or Seward deliberately ignored it, for, on Dec. 26, he wrote Lincoln that he had received the written resolutions that morning, and that "the Republican members of the committee, with Judge Trumbull and Mr. Fessenden, met at my house to consider your written suggestions," that evening. Seward, *Seward,* II, 484.

resolutions was, in large measure, disregarded. Seward avoided admitting this, and told Lincoln that the measures which he introduced "seemed to me to cover the ground of the suggestion made by you, through Mr. Weed, as I understood it."[59] But, in fact, his proposals included a guarantee, which Lincoln had not suggested, for slavery in the states; they ignored Lincoln's desire for a declaration that "the Federal Union must be preserved"; they deliberately rejected Lincoln's proposed endorsement of Congressional enforcement of the Fugitive Slave clause of the Constitution on the ground that it might alienate those Republicans who believed in state enforcement;[60] they also failed to embody Lincoln's proposal to remove the existing requirement that private persons help enforce the Fugitive Slave Law. In fact, they coincided explicitly with Lincoln's proposals only in their recommendations that the states should repeal all Personal Liberty Laws, and that fugitive slave cases should be tried before a jury.[61]

These variations suggest either that Seward had not been properly informed by Weed of Lincoln's wishes, or that, at the outset, Seward was ready, as he was often in succeeding months, to deviate from Lincoln's program. But though Seward's innovations may have been significant as a foreshadowing of his impulse to direct matters himself, they did not clash with the spirit of Lincoln's program. In fact, all the differences of the two sets of resolutions pale to insignificance when account is taken of their

59. Seward to Lincoln, Dec. 26, in Seward, *Seward,* II, 484.

60. *Ibid.,* II, 485. "While we think the ground has been already covered, we find that, in the form you give it, it would divide our friends, not only in the Committee, but in Congress, a portion being unwilling to give up their old opinion, that the duty of executing the constitutional provisions, concerning fugitives from service, belongs to the States, and not at all to Congress."

61. Cf. the two sets of resolutions, above, pp. 167–168, 173, note 54.

Certain historical errors have resulted from the literal acceptance of Seward's implication that the two sets of resolutions were equivalent: e.g., George Fort Milton's assertion that Lincoln suggested an amendment to guarantee slavery in the states. *The Eve of Conflict,* p. 527.

agreement in tacitly vetoing the Crittenden proposals, and rejecting any attempt at territorial compromise. On this basic point, Seward followed Lincoln's lead. And inasmuch ₴ no settlement which ignored the territorial question could possibly gain a hearing in the cotton states, it is not too much to say that the introduction of these proposals marked a renunciation, by the Republicans, of any attempt to appease the secessionists of the lower South.

In a sense, too, the introduction of Seward's resolutions marked his acquiescence in the leadership of Lincoln. If he later attempted to influence Lincoln, to modify Lincoln's policies, even to force Lincoln's hand, he never openly resisted Lincoln's program. Though he did not yet know it, he had enlisted for the duration of the war.

Lincoln's letters to his friends in Congress, and his dextrous measures in gaining Seward's co-operation, show clearly his opposition to compromise. But the significance of these events lies less in the fact of their occurrence, than in the effect which they had upon the Republicans in Congress. Granted that Lincoln struck repeated blows against territorial concession, it remains to be determined whether his policy merely coincided with that of party leaders in Washington, or whether it altered decisively the course of the Republican group. The importance of his action is real or illusory in proportion as its effect was determining, or merely incidental. This, of course, involves an inquiry as to what the congressional group would have done if Lincoln had not intervened. No explicit answer is possible, but still one must examine the indications.

In the radical wing of the Republican party, there were a number of congressmen who needed no urging by Lincoln to reject compromise, for they opposed it more vigorously than he. In the Senate, Ben Wade, Charles Sumner, and Preston King were of this class;[62] in the

62. Wade, in Senate, Dec. 17, *Cong. Globe,* pp. 99–104; Sumner to F. W. Bird, Jan. 28, in Pierce, *Sumner,* II, 16, saying, "I insist upon

House, Owen P. Lovejoy of Illinois, Thaddeus Stevens of Pennsylvania, John A. Gurley of Ohio, and Charles B. Sedgwick of New York were equally stalwart.[63] It must also be recognized that the delegations of certain states— especially, of Vermont and of Wisconsin—were consistently and thoroughly hostile to compromise.[64]

Although never universal, this attitude characterized a substantial portion, and perhaps a majority, of the Republican membership. Throughout the crisis, some observers stressed the importance of this stalwart element, and asserted that compromise was making little headway among the members of the victorious party. Senator

an inflexible 'No' to every proposition. 'No,' 'No,' 'No,' let the North cry out to every compromise"; Mrs. Lyman Trumbull to Walter Trumbull, Jan. 26, in White, *Trumbull*, p. 122, containing an account of a committee urging compromise upon King, to which he replied, "I would rather resign my seat first and I think I would rather die."

63. Speeches in House, in *Cong. Globe*, by Lovejoy, Jan. 23 (appendix, pp. 84–87); Stevens, Jan. 29 (pp. 621–624); and Sedgwick, Feb. 7 (pp. 795–798). Gurley to Chase, Jan. 24, in Chase MSS.

Lovejoy's theocratic approach to politics was well expressed in a speech to the Republican caucus in which he said: "There never was a more causeless revolt since Lucifer led his cohorts of apostate angels against the throne of God, but I never heard that the Almighty proposed to compromise the matter by allowing the rebels to kindle the fires of hell south of the celestial meridian of 36° 30'." New York *Herald*, Jan. 6.

Sedgwick was a Representative from the Syracuse district, New York, and was a man of such stern temper that Henry Adams said he "would have done well for a member of the Long Parliament." Letter of Adams, Feb. 7, in Boston *Advertiser*, Feb. 11.

Henry Adams listed, as characteristically staunch men, John F. Potter, Cadwallader C. Washburne, Charles B. Sedgwick, John Bassett Alley, and Thomas Dawes Eliot. Adams to C. F. Adams, Jr., Dec. 9, in Ford, ed., *Henry Adams Letters, 1858–1891*, p. 63.

64. Henry Adams wrote to C. F. Adams, Jr., Dec. 18, deploring the lack of firmness among the Republicans, but rejoicing that "Wisconsin is a new Vermont." Ford, ed., *Henry Adams Letters, 1858–1891*, p. 67.

Henry Waldron, Representative from Wis., writing in the Detroit *Free Press*, Jan. 25, declared, "The sentiment of our delegation is that we have nothing to concede, compromise, or apologize for." Harris, *Chandler*, p. 53.

Justin Morrill, Representative from Vermont, wrote Mrs. Morrill, Dec. 7, that every proposed compromise required a surrender of principles, which he would not make. William Belmont Parker, *The Life and Public Services of Justin Smith Morrill* (Boston, 1924), p. 119.

Grimes remarked placidly, "There is . . . much talk about all sorts of compromises, but there is not the slightest probability that anything will be done." James Buchanan, looking wistfully for signs of conciliatory feeling, was disappointed to find "no reason to believe that this [the Crittenden plan] is at present acceptable to the Northern senators and representatives," and his only hope lay in the growing tendency among them to accept it. Very shortly afterward, Seward reported to Lincoln that he did "not see the slightest indications of its [the Crittenden compromise's] adoption, on the Republican side of Congress. The members stand nearly, or quite as firm against it, as the country is."[65] Somewhat later, Senator Fessenden recorded that "the great majority of Northern representatives in both houses of Congress seem to be of my opinion [that no concession should be offered]"; Senator Latham of California found, among his Republican opponents, an attitude of stolid indifference to the crisis; and Henry Adams, who had previously expected a compromise, wrote on January 7, "Mr. Weed, . . . who came . . . here with various compromise measures . . . has gone back today, without having found the first Republican to give them countenance."[66]

As contrasted with these commentators, there were others who emphasized the prevalence of a desire for compromise among a growing minority of the Republican members. The rapid increase of this group was the more

65. Grimes to his wife, Dec. 11, in Salter, *Grimes,* p. 132; Buchanan to Royal Phelps, Dec. 22, in Horatio King, *Turning on the Light, A Dispassionate Survey of President Buchanan's Administration from 1860 to its Close* (Philadelphia, 1895), p. 46; Seward to Lincoln, Dec. 26, in Seward, *Seward,* II, 484–485

In the same vein were statements by Seward to Weed, Dec. 3, "The Republican Party today is as uncompromising as the secessionists." Barnes, *Weed,* p. 308; and by Preston King to Bigelow, Dec. 3, "I do not find any Republican willing to entertain the idea of extending slavery." Bigelow, *Retrospections,* I, 316.

66. Letter of Fessenden, undated, apparently Feb., in Fessenden, *Fessenden,* I, 121; Milton Scott Latham to Franklin Pierce, Feb. 6, in the Franklin Pierce Papers in the Library of Congress; letter of Adams, Jan. 7, in Boston *Advertiser,* Jan. 11.

notable in that scarcely any enthusiasm for emergency measures had appeared at the opening of Congress, because there was slight recognition that an emergency existed. Eight days after the Congress assembled, before the emergency psychology could mature, Lincoln sent the first of that series of notes which advised congressmen against compromise. Thus Republican conciliatory inclinations experienced a normal development for only eight days, but, in that brief interval, burgeoned rapidly enough to lead Henry Adams to foretell "a complete disorganization of our party."[67]

While this startling prediction was never fulfilled, numerous other indications showed that compromise found supporters on the Republican side of House and Senate. Hamilton Fish believed that it did, and even reached the conclusion that both the Northern and the Southern factions were "willing to accept less than the others would grant," but that they were afraid of their constituents, and of certain demagogic rivals.[68] Representative S. S. Cox later listed five of the Republican senators—Simon Cameron of Pennsylvania, Edward D. Baker of Oregon, Jacob Collamer of Vermont, and James Dixon and Lafayette S. Foster of Connecticut—as men not unfriendly to the idea of compromise.[69] Henry B. Anthony and James F. Simmons of Rhode Island were regarded as "very fishy and weak-kneed," in the Adams household, where Collamer, Dixon, and Foster were also suspected.[70] Seward was widely regarded as a would-be pacificator. Thus, at least one-third of the Republican members in the Senate were not trusted by the militant group within their own party. And it is evident that this feeling was not altogether without foundation, for Dixon agreed, on the Senate floor, to

67. See above, pp. 130–131.
68. Fish to Charles S. Davies, Jan. 18, in Nevins, *Fish*, p. 81. Fish himself thought that "concessions should be offered." See above, p. 115.
69. Samuel S. Cox, *Three Decades of Federal Legislation, 1855 to 1885, etc.* (Providence, 1885), p. 64.
70. Henry Adams to C. F. Adams, Jr., Dec. 9, in Ford, ed., *Henry Adams Letters, 1858–1891,* pp. 63–64.

"make any sacrifice which a reasonable man can ask, or an honorable man can grant."[71] Cameron, going to the extreme limit of concession, made the very strong (or, as his colleagues would have thought, very weak) statements that "anything I can do by my vote here as Senator, I will do, to prevent the separation of the South from the North. . . . I desire to preserve it [the Union] by any sacrifice of feeling, and, I may say, of principle. . . . I will go for the proposition of my colleague [Senator Bigler's resolution to hold a popular referendum on the Crittenden proposals] or for any other proposition to save the country."[72]

But, however much Republican solidarity was impaired in the Senate, it was worse shattered in the House. As evidence of this, it is only necessary to recall the resolutions of Republican members, such as Kilgore, Thayer, and John Sherman in the House; the conciliatory tone of proposals and speeches, by Ferry, Humphrey, Corwin, Kellogg, Morse, and Curtis in the Committee of Thirty-three; and, particularly, the resolution of eight Republican members of this committee that they would offer "additional and more specific and effectual guarantees" for the South.[73] In the light of such developments, one can readily understand the anxiety of the staunch Republicans, who, like Joshua Giddings, felt "sorry to find so many cowards even among Republicans." A Pennsylvania Republican wrote, "There has been a great cave-in by the Republicans in the [Pennsylvania] Senate."[74] Meanwhile, Henry Adams expressed disgust with the Republican

71. In Senate, Dec. 10. *Cong. Globe,* p. 32.

72. In Senate, Jan. 21. *Ibid.,* pp. 494–495.

73. See above, pp. 92–99.

74. Giddings to Charles Sumner, Dec. 3, and E. W. Capron to William Lloyd Garrison, quoted by J. G. Randall, "The Civil War Restudied," in *Journal of Southern History,* VI (1940), 454. These items, excerpted from the Sumner and Garrison MSS. respectively, are accompanied by Professor Randall's comment that, "This note of disgust at Republican concessions runs all through the correspondence of Garrison, Sumner, Andrew, and other antislavery men."

delegations from Pennsylvania ("rotten to the core"), Ohio ("not all she should be"), and Indiana ("all she should not be, just as that mean state always was").[75] Since these states contributed more than one-third of the Republican membership, their possible defection was a serious matter.[76] Perhaps it was not serious enough to warrant Adams' alarmist estimate that a complete disorganization might ensue, reducing the party strength by two-thirds in the House, but it was certainly grave enough to justify a report by Seward that bewilderment and demoralization existed in the Republican ranks, and that "the timid will rush into the Democratic party." The New York *Herald* suggested that many of the victorious party wanted an adjustment, and were restrained only by fear of anathemas from the party press.[77]

Certain historians, being convinced of the conciliatory disposition of the Republicans in Congress, have argued that the Crittenden plan might even have succeeded in the Committee of Thirteen, if Lincoln's influence had not prevented such a consummation. William E. Dodd, for instance, suggested that Grimes and Doolittle would have followed Seward, if he had chosen the path of compromise.[78] If such a combination could have been formed, it would have assured the success of the Crittenden plan in the committee, but the conjecture that these senators might have supported such a program directly contra-

75. Adams to C. F. Adams, Jr., Dec. 18, in Ford, ed., *Henry Adams Letters, 1858–1891*, p. 67.

76. Republicans in House, 114; from Pa., 20; from O., 16; from Ind., 7.

77. Adams to C. F. Adams, Jr., Dec. 13, in Ford, ed., *Henry Adams Letters, 1858–1891*, p. 66; Seward to his wife, Dec. 9, in Seward, *Seward*, II, 481; New York *Herald*, Jan. 3.

78. William E. Dodd, *Jefferson Davis* (Philadelphia, 1907), p. 196, says, "Seward had been writing letters to his wife for nearly a month, which show that he was ready to abandon the irrepressible conflict, and this change of heart was vaguely understood among his followers. If the New York senator gave his consent to Crittenden's plan, Grimes and Doolittle would have easily added their votes, and only Collamer and Wade would have been left to protest the report."

venes their own specific utterances. Grimes, on December 16, wrote that the secessionists "want to debauch the moral sentiment of the people of the North, by making them agree to the proposition that slavery is a benign, constitutional system"; he could not have voted for the Crittenden proposals without giving explicit constitutional recognition to slavery. Doolittle, with equal decisiveness, said, "Let it be settled there shall be no more slave territory";[79] it may be that pressure would have induced him to abandon this position and vote for compromise, but certainly no evidence indicates that he was disposed to do so, nor that he was more likely than other Republican senators to take such a course. As for Senator Wade, he was at all times violently opposed to concessions.

Collamer, on the other hand, might have been persuaded to sacrifice the Chicago Platform. He remained noncommittal on the Senate floor, but his firmness was suspected in the well informed Adams household, and he is said to have told Senator Clingman of North Carolina, "You must let us know your terms, for we do not want to part with you." It is notable that, when the Crittenden proposals later came to a vote on the Senate floor, Collamer did not vote.[80]

As for Seward, he was an enigma, and, in all likelihood, will remain one. His close association with Weed creates a strong presumption that he was not hostile to the revival of the Missouri line. Moreover, his customary, and rather cryptic optimism, suggested that he willingly anticipated a compromise. It was reported at the time, and for thirty years following, that Seward had assured various people

79. Grimes to his wife, Dec. 16, in Salter, *Grimes,* p. 132; Doolittle to his wife, Dec. 2, in Duane Mowry, "An Appreciation of James Rood Doolittle," p. 290, in State Historical Society of Wisconsin, *Proceedings,* 1909. Also a very strong anti-compromise letter, by Doolittle, Nov. 16, in *Cong. Globe,* p. 9.

80. Henry Adams to C. F. Adams, Jr., Dec. 13, in Ford, ed., *Henry Adams Letters, 1858–1891,* p. 64; *Selections from the Speeches and Writings of Thomas L. Clingman* (Raleigh, 1877), p. 523; vote in Senate, Mar. 2, in *Cong. Globe,* p. 1405.

that he would accept the Crittenden plan.[81] Most of these reports were tainted with anonymity, but an exception exists in the case of James Barbour, an outstanding and trustworthy Virginia Unionist, who gave circumstantial accounts of two interviews in which Seward offered such assurances. According to Barbour, Seward told him, "I am of your opinion that nothing short of that [the Crittenden plan] will allay the excitement, and therefore I will favor it substantially."[82] It is easy to understand the conflicting reports as to Seward's policy, when one observes the uncertain tenor even of his letters to his family. On December 8, he assured his wife, "I am, thus far, silent, not because I am thinking of proposing compromises, but because I wish to avoid . . . intermeddling, just now— when concession, . . . or solicitude, would encourage, and demonstrations of firmness of purpose would exasperate." But two days later the policy of non-intervention seemed less attractive, and he was pondering the "difficult task, of trying to reconcile the factious men who are bent on disunion."[83] However, Seward's words were frequently intended to mask his purposes, and no analysis of them will reveal his position. The only possible clew to his attitude lies in his actions, and these suggest that, if Lincoln had not dominated him, he would have accepted

81. New York *Herald*, Jan. 4. James DePeyster Ogden, Jan. 29, wrote to Crittenden, "A gentleman this morning told me that a perfectly reliable party assured him that Seward said, ten days since . . . that he was resolved not to yield an inch. Whereas, three days since, another party assured him that he had just had a long conversation with the same *Statesman* and that he speaks in decided terms of the necessity of a compromise"; exactly one month earlier, Ogden had written, "Those who pretend to know say that Weed and Seward will move, and are in reality acting together"; both letters in Crittenden MSS.

82. James Barbour to F. Bancroft, Aug. 24, 1893, in Bancroft, *Seward*, II, 32, discusses the interview of thirty-two years before. The letter seems thoughtful and accurate, and is free of the dramatics and inaccuracies which usually cast suspicion on letters written in old age. The fact that an interview took place is confirmed by letters of Barbour to Seward, Feb. 8, in *ibid.*, II, 534–536, and of Seward to Lincoln, Jan. 27, in Nicolay and Hay, *Lincoln*, III, 365.

83. Seward to his wife, Dec. 8 and 10, in Seward, *Seward*, II, 480–481.

the Crittenden proposals. Implication and circumstance point directly to the conclusion that he would have favored a territorial line.[84]

There is good reason for supposing, tentatively, that Seward and Collamer would have voted with Crittenden in the Committee of Thirteen, and that Grimes, Doolittle, and Wade would have voted against him. This, under the rule requiring majorities of each faction, would have defeated the Crittenden proposal in committee. Therefore it seems unsound to emphasize Lincoln's responsibility, as some historians have done, to the point of attributing the committee action to his influence.[85]

But this is not to deny that Lincoln's intervention was a vital one. For the Crittenden proposals did not receive their *coup de grace* on December 22 at the hands of the Committee of Thirteen, but on January 16, when the Senate adopted, by a vote of 25 to 23, a substitute to prevent the Crittenden resolutions from being brought to a vote on the Senate floor.[86] The substitute was adopted in part because of the non-voting of six Southern Democrats (whose responsibility will be discussed subsequently), but primarily because the entire bloc of Republican senators[87] cast their full strength for the substitute, giving for it every vote which it received. In these circumstances, the change of a single vote would have caused a tie, leaving Vice President Breckinridge to cast a deciding vote, as he undoubtedly would have, to bring the Crittenden proposals to the Senate floor. But there was no tie, partly be-

---

84. Rhodes, *Hist. of U. S.*, III, 164, and Bancroft, *Seward*, II, 26–29, both held this view.

85. Rhodes, *Hist. of U. S.*, III, 165–167; Dodd, *Jefferson Davis*, p. 196. On the question of responsibility for the action of the Committee of Thirteen, see also W. E. Tilberg, "The Responsibility for the Failure of Compromise in 1860," in *The Historical Outlook*, XIV (1923), 85–93, and Clinton Everett Knox, "The Possibilities of Compromise in the Senate Committee of Thirteen and the Responsibility for Failure," in *Journal of Negro History*, XVII (1932), 437–465.

86. *Cong. Globe*, p. 409.

87. Except Hannibal Hamlin, whose resignation was effective next day (Jan. 17) and who was not in attendance.

cause no one of the senators—Anthony, Baker, Cameron, Collamer, Dixon, Foster, Seward, and Simmons—who had evinced a disposition toward compromise, cast a vote for the extremely mild proposal to make the Crittenden measures the order of business. With a probability not far short of certainty, it appears that Lincoln's intervention contributed decisively to the sudden intransigence of these men, and thus played the major part in preventing the Crittenden resolutions from coming to a vote until after the formation of the Southern Confederacy.

Lincoln's decisive rôle was recognized at the time. Sumner knew of it and was comforted. "Mr. Lincoln," he recorded, "is perfectly firm. He says that the Republican party shall not with his assent become 'a mere sucked egg, all shell and no meat,—the principle all sucked out.'" Preston King, almost as much of a zealot as Sumner, reported an "apparent firmness" in the Republican ranks, and observed that, "All we hear of Lincoln contributes to this steadiness." Henry Adams confided to his brother that "Lincoln is all right. You can rely on that. He has exercised a strong influence through several sources on this committee [of Thirty-three] and always right." Two days later, he returned to the same important topic, and wrote: "The President elect has signified too in more ways than one, what the Committee [of Thirty-three] had better do and what leave undone."[88]

The Republican solidarity in rejecting compromise in mid-January marked a complete reversal of the tendency of mid-December, when conciliatory measures seemed to be steadily gaining Republican adherents, and when the prospect of a split in the party had caused grave anxiety to Republican leaders. Yet the crisis was no less ominous,

88. Sumner to F. W. Ballard, Jan. 26, in Pierce, *Sumner,* IV, 16; King to Bigelow, Jan. 30, in Bigelow, *Retrospections,* I, 355; Adams to C. F. Adams, Jr., Dec. 20 and 22, in Ford, ed., *Henry Adams Letters, 1858–1891,* pp. 68–69. Adams probably had reference to Lincoln's letters to Kellogg, Trumbull, and Washburne (see above, pp. 157, 160, note 11, 158), for Lincoln had not completed his arrangements with Seward when Adams wrote.

and the pressure from conciliationist groups had not abated. The change in temper, therefore, resulted from no amelioration in crisis conditions, but from new forces at work within the party. These forces may have been multiple, but certainly none was more potent than the intervention of Lincoln. Almost unobserved, except in the most limited circles, the President-elect had held the ranks of his party solid when a schism appeared imminent.

The later history of the Senate Committee of Thirteen, and of Seward's resolutions therein, contributed no new factor in the development of the crisis. It may suffice to remark that neither the Republican resolutions, nor any others, were ever reported by the committee.[89] Other proposals of territorial compromise were introduced by Douglas, Bigler, and Rice. But when these were rejected,[90]

89. Seward's first resolution was adopted, 11 to 2, with Davis and Toombs in the negative; the second was amended, on the motion of Douglas, to require that jury trials of alleged fugitives should be held in the state from which the flight was claimed to have occurred, and, in this amended form, was defeated by the Republicans, who had opposed the amendment; the third was rejected by the Southern senators, on the ground that it would affect the laws of slave states concerning Negro seamen; the last was amended, by the Democrats, to give a broader definition to the punishable offense, and was defeated by the Republicans, who had opposed the amendment. *Journal of Committee of 13,* pp. 11, 13.

On Dec. 28, the committee adopted a resolution that it had "not been able to agree upon any general plan of adjustment," and so reported to the Senate. *Ibid.,* p. 18; *Cong. Globe,* p. 211.

90. Douglas proposed two Constitutional amendments, providing chiefly that the existing status of slavery in the existing territories should remain unchanged until they became states, that new territory should be acquired only by treaty or by two-thirds of both houses of Congress, and that the status of slavery in such new territory should remain as at the time of acquisition.

Bigler proposed Constitutional amendments dividing all territory on the line 36° 30′, with four slave territories south, and eight free territories north of that line, these territories to be admitted later as states.

Rice proposed a resolution to admit the entire territory north of 36° 30′ as the "State of Washington," and all south of it as the "State of Jefferson," with provision for subdividing into smaller states as the population grew. Seward offered to amend this to exclude Kansas from the arrangement—that is, to secure two free states for one slave state.

it was, in essence, a mere repetition of the Republican refusal to offer a territorial adjustment.

Their adherence to this position virtually eliminated the possibility of a compromise with the secessionists. It was a bitter blow to the so-called "Union-savers," and they reacted by taxing the Republicans with sole responsibility for preventing reconciliation. Moreover, they assumed that the only Republican motive for this act was a bellicose determination to force the South to submit—a preference for coercive, rather than conciliatory measures. These accusations, in effect, would fix upon the Republicans the responsibility of causing a needless tragedy, and the guilt of choosing deliberately the course of war. In the apportionment of responsibility for the American Civil War, however, no such simple formulae will suffice. Though the Republicans opposed territorial concessions, the question remains whether the Northern people would have supported an offer of compromise, and whether the Southern people would have accepted one. And even if it should appear that compromise was, in fact, practicable, Republican rejection of compromise cannot validly be interpreted as an evidence of a spirit of aggression, without specific examination of the beliefs which led the members of the party to determine upon their course.

The amendment failed, 6 to 6, Douglas voting with the Republicans, Bigler not voting.

The vote on these measures was as follows: Douglas resolutions, defeated 2 (Crittenden and Douglas) to 11, on Dec. 24; Bigler resolutions, defeated without a record vote, Dec. 28; Rice resolution, defeated 3 (Bigler, Davis, Rice) to 10, Dec. 28. It is notable that in all recorded cases, the Republicans solidly opposed compromise proposals. *Journal of Committee of 13,* pp. 8–18.

CHAPTER VIII

PARTISAN LEADERS AND THE POPULAR WILL

IN the problem of the secession crisis, all disputed questions of personal or sectional justification signify far less than the basic, undisputed fact that the public men of 1861 failed to effect the voluntary perpetuation of the Union. In a larger sense, this breakdown of peace began with the sectional antagonism of the preceding decades. In a more immediate sense, it ensued from the condition that no compromise—and, explicitly, no territorial compromise—was either offered by one section or requested by the other.

In the analysis of this failure, attention naturally focuses upon the manner in which Lincoln and his party resisted territorial adjustment. But the fact that they opposed the plan does not necessarily mean that they prevented the fulfillment. A major question remains as to whether the Republicans defeated a practicable and publicly approved device for the maintenance of the Union, or whether they merely dispatched at once an illusory scheme which was certain to fail in due time because of other factors. If it be true, or if the data indicate, that the compromise proposals were desired by the Unionist states, and acceptable to the South, then the accountability of the Republicans must be regarded as very grave. If, on the other hand, the Crittenden proposals and others like them faced insuperable obstacles from the beginning, in the form of public disapproval or of Southern distaste for the maintenance of Union on any terms, then the policy of the Republicans cannot be regarded as being, in any sense, decisive. Much turns upon the question as to what the Unionist states desired, and what the seceding states would have accepted.

Neither polls nor straw votes existed to record the shifting currents of public opinion in the sixties. Nevertheless, it is necessary to read such gauges as were available to determine whether or not that opinion predominantly favored a territorial compromise. Among the evidence which bears on this question, none is more complete and more revealing than the popular vote in the election of 1860. For this vote shows plainly that a majority, not only of the voters as a whole, but even of the voters in states which remained loyal to the Union, regarded the exclusion of slavery from the territories as non-essential or even undesirable, and voted against the candidate who represented this policy. When Lincoln was inaugurated, the states which accepted him as President were states which had cast a majority of more than half a million votes against him, and even when the outbreak of war caused four more states to join the Confederacy, the remaining Union still contained a population in which the majority of the electorate had opposed the Republican ticket.[1] Inasmuch as this majority was divided between Breckinridge, who denied the right of congressional intervention in the territories, Douglas, who offered popular sovereignty as a solution, and Bell, who favored anything that would insure harmony, it appears that the proponents of slavery exclusion lacked a majority, even before the secession crisis.

How far they fell short of attaining a majority is uncertain, but clearly their numerical strength was appreciably less than that of the Republican party as a whole. For many of the citizens who cast their ballots for

1. The following table, based upon data in Edward Stanwood, *A History of the Presidency from 1788 to 1897* (Boston, 1898), p. 297, illustrates Lincoln's minority position in states which remained in the Union:

| | Election of 1860 | |
	Lincoln	Other candidates
vote of entire United States	1,866,452	2,815,617
vote of states which rejected secession prior to war	1,866,452	2,421,752
vote of states which fought for Union (including Ky. and Mo.)	1,864,523	1,960,842

Lincoln, did so in spite of, rather than because of, his advocacy of slavery exclusion. It is a well known fact that the platform of 1860 made a clever and successful bid for the support of protectionists, advocates of free homesteads, and promoters of a transcontinental railway. Add to this the strength which the Democratic party forfeited through its corruption and that which Lincoln gained simply as a man of the people, and the intrinsic strength of the slavery exclusion program seems very indeterminate, indeed.[2] Honest Abe, the rail-splitter, probably ran fully as strong at the polls as Abraham Lincoln, the friend of the enslaved.

If the advocates of slavery exclusion did not command a majority at the outset of the crisis, they certainly never possessed one thereafter, for it is an incontestable fact that many Republicans who had endorsed the entire Chicago Platform during the campaign, hastily modified their position as the secession crisis developed. Copious evidence proves that defections occurred on a large scale. In Massachusetts, for instance, a number of local elections took place in early December, and in these contests the heavy Republican majorities of the preceding month were heavily reversed in such important towns as Worcester and Newburyport. Where no actual reversal took place, the proportion of Republican strength was reduced, as in Boston, Charleston, and Lowell.[3]

Many observers, both within and without the Republi-

2. "Now our triumph was achieved more because of Lincoln's . . . honesty and the known corruption of the democrats, than because of the negro question." James W. Grimes, Burlington, Ia., Nov. 13, to Lyman Trumbull, in Trumbull MSS.

3. New York *Herald,* Dec. 14, recorded these elections as follows:

	November		December	
	Republican	Opposition	Republican	Opposition
Boston	9723	10649	5674	8834
Charleston	785	1528	697	1671
Roxbury	1408	1632	1023	1223
Worcester	1195 maj.			176 maj.
Lowell	2779	1593	2073	1661
Newburyport	939	679	690	1135

can party, noted this thinning of the ranks. Zachariah Chandler had deplored the signs of wavering even among "good reliable Republicans" and had feared that the panic might infect Lincoln. Norman B. Judd, meeting with the Republican members of the Illinois legislature, experienced "trouble in holding them steady" even in the hyper-Republican atmosphere of Springfield. Moses Grinnell confided to Seward his fear that "many of our Republican friends have strong sympathies with those who are ready to yield to . . . the Crittenden . . . propositions."[4] This fear was amply justified by the large number of cases in which Republicans became converts of the Crittenden plan. Several of these partisans wrote to assure Crittenden of their support. A Pennsylvanian of this class believed that he was only one of a host of Republicans who sympathized with the Kentucky senator. Another writer said that he represented a great number who had voted for Lincoln only because they wanted honesty to displace corruption, and not because of any inflexible conviction on the territorial question.[5]

Still another group, who had never been Republican, wrote in a different mood, but with the same theme: the Republican masses wanted compromise. One of the most distinguished of this group, Martin Van Buren, surmised that the Republicans would never openly support the Crittenden proposal, but would "suffer [it] . . . to pass by the aid of the most conservative and least partisan portions of their body, when they know that its passage would be acceptable to, if not desirable to, a large portion, not to say a majority of their own supporters. . . ."[6] John Brodhead claimed for Crittenden the support of

4. Chandler to Trumbull, Nov. 17, in Trumbull MSS.; Judd to Chase, Jan. 16, in Chase MSS.; Grinnell, New York, Jan. 28, to Seward, in Bancroft, *Seward,* II, 532–533.
5. Letters to Crittenden from S. E. Woodruff, Girard, Pa., Jan. 2; J. H. Reed, Greenwich, Conn., Jan. 17; in Crittenden MSS. Also see letters from A. S. Fiske, New York, Jan. 21, and E. Spoford, Brooklyn, N. Y., Jan. 16, in *ibid.*
6. Van Buren to Crittenden, Dec. 24, in Van Buren MSS.

half of the Pennsylvanians who had voted for Lincoln.[7]
This was probably an exaggeration, but it seemed to be
partially justified when a group of Philadelphians, numbered at 2000, and claiming to have supported Lincoln,
presented to Congress a petition in favor of the Crittenden
compromise.[8] In New York, it was said that the conservative element was leaving the Republican party, that the
political ranks were dividing in Albany, and that the
moderate Republicans of New York City were pressing
the radicals in Congress to adopt a more conciliatory
policy.[9] One observer of these trends wrote, "I am not a
republican nor did I vote their ticket. I move daily among
those who did vote that ticket and I believe could they
tomorrow they would recall their votes." August Belmont,
meanwhile, suggested to Stephen A. Douglas that he work
for a revival of the Missouri Compromise, "because I have
good reason to know that the conservative portion of the
Republican leaders are in favor of it." Crittenden himself
was heartened by his "commendation . . . from *high Republican* sources."[10]

While certain elements in the Republican party began
to champion the cause of compromise, there were other
elements which remained stalwart. Certainly, the Republican masses were by no means stampeded, and in some
regions—the rural areas in general, and upper New
England and the Western states in particular—their lines
remained almost intact.[11] Despite the widespread desire

7. John Brodhead, Philadelphia, Jan. 4, to Crittenden, in Crittenden
MSS.

8. *Cong. Globe,* p. 777.

9. Letters to Crittenden, from James DePeyster Ogden, Jan. 29;
James William Beekman, Jan. 24; in Crittenden MSS. Letter from
John A. Dix to Horatio King, Dec. 29, in King, *Turning on the Light,*
p. 36–37.

10. Washington Murray to Crittenden, Dec. 24; Crittenden to S. S.
Nicholas, Dec. [?]; in Crittenden MSS. Belmont to Douglas, Dec. 31;
also to Herschel V. Johnson, Dec. 30, and to John Forsyth, Dec. 19; in
Belmont, *Letters,* pp. 36–39, 42, 45.

11. George D. Briggs of N. Y., Feb. 4, in House; Morton S. Wilkinson
of Minn., Feb. 14, in Senate ("if Senators . . . would ascertain what
the true sentiment of the country is, they must get off from the side-

for compromise, opposition to it remained so strong in
some quarters that when the Republican members of the
Committee of Thirty-three voted for the Dunn resolution,
they were "dreadfully pulled over the coals for it by their
constituents,"[12] and consequently veered back toward the
Chicago Platform. Several Republicans in the Senate
also observed a firm tone among their constituents. For
instance, the vast majority of Lyman Trumbull's numerous correspondents exhorted him to stand firm;[13] the
Republicans who wrote to William Pitt Fessenden were
"almost unanimous" in their opposition to compromise,
although other groups urged him to make concessions; the
correspondence of Seward was very heavy, and it left him
with the impression, not consistently held, that the people
of the North were firmly opposed to the Crittenden plan;
when Senator James Harlan of Iowa made a speech
against compromise, it brought him an unusually heavy
shower of commendatory letters; and Preston King rejoiced to find "an apparent firmness in the great body of
our folks."[14] Outside of Congress, the extensive corre-

walks of our cities; they must go away from the commercial districts
. . . ; they must penetrate into the interior."), *Cong. Globe,* pp. 729,
896. New York *Times,* Nov. 19, Dec. 7 ("The people in the interior do
not believe that there is danger of disunion.").

12. Henry Adams to C. F. Adams, Jr., Dec. 22, in Ford, ed., *Henry
Adams Letters, 1858–1891,* p. 69.

13. Letters to Trumbull from A. C. Clayton, Jerseyville, Ill., Dec. 10;
G. Koerner, Belleville, Ill., Dec. 10; J. H. Alderman, Jacksonville, Ill.,
Dec. 13; George P. Edgar, Chicago, Ill., Dec. 14; Thomas Richmond, Chi-
cago, Ill., Dec. 14; Wait Talcott, Mattoon, Ill., Dec. 16; Wm. E. Griffin,
Richland Grove, Dec. 17; George T. Brown, Alton, Ill., Dec. 18; R. C.
Mann, Preston, Ill., Dec. 18; A. B. M'Chesney, Alton, Dec. 18; A. Bal-
linger, Alton, Dec. 18; A. W. Metcalf, Edwardsville, Ill., Dec. 18;
W. H. Hanna, Bloomington, Ill., Dec. 19; E. Stafford, Carondelet, Mo.,
Dec. 20; Seth McCormick, Racine, Wis., Dec. 20; John R. Woods, Wood-
wild, Ill., Dec. 20; Edward Harte, San Francisco, Cal., Dec. 20; W. H.
Herndon, Springfield, Ill., Dec. 21; John Olney, Shawneetown, Dec. 21;
David J. Baker, Alton, Dec. 22; and many others.

14. White, *Trumbull,* p. 117; Fessenden, *Fessenden,* I, 117; Seward to
his family, Dec. 24, and to Lincoln, Dec. 26, in Seward, *Seward,* II, 483–
485; Johnson Brigham, *James Harlan* (Iowa City, 1913), p. 154, with
citations to Harlan's autobiographical MSS. and papers; King to Bigelow, Jan. 30, in Bigelow, *Retrospections,* I, 355.

spondence of Salmon P. Chase revealed a large body of
Republican opposition, in Ohio, to compromise.[15] Francis
P. Blair, Jr., reported a similar sentiment in Illinois.[16]
Richard Yates, of the same state, wrote, "The Republicans, however, are firm. Much as they dread the prospect
of civil war, yet they feel in no way responsible for any
such result."[17]

To reconcile these statements of hostility toward
compromise with other statements of receptiveness, is
impossible. To believe one and reject the other is equally
impossible. To average the two and produce a neutral
result would be most misleading of all. No valid conclusion
can follow except that the party was splitting into factions
on the issue of compromise, and that the "irrepressible
conflict in the Republican party," already predicted by
the *Herald,* was now about to break forth. Certainly this
was the result most feared by Republican leaders. Salmon
P. Chase had declared, at the very inception of the crisis,
that "No disunion need create alarm except the disunion
of the Republican Party,"[18] and Henry Villard showed the
fulfillment of Chase's fears in an early February dispatch
from Springfield: "It is not only in Congress that
dissonances are audible in the republican ranks in
reference to the compromise question. It is not only in
their party organs that flagrant discrepancies of opinion

15. See especially letters to Chase from: George A. Nourse, St. Paul,
Minn., Nov. 17; Edward D. Mansfield, Morrow, O., Nov. 26; L. Clephane,
Washington, Dec. 7; J. H. Baker, St. Paul, Minn., Dec. 10; E. B. Taylor,
Greenville, [no state], Dec. 14; T. A. Cheney, Chautauqua County, N. Y.,
Dec. 14; J. C. Brand, Urbana, Ill., Dec. 21; George Hoadley, Cincinnati,
Dec. 7, "The north is of one mind . . . in preferring dissolution and
even war to the nationalizing of slavery"; George G. Fogg, Washington,
Dec. 12, "Our friends here are generally standing firm"; George Opdyke,
New York, Dec. 26, "The republicans generally . . . are for standing
by their principles, come what may"; Milton Sutliff, Warren, O., Feb. 14,
saying that a large majority of Republicans would vote against territorial compromise. All in Chase MSS.
16. F. P. Blair, Jr., to Montgomery Blair, Jan. 24, in Blair MSS. "Our
friends in Illinois are not for any compromise."
17. Yates to Trumbull, Jacksonville, Ill., Dec. 21, in Trumbull MSS.
18. Chase to Trumbull, Columbus, O., Nov. 12, in *ibid.*

are becoming manifest—nay, in almost every State that rolled up a majority for Lincoln and Hamlin, a division of the party in power into pro- and anti-compromises [*sic*], or conservatives and radicals, appears to be imminent. . . . That profound apprehensions of a wreck of the republican party against the compromise rock prevail in Presidential circles is certain."[19]

When the faction of Republican moderates is added to that of Breckinridge Democrats, Douglas Democrats, and Constitutional Unionists, assurance seems doubly certain that the majority opinion of the Unionist states would readily have offered concessions in the territories if thereby they could have secured the perpetuation of the Union. Testimony as to the desire of the majority for compromise is voluminous. On the floor of the Senate, Douglas, Pugh of Ohio, and Bigler of Pennsylvania made explicit statements of their own conviction that the majority favored territorial concessions and wanted only an opportunity to vote on the issue.[20] Crittenden himself declared, "I firmly believe that a great majority of the people would accept my plan of settlement."[21] That this opinion was no mere wishful thinking, is abundantly evident from the Senator's letter-files.

From all parts of the Union, Crittenden received not only pledges of personal support, but also, assurances by astute political observers of widespread public support. His correspondents included many of whom history preserves no record, but a significant proportion of communications came from men with influence to shape opinion and with insight to discern it. Martin Van Buren assured Crittenden that his proposals would certainly receive the endorsement of the requisite number of states. John A. Dix likewise possessed "strong confidence that we could carry three-fourths of the States." Governor Hicks of Maryland

19. New York *Herald,* Feb. 16 (Springfield, Feb. 3).
20. Statements in *Cong. Globe;* by Pugh, Dec. 10 (p. 33); by Bigler, Dec. 11 (p. 48); by Douglas, Jan. 3 (appendix, p. 42).
21. Crittenden to S. S. Nicholas, Dec. [?], in Crittenden MSS.

believed, on December 13, that the cause of compromise already commanded the loyalty of millions and was growing rapidly.[22] From New York, Horatio Seymour assured Crittenden that a referendum would show a state-wide majority of 150,000 in favor of his proposed amendments.[23] For Pennsylvania, Jay Gould estimated "not less than a hundred thousand majority," as the margin of public support for Crittenden. On the same day that Gould wrote, another railway executive, John Brodhead, reported: "I have taken pains to ascertain the sentiments of our people in regard to your proposition . . . and I am satisfied that three fourths of the people of Pennsylvania and New Jersey warmly approve your plan."[24] This estimate for New Jersey was borne out by ex-Senator Philemon Dickinson, who predicted that, on a referendum, the Crittenden proposals would be endorsed by an overwhelming majority.[25]

These assurances derive especial importance from the prominence of their authors. But many similar assurances came from other men who, though less distinguished, were perhaps no less able as analysts. Great numbers of them wrote to Crittenden to assure him that he headed a popular movement. One of these had talked to "a number of . . . prominent men of both parties" in New York,

22. Van Buren to Crittenden, Dec. 24, in the Martin Van Buren Papers in the Library of Congress; Dix to Crittenden, Dec. 22, in Coleman, *Crittenden*, II, 237; Thomas H. Hicks to Crittenden, Dec. 13, in Crittenden MSS.

23. Seymour to Crittenden, Jan. 18, in Coleman, *Crittenden*, II, 254–255. See also letters to Crittenden from Daniel Lord, New York, Dec. 29; S. Baldwin, New York, Jan. 11; and Appleton Oaksmith, New York, Jan. 19; and from Crittenden, Dec. [?], to S. S. Nicholas; in Crittenden MSS. Oaksmith wrote, "The true sentiments of *the People* of this City are in favor of . . . the Crittenden Compromize [*sic*]." Crittenden wrote, "from New York I have received any amount of commendation. . . ."

24. Letters to Crittenden from Gould, Jan. 4, 1861 [incorrectly dated, 1860, and so recorded in published calendar], and John Brodhead, of the Camden and Atlantic R. R., Jan. 4, in Crittenden MSS. In same collection, see also letters of S. E. Woodruff, Girard, Pa., Jan. 2, and D. Rodney King, Philadelphia, Pa., Jan. 3.

25. Dickinson to Crittenden, Trenton, N. J., Jan. 16; also, John Hulme, Philadelphia, Pa., Jan. 20, in Crittenden MSS.

and had found a consensus among them that if the masses could be reached, they would sustain the policy of conciliation. Another could find among "my *whole acquaintance*" only one man who would vote against Crittenden's resolutions. Still another felt sure that the majority of inarticulate conservatives desired compromise. From his home state, a telegram to Crittenden suggested that a popular referendum would sustain him by a vote of five to one. From Virginia, an irate citizen surmised that "Your plan . . . would be adopted gladly by the people of the country, if they could so far get the upper hand of their masters, the politicians, as to get a straight *up and down* vote upon the question." Day after day, similar opinions from all parts of the country poured in upon the Kentucky Senator,[26] and found widespread expression elsewhere. Correspondents of Robert J. Breckinridge were no less certain of the popular trend than were those who wrote to Crittenden, and they estimated that three-fourths or

26. The persons writing to Crittenden were, in the order mentioned: Jas. B. Murray, Dec. 22; Samuel T. Suit, Jan. 20; Edwin Croswell, Dec. 24; F. T. and B. W. Ward of Maysville, Ky., Dec. 27; H. M. Fowlkes of Wintopock, Va., Jan. 13; all in Crittenden MSS.

Of the many writers who assured him of the public sentiment in favor of his compromise, the following, all in the Crittenden MSS., are especially relevant: James DePeyster Ogden, New York, Dec. 29, Jan. 12 and 19; S. Baldwin, New York, Jan. 11; Charles Augustus Davis, New York, Jan. 7; Enoch Van Aken, New York, Jan. 19; S. S. Haddock, West Lebanon, N. Y., Dec. 18; O. Blenis, Salina, N. Y., Jan. 29; Matthew Carey Lea, Philadelphia, Pa., Jan. 7; Robert S. Kennedy, Stewartsville, N. J., Jan. 5; J. H. Reed, Greenwich, Conn., Jan. 17; James F. Noble, Cincinnati, O., Dec. 3; Wallace Perkins, Canton, O., Dec. 20; Isaac N. Phipps, Indianapolis, Ind., Jan. 18; John Dougherty Defrees, Washington, Jan. 5, claiming that a majority of 50,000 in Indiana favored the Crittenden plan; Benjamin S. Adams, Louisville, Ky., Dec. 28, claiming the region south of the National Road almost unanimously for compromise; Thomas G. Edwards and others, Dubuque, Ia., Jan. 26; W. Selden Gale, Galesburg, Ill., Jan. 24; R. M. Clelland, Detroit, Mich., Jan. 30, to Moses Kelley; David Wilson, Baltimore, O., Jan. 16; J. P. Hall, Glasgow, Ky., Jan. 8; John Eaker, Mayfield, Ky., Jan. 23; "Your Friend," Scott County, Ky., Feb. 3; Benjamin J. Darneille, Buckingham C. H., Va., Jan. 10; Thomas Whitworth, Mayfield, Va., Jan. 19; C. W. Andrews, Shepherdstown, Va., Dec. 31; Edward Dumas, Barnesville, Ga., Jan. 23; N. M. Ludlow, Mobile, Ala., Jan. 1.

four-fifths of the Northern people would sanction any reasonable concession.[27]

Aside from these personal utterances, various other developments testified to the force and extent of the public desire for compromise. One such evidence is to be found in the petitions which were presented to Congress during the winter. While the evaluation of petitions is always a tricky problem, one can safely assert that such numerous and widely distributed signatures as appeared on these petitions could not possibly have been gathered without substantial public support. If they were, in fact, what they purported to be, it meant that, in New York City alone, 63,000 signers endorsed the Crittenden plan; in Pennsylvania, 4,000 working men, at a public meeting, did likewise; in Massachusetts, several towns produced a greater number of signers for Crittenden in December than of Republican voters in the preceding month; for other states and local communities, from Maine to Missouri, petitions, to be presented to Congress, poured in almost daily during the period when the Crittenden Compromise remained a live issue.[28]

Another type of evidence, of which no analysis will be attempted here, is the evidence of the public mass meetings in Northern metropolitan centers. In New York, one of the greatest of these rallies was held, under relatively placid circumstances, at the Cooper Union on January 28.[29] But in Philadelphia, the Union meeting was called

27. Letters to Robert J. Breckinridge from Charles Hodge, Princeton, N. J., Jan. 10 (estimate, 4/5); R. L. Allen, New York, Jan. 21 (estimate, 3/4); William McDaniel, Canonsburg, Pa., Jan. 21; all in Breckinridge Papers in Library of Congress.

28. For the New York City petitions, see *Cong. Globe,* p. 657; workers' petition, *ibid.,* p. 634; petitions from Massachusetts, *ibid.,* p. 862. In presenting the Massachusetts petition, Crittenden stressed the fact that Boston, with 19,000 voters, had yielded 14,000 signatures. Scituate, with 350 voters, of whom 195 had been Republicans, yielded 318. Ballardville, 54 voters, 41 signatures; Wendell, 77 Republican voters, 107 signatures; Cohasset, 128 Republican voters, 142 signatures. The *Globe* contains numerous entries throughout the session showing the introduction of petitions in favor of compromise. Petitions in favor of the Crittenden proposals appear in profusion from Jan. 2 to Mar. 1, pp. 237-1300.

29. See above, p. 122.

by Mayor Henry (a supporter of Lincoln) for December 13, in Independence Square, after he had warned the owner of Concert Hall that a lecture by George William Curtis, abolitionist sympathizer, might cause a riot— a prospect which the mayor evidently viewed with equanimity, for he had publicly deplored his lack of power to prevent Curtis from speaking. Curtis' speech was thereupon canceled, and the rally in Independence Square drew a huge audience. In Boston, also, the radicals fared ill. A meeting in memory of John Brown was broken up; Wendell Phillips was menaced by a mob of a thousand hostile Bostonians; and, in February, the mayor presided over a great Union meeting in Faneuil Hall.[30]

Editorial comment, too, might be cited to show the strength of the compromise movement,[31] but, perhaps, two other general observations will suffice. One comes from the pen of that zealous Republican and slavery exclusionist, Horace Greeley, who, some years after the crisis, expressed his belief that the advocates of the Crittenden Compromise had, "with good reason, claimed a large majority of the people in its favor," and that, if it had been submitted to a popular vote, many Republicans "would have refrained from voting at all, while their adversaries would have brought every man to the polls in its support, and carried it by hundreds of thousands."[32] The other comment is that of James Ford Rhodes, who

30. For Philadelphia, see Rhodes, *Hist. of U. S.*, III, 172-173; for Boston, see *ibid.*, and also Pierce, *Sumner*, IV, 18. The latter shows that, at the Faneuil Hall meeting, Edward Everett, A. A. Lawrence, and Robert C. Winthrop accepted service on a committee to go to Washington to work for the Crittenden Compromise. Letters to Crittenden from Everett, Dec. 23, and Lawrence, Jan. 12, appear in Crittenden MSS.

31. "There can be no doubt that Crittenden's plan of adjustment, if submitted to a direct vote of the people, would be adopted by such a vote as never was polled in this country." Richmond *Whig*, Jan. 28, and a similar statement, Jan. 17, quoted by Rhodes, *Hist. of U. S.*, III, 263; the New York *Herald*, Dec. 9, 14, 15, 16, 21, Jan. 12, and other dates emphasized the extent of the popular demand for compromise.

32. Horace Greeley, *The American Conflict, etc.* (Hartford, 1864–66), I, 380; Horace Greeley, *Recollections of a Busy Life* (New York, 1868), p. 397.

had no predisposition to underestimate Republican strength, but who nevertheless concluded that "no doubt can now exist, and but little could have existed in January 1861, that if it [the Crittenden plan] had been submitted to the people, it would have carried the Northern States by a great majority [and] . . . that it would have obtained the vote of almost every man in the border States."[33] If these conclusions are valid, as the preponderance of evidence indicates, it means that when Lincoln moved to defeat compromise, he did not move as the champion of democracy, but as a partisan leader.

In order to achieve any compromise, two conditions are essential: one party must agree to offer concessions, and the other must agree to accept them. Therefore, unless the South wanted compromise and would have accepted it, it would be fallacious to regard Republican refusal to offer terms as equivalent to Republican defeat of compromise proposals. If the secessionists *per se*, with their hatred of the Union, and the Southern nationalists, with their dream of a separate Southern destiny, represented Southern sentiment, then compromise aspirations were at all times illusory. Thus, a final evaluation of the merit of Republican policy must rest upon a consideration of the temper of the Southern groups with whom the Republicans had to deal.

Just as the abolitionists held a conspicuous place in the Northern political scene, so the "fire-eating" secessionists enjoyed great prominence in Dixie. In both cases, however, the extremism and melodramatic behavior of the spokesmen gained for their causes publicity quite incommensurate with the popular strength of their programs. Consequently, in an analysis of the temper of the South in the secession crisis, it is necessary to take account of the fire-eaters, without accepting literally their pretensions.

Unfortunately for the cause of peace, the more rabid type of secessionist was fully represented in Congress. In

33. Rhodes, *Hist. of U. S.,* III, 261.

the Senate, Alfred Iverson of Georgia, Louis T. Wigfall
of Texas, James M. Mason of Virginia, and Thomas L.
Clingman of North Carolina, displayed great fierceness
toward the "Black Republicans." In the House, there was
an array of such men, of whom Thomas C. Hindman of
Arkansas may be mentioned as typical because "it seemed
as if he was perpetually anxious to have a duel."[34] Men of
this sort incessantly denied that any compromise could
prevent secession,[35] demanded the extension of slavery to
all the territories,[36] and expressed such arrogance and
animosity as to chill every impulse of good will in the
Republican ranks.[37] On two occasions, at least, they
repelled friendly overtures with exceptional brusqueness:
first, on the passage of the motion authorizing the Committee of Thirty-three, when twelve of them refused to
vote on the ground that no action by the House could
avail, since secession was already determined;[38] second, on

34. Cox, *Three Decades,* p. 96.

35. E.g., Iverson, declaring himself opposed to the appointment of
the Committee of Thirteen, inquired, "I want to know of what value any
concessions, any guarantees, or any pledges from the northern States
will be to the South? None, as long as this vitiated public sentiment of
anti-slavery exists." In Senate, Dec. 11, *Cong. Globe,* p. 50. Wigfall asserted that nothing short of a resolution affirming the right of secession
would induce the Gulf States to entertain compromise proposals. In
Senate, *ibid.,* p. 1373.

36. *Cong. Globe* shows such demands in Senate, by Wigfall, Dec. 11
(p. 57); resolutions of Jefferson Davis, Dec. 24 (p. 190); and speech of
Toombs, Jan. 7 (p. 268).

37. Iverson declared in the Senate, Dec. 5, "There is an enmity between the northern and southern people that is deep and enduring, and
you never can eradicate it—never! . . . I believe that the northern people
hate the South worse than ever the English people hated France; and I
can tell my brethren over there that there is no love lost on the part of
the South." *Ibid.,* p. 12. Wigfall deliberately baited the Northern
senators with such provocations as the statement, "The Star of the West
swaggered into Charleston harbor, received a blow planted full in the
face, and staggered out. Your flag has been insulted; redress it, if you
dare. You have submitted to it for two months, and you will submit to
it forever." In Senate, Mar. 2, *ibid.,* p. 1373.

Also note the rude rejection by Iverson and Mason of friendly overtures by Hale, Dec. 10, and Cameron, Jan. 21. *Ibid.,* pp. 34, 494–495.

38. In House, Dec. 4, *ibid.,* p. 7. On that occasion, Singleton of
Miss. said, "I was not sent here for the purpose of making any com-

the day after the Committee of Thirty-three voted to offer "any reasonable, proper, and constitutional remedies, and additional and more specific and effectual guarantees,"[39] when thirty Southern senators and representatives rejected this appeasement in a manifesto to their constituents declaring that "The argument is exhausted. All hope of relief in the Union through the agencies of committees, Congressional legislation, or constitutional amendments is extinguished, and we trust the South will not be deceived by appearances or the pretense of new guarantees."[40]

The Republicans, in response to this treatment, either felt or pretended to feel that it was vain for them to offer concessions. When Seward, after long delay, at last spoke of the possibility of coercion, he explained that he did so only because "I have learned . . . that neither any suggestion that has been made yet . . . nor any that that convention [the Washington Peace Convention] can make . . . or any other that has yet been projected, will be satisfactory to [the] . . . interest of secession or disunion." In a similar vein, he wrote to his family that there was much "Vaporing by Southern Senators. Setting forth the grievances of their section and requiring Northern Senators to answer, excuse, and offer terms, which they are told, in the same breath, will not be accepted." To

promise, or to patch up existing difficulties." Hawkins of Fla. said, "I am opposed, and I believe my state is opposed, to all and every compromise." Clopton of Ala. said, "Believing that . . . the only remedy for present evils is secession, I will not hold out any delusive hope, or sanction any temporizing policy." Miles of S. C. said, "The South Carolina delegation have not voted on this question because they conceive they have no interest in it. We consider our state as already withdrawn from the Confederacy in everything except in form." Pugh of Ala. said, "As my State of Alabama intends following South Carolina out of the Union, . . . I pay no attention to any action taken in this body."

39. See above, p. 97.

40. Text of manifesto in Nicolay and Hay, *Lincoln*, II, 436. The signers were Senators Iverson of Ga., Davis and Brown of Miss., Slidell and Benjamin of La., and Wigfall and Hemphill of Texas, and 23 representatives; Ga., 5; Ala., 5; S. C., 4; Miss., 3; N. C., 2; and Tex., La., Fla., and Ark., 1 each.

Lincoln he wrote, "I think that they [the Gulf States] could not be arrested, even if we should offer . . . the restoration of the Missouri Compromise line. But persons acting for those States, intimate that they might be so arrested, because they think that the Republicans are not going to concede the restoration of that line."[41] This consideration was also recognized outside of the Republican camp, for the New York *Herald* observed: "Of all the obstructions which stand in the way of a Union saving compromise, the most embarrassing to Northern conservative men is the belief that so overwhelmingly strong, impetuous, and irresistible is the cause of disunion in the Southern states that it cannot be now arrested by any peace offerings whatsoever. The impression has become almost universal in the North that all parties and all classes of our Southern brethren have been drawn into and are borne along by this resistless current of revolution so that none of them are disposed any longer to believe in or listen to any terms of reconciliation."[42]

Without denying the evident fact that the animosity of the fire-eaters repelled conciliatory expressions from the Republican ranks, it is important to avoid assuming the ostensible corollary that the Republican refusal to offer terms was motivated primarily by a conviction that such terms would be rejected because of a Southern preference for secession *per se*. Far from overestimating the separatist tendencies of the South, the Republicans actually underestimated them, and were constantly expecting a Unionist element to assert itself and gain the ascendancy.[43] With such an emphatic belief that Unionism in the South needed only to be encouraged, they could not have sincerely believed that conciliatory offers would evoke no response among Southerners.

41. Seward, speech in Senate, Jan. 31, in *Cong. Globe,* p. 680; letters to his wife, Dec. 11, and to Lincoln, Dec. 26, in Seward, *Seward,* II, 481, 485. Henry Adams, "Secession Winter," in Mass. Hist. Soc., *Proc.,* XLIII, 667, expresses the same idea.

42. New York *Herald,* Jan. 16.

43. See below, ch. IX.

Moreover, if they had felt certain that the South would reject all peace offers, it would have been to their tactical and moral advantage to make an offer and force the South to accept the responsibility for defeating it.[44] But they preferred not to jeopardize their hypothesis of Southern intransigence by attempting to demonstrate it, and no feasible plan of adjustment was ever tendered.

Rather than admit, however, that they had been instrumental in denying the South an opportunity to accept compromise terms, Republican apologists sought to fix upon Southerners the responsibility for rejecting them, and in lieu of a genuine rejection they made much of the fact that Toombs and Davis voted against the Crittenden Compromise in the Committee of Thirteen,[45] and that six Southern senators—Benjamin and Slidell of Louisiana, Hemphill and Wigfall of Texas, Iverson of Georgia, and Johnson of Arkansas—refrained from voting when two of their votes would have brought the Crittenden resolutions before the Senate.[46]

44. Gov. Thomas H. Hicks of Md. wrote to Crittenden, Jan. 25, "Why do the Northern members say 'we will do certain things if you of the South will be satisfied with it'. Why will not the fools, *do them,* if they think it right, and put such fool hardy Southern members at fault. . . ." Crittenden MSS.

45. John Minor Botts in 1866 (*The Great Rebellion,* p. 189) asserted that Davis and Toombs defeated the Crittenden Compromise. For an example of the continued currency of this error in 1941, see Henrietta Buchmaster, *Let My People Go, The Story of the Underground Railroad and the Growth of the Abolition Movement* (New York, 1941).

46. On a motion in Senate, Jan. 16, to take up the Crittenden resolutions, resolutions of Senator Clark were adopted as a substitute by a vote of 25 to 23, with the six Democrats not voting. *Cong. Globe,* p. 409. Had the Clark resolutions been defeated, the Crittenden resolutions would have come before the Senate.

The effort to fix blame for this action upon Southern senators began, Jan. 17, when Crittenden telegraphed to Unionist friends in North Carolina, "the vote against my resolutions will be reconsidered. Their failure was the result of the refusal of six Southern Senators to vote. There is yet good hope of success." Nicolay and Hay, *Lincoln,* III, 227. Stephen A. Douglas condemned the nonvoting senators, in Senate, Jan. 31. *Cong. Globe,* p. 661. Andrew Johnson emphasized their responsibility in a Senate speech, Jan. 31, 1862. *Cong. Globe,* 37th cong., 2nd sess., p. 587.

In two respects, validity is lacking in this contention that Southern senators deliberately caused the defeat of compromise. First, some of the senators in question were actuated not by hostility to Crittenden's plan but by a suspicion that the hope of compromise, destined never to be fulfilled, was being used deliberately to divide the South and to delay secession past the opportune moment— perhaps until coercive measures could be prepared. Later events were to show that this suspicion was not entirely baseless.[47] In the case of the Committee of Thirteen, it is evident that Toombs and Davis voted as they did primarily because they did not wish to deceive the South and to delay Southern action by arousing false hopes of compromise. Accordingly, they gave notice in the committee that they would oppose any measure which the Republicans should oppose.[48] This action was not necessary under the rule requiring a majority of each faction in favor of any measure, before it could be reported to the Senate.[49] But the testimony of Vice President Breckinridge, of Senators Crittenden and Douglas, and even of Toombs himself, establishes the fact that Davis and Toombs would have voted for the Crittenden resolutions if the Republican senators had done so.[50] Toombs is credited

47. See below, pp. 295–297.
48. Ulrich B. Phillips, *The Life of Robert Toombs* (New York, 1913), p. 207.
49. Toombs and Davis evidently wished to fix the blame for the defeat of the compromise upon the Republicans. Yet they voted against it when Republican votes alone would have defeated it, under the rule. Why?
No evidence furnishes even a tentative solution of this problem. Perhaps the most likely surmise is that of U. B. Phillips, in *ibid.*, p. 207, that the rule, although listed in the journal as the first business of the committee, was not adopted until after the first vote on the Crittenden resolutions, and that the votes of Davis and Toombs were therefore cast, in accordance with their notice, to prevent the adoption of the resolution over a united Republican opposition. One might also surmise that the two cotton-states senators did not wish to cast votes abandoning their claim that all territories should be open to slavery, unless Republicans abandoned the contrary claim that none should. Or perhaps they were avoiding the humiliation of asking for a settlement which was sure to be refused.
50. Rhodes, *Hist. of U. S.*, III, 154-155, presents copious evidence to

with the remark, in committee, that he personally did not regard the compromise as acceptable, but that his state would accept it, and he would go with his state.[51]

In the case of the six senators who withheld their votes, their purposes were probably less uniform than those of Toombs and Davis, but some of them seem to have been motivated primarily by a belief that the Republicans would never permit the fulfillment of compromise plans, and that the illusion of compromise was deliberately used to inhibit Southern action. All of them were influenced in some measure by the fact that, on the same motion, the Republicans voted unanimously to prevent the Crittenden resolutions from coming to the Senate floor.[52]

prove this point. The ten sources which he cites are corroborated by a speech of John C. Breckinridge, in Senate, July 16, 1861: "I happened personally to know . . . that the leading statesmen of the lower southern States were willing to accept the terms of settlement which were proposed by the venerable Senator from Kentucky, my predecessor [Crittenden]." *Cong. Globe*, 37th Cong., 1st sess., p. 142.

51. Crittenden told S. S. Cox of this remark. Cox, *Three Decades*, p. 77.

52. Two of the Southern senators, Johnson of Arkansas and Wigfall of Texas, stated these motives on the Senate floor, Jan. 31. *Cong. Globe*, pp. 661, 665–667.

The statement of Wigfall, while not entirely candid on the part of an ardent secessionist, was very forceful: "They [the Republicans] happen temporarily to be in a minority . . . but . . . they represent the majority party. Without their assent, without their cordial aid and cooperation, we know that the Constitution cannot be amended; that no compromise can be made. What, then, was the use of our stultifying ourselves? What was the use of our sitting here, and voting down resolutions which expressed the opinion of the dominant party of the country, in order that the Senator from Illinois [Douglas] might write letters, or telegraph to different States, that the Union was about to be saved; . . . I did not intend to make myself a party to the fraud; and therefore, . . . I, for one, forebore to vote. . . .

"Under these circumstances, I chose to vote against reconsidering the vote on Mr. Clark's resolution; because the entire Republican party had voted against reconsidering; because the Republican who had moved a reconsideration [Cameron] himself voted against it; because I saw not the slightest evidence of relenting; because I had heard from that side nothing which looked to compromise or concession, or a recognition of our rights. . . . And then, because I do not choose to make a ninny of myself, because I do not choose to stultify myself, and vote for resolutions that mean nothing, in order that Senators may telegraph over the

Regardless of the objects of these Southern senators, however, the argument which would fix upon them the responsibility for the congressional defeat of compromise is fallacious in a second respect: from a quantitative standpoint, it is evident that the adverse votes of Davis and Toombs had no decisive effect, while those of the five Republicans defeated the Crittenden plan in committee. It is equally evident that the hostile votes of twenty-five Republicans were far more decisive than the abstention of six Democrats, in denying the same resolutions a hearing before the Senate. Granted the provocation offered, and the rancor generated, by the fire-eaters, it still does not appear that they prevented Congress from offering compromise.

It is one of the misfortunes of the literature of vindication, by both Northern and Southern apologists, that it has overemphasized these tactical maneuvers in Congress. Far more significant than all the disputed by-play of congressional manipulation is the undisputed fact that no compromise was tendered by one section, or requested by the other. This was true, in one case, because the leaders who might have made such a tender preferred to adhere to the Chicago Platform; and, in the other case, because the leaders who might have made such a request preferred to invoke secession. Yet in neither instance is there any convincing evidence that the policies adopted were the policies desired by the ordinary men and women who had to bear the consequences. The Unionists of the country—even the unconditional Unionists—were not preponderantly in favor of the Chicago Platform. Similarly, the Southerners, who almost unanimously upheld what they believed to be their sectional rights, were not preponderantly in favor of secession. The fire-eaters, occupying a strategic political position, forced it upon them, just as Lincoln and his faction, in their strategic position, over-

country that all is peace and quiet—because I do not choose to do that, or to be led by the nose as tenderly as asses are, I am charged with a conspiracy with the Black Republicans . . . to prevent any compromise."

rode the conciliationists of the North. It was this policy of the fire-eaters toward the lower South, and not their hectoring of the Republicans in Congress, which gave them such fateful importance in the failure of peace.

At no time during the winter of 1860–1861 was secession desired by a majority of the people of the slave states. In proof of this, it is only necessary to cite the miserable failure, until after the war began, of the secession program in Arkansas, Missouri, Kentucky, Tennessee, Maryland, Delaware, Virginia, and North Carolina.[53] Furthermore, secession was not basically desired even by a majority in the lower South, and the secessionists succeeded less because of the intrinsic popularity of their program than because of the extreme skill with which they utilized an emergency psychology, the promptness with which they invoked unilateral action by individual states, and the firmness with which they refused to submit the question of secession to popular referenda.

In the earliest stage of the secession activity, shortly after Lincoln's election, an ardent South Carolina separationist frankly conceded that public opinion did not support disunion. "I do not believe that the common people understand it," he wrote, "in fact I know that they do not understand it; but whoever waited for the common people when a great move was to be made. We must make the move and force them to follow."[54]

Although few other secession leaders were equally candid, this statement seems to have expressed an attitude which was typical of many of them. Instead of encouraging any true deliberation, the secessionists dramatically urged haste, with such emotional appeals as that of Judge Charles Gayarré: "The fourth of March is rushing upon the citizens like a fiery steed; and deliberation must now give way to action when Barbarians are at the foot of the

53. See below, pp. 312–313.
54. A. P. Aldrich to James H. Hammond, Nov. 25, quoted from Hammond MSS. by Lillian A. Kibler, "Unionist Sentiment in South Carolina in 1860," in *Journal of Southern History*, IV (1938), 358.

capitol."[55] Clearly, they wished to make the most of the excitement and apprehension which Lincoln's election had aroused, to induce action under the stimulus of such excitement, and, once such action had been taken, to prevent its submission to the test of public approval.

Of the seven states of the original Confederacy, only one, and it the last—Texas—submitted its ordinance of secession to popular ratification. In each of the others, except South Carolina, moderate delegates in the conventions argued that so drastic a measure as secession, or, later, adherence to the Confederate Constitution, ought to be sanctioned by direct popular endorsement, and in each such case their proposals for a referendum were defeated in convention.[56] James L. Petigru had already foreseen that the secessionists were afraid "to trust the second thought of even their own people,"[57] and many other Southerners condemned this precipitate policy. The Alexandria (La.) *Constitutional* flatly charged that the secessionists "will not submit the constitution to the people, because there are sufficient co-operationists to vote it down."[58] A delegate, from one of the up-river parishes, in the Louisiana convention, solemnly protested that, "Convened without authority from the people of the State, and refusing to submit its action to them for their sanction in the grave and vital act of changing their government, this Convention violates the great fundamental principle of American government, that the will of the people is supreme."[59] The New Orleans *Picayune* expressed an even

55. Quoted in Willie Malvin Caskey, *Secession and Restoration of Louisiana* (University, La., 1938), p. 22.

56. The various motions to submit secession to popular referendum appear in the published journals of the conventions of the respective states.

57. Petigru to Mrs. Jane Petigru North, Nov. 13, 1860, quoted by Kibler, "Unionist Sentiment in S. C.," in *Jour. Southern Hist.*, VI, 362.

58. Alexandria *Constitutional*, Mar. 30, quoted by Caskey, *Secession and Restoration of La.*, p. 242, note 46. Also see p. 244, note 67.

59. Statement of James G. Taliaferro, delegate of Catahoula parish, first published in New Orleans *Crescent*, Jan. 31, and reprinted by Roger Wallace Shugg, ed., "A Suppressed Co-operationist Protest Against Secession," in *Louisiana Historical Quarterly*, XIX (1936), 199–203.

more sweeping criticism: "We charge that the Alabama, Georgia, and Louisiana Conventions by usurping the rights of the people to decide on the merits of the Constitution framed for their government . . . gave new and startling evidence of their distrust of the people, and thus furnished strong testimony . . . that the South was divided, and that the movement in which we are now engaged, has not the sanction of the great body of the people."[60] Most pointed of all criticisms, however, was that of the New York *Express*, which shrewdly pointed out the analogy between the Northern slavery exclusionists who refused to submit territorial compromise to a popular referendum,[61] and the Southern separationists who refused to submit the ordinances of secession to popular ratification.[62]

If the secession cause lacked substantial popular support within the individual states, even more did it lack strength in the South as a whole. Consequently, secessionists were obliged to achieve their purpose through the piecemeal acts of the individual states rather than through the action of the South in unison. This disunion activity, which its protagonists publicized, and which historians have accepted, as a "Southern movement," was

60. New Orleans *Daily Picayune*, Mar. 29, quoted by Caskey, *Secession and Restoration of La.*, p. 38.

Northern papers in general, and the New York *Tribune* in particular, repeatedly asserted that the secessionists were afraid, because of their weakness, to submit secession to a popular vote. On Feb. 1, James S. Pike wrote in the *Tribune*, "They [the secessionists] are even weak now at home, as the refusal in several of the seceding States to submit the Secession ordinances to the people, and the light vote for the Secession Conventions, plainly show." On April 11, the *Tribune* remarked upon the statement of a certain fusionist that it was a mistake to suppose that a strong Union sentiment existed in the South. "A mistake is it?" said the *Tribune*. "Then why don't the rebels submit their Confederate Constitution to a vote of their own people?"

61. After Senator Crittenden failed to gain congressional support, he sought to appeal to public opinion. To this end, he introduced, on Jan. 3, a resolution declaring that his resolutions of territorial compromise ought to be submitted to popular referendum. *Cong. Globe*, p. 237. Thereafter, the compromisers in Congress made this resolution their chief issue.

62. New York *Express*, quoted by New York *Tribune*, Mar. 22.

not, in the sense of volition, a "Southern" movement at all, and no one knew this better than the secessionists themselves. Because of this knowledge, they renounced at the outset any "co-operationist" effort to coordinate the action of the several states through a convention in which all Southern states would be represented. Because of this knowledge, also, they resorted to unilateral action, in order that the secessionist act of one state might influence the decision and force the hand of neighbor states.[63] In this unilateral action, they possessed the great strategic advantage of being able to change the issue from one of the desirability of secession, on which the South was hopelessly divided, to one of the right of secession, on which the South was approximately united. The states of the upper South did not want the issue to take this form, for they believed in the doctrine and deplored its exercise, but they were helpless in the hands of the precipitationists. When war came, four states which had refused to invoke secession on their own account, felt themselves compelled to invoke it in support of seceded states.

The four years of conflict which ensued caused most Southerners to forget how sharply they had been divided, but, for a time, the men of the upper South knew that their hand was being forced, and they resented it. In January, Governor Letcher of Virginia protested publicly, in his message to the legislature, against the efforts of South Carolina and others to draw the Border into secession.[64] The same protest appeared more freely in the press, where

63. "Commercial relations will force Georgia out [of the Union], for she cannot afford to have a string of customs houses on her Alabama, Florida, South Carolina, and perhaps Tennessee frontiers." Augusta [Ga.] *Daily Constitutionalist*, Dec. 30, quoted by Dumond, ed., *Southern Editorials on Secession*, p. 380.

In the "Declaration of the Causes which impel the State of Texas to secede from the Federal Union," appears the statement: "By the secession of six of the slaveholding States, and the certainty that others will speedily do likewise, Texas has no alternative but to remain in an isolated connection with the North, or unite her destinies with the South." *Journal of the Secession Convention of Texas, 1861* (Austin, 1861), pp. 61–66.

64. Bancroft, *Seward*, II, 11, citing Richmond *Enquirer*, Jan. 8. Shanks, *Secession in Virginia*, p. 143.

the Raleigh *North Carolina Standard* warned that "if any one State shall secede, with the expectation of drawing other States after her . . . the states thus forced out . . . will dislike her and watch her as an evil star in the new constellation."[65] Later in the course of the crisis, the Charlottesville (Va.) *Review* declared, "we entertain toward South Carolina the most bitter resentment. We feel that she has not only precipitately thrown down the bulwarks of the Union, and inaugurated on her own responsibility revolution and anarchy; but she has done so with the full knowledge—aye, the intention—to hold Virginia and the border States between her and the Storm, and to carry out her caprices while relying on them."[66]

This foreboding of the Border moderates that the lower South would precipitate a conflict in order to force them to take sides, was, in a measure, justified. Some of the ardent secessionists did deliberately seek to create a situation —even one of hostilities—which would compel the Border to abandon its position of peaceful Unionism. It was in the avowed pursuance of this purpose that Governor Pickens of South Carolina proposed, on February 12, to begin military operations against Fort Sumter. "He did not desire," according to his own statement, "that the border states should patch up a . . . disgraceful Union with the North, and he thought that perhaps the immediate

65. Raleigh *North Carolina Standard*, Dec. 1, in Dumond, ed., *Southern Editorials on Secession*, p. 286.

66. Charlottesville *Review*, Jan. 4, in Dumond, ed., *Southern Editorials on Secession*, p. 389. Dumond also reprints editorials from the New Orleans *Daily Picayune*, Dec. 8, discussing the "New Lines of Sectionalism" between upper and lower South (p. 309); the Louisville [Ky.] *Daily Courier*, Dec. 20, remarking upon the complaint voiced in the Border states against the precipitancy of South Carolina (p. 357); the New Orleans *Bee*, Dec. 28, on the same subject (p. 375); and the Wilmington [N. C.] *Daily Herald*, Nov. 9, putting a question as to the people of North Carolina: "Will they *submit*, to be dragged into revolution and anarchy, and all to please the State of South Carolina, who, by her insufferable arrogance . . . has been a constant source of annoyance . . . to the whole country. . . . We say unhesitatingly, that there are no two adjoining States in the Union, whose people have so little community of feeling as North and South Carolina" (pp. 227–228).

possession of the Fort might be necessary to open a gulf between the border states and the North so deep that it could never be closed, and perhaps it would be politic to do this, even at the expense of bloodshed."[67] Roger A. Pryor proposed the same dire policy more succinctly when he declaimed to a Charleston audience, *"I will tell you, gentlemen, what will put her [Virginia] in the Southern Confederation in less than an hour by Shrewsbury clock—STRIKE A BLOW! The very moment that blood is shed, old Virginia will make common cause with her sisters of the South."*[68]

By an unhesitating use of their strategic advantages—that is, by making the decision of hastily elected conventions final on the question of secession, and by exercising an unmerciful leverage upon the state-rights Unionists of the Border states—the fire-eaters ultimately carried their program to completion. Even in these circumstances, however, the opposition which they encountered was stubborn and the margin of their success was far more narrow than the later solidarity of the Confederacy indicated. In every one of the Gulf states, except South Carolina, secession was accomplished only after a sharp contest, and even in the Palmetto State, Unionist elements were far stronger than they appeared to be.[69] Without examining these state contests in detail, it will suffice to note certain basic facts. First, in the election of delegates to the conventions, the moderates fought hard against immediate secessionists.

67. Letter of Pickens to Toombs, Feb. 12, in Samuel W. Crawford, *The Genesis of the Civil War. The Story of Sumter* (New York, 1887), p. 270. The quotation is not of Pickens' direct words, but of Crawford's paraphrase.

68. Speech of Apr. 10, quoted from Charleston *Mercury,* in Edward McPherson, *The Political History of the United States . . . during the Great Rebellion, etc.* (Washington, 1865), p. 112. McPherson also cites a statement by Jeremiah Clemens of Ala., that secessionists in that state had demanded military action because "unless you sprinkle blood in the face of the people of Alabama they will be back in the old Union in less than ten days."

69. Lillian A. Kibler, "Unionist Sentiment in S. C.," in *Jour. Southern Hist.,* IV, 346-366, provides a very able discussion.

For the most part, the election returns for these contests are not available, or do not lend themselves to exact interpretation. But in cases where tentative analyses are possible, the opposition to immediate secession consistently appears substantial. After the elections in South Carolina and Florida, Mississippi elected her secession convention on December 20. In a total of 41,000 votes cast, nearly 12,000 are not subject to analysis. Of the remainder, 16,874 were cast in favor of immediate secessionists and 12,218 against them. Four days later, in the Alabama election, the opponents of immediate secession cast a vote estimated at 28,181, but 35,693 ballots were against them. Georgia went to the polls on January 2, and registered a decision in favor of immediate secession by a vote of 50,243 to 37,123. Five days in the wake of Georgia, Louisiana indicated a similar preference, on the same question, by a vote of 20,448 to 17,296.[70] If these figures err seriously, it is apparently on the side of the separationists. But, even accepting them at face value, they show the strength of the moderates and the weakness of the secessionists in two striking aspects: first, in each one of the states in question, the foes of immediate secession are credited with at least 42 per cent of the determinable vote;[71] second, in not one case did the precipitationists secure a vote large enough to have constituted a majority of the vote cast by the state in the presidential election of a few weeks earlier.[72]

70. Rainwater, *Mississippi, 1856–1861*, p. 200; Denman, *Secession in Alabama*, p. 116; I. W. Avery, *History of the State of Georgia from 1850 to 1881* (New York, 1881), p. 149; Caskey, *Secession and Restoration in La.*, p. 37.

71. The percentage vote against immediate secession is: Miss., 41.9; Ala., 44.2; Ga., 42.4; La., 45.8.

72. In the two columns below, are the total vote cast in the presidential election (as shown in Stanwood, *History of the Presidency, 1788–1897*, p. 297), and the vote for immediate secessionists.

Mississippi	69,120	16,874, plus part of 12,000 indeterminate
Alabama	90,357	35,693
Georgia	106,365	50,243
Louisiana	50,690	20,448

Apart from the popular election of the conventions, the strength of the moderates was again manifested within the conventions themselves. At first glance, the extent of their force is not evident, for they did not show their full strength on the adoption of the ordinances of secession. Because of a desire to present a united front in the crisis, they avoided making an issue of these final acts. But on proposals to delay, or to make their action contingent on something else, they deployed their entire force, which, except in Mississippi, was strong. There the conservatives lost, by a vote of 70 to 29, their motion to submit secession to a popular ratification.[73] But in Florida, 30 delegates voted to await the action of Georgia and Alabama, and only 39 opposed.[74] In Alabama, 45 delegates recommended a convention of Southern states at Nashville, voted to await the action of such a convention, and proposed a basis for settlement of sectional issues within the Union. This policy met the opposition of 54 delegates, and was defeated.[75] In Georgia, the conservatives were prevented from securing a direct vote on their resolution naming terms on which Georgia would remain in the Union, but the parliamentary skirmishing showed that their minority was only 130 to 166.[76] Thus the secessionists were in the ascendancy by a margin of only 9 delegates out of 69 in Florida, of only 9 out of 99 in Alabama, and of only 36 out of 296 in Georgia. A reversal of 5 votes in Florida, 5 in Alabama, and 19 in Georgia would have gone far to arrest the whole secession movement.[77]

73. Rainwater, *Mississippi, 1856–1861,* p. 211.

74. Dorothy Dodd, "The Secession Movement in Florida, 1851–1861," in *Florida Historical Quarterly,* XII (1933), 61.

75. Dumond, *Secession Movement,* p. 203.

76. Ulrich B. Phillips, *Georgia and State Rights,* in American Historical Association, *Annual Report,* 1901, II, 203.

77. This opposition to immediate secession was not openly Unionist, except in a very few cases, but was usually designated as "co-operationist." Much confusion of interpretation results from the fact that some historians treat "co-operation" as a mere modification of secessionism, while others treat it as if it were equivalent to Unionism (e.g., see Caskey, *Secession and Restoration of La.,* p. 243, note 57). The New

In each of these sharp contests, the secessionists had one great advantage: they could assert, without contradiction, that there remained no hope of receiving guarantees from the Republicans. Thirty of their congressmen had told them so in a manifesto on December 14;[78] Robert Toombs had warned that "all further looking to the North for security . . . ought to be instantly abandoned";[79] twelve of their senators, on January 5, had advised them that, "in our opinion each of the Southern States should, as soon as may be, secede from the Union";[80] news had come that the Committee of Thirteen reported itself unable to reach an agreement;[81] Southern congressmen had withdrawn from the Committee of Thirty-three;[82] and no action of

Orleans *Crescent,* Jan. 5, (quoted in *ibid.,* p. 239, note 19), said, "Here in New Orleans nobody knows exactly what cooperation means. With some it means delay, with some conference with other states, with some it means submission." Walker Brooke, delegate in the Mississippi convention, spoke of himself as a "cooperationist—which means, as I understand it, one who was in favor of united Southern action for the purpose of demanding further guarantees from the North, or failing in that, the formation of a Southern Confederacy. . . . Previous cooperation, or cooperation before secession, was the first object of my desire. Failing in this I am willing to take the next best, subsequent cooperation or cooperation after secession." Quoted by Dumond, *Secession Movement,* pp. 200–201, from *Weekly Mississippian,* Jan. 16. Cooperation certainly did not mean unconditional Unionism, for that was negligible in the lower South, but it did mean, in effect, consistent opposition to the secession program as executed.

78. See above, p. 98.

79. Telegram of Toombs to "Fellow-citizens of Georgia," Dec. 22, in Phillips, *Toombs,* p. 209.

80. Resolutions adopted by a caucus of Southern senators, Jan. 5, in *The War of the Rebellion, A Compilation of the Official Records of the Union and Confederate Armies* (Washington, 1880–1901), Series I, Vol. I, pp. 443–444 (cited hereafter as *Official Records*). The senators who sponsored this resolution were Davis and Brown of Miss., Hemphill and Wigfall of Tex., Benjamin and Slidell of La., Yulee and Mallory of Fla., Iverson and Toombs of Ga., Johnson of Ark., and Clay of Ala.

81. Report of Sen. Powell, chairman of committee, in Senate, Dec. 31, in *Cong. Globe,* p. 211.

82. The Committee of Thirty-three first met on Dec. 11. Hawkins of Fla. did not attend at all. Boyce of S. C. attended only on Dec. 12. Reuben Davis of Miss. quit the committee permanently on Dec. 19. In addition to these three "secessionists" from the committee, others absented themselves beginning on Dec. 28 (Love of Ga.), 29 (Rust of

the Republicans served to counteract these developments.

In these circumstances, without a shred of evidence that the North would extend guarantees, the Southern conservatives in Alabama, Georgia, and Florida narrowly missed committing their states to a policy of negotiating for such guarantees. If they had succeeded, there would have been no secession in Louisiana and Texas.

In a period of nine days between January 9 and 18, the four states of Mississippi, Florida, Alabama, and Georgia adopted ordinances of secession. In each of these states, a group of conservatives fought against disunion vigorously, and, in three states, almost successfully. They waged these contests under a fatal handicap: they could show no offer of compromise, nor even a gesture of good will from the party which was about to take control of the Federal government. When the secessionists said "The argument is exhausted. All hope of relief in the Union . . . is extinguished," or "All further looking to the North for security for your Constitutional rights in the Union ought to be instantly abandoned," the conservatives had no effective reply, and without it, pleaded the cause of Union in vain. Had they been armed with a reply, they could scarcely have failed to gain the narrow margin of strength which would have enabled them to uphold the Union.

It was the tragedy of the Southern state-rights Unionists—perhaps the basic tragedy of the war—that they were not supported by adequate assurances of the good will and the equitable purpose of the national Unionists of the North. Intrinsically valueless as territorial concession would have been,[83] it would have served as a symbol

Ark.), and 31 (Winslow of N. C., Taylor of La., and Houston of Ala.). These returned for the final sessions, presumably for the purpose of submitting minority reports. *Journal of Committee of 33, passim.*

This disproves the statement of Reuben Davis, in his *Recollections,* pp. 399–401, that the Southern members withdrew collectively on Dec. 16.

83. For an able discussion of the physical obstacles to the expansion of slavery, see Charles W. Ramsdell, "The Natural Limits of Slave Extension," in *Mississippi Valley Historical Review,* XVI (1929), 151–171.

of Northern recognition of Southern parity in the Union and would have strengthened Southern Unionists immeasurably. Preponderantly, citizens of the North were willing to make such a concession for such a purpose, but Republican partisan leadership prevented this gesture. Preponderantly, citizens of the South were willing to accept, and even to request, such a concession, but secessionist partisan leadership, with its reliance upon public excitement rather than public judgment, and with its unscrupulous compulsion of the Border states, prevented this. Abandoned by their potential Northern allies, Southern Unionists waged their contest in vain against the fire-eaters, and partisan leadership triumphed over the popular will.

CHAPTER IX

THE ALTERNATIVE OF VOLUNTARY
RECONSTRUCTION

AS Lincoln confronted the future in the winter of 1860–1861, he had to choose whether he would attempt to hold the Union together with or without compromise. Because compromise had connotations of peace, and the failure of compromise had connotations, increasingly, of war, it is an easy fallacy to translate the problem into a choice between the evident alternatives of peace or war. Yet the fact is that acceptance of the Crittenden Compromise did not signify, in Lincoln's mind, future tranquillity, and rejection of it did not signify a resort to arms.

As viewed from the twentieth century, the Crittenden Compromise inevitably suggests a nominal slavery status for a fixed area—the territorial region between the line 36° 30′ on the north and the Mexican border on the south. In such a concept, there is an implication of permanence, for the boundary of the Republic has not been altered since 1853, and expansion into contiguous territory has not been a political issue for three-quarters of a century. But to Lincoln in 1860, the Crittenden proposal suggested a line of demarcation for slavery on the north, and a movable Mexican border as a temporary barrier on the south. As he visualized it, there was no implication of permanence, for the boundary had been altered twice in the preceding twelve years, and a constant agitation for further expansion indicated the determination of ambitious Southerners to enlarge the slavery region.

This slavery-expansion program commanded the attention of everyone interested in public affairs, for it had been the most prominent feature of the foreign policy of the Pierce and Buchanan administrations, and it had also manifested itself in a series of spectacular filibustering expeditions which enjoyed great popularity in the South. The movement was directed against Cuba and against northern Mexico, because it was believed that slave states could readily be created in these regions.

In its diplomatic aspect, the attempt to acquire lands to the south entered an active phase during the presidency of Franklin Pierce. He concerned himself primarily with the annexation of Cuba, and instructed his minister to Spain, Pierre Soulé, to negotiate for the purchase of the island. The mission failed because of Soulé's ineptitude, coupled with the blunder of the Ostend Manifesto, which proposed that the United States procure the island by purchase, or, if that were rejected, by "wresting it from Spain."[1] But when Buchanan, a signer of the Ostend Manifesto, ran for the presidency, it was on a platform urging annexation. Like Pierce, he found the obstacles insuperable, but in three of his four annual messages he recommended the prosecution of this policy, and, in 1860, the project still received endorsement in the platforms of both branches of the Democratic party.

While giving their major attention to Cuba, neither Pierce nor Buchanan ignored the possibility of acquiring territory in Mexico. Pierce attempted to buy a large area in northern Mexico, and was successful only in achieving the Gadsden Purchase.[2] Buchanan, striving even harder, met with complete disappointment. When he made proposals of purchase, they were rejected by Mexico; when he secured from Mexico the McLane-Ocampo Treaty, which would have reduced that country almost to a protectorate, it was defeated by the American Senate; when he asked Congress for powers to assume a "temporary protectorate" over northern Chihuahua and Sonora, the request was refused, as was another request for authority

1. A. A. Ettinger, *The Mission to Spain of Pierre Soulé, 1853–1855* (New Haven, 1932).
2. P. N. Garber, *The Gadsden Treaty* (Philadelphia, 1923).

to send a military force into Mexico to obtain "indemnity for the past and security for the future."[3] But though none of these measures came to fruition, they all showed the consistent purpose of the South (as manifested through the Democratic party) to extend the area of slavery.

While these developments took place on the diplomatic front, men who yearned for prompt action turned to more direct methods. The result was a series of filibustering expeditions, first against Cuba, under the leadership of General Narciso Lopez;[4] and later against Mexico and Nicaragua, under William Walker's command.[5] Both men enjoyed a strong following in the South; both were tried and acquitted by friendly juries in New Orleans; Lopez died at the hands of a firing squad during his third attempt on Cuba, and Walker met his death in the same fashion during his third expedition to Nicaragua. But the failures of these men did not diminish the zeal of other adventurous Southerners, and in 1861 a secret organization, the Knights of the Golden Circle, was preparing to embark upon the most grandiose scheme of all—a plan to unite in one great slave empire all the rich lands that lay in a vast "golden circle" along the shores of the Gulf of Mexico.[6]

3. H. L. Wilson, "President Buchanan's Proposed Intervention in Mexico," in *American Historical Review,* V (1900), 687–701; J. M. Callahan, "The Mexican Policy of Southern Leaders under Buchanan's Administration," in American Historical Association, *Report,* 1910, pp. 125–161. J. Fred Rippy, *The United States and Mexico* (New York, 1926), pp. 212–229.

4. Robert G. Caldwell, *The Lopez Expeditions to Cuba, 1848–1851* (Princeton, 1915).

5. W. O. Scroogs, *Filibusters and Financiers: the story of William Walker and his associates* (New York, 1916); on Walker's activities in Mexico, see J. M. Clarke, "Antonio Melendrez, Nemesis of William Walker in Baja California," in *California Historical Society Quarterly,* XII (1933), 318–322.

6. Ollinger Crenshaw, "The Knights of the Golden Circle" in *American Historical Review,* XLVII (1941), 23–50; C. A. Bridges, "The Knights of the Golden Circle, A Filibustering Fantasy," in *Southwestern*

The Republicans were, of course, not oblivious to the implications of this persistent and energetic movement, and they very readily foresaw that an agreement as to the limits of slavery within the Union would in no way stabilize the situation, so long as the limits of the Union possessed no stability. In fact, the Crittenden Compromise, with its application to territory "hereafter to be acquired," seemed actually to contemplate the acquisition of additional territory south of 36° 30′. At least, such was the conviction of Republican Senator Ten Eyck of New Jersey, who asserted that he could not vote for Crittenden's territorial amendment because "In view of what I now believe to be a well-established purpose . . . in certain quarters, as shown by past events, to extend the power of this Government over Mexico, Central America, Cuba, and the islands of the sea, such an amendment . . . would, soon or late, consign this continent, south of us and north of Darien, to the influences of slavery, political and social."[7] At the previous session of Congress, Senator Doolittle likewise had condemned the Southern program of "acquisition of Cuba, Mexico, Central America, all tropical America . . . for the purpose of counter-balancing the growing power . . . of the great Caucasian race in the North and the West. Call this solution by what name you please—the solution of Walker and his filibusters; the solution of the slave propagandists, or of the Knights of the Golden Circle."[8]

This same expectation of an increasing pressure by Southern expansionists was a major reason for Lincoln's opposition to the Crittenden plan. Though his statements on the subject were few and brief, he adduced this reason on at least three occasions. In a letter to Washburne, De-

Historical Quarterly, XLIV (1941), 287–302. George Bickley, leader of the Knights, allured his followers with a prospect of 25 new slave states, and 50 new pro-slavery senators, for the American Union.

For a plan of Sam Houston for the annexation of all Mexico, see Walter P. Webb, *The Texas Rangers* (New York, 1935), pp. 197–216.

7. In Senate, Feb. 1, *Cong. Globe,* p. 682.

8. In Senate, Apr. 12, *ibid.,* 36th Cong., 1st sess., p. 1632.

cember 13, warning against adopting either popular sovereignty or territorial compromise, he predicted, "Let either be done, and immediately filibustering and extending slavery recommences." In a letter to James T. Hale, January 11, he declared that, if the concessions proposed by Crittenden should be granted, "a year will not pass 'till we shall have to take Cuba as a condition upon which they [the Southerners] will stay in the Union."[9] Finally, on February 1, when Seward and Charles Francis Adams were pressing Lincoln to consent to a measure for the admission of New Mexico as a state, presumably with slavery, he gave his reluctant assent, with certain reservations and badgered protests: "I am for no compromise which assists or permits the extension of the institution on soil owned by the nation. And any trick by which the nation is to acquire territory, and then allow some local authority to spread slavery over it, is as obnoxious as any other. I take it that to effect some such result as this, and to put us again on the high road to a slave empire, is the object of all these proposed compromises. I am against it. As to fugitive slaves, District of Columbia, slave trade among the slave States, and whatever springs of necessity from the fact that the institution is amongst us, I care but little, so that what is done be comely and not altogether outrageous. Nor do I care much about New Mexico, if further extension were hedged against."[10]

In an analysis of the validity of Lincoln's forebodings, it may be argued, with some force, that he was "borrowing" trouble, that if annexationist schemes had not succeeded under Pierce and Buchanan there was little reason to fear their success under a Republican administration, and that the choice to precipitate an existing crisis, rather than to await a possible future showdown, was an unwise decision. But, apart from all these controversial considerations, the fact remains that, to Lincoln, compromise meant

9. For texts of both letters, see above, pp. 158, 160, note 11.
10. Lincoln to Seward, Feb. 1, in Nicolay and Hay, eds., *Works of Lincoln*, VI, 102–104.

neither peace nor stability. It meant only the transition of the slavery expansion movement into a new phase. To him, therefore, the rejection of compromise did not mean the rejection of peace.

If the maintenance of the Union by compromise did not mean peace, as Lincoln saw it, it is equally true that the maintenance of the Union without compromise did not carry, for him and for many of his associates, any clear implication of war. This major fact has been widely ignored in the decades since Appomattox, because the later events of the war gave to the initial acts of secession a significance which was entirely lacking at the time of their passage. Because the assertion of Southern independence was later contested at such epic cost by so great a number of men, one naturally assumes that it bore, from the outset, the stamp of grim finality which later events gave to it. Anyone who views it thus must necessarily suppose that the acts of secession awakened everyone to the realization that the Union could be saved only by unstinted compromise or unstinted bloodshed. Or, more explicitly, he must assume that the Republicans squarely confronted and fully recognized the alternatives of compromise or war as the price of Union.

Much of the best history of the war period is constructed on this assumption. Thus Channing declared that, "With his Southern connections and the accurate information that Lincoln must have possessed as to the motives and temper of the Southern people, it must have appeared to him . . . that if there were no more compromise, either the South must be permitted to remain outside of the Union or be brought back at the cost of hundreds of thousands of lives and of billions of property and treasure." Oberholtzer, on the same subject, averred that "most men were well persuaded that the South could not be recovered without war." These statements are unguarded, but they do not approach in rashness the statement in a volume of the *American Nation Series* that, at the time of the inauguration, "Lincoln saw, as everyone now must see, that eventually war was in any case inevitable."[11]

In all these accounts, the writers rely upon a syllogism and not upon evidence. Without offering any data on Lincoln's mental attitude at the time, they resort to a very simple deduction: the alternatives were visible, or, at least, they are now visible by hindsight; therefore Lincoln must have seen them. Plausible as this reasoning may seem, it fails fatally to view the crisis from the other side of Appomattox, and it ignores a great mass of evidence showing that many people expected to see the Union preserved neither by war nor by compromise, but by a third alternative.

This alternative was the peaceful "reconstruction" of the Union by the voluntary action of the Southern states. The reconstruction theory predicated a substantial body of overawed, but ever faithful, Unionists in the South. It assumed that the majority of Southerners temporarily supported secession because they feared Republican hostility and unconstitutional aggressions. But, as soon as the Republican administration demonstrated its peaceful and law-abiding purpose, Southern alarm would abate, the Southern masses would repudiate the secessionists, and Unionist leaders would bring their states trooping back into the Union. Such was the course of events anticipated by many.

This anticipation, though ultimately fallacious, rested upon a sound basis, for there actually existed, even among the secessionists, some desire for reconstruction, some expectation of it, and a certain amount of deliberate effort to lead Republicans to expect it.

The bitter years of war caused Southerners to forget, almost completely, that many of their own people had regarded secession as a mere transient manifestation. Yet

11. Edward Channing, *A History of the United States,* Vol. VI, *The War for Southern Independence* (New York, 1925), p. 296; Ellis Paxson Oberholtzer, *Abraham Lincoln* (Philadelphia, 1904), p. 185; French E. Chadwick, *Causes of the Civil War* (New York, 1906), p. 289.

every well-informed Southerner, during the crisis, encountered this point of view. It was freely recognized and publicly advocated. In Mississippi, the Governor of the state became its champion and found for it a metaphor when he urged that Mississippi must "go down into Egypt while Herod rules in Judea. . . . And when in after years it shall be told you that they [the Republicans] who sought the life of this Prince of Peace [the right to secede from oppression] . . . are dead, you may come up out of Egypt and realize all the fond hopes of . . . peace on earth and good will among men, under the benign influence of a re-united government."[12] In expressing this hope for an ultimate restoration of the Union, the Governor was not without a substantial body of support. L. Q. C. Lamar had approved of the secession of South Carolina, because it would insure either a Southern republic or a restored Union under an amended Constitution.[13] Another prominent Mississippian, A. H. Handy, sent by his state to urge Maryland to secede, asserted at Baltimore that, "We do not propose to go out of the Union for the purpose of breaking up this government. . . . We will . . . say to the aggressive States of the North, when you can learn to respect this sacred instrument [the Constitution], and will mark your sincerity by conceding to us new and sufficient guarantees, we will gladly renew our fraternal relations with you." In elaborating this viewpoint, Handy expressed confidence that a widespread secession would quickly elicit the desired guarantees.[14] While Handy may have seasoned his secession program with the flavor of reconciliation to suit the strongly Unionist taste prevalent in Maryland, he would scarcely have misrepresented

12. Message of Governor John J. Pettus to the Mississippi Legislature, quoted in Rainwater, *Mississippi, 1856–1861*, p. 170.

13. Lamar to Augustus B. Longstreet, Nov. 13, saying, "If South Carolina will only have the courage to go out, all will be well. We will have a Southern Republic, or an amended Federal Constitution. . . ." Edward Mayes, *Lucius Q. C. Lamar, His Life, Times, and Speeches, 1825–1893* (Nashville, 1896), p. 86.

14. Handy, commissioner from Miss. to Md., speech at Baltimore, Dec. 19, reported by Baltimore *Commercial Advertiser*, Dec. 20, quoted by Rainwater, *Mississippi, 1856–1861*, pp. 170–171.

Mississippi's aspirations altogether. And the fact that he did not is attested by other witnesses. One Mississippian wrote, "I would like to see the border states coming with us and then talking about a re-union afterwards."[15] Another noted the presence of a party of "Union-secession[i]s[ts], who advocate secession as a necessity, a united convention, and a demand of reasonable guarantees from the North." From his conversations with the experienced people of his community, this observer concluded that the reconstruction party might gain the ascendancy.[16] The perseverance of this sentiment is evident from the observation of Jefferson Davis that, as late as February, 1861, there was "in the minds of many the not unreasonable hope" that the North would offer "suitable guarantees" and thereby make possible a "reunited nation."[17]

From other quarters, too, came evidences of a feeling that secession was impermanent. In Kentucky, Garrett Davis, an experienced public man, reported the presence of a group of secessionists whose "aim is to force [se]cession upon K[entuck]y and to reconstruct the Union, or establish a slave state confederacy, as the one project or the other shall be most feasible. . . ." Ex-senator Archibald Dixon expressed publicly his hope that reconstruction would follow secession. Another Kentuckian declared that he would not abandon hope of reunion, unless the shedding of blood should make it impossible. Still another, as late as March 25, cherished the belief that those Southerners who had voted for Bell and Douglas would soon declare their allegiance to unconditional Unionism.[18]

15. Addison Craft, Holly Springs, Miss., Jan. 18, to William Breckinridge, in Breckinridge MSS.

16. G. Webb, Greenville, Miss., Dec. 26, to William Breckinridge, in Breckinridge MSS.

17. Manuscript record by Jefferson Davis, cited in Rainwater, *Mississippi, 1856–1861*, p. 171.

18. Davis, Paris, Ky., Feb. 9, to R. McMurdy, in Chase MSS.; Archibald Dixon, Henderson, Ky., Dec. 12, to Gov. Magoffin, a printed letter, in Crittenden MSS.; John L. Helm, Elizabethtown, Ky., Jan. 15, to Crittenden, in *ibid.*; S. Lester Taylor, Covington, Ky., Mar. 25, to Chase, in Chase MSS.

Among Crittenden's correspondents, there were several who hoped to restore the Union by constructing a central union, or a Mississippi Valley Confederacy, around which the separated states of the old Union might be reunited. One of these writers wished to hold together "the middle cluster of 'stars,' around which in the future all may be attracted." Writing in the same vein, a close friend of Crittenden hit upon a Mississippi Valley Confederacy as a magnetic nucleus, around which he believed "the blessed old Union would soon be reinstated in its entirety." The same idea found expression in a letter from Alabama, urging Crittenden to attempt the formation of a *"Central Union"* of conservative states. To this Union, other less conservative states would be gradually added, and, as the new entity increased in size, it would be more and more difficult for the remaining states to stand aloof. Thus "the wandering stars might once more concentrate—after having jostled one another in their eccentric paths. . . ."[19] This project apparently found some support in high quarters, for Benjamin F. Butler claimed that the "more advanced of the Southern men" in Washington during the Christmas season wanted to construct a government "into which piecemeal portions of the North should seek admission."[20]

Many of the Southern leaders endorsed the idea of reconstruction, either openly or tacitly. James L. Orr of South Carolina and Judah P. Benjamin of Louisiana both expressed themselves rather guardedly in favor of such a policy.[21] One of the Florida senators, David Yulee, was

19. Letters to Crittenden, in order mentioned, from H. B. Allis, Pine Bluff, Ark., Jan. 7; S. S. Nicholas, Louisville, Ky., Dec. 27; N. M. Ludlow, Mobile, Ala., Jan. 1; in Crittenden MSS.

20. Butler to Gen. William Schouler, July 10, 1870, in *Private and Official Correspondence of Gen. Benjamin F. Butler During the Period of the Civil War* (Privately printed, 1917), I, 7–8.

Henry Adams, "Secession Winter," in Mass. Hist. Soc., *Proc.*, XLIII, 661, asserted that "The more moderate or the more astute [Southern leaders] who followed the footsteps of the Virginia leaders, men like Senator Mason and his colleague [Hunter], and Mr. Breckinridge were all agog with the idea of a dissolution and a reconstruction of the Union with the anti-slavery element left out."

accused of supporting secession solely for the purpose of forcing the North to offer guarantees to lure his state back into the Union. If this were true of him, it was probably true of his colleague also, for Stephen Mallory, who urged secession himself, later wrote that he had expected compromise and conciliation even after the secession of South Carolina.[22] His expectation was even less extravagant than that of another Southerner who afterward served with him in the Davis cabinet. This was John A. Reagan, Representative from Texas, who offered the opinion, even after the secession of his state, that the South would remain out of the Union for a season and then return voluntarily.[23]

The possibility of reconstruction, in fact, had a strong hold on the Southern popular mind, and an astonishing degree of influence with the Montgomery government. So far as public opinion was concerned, it may even be argued that the January secessionists could not have recruited majorities to take their states out of the Union if they had treated the departure as a permanent one. In the

21. Orr did not care for a Southern Confederacy because it made reconstruction more difficult. Benjamin thought the crisis might lead to reunion under a drastically revised constitution. "Diary of a Public Man," Dec. 28, Jan. 13, in *North Am. Rev.*, CXXIX, 128, 133-134.

22. For the position of the Florida senators, see Dodd, "Secession Movement in Florida," in *Fla. Hist. Quart.*, XII, 56–57, citing the New York *Tribune*, Jan. 15, on Yulee, and a letter of Mallory to Zachariah Chandler, July 2, 1865, in *Official Records*, Ser. II, Vol. VIII, p. 737.

The New York *Times*, Dec. 8 (Washington, Dec. 7), reported that a South Carolina gentleman, member of both legislature and convention, "thinks that when the experiment [of secession] has been tried, she [S. C.] will come back. . . ."

Preston King wrote to John Bigelow, Dec. 25, "Some of them [the secessionists] talk of the secession as only a temporary thing—of making terms and of reunion." Bigelow, *Restrospections*, I, 317.

New York *Tribune*, Dec. 19 (Washington, Dec. 9), reported that the Southern program called for the Gulf states to secede, and for the Border slave states to remain in the Union to negotiate for the return of the others.

Gouverneur Kemble, Cold Springs, N. Y., Jan. 24, wrote to Martin Van Buren, after a trip to Washington, that "[R. M. T.] Hunter says that Virginia and the border states will retire from the Union, not with the intention of remaining separate, but to procure . . . modifications of the constitution." Van Buren MSS.

23. Cox, *Three Decades*, p. 65.

crucial state of Georgia, it was the opinion of Alexander H. Stephens that "Two-thirds at least of those who voted for the Ordinance of Secession did so, I have but little doubt, with a view to a more certain Re-formation of the Union. . . . In other words they acted under the impression and belief that the whole object . . . could better be accomplished by the States being out of the Union than in it."[24]

Two-thirds may seem a very high estimate for the portion of the Georgia electorate which expected a return to the Union, but the trend of events at the inception of the Montgomery government proved that the reconstruction movement was genuinely formidable. It was, in fact, rumored to be the administration policy. Such rumors were easily credible, for Jefferson Davis had shown great caution in supporting secession, and had apparently looked with equanimity, if not with favor, upon the prospect of reconstruction.[25] He was already suspected by the fire-eaters, therefore, and when he surrounded himself with moderates like Mallory, Reagan and Memminger,[26] to the

24. Stephens, *Constitutional View,* II, 321. In the same passage quoted, Stephens asserted that T. R. R. Cobb, addressing the Georgia legislature, had used very effectively the argument that, "We can make better terms out of the Union than in it." This has been often repeated, but U. B. Phillips showed that Cobb did not use such an argument in his address to the legislature, though he may have used it elsewhere. Phillips, *Toombs,* p. 199.

When Sen. Iverson of Ga. withdrew from the Senate, Jan. 28, he declared that he would always oppose a reconstruction of the Union, but added, "I may be overruled by the people of my State, and of other Southern States." Nothing, however, would bring them back, he added, except the full recognition and guarantee of the safety of slavery. *Cong. Globe,* p. 589.

New York *Herald,* Dec. 20 (Washington, Dec. 19), reported that Joshua Hill, Representative from Georgia, believed that a Unionist reaction was at work in his state.

25. Joseph E. Davis wrote to Jefferson Davis, Jan. 2: "John Perkins was here yesterday. . . . [I] read to him a part of your letter, he seemed greatly pleased at its statement except the possibility of reconstruction. . . ." Rowland, ed., *Davis,* IV, 561.

26. White, *Rhett,* p. 196, quotes the British Consul, Feb. 28 (British Foreign Office 5, Vol. 781), to the effect that Memminger's enthusiasm was not really enlisted in the secession movement, which he had long ridiculed.

exclusion of such firebrands as Rhett and Yancey, the extremists feared the worst. When, in addition, he supported proposals to postpone the adoption of a permanent Constitution, to follow the form of the old Republic as closely as possible, and to permit the admission of non-slaveholding states, the fire-eaters concluded that he was "leaving the door open" for a reconstruction of the hated Union.[27] Perhaps no one felt this more bitterly than Barnwell Rhett, and he probably inspired the series of vigorous editorials in which the Charleston *Mercury* revealed the divided counsels within the Davis government, and denounced the policy of reconstruction. The *Mercury* resented the idea of "being dragged back eventually into the old political affiliations" from which the South had "just cut loose,"[28] and it launched, at this time, its violent campaign against Jefferson Davis. Meanwhile, at Montgomery, Thomas R. R. Cobb was reading the signs of the times, and finding them very alarming to a man of his anti-Unionist views. His first disillusionment came with the discovery that the Alabama delegates were "not only reconstructionists but absolutely union men." Soon after, he was worse discouraged by persistent rumors that Davis himself was a reconstructionist. But it was not until after the inauguration of Lincoln that his outlook became black-

27. *Ibid.*, p. 194, with copious citations.
28. *Ibid.*, p. 203, quotes Charleston *Mercury*, Mar. 25 and Apr. 1 (given in separate paragraphs):
"A struggle has occurred in the secret sessions of the Montgomery Congress, in which those refusing to close the door against the reception of anti-slave states have achieved a victory. Thus the policy of ultimately admitting the anti-slave states of the Northwest first, and afterwards, Pennsylvania, New York, etc. . . . is obviously the programme . . . of the Montgomery Congress. The Union . . . is to be reorganized on the new basis, and we are in danger . . . of being dragged back eventually into the old political affiliation with the States and peoples from whom we have just cut loose."
"Friends of Mr. Douglas, including the near and dear George N. Sanders are already declaring that the Northwestern states should apply for admission into the Confederate States. Mr. Breckinridge, in the United States Senate speaks of this as the probable result. The Border States all look to it. The New York *Herald* daily urges the advantage of New York doing the same thing."

est. On March 6, he wrote: "I found out yesterday, why George Sanders was here, he is an agent from Douglas and is working to keep out of the Constitution any clause which will exclude 'Free States.' The game, now, is to reconstruct *under our Constitution*. There will be a hard fight on this question. . . . Stephens and Toombs are both for leaving the door open. . . . *Confidentially* and to be kept a secret *from the public, Mr. Davis* is opposed to us on this point also and wants to keep the door open. . . . I am much afraid of the results."[29]

A little more than a month later, war came to obviate the possibility of voluntary reconstruction—and to take Cobb's life on the battlefield. One cannot know what success the policy or the man would otherwise have attained. Thus, the practicability of the plan as a peace-time project was never tested. From the vantage point of another century, it seems visionary and impossible of fulfillment. But practicable or not, it carried conviction to many minds, won a considerable number of voters to the support of a secession policy which they might otherwise have opposed, and commanded enough importance as an issue to split the Confederate Congress into two rival factions. Shadowy as it may seem today, peaceable reconstruction was a very real possibility to countless Southerners in the first months of 1861.

When Republican observers witnessed the many evidences of a movement within the slave states, and even within the seceded states, for a reconstruction of the Union, they naturally felt that their earlier incredulity of secession was justified, and that the Union might be saved without the necessity of any resort to extraordinary measures. This attitude, in fact, gained such wide currency in the Northern states that it caused concern among Southern disunionists. The New Orleans *Crescent*, for instance,

29. Cobb to his wife, Feb. 4, 15, Mar. 6, in "The Correspondence of Thomas Reade Rootes Cobb, 1860–1862," in Southern History Association, *Publications*, XI (1907), pp. 161, 178–179, 255.

published an editorial on "The Northern Delusion," in which it observed "the strange misconception by the Northern people of the temper and spirit of the South, in respect of a reconstruction of the Union. . . . All this is a delusion, and a most fatal one," continued the *Crescent*. "But we are inclined to the belief that the Northern people are not so much to be blamed for making this mistake as we at first supposed them to be. We believe, in many cases, they have reached this conclusion from wrong information *given to them from the South!* . . . We have reason to suspect that there are people in the South . . . who are constantly writing letters to the North and to the Border Slave Sates [*sic*], misrepresenting Southern sentiment and creating wrong impressions. . . . These letters are handed about and circulated privately, and in some cases extracts from them are published in the papers." The *Crescent* continued, to suggest that "the Northern people . . . would gain a clearer insight . . . by watching the Southern press. . . . If there has been any indication, in any quarter of the seceded States of a disposition to return to the Union on the Crittenden or any other proposition, we have yet to see it."[30] Despite this condescending assurance, the Southern press had shown no such unanimity as the *Crescent* suggested. On the contrary, the New Orleans *Bee* had declared: "It is to our knowledge that a large proportion of the citizens of New Orleans who . . . are now ardent advocates of secession, are greatly influenced in the decision they have reached by this very idea of forming at some future period another and a better Union. . . . The reconstruction of the Government hereafter is by no means a chimerical notion—especially if the Federal powers throw no insuperable obstacles in the way, by an insane effort at coercion."[31]

The Montgomery *Weekly Post* agreed with the *Crescent* that, "for the hope of a reconstruction entertained by the

30. New Orleans *Daily Crescent*, Mar. 2, in Dumond, ed., *Southern Editorials on Secession*, pp. 472–474.
31. New Orleans *Bee*, Dec. 22, in *ibid.*, p. 365.

people of the North, misguided friends of the Union in the South are mainly to blame." The *Post* denounced these "dreams of reconstruction" as an *"ignis fatuous"* [*sic*], a "delusive hope . . . that soon the stray sheep of the South will return and bleat for admission into the original fold," and it warned that such expectations would cause Northern leaders to defer "as long as possible, an acknowledgment of our position, and a recognition of our rights." The *Post*, furthermore, believed that "the Border States have maintained their States in the Union for no other reason than to exercise their influence in behalf of reconstruction."[32]

Clearly enough, by the admission of the *Crescent* and the *Post*, two versions of the Southern attitude were available to men of the North, and most of them chose to believe that "reconstruction . . . is by no means a chimerical notion." Some few, like Zachariah Chandler and Preston King, eagerly anticipated war;[33] a few others, like John P. Hale and James W. Grimes, anticipated it regretfully.[34] But among the mass of Republicans, no such eventuality was foreseen. After years of scoffing, they had been very slow to believe that the Southern states would secede at all. Gideon Welles, William H. Seward, Henry Adams, Edward Bates, William Pitt Fessenden, and other leading Republicans had either exemplified this attitude themselves, or commented upon it in others.[35] With such a mental "set," they refused to be convinced even by the

32. Montgomery *Weekly Post,* Mar. 26, in Dumond, ed., *Southern Editorials on Secession,* p. 490–492.

33. Chandler to Gov. Blair of Minn., Feb. 11, said, "Without a little blood-letting this Union will not, in my estimation, be worth a rush." Letter in *Cong. Globe,* p. 1247.

King to Weed, Dec. 7, said, "You and Seward should be among the foremost to brandish the lance and shout for war." Barnes, *Weed,* p. 309.

34. Hale said, in Senate, Dec. 5, "This state of affairs looks to one of two things: it looks to absolute submission . . . of the North . . . or it looks to open war." *Cong. Globe,* p. 9.

Grimes wrote to his wife, Dec. 16, "There will be an effort to go peacefully, but war of a most bitter and sanguinary character will be sure to follow in a short time." Salter, *Grimes,* p. 132.

35. See above, pp. 77–80.

Southern ordinances of secession, and continued to regard secession rather as a gesture than as an actuality.

This viewpoint annoyed members of other political groups, and elicited many irritated comments. Senator Latham of California wrote, "I cannot tell you how blind the Republican leaders seem in this body. The 'accomplished fact' of secession seems to them a grand joke."[36] Senator Crittenden observed, in connection with the defeat of his measures, that the Republicans "are disposed to believe that the threatening appearances in the South will pass away and that *their* policy is to stand firm and *do nothing*." Outside the Senate, August Belmont asserted that, "The Republican leaders seem utterly blind to the dangers which they have begirt us with."[37] Correspondents of Crittenden and Breckinridge also made several revealing comments: one of them noted, in mid-January, that "some (many) [Republicans] are still ignorant of the state of feeling at the South"; another condemned the "stolid indifference" of the Congressmen of the northeast; still another shrewdly observed that the loyalty of Kentucky to the Union had had the unfortunate "effect of deceiving and emboldening the people of the North by the prospect held out of divisions at the South. . . . I believe the North is still not entirely undeceived. . . ."[38]

The basic conviction underlying all the apparent indifference of the North was the belief that a majority of the Southern people were still loyal to the Union, even after secession. This supposition was not confined to Republicans, but was widely entertained. Benjamin F. Butler

36. Milton S. Latham to Franklin Pierce, Feb. 6, in Pierce MSS. However, Latham, too, had some expectation of reconstruction, for his letter continues, "I believe permanent guarantees will be conceded to the South, after which a party will spring up in the states now gone, which I hope will eventually bring them back."

37. Crittenden to Samuel S. Nicholas, Dec. [?], in Crittenden MSS.; Belmont to Stephen A. Douglas, Dec. 26, in Belmont, *Letters,* p. 40.

38. Letters to Crittenden from Jas. DePeyster Ogden, New York, Jan. 12, and N. M. Ludlow, Mobile, Ala., Jan. 1; in Crittenden MSS. G. B. Anderson, Louisville, Ky., Dec. 27, to William Breckinridge, in Breckinridge MSS.

held to this notion after South Carolina's Ordinance; Charles A. Davis believed that the secessionists would come back of their own accord, and proposed to let them "experiment," if they wished; a Bostonian argued that all fifteen of the slave states should be encouraged to secede, on the theory that their combined influence would enable them to dictate terms of reconstruction, whereas a smaller group of seceded states would lack strength to secure the desired terms, and would therefore remain outside the Union; August Belmont urged peaceable separation, because he believed that it would give free play for a Unionist reaction which would result in an "early reconstruction"; and Senator Lane of Oregon anticipated a "reorganization" in which the seceding states would participate.[39] Even the New York *Herald*, which criticized the unrealistic attitude of the Republicans, published dispatches from Baltimore declaring that the South proceeded with secession only because she expected to make better terms after secession than before, and from Washington, asserting that "the bone and sinew of the South are still in favor of the preservation of the Union."[40]

Nowhere was this widespread conviction more prevalent than among the Republicans. On this point, the testimony of the leaders themselves is almost conclusive. Alexander K.

39. Benjamin F. Butler, *Autobiography and Personal Reminiscences, etc.* (Boston, 1892), p. 151; Charles A. Davis to Winfield Scott, New York, Dec. 26, in Crittenden MSS.; Francis H. Forbes, Boston, Jan. 17, to Crittenden, in *ibid.;* Belmont, New York, May 21, 1861, to Baron Lionel de Rothschild, in Belmont, *Letters,* p. 49; Lane in Senate, Dec. 21, *Cong. Globe,* p. 145. See also John T. Doyle, New York, Mar. 2, to Montgomery Blair, in Blair MSS.

40. New York *Herald,* Nov. 27 (Baltimore, Nov. 22) and Jan. 18 (Washington, Jan. 17). The *Herald* also, on Nov. 5 (Baltimore, Nov. 2), declared that it was agreed that the Gulf states should secede and then issue an address calling on the Northern states to meet them in a Constitutional convention, at which a reunion would be arranged. On Dec. 22, a Baltimore dispatch of Dec. 12 observed that no one in Maryland believed the secessionists were in earnest.

On Dec. 21, a Washington dispatch of Dec. 20 observed that the Crittenden Compromise would "ultimately satisfy the South and repair the fractured Union."

McClure, one of the most active of Pennsylvania Republicans, wrote that "A very large portion of the Republican party, including some of its ablest and most trusted leaders," favored "peaceable secession, that might reasonably result in early reconstruction."[41] One of the leaders who conformed to this description was Edward Bates, for he held that the seceding states would fail to prosper outside the Union, and that "the real people" would "rebel against the traitors, and compel a return to allegiance."[42] Hamilton Fish was less optimistic than Bates, but he urged concessions to hold the Border states in the Union, in order that they might serve "for the purpose of bridging over the space and bringing back the Southern States."[43] Salmon P. Chase likewise underestimated the crisis and observed that, "The disunion madness makes us much trouble, but I think old Ironsides won't go to pieces yet."[44] Many of Chase's correspondents shared this view. One of them still doubted, six days after South Carolina's secession, that the frenzy in the South would lead to dissolution.[45] Others indulged a belief, even after the inauguration, that Lincoln could win the Gulf states back by some simple expedient, such as nominating Crittenden for the Supreme Court; or merely assuming a menacing but inactive policy, thereby causing the Gulf states to bankrupt themselves in military preparation, whereupon they would be prepared to return to the Union; or issuing a ringing proclamation against secession, for the purpose

41. Alexander K. McClure, *Abraham Lincoln and Men of War Times* (Philadelphia, 1892), p. 292–293.

42. Account of interview with Bates in diary of O. H. Browning, Feb. 24, in Theodore Calvin Pease and James G. Randall, editors, *The Diary of Orville Hickman Browning,* I, 457, in Illinois State Historical Society, *Collections,* XX.

When the South Carolina Convention moved from Columbia to Charleston because of an epidemic, Bates thought it was because the secessionists wanted the outside support which Charleston would offer and Columbia would not. Entry for Dec. 19, in Beal, ed., *Bates Diary,* p. 167.

43. Fish to W. S. Thayer, Dec. 15, in Nevins, *Fish,* p. 80.

44. Chase to James A. Briggs, Nov. 26, in Chase MSS.

45. George Opdyke, New York, Dec. 26, to Chase, in *ibid.*

of consolidating Union sentiment in the South, "where nearly half the people are yet for the Union."[46]

On the Republican side of Congress, the same underestimate of the Southern crisis prevailed. William P. Fessenden, for instance, wrote on December 15 that, if Buchanan had done his duty, the crisis would have subsided promptly, but that, even without such treatment, "I am inclined to think that the force of the storm is spent." Two weeks later, Lyman Trumbull still believed that if the President would only do "his duty . . . even at this late day, . . . the states which resolved themselves out of the Union would be coming back before many months." Even after the secession of the lower South was complete, John Sherman asserted that, "In thirty days we could have a large minority or even a majority in every seceding state for maintaining the Union, if the leaders in resisting secession could feel sure of backing."[47]

While congressmen soothed themselves with this comforting assumption that the Southern situation would correct itself, the Republican press consistently belittled the secession movement. The *Tribune* was especially active in this pursuit, and it constantly asserted that "Their [the

46. Letters to Chase, from, respectively, John Stewart, Baltimore, Md., Mar. 9; J. W. Schaumberg, Cincinnati, O., Mar. 9; William Lawrence, Logan County, O., Mar. 26; in Chase MSS.

"An Earnest Republican" of New York wrote to Chase, on Mar. 14, that the Unionist element was strong in Georgia, Louisiana, and Texas, but that it had evidently been cowed. Chase MSS.

Daniel Ammen, Baltimore, Jan. 18, wrote to Chase, "If their [the seceding states'] mails are stopped and they could be let alone for a few months anarchy would prevail that would render their condition unbearable for any length of time. They would then I would suppose, appreciate the advantages of the Union which are now ignored, and if so, the lesson would be ten times as instructive as if coerced." Chase MSS.

47. Fessenden to Hamilton Fish, Dec. 15, in Nevins, *Fish*, p. 80; Trumbull to Richard Yates, Jan. 2, in White, *Trumbull*, p. 120; Sherman to F. P. Blair, Jr., Feb. 9, in Blair MSS. Also see the speculations of Rutherford B. Hayes on this subject, given in Charles Richard Williams, editor, *Diary and Letters of Rutherford Birchard Hayes* (Ohio State Archeological and Historical Society, 1922), I, 566.

secessionists'] whole scheme is likely to prove a total failure if nothing is done to help them out. . . . It only needs time and patience to bring about a counter-revolution. . . . The benefits of the Union are really so much greater to them than its evils, that the commonsense of the People will make the runaway States soon beg for readmission into the Old Union, provided that open war can be avoided."[48] A few days after this assertion, the *Tribune* observed that, "It is well known that both Jefferson Davis and Alexander Stephens . . . are wholly averse to separation, and would gladly get back into the Union."[49] On February 25, Greeley's paper classified the secessionists as being of two parties, the "sanguinary secessionists" who were bellicose in their disunionism, and the "diplomatic secessionists . . . with the *arrière pensée* of eventual reconstruction."[50] On March 15, it published a dispatch from New Orleans, asserting as "beyond dispute" the fact that "throughout Mississippi and Alabama, especially in the Northern portions, there is . . . emphatic dissatisfaction. Many have opposed secession from the outset. Some went into it with no idea that it was to be carried out, but simply to force the North into concessions. A feeling is now openly expressed that the whole thing has been too fast. In some localities, the stars and stripes are still flying."[51]

With reports like these coming in, Republican leaders found it easy to maintain an unruffled calm.

48. New York *Tribune,* Feb. 1 (Washington, Jan. 30, signed J. S. P[ike].).

49. *Ibid.,* Feb. 14 (Washington, Feb. 12). On Feb. 25, a dispatch from Charleston, Feb. 20, suggested that the appointment of C. G. Memminger to the cabinet was an evidence that the Davis administration favored reconstruction. On Mar. 15, a Baltimore dispatch of Mar. 14 declared that, "On Monday last, Judge [Jeremiah S.] Black, who ought to know, is said to have openly predicted that there will be no war on the part of the rebels, that Jeff. Davis will, within ninety days, have the Cotton States all under the Federal flag again nice and snug, and will be the Democratic candidate for the Presidency of the United States in 1864!"

50. New York *Tribune,* Feb. 25, editorial.

51. *Ibid.,* Mar. 15 (New Orleans, Mar. 8).

All of the foregoing quotations are indicative of the climate of opinion in the Republican ranks. But ultimately, the opinions which were decisive in the formation of party policy were those of Lincoln, with whom future leadership lay, and Seward, who was charged with the immediate direction of the party until the inauguration. The extent to which these two leaders were lulled by the hope of peaceable reconstruction, therefore, was of surpassing importance.

As for Seward, no one was more confident of a restoration of the Union than he. Although opportunistic in his conduct, and devoid of dogmatic tendencies, Seward relied heavily upon abstract reason in his appraisal of the disunion movement. He assumed that, physically and economically, the United States was one nation; that, by many common bonds, the people of the states were one people. From this he concluded that the seceding states could not permanently resist the impulse to return to the Union. This may have been true—the theory was never tested. But when Seward attempted to translate this long-range viewpoint into short-term policy, he ran into absurdities. When he supposed that the Southerners could not actually wish to leave a Union with which their true interest was identified, his fallacy lay in the assumption that men will always recognize where their interest lies. When he assumed that mere patient waiting would suffice to bring the secessionists back, he underestimated the time required for such a process, the loss of strength which the Federal Union would incur by the suspension of its authority, and the danger of friction leading, in the interim, to war.

Ignoring all these factors, however, Seward held, from first to last, that a reaction in the South would bring the seceding states voluntarily back to the Union. As early as September, in campaign speeches for Lincoln, he had replied to Southern assertions that the North would not dare to plunge the nation into war by agreeing that, "They are right. We do not propose to do any such thing."

If his own people, he continued, should secede, he would expect the other states to "let them stay out just as long as they behaved themselves," and this policy, he, in turn, would use toward all others.[52] Just what constituted proper behavior, and just what measures he would use to punish its infraction, he did not say; and, throughout the crisis, he continued to be evasive on this vital question. He did not wish to consider what measures the North was legally entitled to take, but what course it would most wisely pursue. Thus on the night of Lincoln's election, in a speech to his neighbors, he observed that some elements regarded secession as the shortest way in which to attain their ends. "But let us not doubt," he continued, "that if we commend our way [of action within the Union] by our patience, our gentleness, our affection towards them, they, too, will, before they shall have gone too far, find out that our way, the old way, their old way as well as our old way, is not only the shortest, but the best."[53]

Seward held faithfully to this magnanimous view throughout the crisis. When Congress convened, he carefully avoided all tactics of threat and crimination, and, so far as he could, restrained his colleagues from such tactics.[54] Almost at once, he thought, this policy of restraint bore fruit, and he assured Hamilton Fish, "We think that here we see already apprehensions among the fire-eaters that they may not succeed in getting out of the Union unless they can provoke some violence or intemperance on our side."[55]

Until after Weed's trip to Springfield, Seward's view of the crisis was not widely known, for he made no Senate

52. Speech at LaCrosse, Wis., Sep. 14, in Baker, ed., *Works of Seward,* IV, 421. Also, p. 248.

53. Speech at Auburn, Nov. 6, in *ibid.,* IV, 115.

54. Seward to his wife, Dec. 7, "The mad-caps of the South want to be inflamed, so as to make their secession irretrievable. Good men there want moderation, on the part of the government, so that they may in time produce a counter-movement. Our senators agree with me to practice reticence and kindness." Seward, *Seward,* II, 480.

55. Seward to Fish, Dec. 11, in Nevins, *Fish,* p. 79.

speech during the early part of the session. But on December 22 he broke his silence, and announced his attitude under circumstances which lent unusual importance to his words. He had just been offered the portfolio of State, and while this offer was not known, it was known that he had just held important communication with Lincoln through the intermediation of Weed. He was in New York, on his way back, as many people believed, to represent Lincoln's views in Congress. South Carolina had seceded two days before. The New England Society dined at the Astor House that night, and Seward was invited to speak. It was evident that his words must command extraordinary attention from an audience fearful of crisis and eager for a policy.

Seward's speech showed so well the extent of his misconception, and the sound abstract reasoning which had led him astray, that it is worth quoting at length: "There is no such thing in the book, no such thing in reason, no such thing in philosophy, and no such thing in nature as any State existing on the continent of North America, outside of the United States of America. . . . I have the presumption and vanity to believe that if there were nobody to hear the State of South Carolina when she is talking, she would confess that she liked us tolerably well. I am very sure that if anybody were to make a descent on New York to-morrow—whether Louis Napoleon or the Prince of Wales, or his mother, or the Emperor of Russia, or the Emperor of Austria, all the hills of South Carolina would pour forth their population for the rescue of New York. . . . Therefore they do not humbug me with their secession. And I do not think that they will humbug you; and I do not believe that . . . they will much longer succeed in humbugging themselves. . . . I do not know a man on earth who—even though his wife was as troublesome as the wife of Socrates—cannot keep his wife if he wants to do so; all that he needs is, to keep his own virtue and his own temper. . . . If we keep entirely cool, and entirely calm, and entirely kind, a debate will ensue which will be kindly in itself; and it will prove very soon either that we are wrong—and we shall concede to our offended brethren—or else that we are right, and they will acquiesce and come back into fraternal relations with us. . . . Many . . . demand at once to know . . . whether we propose to coerce our Southern brethren. . . . All I have to say on that subject is, that so long ago as the time of Sir Thomas More, he discovered, and set down the discovery in his writing, that there were a great many schoolmasters, and that while there were a very few who knew how to instruct children, there were a great many who knew how to whip them. I propose to have no question on that subject, but to hear complaints, to redress them if they ought to be redressed, and if we have the power to redress them, and I expect them to be withdrawn if they are unreasonable, because I know that the necessities which made this Union . . . are stronger to-day than they were when the Union was made, and that those necessities are enduring, while the passions of men are short-lived and ephemeral. I believe that secession was stronger on the night of the 6th of November [election night] . . . than it is now. That is now some fifty days since, and I believe that every day's sun which set since that time has set on mollified passions and prejudices, and that if you will only give it time, sixty days' more suns will give you a much brighter and more cheerful atmosphere."[56]

In this extemporaneous after-dinner talk, Seward showed all of the traits of temper, and all the convictions of mind, which governed his policy in the ensuing months. His optimism, his levity, his forbearance, were in evidence. And along with these came his overriding convictions that the bonds of Union were actually unbreakable, that time would heal the difficulties without the use of force, and that, at bottom, the people of the South were loyal to the

56. Speech in New York *Herald*, Dec. 24. In Baker, ed., *Works of Seward*, there is an altered version of the same speech.

Union. In his assertion that South Carolina would aid New York in case of foreign invasion, one finds even the germ of his famous proposal to win back the South by provoking foreign war.[57]

As Seward's policy unfolded, it showed the perfect fidelity with which he adhered to these views, for it was obviously adapted to facilitate the type of reconciliation which he envisioned.[58] There is no need to examine his position further at this time, except to observe that if he later came to doubt the happy ending which he predicted, he gave no sign of it.[59] He held tenaciously to his expectation, encouraged by certain Southerners, who predicted the peaceful return of the seceding states. John A. Gilmer of North Carolina, later a member of the Confederate Congress, assured him that, "If the border states can be retained, Mississippi, Louisiana and Texas will soon be back. If the others never come back, there will be no great loss. But I believe Georgia and Alabama will also soon want to return."[60] Gilmer was apparently sincere in his predictions, but other Southerners, who spoke similarly, were motivated by ulterior purposes. When Confederate Commissioners came seeking recognition, in March, they were careful to encourage what they regarded as Seward's delusion, for they knew that his efforts to achieve a peaceable reconstruction might facilitate a peaceable separation. "It is well," wrote John Forsyth, "that he should indulge in dreams which we know are not to be realized."[61] But

57. See below, pp. 368–371.

58. See below, Chapters X and XI.

59. Gouverneur Kemble to Martin Van Buren, Jan. 24: "Seward . . . maintains that all will be right after a short time, and the seceding states glad to return into the Union." Van Buren MSS. "Seward ridiculed the idea of serious civil war, and then and thereafter renewed his bond for peace in sixty days, only to be protested from month to month and from year to year." McClure, *Lincoln and Men of War Times,* p. 52. Such quotations might be extended *ad nauseam.*

60. Gilmer to Seward, Mar. 8 (also Mar. 7 and 12), in Bancroft, *Seward,* II, 545–547.

61. Forsyth, C. S. A. Commissioner, to Robert Toombs, Mar. 8, quoted in Nicolay and Hay, *Lincoln,* III, 399.

though an occasional fire-eater may have imposed upon Seward, primarily he was not the dupe of the secessionists. Basically, his miscalculation grew out of the nature of his mind and temperament. With these factors shaping his opinion, he felt such assurance of a peaceful reconciliation that he was quite capable of voting against the Crittenden resolutions without thinking of war as a likely eventuality. Probably no public man in the North rejected the alternative of compromise with more complete ignorance of the grimness of the alternative which remained.

While Seward voiced his opinions with almost promiscuous freeness, Lincoln continued to refrain from making any statement foreshadowing his presidential policy. His partnership with Seward enabled him to maintain this passive policy, for he could devolve upon his Secretary-elect the leadership of the party until the inauguration, and could thus avoid active participation himself.

Consequently, Lincoln gave but few advance indications that he relied upon Southern loyalists to reconstruct the Union without compromise and without war. When the time arrived for him to announce himself, he gave abundant proofs, by word and by act, that his policy was directed toward that objective. To discuss them at this point would be in advance of the narrative, but it is distinctly pertinent to record that the President-elect had already showed and continued to show a complete misunderstanding of the Southern temper, and a complete misconception of the extent of the crisis. On this misconception, his later policy was constructed.

For the first evidence of this, one may go back as far as 1856, when Lincoln had declared, in a speech at Galena, that "All this talk about the dissolution of the Union is humbug, nothing but folly."[62] "Humbug," as it happens, is the same term which Seward applied to secession in his speech at the Astor House four years later. But did Lin-

62. Speech at Galena, Ill., Aug. 1 [?], 1856, in Nicolay and Hay, eds., *Works of Lincoln*, II, 295.

coln himself still apply it after four years of sectional strife? Evidently he did, for during his election campaign he told a correspondent that he received from the South many assurances that "in no probable event will there be any very formidable effort to break up the Union. The people of the South have too much of good sense and good temper to attempt the ruin of the government. . . . At least, so I hope and believe."[63]

This is to say that Lincoln shared with his party the pre-election belief that the secession threat would not be executed. After the election, he, like other Republicans, was brought abruptly to a situation where he must either re-orient his views or blink the facts. He took the easier and more dangerous course. This error he betrayed emphatically in the remarks which he prepared for Trumbull's speech at Springfield in November. In that speech, one may recall, Trumbull was made to say, "Disunionists *per se*, are now in hot haste to get out of the Union, precisely because they perceive they can not, much longer, maintain apprehension among the Southern people. . . . With such, '*Now, or Never*' is the maxim. . . . I am rather glad of this military preparation in the South. It will enable the people the more easily to suppress any uprisings there, which their [the secessionists'] misrepresentations . . . may have encouraged."[64]

Late in November, then, Lincoln still believed that the secessionists were sowing the seeds of their own destruction. If any single event ought to have startled him out of his complacency, one would suppose that the formal secession of South Carolina might have done it. After a period of seventy years of steady growth from thirteen states to thirty-three, the Republic was for the first time reduced, when, on December 20, one of the original thirteen, with all solemnity, withdrew. It was an event to chill the warmest optimism, to shake the most fixed ideas, and to impress

63. Lincoln to John B. Fry, Aug. 15, 1860, in Nicolay and Hay, eds., *Works of Lincoln*, VI, 50.
64. See above, p. 141.

the least impressionable. It concerned no man more deeply than Lincoln. Yet he did not spend the day of that action meditating the problems involved, or taking counsel of his associates as to what his course should be, or waiting at the telegraph for news from Charleston, as he later awaited news from northern Virginia. He spent it discussing cabinet appointments with Thurlow Weed, and when Weed tried to bring him to a recognition of the crisis, he replied that "while there were some loud threats and much muttering in the cotton States, he hoped that by wisdom and forebearance the danger of serious trouble might be averted, as such dangers had been in former times."[65] Later in the winter, two of his most intimate associates, Herndon and Ward Lamon, found him as oblivious to the crisis as Weed had found him. Herndon afterward wrote that, during the last winter in Springfield, Lincoln said that he "apprehended no such grave danger to the Union as the mass of people supposed would result from the Southern threats," and that "he could not in his heart believe that the South designed the overthrow of the Government."[66] Lamon was the witness of similar remarks by Lincoln, and was one of the few men who did not loyally forget them later. When he afterward wrote his life of Lincoln, he distinguished it among Lincoln biographies by pointing out explicitly that his subject had hoped for a peaceful restoration of the Union, even after the formation of the Southern Confederacy.[67]

Lincoln's unrealistic perception was, of course, highly significant insofar as it contributed to his opposition to compromise, and as it entailed, later, an unrealistic policy which did not save the country from war. But, after the defeat of compromise in December, his views did not again operate to shape the course of events until March. In the interim, the immediate problem was not whether Lincoln would involve the government in war, but whether it would

65. Weed, *Autobiography,* p. 605.
66. Herndon and Weik, *Lincoln,* p. 473.
67. Lamon, *Lincoln,* pp. 507–511.

be at peace when he came to the presidency, and whether insuperable obstacles to reunion would appear before he could attack the problem. The prevention of such developments and the maintenance of the existing status were essential prerequisites for the successful launching of the new administration. To achieve these ends was a delicate and absorbing task requiring the utmost skill of a resourceful leader. The task fell, of course, to Seward, and the story of Republican policy during January and February is largely the story of Seward's successful efforts to keep the situation open for the incoming administration.

CHAPTER X
PREREQUISITES TO REUNION

FROM the defeat of the Crittenden Compromise in committee, until the inauguration of Lincoln, the history of Republican policy is, throughout, the history of an effort to facilitate an expected Unionist reaction in the South, and to guard against any developments which might prevent a harmonious reunion. This was in no sense a policy of concession, for that would involve "appeasing," and thus strengthening, the secessionists. For the cultivation of a true Unionist reaction, it was believed that the secessionists must be left free to destroy themselves by leading the cotton states into an untenable situation.

To persons who held this view, the act of secession, itself, was not a cause for alarm. Senator Fessenden wrote in February that, "We have become so accustomed to the secession movement that it frightens nobody." On January 17, with four states out of the Union, Henry Adams said, "I regard the critical point as passed." The New York *Herald*, habitually alarmist, forgot itself to the extent of saying, early in the same month, that the passing of the crisis resulting from Major Anderson's move to Fort Sumter gave new hope for peace. Cooler than any of these, William H. Seward blandly remarked, two days after the defeat of the compromise, that, "We shall . . . see the fuller development of the secession movement," and after the secession of the Gulf states was almost complete he observed that, "Either the revolution grows more moderate, or we become more accustomed to it, and society begins to resume its tone."[1] These attitudes were charac-

1. Fessenden to his family [Feb., 1861], in Fessenden, *Fessenden*, I, 124; Henry Adams to C. F. Adams, Jr., Jan. 17, in Ford, ed., *Henry Adams Letters, 1858–1891*, p. 82; New York *Herald*, Jan. 8; Seward

teristic, and, paradoxical though it may seem, the Republican leaders as a class regarded the secession movement with remarkable calm. They had reckoned that it would wax, and they reckoned with equal confidence that it would wane, so soon as the cotton states should experiment with independence.

But this does not mean that they approached the crisis with complete insouciance. On the contrary, the more thoughtful among them clearly understood that they were staking everything on their ability to maintain a very delicate status while the expected reaction worked itself out. As part of this status, they felt it necessary to maintain an assertion of the national authority, and as a tangible symbol of this they attached great importance to the position of Major Anderson in Charleston Harbor.[2] Moreover, the maintenance of the government intact, and the protection of the capital were problems that caused grave concern, for with many Southern sympathizers in the government service and with the city of Washington lying wholly within the slave states, there was a possibility that the army, the navy, or some other essential branch of the Federal organization might be betrayed, or even that the capital might fall into the hands of secessionists. Any such occurrence would have greatly impaired the prospect of a peaceful reunion.

The success of Republican policy, therefore, depended on the maintenance of Federal authority in full vigor.

to his family, Dec. 24 and Feb. 3, in Seward, *Seward,* II, 483, 502. The crisis to which the *Herald* alluded was not the secession crisis, but the crisis resulting from Carolinian threats to fire on Anderson after he moved from Moultrie to Sumter.

2. Briefly, the Sumter situation was this: public attention had been focused on the Fort when Major Anderson moved his troops there from Fort Moultrie on Dec. 26; Secretary Floyd, seeking a pretext on which to resign, did so on Dec. 29, when Buchanan refused to repudiate Anderson's act; on Dec. 31, after an acute crisis in the cabinet, Buchanan refused South Carolina's demand for Anderson's removal; on Jan. 9, the *Star of the West,* with reinforcements for Sumter, was repelled by South Carolina batteries. All these events were publicly known, and they contributed to give Fort Sumter a symbolic importance wholly disproportionate to that of other fortifications of equal military value.

But, at the same time, it also required that such authority be exercised with forbearance and tact, in order to avoid war, which would be ruinous to the cause of reunion.

Furthermore, while upholding Federal claims and averting hostilities, so as to leave the way clear for reconstruction, it behooved the Republicans, by some means, to keep the Border states voluntarily in the Union. So long as these Border states remained, the seceded cotton states might be expected to feel a sense of inadequacy in their independence, and a kinship with the Unionist slave states which would draw them back to the Union. But if all the slave states should secede, the difficulties of reconstruction would be much increased.

Thus the Republican responsibilities were multiple and urgent. If the policy of voluntary reconstruction were to be fulfilled, at least three prerequisites must be satisfied: first, the Buchanan administration must be prevented from betraying the national authority, and the Lincoln administration must be launched without disorder; second, armed conflict must be averted; and most important, the Border states must be retained in the Union. To these objectives, the Republicans dedicated themselves in the first months of the year 1861.

The leader of the Republicans in this new phase was Seward. His leadership was far firmer than it had been at the opening of Congress. Whereas he had failed conspicuously in December to assume an effective control, or even to exert himself perceptibly, his action in the month following was vigorous and decisive.

Seward's sudden renewal of self-confident activity apparently resulted from his new relationship with Lincoln. As late as December, he had still felt hurt and sensitive because his party had refused him the nomination. He had felt little inclination to assume the function of leadership where the status of leadership had been denied, or to expose himself to repudiation by the President-elect. But in January, his position was altogether different. By that time Lincoln had offered him the State Department. This offer solaced his wounded feelings, and aroused in him the liveliest expectations of dominating the new administration. He was not disillusioned of this prospect until after April 1, when the President politely declined his offer to assume full responsibility for the conduct of the government. Meanwhile, from December 28, when he accepted Lincoln's offer, until April 1, when he learned its limitations, he assumed that he was head of the state, and, one must add, acted with the energy and decision appropriate to that post. Jeremiah S. Black alluded to his *ego et meus rex* attitude, and sarcastically dubbed him the "Wolsey of the new administration."[3] Others, also, noted his tendency to overestimate himself, but, on this point, it will suffice to quote his own statements that, "Only the soothing words which I have spoken have saved us," and (when he abandoned an impulse to renounce the portfolio of State), "I did not dare to go home, or to England, and leave the country to chance."[4]

Thus Seward's rôle in January, with his new dignity and his new responsibility, was far more conducive to action than his position in the previous month. But it is also true that the task of January was a more congenial one. In December, the problem was to formulate a policy with reference to compromise. But in January, it was to play for time, to improvise, to maintain good will, to equivocate skillfully. It was in this type of action that Seward was most gifted. Therefore, he assumed command of the situation with a promptness and an effectiveness which led Henry Adams to believe, in mid-January, that Seward "is now . . . virtual ruler of this country."[5]

3. Letter of Black, entitled "The Character of Mr. Seward. Reply to C. F. Adams, Sr.," in Chauncey F. Black, *Essays and Speeches of Jeremiah S. Black* (New York, 1886), p. 156.

4. Seward to Lincoln, Feb. 24; Seward to his wife, Mar. 8; in Seward, *Seward*, II, 512, 518.

5. Adams to C. F. Adams, Jr., Jan. 17, in Ford, ed., *Henry Adams Letters, 1858–1891*, p. 81.

The first task of Seward, in preparing the way for a reunion, was to take care that the national authority and the Federal functions should be maintained in full vigor, and transmitted without obstruction or disorder to Lincoln. This duty was rendered especially difficult by the fact that the Republicans had no authority in the administration and, moreover, had no way of knowing what occurred in its councils. Thus they were doubly helpless, inasmuch as they could not invoke governmental force to protect national authority, and could not even exercise surveillance to detect disloyalty. Consequently, they seemed almost helpless against two contingencies: first, that Buchanan might abandon the Federal cause in the South by surrendering the Federal property there; second, that the secessionists might profit by the disloyalty or the supineness of the administration, to strike a vital blow to the government, or to prevent it from passing into Republican hands. Thus, Southern partisans might betray the national defense, obstruct the counting of the electoral vote, resist the inauguration of Lincoln, or even seize the capital itself.[6]

All these perils frightened the Republicans at one time or another, but the first to alarm them was the possibility of an abandonment of Federal property in the South. On December 28, when Seward accepted Lincoln's offer of the State Department, and assumed active command of the party, the question of Fort Sumter was at a critical stage. Two days before, Major Robert Anderson had moved his forces in Charleston Harbor from Fort Moultrie to Fort Sumter. This had enraged the Carolinians, who regarded the movement as a violation of a pledge, given, as they

6. New York *Herald,* Feb. 2 (Washington, Feb. 1), said, "It is in evidence before the House Select Committee on Treason, that a variety of plans have actually been discussed . . . to break up the Union. First . . . a convention of the two houses could be prevented on the 15th inst. . . . thereby avoiding a constitutional count of the electoral vote. Second, to prevent Mr. Lincoln from coming here, by assassination. . . . Third, to take the capital by violence and prevent his inauguration."

claimed, by President Buchanan, not to alter the status of the forts. On the same day that Seward agreed to serve under Lincoln, commissioners from South Carolina formally demanded that Sumter be evacuated. For three days following, Buchanan wavered in indecision which he did not throw off until two of his cabinet officers exacted a rejection from him as the price of their continuance in the administration. Meanwhile, the people of the North waited in extraordinary suspense to know whether the national authority would be upheld. Finally, on December 31, the President refused to accede to the South Carolina demand, and the first crisis subsided.

Even before it was passed, however, other fears for the government began to be manifest. Early in January these fears grew into panic, as half of Washington awaited a Southern attempt to seize the capital. The idea of such a *coup d'état* today seems unconvincing. But to residents of Washington, it was vividly real. The Richmond *Enquirer* had used menacing language; Vallandigham of Ohio had asserted that Lincoln would not be inaugurated without resistance;[7] Edwin Stanton was busily engaged in spreading alarms;[8] and rumor credited Henry Wise of Virginia with an intention to march on the capital with a force of 25,000 "minute men." It was even regarded as a most sinister thing that Wise had been to South America, and had there observed the technique of revolution.[9] Few Republicans doubted that Washington would need a new Horatius to hold the Potomac bridge against this terrible man,[10] and the residents expected the town "to be de-

7. Vallandigham made these threats on Dec. 17, in a meeting of the Ohio delegation in Congress, according to his colleague, J. M. Ashley. Ashley to Chase, Dec. 18, in Chase MSS.

8. See below, pp. 259–260.

9. For the plot of Wise, see Daniel Ammen, Baltimore, Jan. 18, to Chase, in Chase MSS. For Wise's South American experience, see W. P. Buckner, Annapolis, Md., Jan. 14, to Crittenden, in Crittenden MSS.

10. Fear of violence at Washington was entertained by Fessenden (letter by him, Dec. 29, in Fessenden, *Fessenden,* II, 119), by Trumbull (Trumbull to Yates, Jan. 2, in White, *Trumbull,* pp. 120, 147), by Sumner (Sumner to F. W. Bird, Jan. 9, in Pierce, *Sumner,* IV, 5), and

stroyed by fire and sword."[11] So susceptible were Washington nerves, that a salute in honor of the admission of Kansas sent panic darting through the town.[12]

Seward himself was by no means immune to these fears. He wrote Lincoln categorically that "a plot is forming to seize the capital on or before the 4th of March. . . ."[13] To Mrs. Seward he transmitted a report that the mayor and 2,000 conspirators designed to deliver Washington to the secessionists. To Weed also, he expressed his fears.[14]

The fear for the capital subsided as abruptly as it had flared up. On January 10, Lyman Trumbull was of the opinion that "the danger of an attack on Washington is, I think, over." Eleven days later, Seward informed Weed that "The plots against the city are at an end."[15] Early in February, a special committee of Congress reported that it had discovered no plan to commit acts of violence against the government.[16]

But though Wise and his 25,000 ceased to trouble the capital's peace of mind, other hazards remained. The Republicans still feared obstruction in the counting of the electoral vote on February 13, and, even more, they feared violence at the inauguration. They were, as they realized, very vulnerable at both of these points. The counting of votes could not be conducted without the compliance of

by Henry Adams (Adams to C. F. Adams, Jr., Jan. 2, in Ford, ed., *Henry Adams Letters, 1858–1891*, p. 76. "I tell you we have just escaped a cursed dangerous plot.") Adams remarked in another letter to his brother that Sumner was "the most frightened man round; not personally, that I know of, but in believing and repeating all the reports and rumors round town." Letter of Jan. 17, in *ibid.*, p. 80. Margaret L. Bailey wrote to Chase, Jan. 19, "Lovers of excitement think Washington was never more attractive than now." Chase MSS.

11. Henry Adams to C. F. Adams, Jr., Dec. 29, in Ford, ed., *Henry Adams Letters, 1858–1891*, p. 75.

12. Mrs. Lyman Trumbull to her son, Jan. 26, in White, *Trumbull,* p. 122.

13. Seward to Lincoln, Dec. 29, in Nicolay and Hay, *Lincoln,* III, 265.

14. Letters of Seward to Lincoln, Dec. 28, Jan. 8; to his wife, Dec. 29, Jan. 18; to Weed, Dec. 29; in Seward, *Seward,* II, 486–488, 493, 497.

15. Trumbull to Lincoln, Jan. 10, in White, *Trumbull,* p. 147; Seward to Weed, Jan. 21, in Seward, *Seward,* II, 497.

16. See below, p. 262.

the Senate—a body with a Democratic majority, and with a presiding officer openly sympathetic to the secessionists. Where such opportunities for obstruction were present, many Republicans expected to encounter resistance. Henry Adams observed, two weeks beforehand, that "It is, or is said to be, more than probable that some attempt or other will be made to prevent the counting of votes and declaration of Lincoln's election." Lincoln himself was apprehensive of difficulty at this point, and a very tense atmosphere prevailed in the Capitol when the count was made.[17] Despite apprehensions, the counting proceeded in routine fashion, but this development did not at all allay Republican fears for the inauguration. If a small group of senators could have blocked Lincoln's election, it was no less true that a small body of armed men could have prevented his induction into office. The Republicans lacked the authority necessary to safeguard themselves against violence. Because of this lack, because of the extremely public nature of the inauguration, and because of the element of personal danger involved, party leaders probably feared the fourth of March even more than the electoral count preceding it.

Their fears were greatly augmented, before the inauguration, when detectives for the railway on which Lincoln planned to travel, and agents acting for the army, arrived independently at the conclusion that an attempt might be made on the life of the President-elect when he passed through Baltimore. These alarms resulted in Lincoln's secret journey to Washington.[18] This dramatic episode set a tone of apprehension for the inauguration, and the event was awaited with great anxiety throughout the North. Lincoln himself had anticipated the possibility of

17. Letter to Henry Adams, Jan. 31, in Boston *Advertiser*, Feb. 2; Lincoln to Seward, Jan. 3, in Nicolay and Hay, eds., *Works of Lincoln*, VI, 90; L. E. Chittenden, *Recollections of President Lincoln and his Administration* (New York, 1891), pp. 36–39, 40–46.

18. For a complete and fully documented account of this affair, see Nicolay and Hay, *Lincoln*, III, 302–316.

violence.[19] Seward had warned him of the existence of "all kinds of apprehensions of popular disturbance and disorders connected with your assumption of the Government."[20] These fears did not abate as the inauguration came nearer, and it was not until Chief Justice Taney had administered the oath of office that people "ceased to speculate as to the probabilities of 'a bead being drawn on Mr. Lincoln.'"[21] Charles Francis Adams was only one of thousands who "drew a long breath" when the new President left his carriage to enter the White House safely.[22]

Thus, for more than two months, a series of hazards kept the Republicans in a state of constant alarm, and, as they thought, constantly imperiled the incoming administration. In December it had been the possibility of evacuation or of hostilities at Sumter; in January, the threat of a seizure of Washington; in February, the hazard of counting the electoral votes; in March, danger that Lincoln's assassination might be attempted, or that violence might prevent his inauguration. Each of these situations seemed to jeopardize the installation or the potential effectiveness of the Lincoln government. And even an attempt by Southerners, whether successful or not, to take advantage of one of these situations, would have destroyed the delicate equipoise whose maintenance was necessary for a peaceful reconstruction of the Union.

Amid these hazards, real and imaginary, there was not much that the Republicans could do, devoid as they were of administrative authority. But they could remain on the alert against any betrayal in the administration; they could exercise a legislative supervision over the executive

19. Herndon and Weik, *Lincoln,* pp. 492–493.

20. Seward to Lincoln, Dec. 28, in Nicolay and Hay, *Lincoln,* III, 264.

21. C. F. Adams, Jr., *Autobiography,* p. 97–99, quoting an account by himself in the Boston *Transcript,* Mar. 7, 1860.

22. *Ibid.,* p. 99. On the day after the inauguration, Mary Mann wrote to Chase, "When Horace brought me in the paper this morning with his finger pointing to the words 'No Disturbance,' his face was flushed and he could not speak. It is an education for boys to live in such a time. . . ." Chase MSS.

departments; they could enlist the aid of army officers against potential violence; and all of these things they did—largely under the guidance of Seward.

By the very nature of his position, Seward's opportunities for getting first-hand information of administration policy were extremely limited. With the President, Seward had no social or official intercourse.[23] He was on better terms with the Secretary of State, Jeremiah S. Black, and there were occasions when he visited the State Department and conferred with Black freely. Once the Secretary even tried to reconcile North and South by persuading Seward to accept, as a basis of settlement, simply the Constitution and laws as interpreted by the judiciary. This implied an acceptance of the Dred Scott decision, which Seward refused.[24] He continued to see Black whenever he wished, but the relationship was not at any time an intimate one, and Seward had no visible means of learning what took place in the inner circles of the administration.

As early as December 29, however, Seward began to send to his family, to Thurlow Weed, and to Lincoln, reports suggesting a most remarkable knowledge of affairs in the cabinet.[25] In communicating these items to Lincoln, he added the significant comment, "At length I have gotten a position in which I can see what is going on in the councils of the President. . . . You must not imagine that I am giving you suspicions and rumors. . . . I know what I write."[26]

23. Seward to Henry Wilson, June 6, 1870, in Henry Wilson, "Jeremiah S. Black and Edwin M. Stanton," in *Atlantic Monthly,* XXVI, (1870), 464–465.

24. Letter to Black to C. F. Adams, Sr., entitled "The Character of Mr. Seward," in Black, ed., *Essays and Speeches of Black,* p. 156. For further matter concerning communication between Black and Seward, see Black, "Letter to Henry Wilson," in the *Galaxy,* XI (Feb., 1871), 267, and Baker, ed., *Works of Seward,* V, 454, 457–459.

25. Seward to Weed, and to members of his family, Dec. 29 and 30. Letters in Seward, *Seward,* II, 487–488.

26. Seward to Lincoln, Dec. 29, in Nicolay and Hay, *Lincoln,* III, 264–265.

Seward gained his knowledge of the administration's policy—or lack of it—from an astonishing source. His informer was no less a person than the Attorney General, Edwin M. Stanton—as devious a conniver as American public life has produced. The initiative, of course, came from Stanton, for Seward would hardly have solicited the Attorney General to act as a spy on his own administration. But Stanton, through his friend Peter H. Watson, who was also a friend of Seward, offered to keep Seward informed of developments in the administration. Seward accepted this offer unreservedly; Watson, acting as intermediary, called on him daily, and transmitted oral and written messages between the two principals. Through this channel, Seward received much secret information—which was less reliable than he supposed. He obtained permission to tell Lincoln of the arrangement, and on a few important matters he was authorized to reveal the source of his information to certain other party leaders. But, for the most part, the entire communication was kept secret; he and Stanton met only once, and then by chance, in a hasty and embarrassed street encounter.[27]

Seward, who rather fancied himself as the player of a deep game, seemingly had no conception of what a master intriguer he was engaged with. He apparently supposed that he was the only recipient of Stanton's revelations, but, in fact, he was only one of several. For Stanton was also meeting Sumner furtively after midnight to tell him hair-raising tales of conspiracy in the high places; he was spreading abroad a sensational story of his single-handed battle against the forces of treason in the cabinet; he was even engaged in leaving notes, at designated hiding places, where his confederates could find them and read, perhaps,

27. All of these facts are developed in a letter of Seward to Henry Wilson, June 6, 1870, in Henry Wilson, "Black and Stanton," in *Atlantic Monthly*, XXVI, 464–465. They are evidently of higher authority than Seward's son's garbled recollection that Stanton came in person, using the name of Watson. Seward, *Seward,* II, 492. Weed wrote a statement of the Seward-Stanton arrangement in 1865, and it appears in Barnes, *Weed,* p. 332. It agrees substantially with Seward's later letter.

that the Secretary of the Navy was a traitor who must be arrested immediately, "or all will be lost."[28]

But the true importance of Seward's connection with Stanton lay not in the theatrical aspects of the affair, nor in the specific information which was transmitted, but in the protection of the Republicans against surprise. After the Seward-Stanton arrangement was perfected, there was no longer any possibility that a secretly prepared act of the administration could catch the Republicans entirely unprepared. If Buchanan had chosen to surrender the forts, Lincoln would have been warned in time to offset the surrender by announcing an intent to retake them.[29] If conspirators in the administration had attempted to betray the army, the navy, the capital, or the government, Seward would have been prepared to expose such plans to publicity, and to array Congress against them.

The connection with Stanton assured Seward of information of disloyal acts, but it provided him with no means for combating them. So long as the Democratic party remained in office, he could not invoke governmental action against secessionist plots. But, in the absence of power,

28. For accounts by credulous Republicans, who participated in this melodrama, see Henry L. Dawes, "Edwin M. Stanton, One Chapter of His Life," in *The Congregationalist and Boston Recorder,* XXII, No. 2, p. 1 (Jan. 13, 1870), and "Washington the Winter Before the War," in *Atlantic Monthly,* LXXII (1893), 162–164; Henry Wilson, "Edwin M. Stanton," in *Atlantic Monthly,* XXV (1870), 234–238, and "Black and Stanton," in *ibid.,* XXVI (1870), 463–475.

Gideon Welles asserted distinctly that Seward did not know of these other activities of Stanton. A. Howard Meneely, "Three Manuscripts of Gideon Welles," in *American Historical Review,* XXXI (1926), 492.

A letter of Lyman Trumbull to Gov. Yates of Ill., Jan. 2, 1861, in White, *Trumbull,* p. 120, suggests that he, too, had secret information from the cabinet—probably from Stanton, directly or indirectly. Apparently Zachariah Chandler, too, received his promiscuous confidences. Anon., *Zachariah Chandler, An Outline Sketch* (Detroit, 1880), p. 186.

Jeremiah S. Black attempted to prove that Stanton had not divulged cabinet transactions ("Senator Wilson and Edwin M. Stanton," in *The Galaxy,* IX [1870], 817–831), but was forced to concede his error ("Letter to Henry Wilson," in *The Galaxy,* XI [1871], 257–276).

29. Lincoln contemplated issuing such an announcement. Lincoln to Trumbull, Dec. 24, in Tracy, ed., *Uncollected Lincoln Letters,* p. 173.

he relied upon publicity as a means of deterring acts of violence. As an instrument of publicity, he resorted to that familiar device, the congressional investigating committee.

A committee well adapted to Seward's purposes had been formed in the House on January 9. It consisted of five members, who were authorized to investigate the relations between the administration and the South Carolina secessionists—especially as Charleston Harbor was concerned. The originator of this committee is difficult to identify, for the congressman—William A. Howard of Michigan—who moved that the committee be organized, was not acting on his own initiative. He later revealed that he had merely been selected to introduce the measure, in order that he might be chairman of the committee. He believed that Stanton had devised the plan, which was transmitted to him by a third party. This intermediary, and, perhaps, co-originator, was, in all likelihood, Seward.[30]

But whatever part he had in establishing the committee, Seward converted it completely to his own uses when he wished to investigate, and thus intimidate, disloyal schemers in Washington. For this purpose, he drew another resolution: "Resolved, that the select committee of five be instructed to inquire whether any secret organization hostile to the Government of the United States exists in the District of Columbia; and if so, whether any official or employé of the city of Washington, or any employés or officers of the Federal Government, in the executive or judicial departments, are members thereof."[31] He then arranged for Galusha A. Grow of Pennsylvania to introduce this resolution in the House.[32] Accordingly, it was

30. *Cong. Globe,* p. 295–296.
   Howard did not explicitly state that there was an intermediary, but it is implied in his statement that he believed Stanton had prepared the resolution; yet that he did not see Stanton at any time during the crisis. William A. Howard to Attorney General Hoar, Feb. 7, 1870, in Henry Wilson, "Black and Stanton," in *Atlantic Monthly,* XXVI, 467.

31. *Cong. Globe,* p. 572.

32. Galusha A. Grow gave information on this matter to Frederic Bancroft in 1894. Bancroft, *Seward,* II, 20.

presented and passed, over heated but ineffective opposition, on January 26.[33]

The committee failed to disclose anything very startling. It held hearings, at which the mayor of Washington,
the chief of Capitol police, and others were questioned,
but unless bar-room threats be taken literally, no plot was
unearthed. At times there was a distinct note of anti-
climax, as, for instance, when it developed that the meetings of a certain Democratic marching club were held
secretly in order to evade creditors and not to hatch insurrection. After less than two weeks' investigation of such
unheroic matters, the committee reported that, if any
plan to seize the capital or prevent the inauguration had
ever existed, it was contingent on the secession of either
Maryland or Virginia, or both, and the sanction of one of
these states.[34]

Measured by this final report, the committee was a fiasco.
Probably it disappointed Seward and everyone else who
had credited the rumors current in Washington. But if he
could not claim great success for it, Seward would never
admit that it was a failure. His chief object, as he later
insisted, was to serve notice on the disaffected that Congress was on the alert to detect and expose disloyal acts.[35]

As a further measure of precaution, both Lincoln and
Seward sought to cultivate an understanding with Lieutenant General Winfield Scott, the ranking officer of the
army. Lincoln had gained an early opportunity to open
communication with the aged general, when Scott sent to
him a printed copy of his "Views" of October 29. This
document, with its complaisance toward peaceable secession, could hardly have elicited Lincoln's unqualified approval. But he seized the occasion, nevertheless, to estab-

33. *Cong. Globe,* p. 572. There was no roll call.

34. *Report of the Select Committee of Five on Alleged Hostile Organization Against the Government Within the District of Columbia,*
p. 2, *passim,* in *Reports of Committees of the House of Representatives,*
36th Cong., 2nd sess., Vol. II, No. 79.

35. Grow told Bancroft this was the purpose of the resolution. Bancroft, *Seward,* II, 20.

lish a cordial relationship with Scott, and, to this end, he thanked him for "this renewed manifestation of his patriotic purposes as a citizen, connected as it is with his . . . most distinguished character as a military captain." Scott was not receiving many such laudatory responses to his "Views," and he was not immune to Lincoln's blandishments. Consequently, in December, in a conversation with Elihu B. Washburne, he spoke very highly of Lincoln. When Washburne informed Lincoln of this, the President-elect again utilized the opportunity for a response. He requested Washburne to "present my respects to the general, and tell him, confidentially, I shall be obliged to him to be as well prepared as he can to either *hold* or *retake* the forts, as the case may require, at and after the inauguration." Soon after, when Senators Cameron and Baker visited in Springfield, Lincoln made them the bearers of verbal messages to Scott, in which, apparently, he expressed concern as to the possibility of violence at the inauguration. Scott assured Cameron that order would be maintained, and also wrote to assure Lincoln directly. Lincoln again expressed fulsome appreciation. But evidently he was not entirely satisfied with these extremely general assurances, or perhaps he mistrusted the Unionism of a general whose "Views" indicated a gentleness toward secession, and whose breeding was Virginian. Because of his misgivings, Lincoln sent Thomas S. Mather, Adjutant General of Illinois militia, to interview Scott. Mather was instructed to learn what precautions were being planned, and to determine, as far as possible, whether Scott was entirely loyal. The meeting of the two men resulted in a report to Lincoln that there was no reason to doubt Scott's ability or his loyalty. Apparently this report set at rest the last of Lincoln's doubts, and from that time forward he felt confident that he could rely upon the support of the army.[36]

36. For the communication between Lincoln and Scott, see Nicolay and Hay, *Lincoln*, III, 249–250, account quoting or citing letters Lincoln to Scott, Nov. 9; Washburne to Lincoln, Dec. 17; Lincoln to Wash-

While Lincoln courted Scott's favor from a distance, Seward cultivated him at close range. He did this quietly, for it was his consistent policy, throughout the critical winter, to disclose his activities as little as possible. Yet it appears that he established himself in intimate and influential relationship with the general. Bancroft's intensive study of Seward led him to conclude that the two men were co-ordinating "like hand in glove."[37] In this simile, it is evident that Scott was the glove, manipulated by the Seward hand.

Seward's intimacy with, and ascendancy over, Scott left few written remains, and therefore it cannot be reconstructed in detail. The extent of this influence, however, is suggested by a number of revealing episodes. For instance, when Scott received reports of a plot to assassinate Lincoln, when passing through Baltimore, he did not inform Lincoln, or any official of Baltimore, or any official of the administration. Instead he informed the Senator from New York,[38] and left it to Seward to take necessary precautions. Again, it is a very suggestive fact that, whereas Scott's first public commentary on the crisis took the form of a letter addressed to President Buchanan, his second letter of advice, on March 3, was not addressed to President Lincoln, but to his Secretary of State.[39] In this letter, Scott stated that certain of his ideas had been suggested by Seward, in conversation, and, indeed, there are strong indications that Seward was the author of the letter, as well as of the ideas.[40] Another item, less important but no less revealing, was recorded by William H. Russell. On April 10, he, Seward, and Edward Bates were invited to

burne, Dec. 21; Cameron to Lincoln, Jan. 3; Scott to Lincoln, Jan. 4; and Lincoln to Scott, Jan. 11.

For the account of Mather's mission, see Jesse W. Weik, "How Lincoln Was Convinced of General Scott's Loyalty," in *Century Magazine,* LXXXI (Feb., 1911), 593–594.

37. Bancroft, *Seward,* II, 124.

38. Scott to Seward, Feb. 21, in Nicolay and Hay, *Lincoln,* III, 311.

39. Scott to Seward, Mar. 3, in Winfield Scott, *Autobiography* (New York, 1864), pp. 625–628.

40. Bancroft, *Seward,* II, 96.

dine with General Scott. During the dinner, a message
was handed to Scott. He read it and handed it to Seward
and Bates, but not to Russell, who did not learn, therefore,
that it was, probably, news of Beauregard's demand for
Anderson's surrender. After much head-shaking, Scott
started to pocket the message, but was stopped by Seward,
who suggested that it ought to be destroyed, lest it fall
into unfriendly hands. Scott burned it forthwith.[41] Although this is not a matter of any intrinsic importance,
there is something very arresting in the picture of a
civilian—even the Secretary of State—telling the ranking officer of the army, especially when that officer was Old
Fuss and Feathers, to burn an important military communication. The little episode bears eloquent witness to
the ascendancy which Seward had established over the
head of the army.[42]

The success with which Lincoln and Seward had cultivated Scott's good will was indicated by the energy which
the general displayed in guarding against any violence
to Lincoln, or any interference with his election. If Scott
erred, in fact, it was in the excess of his zeal. For it was
one of his men who reported plots against Lincoln in
Baltimore, and thus caused the President-elect to make
his unfortunate night journey to Washington.[43] Moreover,
on two occasions which seemed especially crucial, Scott
made open and vigorous display of military force. First,
at the count of the electoral vote on February 13, he posted
guards at the entries to the Capitol and at the doors leading to the floor and the galleries of the House. Since the
galleries were closed except to those with tickets from

41. William Howard Russell, *My Diary, North and South* (London,
1863), I, 109–110. Charles Winslow Elliot, *Winfield Scott, the Soldier
and the Man* (New York, 1937), p. 709, surmises that the news, not
revealed to Russell, was of Beauregard's demand.

42. Henry Adams wrote to C. F. Adams, Jr., Jan. 26, "Scott and he
[Seward] rule the country and Scott's share in the rule is but small."
Ford, ed., *Henry Adams Letters, 1858–1891*, p. 83.

43. Report of Col. Charles P. Stone to Scott, Feb. 21, in Nicolay
and Hay, *Lincoln*, III, 311–312.

members of Congress, the effect of Scott's action was to guard the proceedings of Congress from any outside tumult and to deny admission to all but the invited guests of congressmen.[44] Second, on the day of the inauguration, he made an even stronger show of force. Double files of cavalry flanked the carriage in which Lincoln and Buchanan rode. A company of sappers and miners marched before the carriage, and infantry and riflemen followed it. A small force of regular cavalry was detailed to guard the street intersections, and to move from one to another during the progress of the procession. The Capitol was heavily guarded, and the precautions even included the posting of sharpshooters on the roofs of houses along Pennsylvania Avenue, to watch the windows of houses on the opposite side.[45] As the inaugural procession left the Capitol on March 4, Charles Francis Adams, Jr., found General Scott in a carriage, surrounded by mounted staff officers, at a street intersection overlooking Pennsylvania Avenue.[46] There he could survey the whole scene as if it were a battlefield. Not everyone approved of this military display, and the anonymous "Public Man" complained of it in his diary as a "deplorable display of perfectly unnecessary, and worse than unnecessary, military force which marred the inauguration. . . ."[47]

To such criticism as this, Seward might have replied that the important fact was that Lincoln had been safely inaugurated. Since January, the Republicans had escaped the dangers of surrender at Charleston, of betrayal in the government, of a *coup d'état* at Washington, of the assassination of Lincoln, and of violence to prevent Lincoln's formal election and inauguration. Naturally,

44. Chittenden, *Recollections,* pp. 40–41.
45. Account by Gen. Charles P. Stone, who executed these arrangements, in "Washington on the Eve of the War," in Robert Underwood Johnson and Clarence C. Buel, eds., *Battles and Leaders of the Civil War* (New York, 1887–1888), I, 24.
46. C. F. Adams, Jr., *Autobiography,* p. 98.
47. "Diary of a Public Man," in *North Am. Rev.,* CXXIX, 382.

Seward did not attribute this entirely to chance. As he reviewed the events of the three preceding months, he must have reflected that the success of his party in escaping these dangers was largely due to his activities. The party had obtained correct secret information showing it when and where to be vigilant; this information, he had secured from Stanton. It had shown itself alert to detect disloyalty; this alertness, he had exhibited by arranging for the Committee of Five to investigate plots against Washington. It had received the full protection of the military; this he had facilitated by his intimate connection with General Scott.

In these circumstances, Seward felt that he had been instrumental in carrying his party safely past one of the obstacles to peaceable reconstruction—the hazard that national authority might be transmitted to the Republicans in a badly impaired condition, or that it might not be transmitted to them at all.

The real difficulty of the task which Seward had set for himself lay not in the necessity of maintaining the government functions unimpaired, nor in the problem of avoiding the outbreak of war, but in the achievement of both objects at the same time. His cherished plan of peaceable reconstruction was of such a nature that it could be ruined either by belligerence or by supineness in the government. A policy strong enough to cause war in Charleston Harbor would ruin the plan as completely as a policy weak enough to recognize the validity of secession.

Therefore, Seward faced the responsibility of steering between two hazards and avoiding each without running into the other. Much of what he did in pursuance of this dual purpose was, of necessity, secret. The record, therefore, is fragmentary and inferential, but, scant as it is, it indicates that Seward desired an understanding with the Carolinians for the maintenance of the *status quo* at Charleston, and it proves that he restrained his own party from adopting measures that would give offense to the South.

When Major Anderson moved his troops from Fort Moultrie to Fort Sumter on December 26, the whole country assumed that conflict was imminent. Two days later, South Carolina's Commissioners demanded that Federal troops be withdrawn from Charleston Harbor altogether. Though this was their formal demand, they would, in fact, have been well satisfied to have Buchanan disavow Anderson's act, and order him back to Fort Moultrie.[48] The Republicans, of course, deplored the thought of any concession and most of them rejoiced in Anderson's bold act. Neither Seward nor any other Republican of importance wished to see Anderson removed altogether.

In these circumstances, Seward's plan of reconstruction required that the Carolinians should be induced not to precipitate a conflict. At the same time, the public enthusiasm of his party for Anderson's move made it necessary that Seward should not openly advocate any recession from the position at Sumter. If he should move to secure the recall of Anderson's act, it was necessary that he do so with the utmost secrecy. What he did in the circumstances was done with great secrecy. Yet there are evidences that Seward placed himself in communication with the South Carolina Commissioners, to aid them in securing Anderson's return to Fort Moultrie. The fullest evidence of this startling behavior was left by that mysterious diarist who has never been identified except as a "Public Man." On December 28, the Public Man received a visit from James L. Orr, one of the South Carolina Commissioners. Orr told his host that "He had seen Mr. Seward during the day, who had fully agreed with him that Ander-

48. Sen. Hunter of Va., acting for the Carolinians, tried, on Dec. 30, to persuade Buchanan to return Anderson to Moultrie. Narrative of William H. Trescot, who secured Hunter's services, in Crawford, *Story of Sumter*, p. 159.

son's movement was a most unfortunate one, and had suggested that the matter might be arranged if South Carolina would evacuate Fort Moultrie and allow Anderson to reoccupy that post, both parties agreeing that Fort Sumter should not be occupied at all by either."

After this astonishing announcement, Orr continued to express his confidence that Buchanan would issue the order for Anderson's reoccupation of Moultrie. He anticipated this outcome with more optimism than the circumstances seemed to warrant, and Public Man pressed him for a reason. On this point, Orr was reticent: "he hesitated a little, and finally told me that Mr. Seward had given him reason to think the decision could be brought about through the influence of Senator ———, whose term expires in March, but who has great personal weight with the President, and, as a Southern man by birth and a pronounced Breckenridge [sic] Democrat, no inconsiderable hold upon the more extreme Southern men, particularly of the Gulf States. Mr. Seward, in fact, told him that the subject had been discussed by him with this gentleman last night pretty fully, and that he thought Mr. Buchanan could be led to see that the crisis was an imminent one, and must be dealt with decisively at once."[49]

In short, this says that Seward was in communication with one of the commissioners of secession, and that he was secretly engaged with a Southern-born, Breckinridge Democrat to undo the very act which had made Major Anderson the hero of the Republicans. Certainly it is not a story to be believed on the unsupported word of an anonymous and unauthenticated diarist. It is not to be believed on such evidence, even though Seward later held communication with the Commissioners of the Confederate States, and urged Lincoln to evacuate the fort.[50]

However, the word of the Public Man is supported by the testimony of the mysterious Senator ———. This anonymous figure was evidently William M. Gwin of

49. "Diary of a Public Man," Dec. 28, in *North Am. Rev.*, CXXIX, 128.
50. See below, pp. 344–349, 355–356.

California,[51] for no other member of the Senate conformed to Orr's description of a senator whose term expired on March 4, and who was a Breckinridge Democrat, born in the South but, it is implied, representing a non-Southern state (if he had been a Southern man by residence, Orr would not have emphasized that he was a Southern man by birth). In the identification of Gwin on these points, moreover, it is suggestive that he was a good friend of Seward and later served him in other delicate negotiations.[52]

Gwin offered partial corroboration of Orr's story in an article written about 1881. In this, he reviewed his friendship with Seward, and then, turning to the events of the crisis, declared that, "I was so thoroughly convinced of Mr. Seward's sincerity that I agreed to use all the influence I . . . could bring to bear on the outgoing administration . . . to prevent its throwing any obstacles in Mr. Lincoln's way, should he be disposed to adopt Seward's policy. This was for Mr. Lincoln, upon his inauguration, to let things remain *in statu quo* until, by a wise policy, he should induce the seceded states to resume their former condition."[53] In general terms this coincides with Orr, for it indicates that Seward had adopted, during the Buchanan administration, a policy of maintaining the *status quo*. If Seward arrived at this policy as early as January 1, and applied it to the Charleston situation, he must have favored sending Anderson back to Moultrie, for the removal to Sumter had constituted a sharp de-

51. William M. Gwin, 1805–1885, was born in Sumner County, Tenn.; studied medicine at Transylvania University; practiced medicine at Clinton, Miss., 1828–1833; served as Representative from Miss., 1841–1843; moved to New Orleans about 1844; and moved again, to California, 1849. He was Senator from California, 1850–1861; was later interested in the movement of Southerners to Central America; was twice imprisoned for political reasons, 1861, 1865; and died in obscurity in New York City.

52. See below, pp. 343–344.

53. William M. Gwin, "Gwin and Seward. A Secret Chapter in Ante-Bellum History," in *Overland Monthly*, 2nd series, XVIII (Nov., 1891), p. 466.

parture from the *status quo*. Therefore it is safe to assert that, as early as December, Seward adopted a position which he maintained throughout—that concessions should be made so far as necessary to avoid precipitating a conflict in Charleston Harbor. If this meant moving Anderson back to Moultrie in December, Seward accepted it; if it meant evacuating the harbor altogether in April, he still accepted it. If it meant imposing a policy on an opposition President, by indirection, he undertook the task quite as readily as he later sought to shape his own President's policy from within the cabinet.

After Buchanan refused the South Carolina demands, and after the *Star of the West* was repelled from Charleston Harbor, matters again simmered down. Buchanan was wary of entering into any agreement, but, without pledges being exchanged, there developed a tacit understanding that the status of Fort Sumter should remain unchanged. It was later asserted by Gideon Welles and others that Seward participated in this understanding and "was, on the change of administration, to carry forward the non-reinforcement of Sumter."[54] Whether Seward actually entered into any such agreement can not be determined. But if the fact were established, it would not substantially alter what is already known. If the fort stood in the way of peaceable reconstruction, Seward was, at all times, pre-

54. Morse, ed., *Welles Diary*, I, 12. "In the course of the winter, Mr. Seward came to an understanding, as was alleged and as events and circumstances indicated, with certain of the leading Secessionists. Among other things it was asserted that an agreement had been entered into that no assault should be made on Fort Sumter, provided the garrison should not be reinforced. Mr. Buchanan was to observe the status thus understood during the short remaining period of his administration, and Mr. Seward, as the coming premier, was, on the change of administration, to carry forward the policy of non-reinforcement of Sumter."

The principal reason for doubting this statement is that, if Seward had actually made any such promises, he would almost certainly have been publicly denounced by the Southerners when the terms were not fulfilled.

Welles was consistently hostile to Seward, and was always prepared to believe the worst of him.

pared to sacrifice it. In Washington, his policy was firm, even militaristic; in Charleston, at the same time, it was conciliatory and yielding. Yet both were directed toward the same object: the *status quo* must be maintained and a clash averted until the Unionist reaction could take effect in the South.

Another serious threat to the precarious peace of the secession winter was the warlike attitude of the radical Republicans. Many of this group, men like Preston King and Zachariah Chandler, were ever ready to castigate the South orally, and, if opportunity offered, to adopt threatening legislation. Men of this stamp caused Seward much annoyance by their intemperate utterances, and more serious concern by their demands for a policy of force. It was characteristic of him that he let no sign of impatience escape him publicly, but, occasionally, in letters to his family, his vexation burst out. Once he declared himself "the only *hopeful, calm, conciliatory* person" in Washington. "There is no courage, or courtesy, and not one word is said to disarm prejudice and passion, and encourage loyalty." At another time, he observed that two-thirds of the Republican senators were as reckless as the South; and at still another, he exclaimed: "Mad men North, and mad men South, are working together to produce a dissolution of the Union, by civil war."[55]

But in dealing with the zealots, Seward showed characteristic adroitness. Perceiving that they viewed the possibility of adjustment with distaste, he made no effort to persuade them of its desirability, but addressed to them an argument to which he knew that they would be susceptible: they must cast the responsibility, in case of war, clearly upon the South. This argument he used very effectively. Thus, in a letter to the editor of the radical Republican *Independent*, he defended his course by saying: "Twelve years ago, freedom was in danger, and the

55. Seward to his wife, Jan. 18; his family, Jan. 13; his wife, Jan. 23; in Seward, *Seward,* II, 496–497.

Union was not. I spoke then so singly for freedom that short-sighted men inferred that I was disloyal to the Union. . . . Today, . . . freedom is not in danger and the Union is. . . . Now, therefore, I speak singly for Union, striving, if possible, to save it peaceably; if not possible, then to cast the responsibility upon the party of slavery."[56] A similar argument, used even more skillfully, was employed to still the truculent voice of George S. Boutwell. This radical Republican, speaking in the Washington Peace Conference, had marched his rhetorical armies to the Gulf in a highly bellicose manner. News of the speech reached Seward, of course, who sent for Boutwell "and read to him a long editorial from an ardent secession newspaper in Richmond, warning . . . that Seward was merely temporizing with the South so as to get the new administration firmly settled in power. Seward's tones . . . convinced the caller that the article explained his aim, and that, therefore, it was important for the Republicans to avoid arousing the Southerners."[57]

All in all, Seward had a deft touch. He used the accusations of his opponents to mislead his partisans as to his motives. Moreover, he admitted his policy and thereby concealed his purpose. As the Richmond secessionists believed, and as some Republican extremists were led to believe, Seward was temporizing. They were right in this belief. But instead of detecting his true purpose, which was to gain time for a Unionist reaction in the South, they wrongly supposed that he was merely deferring the struggle until he should be in an advantageous position to begin it. Republican zealots caused him less trouble so long as they believed this, so he encouraged them in their delusion, and minimized his aversion to force.

The restraint of extremist individuals, however, was of minor importance compared with the restraint of the party as a whole. It is a singular and strangely neglected fact

56. Seward to Joseph P. Thompson, editor of the *Independent,* Feb. 23, in Baker, ed., *Works of Seward,* V, 613–614.
57. Boutwell's account to Bancroft, in Bancroft, *Seward,* II, 21.

that the Republicans did not make a concerted effort to enact any legislation for the coercion of the secessionists. During the crisis, they frequently pointed to Andrew Jackson's policy in the Nullification Crisis as a model for Buchanan.[58] But seemingly they never adopted it as a model for themselves. They admired Jackson's dramatic nationalism, but they made no effort to re-enact the lapsed provisions of his Force Bill. That Act had provided that, when a Federal district or circuit judge should report the existence, in any state, of obstruction of the Federal authority by a force too powerful to be subdued by the usual officers, the President should issue a proclamation demanding the cessation of such obstruction. If it continued, he should then suppress the resistance by armed force.

This measure was no longer in operation in 1860, and its revival would have been a timely and appropriate action for men who regarded secession as treason. But the Republicans permitted an entire session of Congress to elapse without pressing for the adoption of this or any other coercive measure. In the Senate, no legislation of this type was considered at all; in the House, a few coercive measures were introduced, but no determined effort was made to secure their enactment, although the Republican party was dominant in that chamber. By a strange paradox, the radicals, who knew no policy except force, showed no resolution in preparing to exercise it.

The brief inglorious history of two of these bills will show how feebly they were supported. One of them was the identical Force Bill which had been enacted during the Nullification Crisis of 1833. Representative John A. Bingham of Ohio introduced this measure in the House,[59] on

58. The lament, "Oh! for an hour of Andrew Jackson!" was current among the Republicans. Montgomery Blair, inviting Lincoln to occupy a room in the Blair home, wrote, Dec. 8, "it is the room which General Jackson intended to occupy after he left the White House, . . . and we Blairs would be delighted for you to begin where he left off." Blair MSS.

59. *Cong. Globe,* p. 219.

December 31. It went to a committee of which he was chairman, and he reported it back to the House, on January 3.[60] There a spirited discussion arose as to what place the bill should have in the order of business, and the whole matter was finally put aside, with the understanding that consideration should be resumed on the following Tuesday. But on the following Monday, the House blandly adjourned over to Wednesday, and the measure was ignored.[61] Bingham complained, on January 22, that his measures met "with but little favor on either side of this House,"[62] and the House proceeded to justify his worst suspicions by neglecting his measure until March 2, when it failed to give the two-thirds majority necessary to suspend the rules and bring the measure to a vote.[63] After it was too late, the Republicans voted 97 to 2 in favor of suspending the rules, and the House as a whole gave a majority of 103 to 62. But despite this nominal evidence of Republican approval, it is apparent that if the Republicans had earnestly desired the passage of the measure, they would not have let the whole session pass without using their majority to force the measure to a favorable vote.

Another "force" bill, which fared slightly better, was introduced by Benjamin Stanton, and was designed to extend executive control of the militia. Under existing law, as interpreted by the Attorney General, the President was not empowered to call out the militia to put down a general insurrection against the authority of the United States.[64] The House Committee on Military Affairs therefore reported a bill, on February 18, remedying this deficiency, and authorizing the acceptance of certain classes of volunteers.[65] The measure was debated, February 19,

60. *Ibid.*, p. 246.
61. *Ibid.*, p. 282.
62 *Ibid.*, appendix, p. 81.
63. *Ibid.*, p. 1422.
64. *Ibid.*, p. 1031.
65. *Ibid.*, p. 1001.

20, and 21, and was bitterly denounced by Democrats as a virtual declaration of war.[66] Consideration was then postponed until February 25. On that day and the next there was more debate,[67] followed by a motion to postpone the measure again until February 28. Stanton opposed this motion on the ground that further delay would preclude all possibility of securing the concurrence of the Senate, and that "if this case goes over till Thursday, there is an end to it." Despite his opposition, the motion carried,[68] and the bill was apparently killed. By March 1, however, the bill had been revived, and Southern Unionists were extremely anxious lest it pass. On that day one of these Unionists, Alexander Boteler of Virginia, determined to seek the intercession of Lincoln, who was then in Washington. Accordingly, he called at Willard's, where the President-elect welcomed him with assurances of a desire to reach an understanding with Southern Unionists. Boteler thereupon explained his mission and earnestly asserted that "the passage of this Force Bill will paralyze the Unionists of Virginia." As Boteler relates it, Lincoln pondered the matter, finally smiled, and said, "Well, I'll see what can be done about the bill you speak of. I think it can be stopped and that I may promise you it will be." After cautioning Boteler not to publicize this promise, Lincoln diverted the conversation to more general topics, and there the interview ended.[69]

The extent to which Lincoln intervened in pursuance of his promise is not known. At the night session of March

66. *Ibid.,* pp. 1031–1033, 1066, 1097–1098, appendix, pp. 231–234.

67. *Ibid.,* pp. 1201–1202, 1225–1232.

68. *Ibid.,* p. 1232. On the roll call, 100 members voted for postponement, and 74 against it. The Republicans were divided 20 for, 71 against.

69. Alexander R. Boteler, "Mr. Lincoln and the Force Bill," in *Annals of the War by Leading Participants North and South. Originally Published in the Philadelphia Weekly Times* (Philadelphia, 1879), pp. 220–227. Boteler states that he wrote a record of this interview on the day of its occurrence. For assistance in locating this item, I am indebted to Messrs. Henry E. Pratt, F. Lauriston Bullard, and Carl Sandburg.

1, however, Stanton made a final effort to bring his bill to passage. To thwart this attempt, John Cochrane, New York Democrat, moved to adjourn. "It was well understood on both sides of the House," wrote Boteler, "that Cochrane's motion involved the fate of the Force Bill." On the ensuing roll call, adjournment carried, 77 to 60, and Stanton's measure was never brought to a vote.[70]

While no coercive legislation reached a direct vote in the House, none even reached the floor of the Senate. Here, once more, the hand of Seward is in evidence. At the opening of Congress, a "force" bill was proposed in a caucus of Republican senators. The measure was debated, and there it ended. The only clew to the fate of the proposal lies in one sentence from Seward to Weed: "I, with . . . difficulty, got them to drop that subject, at this immature time."[71] Later, Seward received complaints from the Virginia Unionists that the coercive measures in the House were injuring their cause. Sherrard Clemens wrote, in a letter forwarded to Seward, "Bingham of Ohio and his force bill has [sic] done us more injury than an invading army." Alfred Barbour wrote to Seward directly, "Force Bills . . . paralyze the Union men here." Joseph Segar, another Virginia Unionist, told him, "the passage of this force bill will take from us the strong foothold that we have."[72] These letters, one may surmise, found their way to the appropriate members of the House, and contributed to the Republican indifference which allowed the coercive measures to die.

Another evidence of the mildness of Republican policy at this time is to be found in the territorial acts which were passed at this session. Three territories—Dakota, Colo-

70. *Cong. Globe,* p. 1336. Stanton spoke in favor of his bill on Mar. 2 (*ibid.,* appendix, pp. 300–302), but no attempt to secure a vote was made at that time.

71. Seward to Weed, Dec. 3, in Barnes, *Weed,* p. 308.

72. Sherrard Clemens, Richmond, Feb. 18, to ————; Alfred M. Barbour, Richmond, Feb. 21, to Seward; Joseph Segar, Washington, Feb. 21, to Seward; in Bancroft, *Seward,* II, 536–539.

rado, and Nevada—were organized. But, although Republicans possessed a majority in the House throughout the session, and in the Senate after the withdrawal of Southern senators, no effort was made to provide for the exclusion of slavery in the acts of organization.[73] On previous occasions, Republicans had fought bitterly to insert into territorial acts specific clauses prohibiting slavery. But now, for the first time when there was prospect of success for such an attempt, the territorial acts were permitted to pass almost without debate, and without a slavery-exclusion clause being offered on the floor of either house. Speaking of the Colorado Act, Senator Wade frankly announced: "The different sides of this chamber could not agree in carrying out the principles that they contend for. The one side intended to make the Territory slave territory; and the other contended that there should be a prohibition of slavery in the territorial bill. Finally we agreed informally . . . we talked the subject over, and both sides, feeling the necessity of having a territorial organization there, agreed that there should be nothing said about slavery in the territorial organization, one way or the other, and the bill was framed with that view."[74]

Radical Republicans and administration Democrats had agitated the territorial question for a decade, and had thus brought the country to the brink of war. By a profound irony, they now at last voted together, a few weeks before the bombardment of Fort Sumter.

If Seward paused on March 4, as he may well have done, to compare the situation which he transmitted to Lincoln

73. The acts for Colorado, Dakota, and Nevada appear in *Cong. Globe,* appendix, pp. 326–328, 346–348, 337–338, respectively. The Colorado bill passed the Senate, Feb. 4, without a record vote, and the House, Feb. 18, by a vote of 90 to 44. *Ibid.,* pp. 729, 1005. The Dakota and Nevada bills passed the Senate, Feb. 26, without a record vote, the House, Mar. 1, without a record vote on the Dakota bill, and with a majority of 91 to 52 for the Nevada bill. *Ibid.,* pp. 1207–1208, 1334–1335.

74. In Senate, Feb. 6, *ibid.,* p. 765.

with the situation which he had confronted when he resumed the leadership of his party in Congress, he must have found substantial cause for satisfaction. All hazards to the national capital had been safely passed; the danger of betrayal in the government had been averted; and Lincoln had been elected, transported to Washington, and inaugurated, without mishap. Thus, the national authority had been transmitted to the new administration unimpaired. At the same time, measures that would excite Southern hostility, and thus prevent reconstruction, had been avoided. The situation in Charleston Harbor had been stabilized in such a way that there was no immediate prospect of a conflict there. The force bills which had menaced the South during the session were now buried in the files of rejected measures, while three new territorial acts had been adopted without any attempt being made to insert clauses for the exclusion of slavery. Thus, no measure had been enacted which could be regarded as an aggression upon the South. Two of Seward's great objects had been achieved: the government had been protected, and peace had been preserved. Both of these accomplishments had been difficult. Both had been attained only by energetic, though unpublicized, exertions.

But neither had presented such difficulties, nor demanded such skill, nor concerned Seward so deeply as the attainment of his third objective—that of holding the Border states in the Union, to induce the Gulf states to return.

CHAPTER XI
THE SECESSION FEVER IN QUARANTINE

WHEN the secession movement is viewed in retrospect, the initial withdrawals, of South Carolina and the other cotton states, appear decisive, while the later secession of the states of the upper South seems of secondary importance. Inasmuch as nearly all historical accounts accept this emphasis, it is particularly important to note that Seward and his associates were largely preoccupied, not with the action of the Gulf states, but with the vital decisions to be taken in the Border slave states. Until events had sealed South Carolina's Ordinance of Secession with blood, Seward regarded the measure as a tentative one, and he anticipated without dismay that a similar gesture would be made by most of the states of the lower South. Before Congress met, he assured Weed that "South Carolina is committed. Georgia will debate. Time will operate favorably, but she probably follows. Florida will precipitate. Mississippi and Alabama likely follow. But by that time passion begins to give place to perplexity, as to whether it is best to conciliate or fight." Shortly after, he could inform his family, with perfect composure, that "We shall . . . see the fuller development of the secession movement." Even while advising Lincoln of the futility of trying to arrest the secession movement at once, Seward added this optimistic prophecy: "The United States of America, their Constitution, their Capital, their organization, in all its departments, and with all its military and naval forces will stand, and pass without resistance into your hands. There will be several, perhaps all, of the slave States, standing in a contumacious attitude on the 4th of March. Sedition will be growing weaker, and loyalty stronger, every day, from the acts of secession as they occur."[1]

1. Seward to Weed, Dec. 2, in Barnes, *Weed*, p. 307; to his family,

From the outset, then, Seward allowed for a temporary secession, which he regarded almost with equanimity. It was not his program completely to forestall secession; rather, he expected to reverse it. But the reversal could not be achieved without the aid of the Border states, and as the cause of Union went into eclipse from South Carolina to Texas, he perceived with increasing anxiety that his program of reconstruction would fail if the Border states were lost.

The retention of this Northern tier of slave states seemed essential for a variety of reasons. First, the secession of Virginia and Maryland, or either of them, would lead, so Seward believed, to an attack on the capital, and this open war would destroy the good will which was prerequisite to reunion. The complete confidence with which he held this view is evident from his advice to Lincoln, on the Inaugural Address. He warned that, if certain passages were not deleted, it would "give such advantages to the Disunionists that Virginia and Maryland will secede, and we shall within ninety, perhaps within sixty, days be obliged to fight the South for this capital, with a divided North for our reliance, and we shall not have one loyal magistrate or ministerial officer south of the Potomac. In that case the dismemberment of the republic would date from the inauguration of a Republican Administration."[2]

The loyalty of the Border states seemed essential to reconstruction, secondly, because the Gulf states would not feel their inadequacy outside of the Union unless they were left in a conspicuous minority. If only five or six states should secede, they were expected to experience a

Dec. 24, and to Lincoln, Dec. 26, in Seward, *Seward,* II, 483–485.

Also, Seward wrote to Fish, Dec. 11, "Whatever may be done or said now will not hold back either South Carolina or any Gulf State." Nevins, *Fish,* p. 79.

2. Seward to Lincoln, Feb. 24, in Nicolay and Hay, *Lincoln,* III, 319–320. For the rumors of a plot against Washington, the dependence of such a plot on the secession of Virginia or Maryland, and Seward's credence of such rumors, see above, pp. 254–255, 262.

sense of ineffectuality, and to feel the pettiness of their new republic. If fifteen went out, however, they would constitute a Confederacy scarcely less formidable than the remaining Union. Many people commented on this aspect of the secession movement. Ex-Governor Tallmadge of New York predicted that "if the border slave states will maintain their position in the Union all will come right without a drop of blood being shed." Postmaster General Horatio King wanted the North to make concessions, in order to "take the wind out of the sails of secession in all the border States," because he believed "this would dampen the ardor of the rebels further South." One of Seward's Virginia correspondents asserted that without the Border states "the squad of traitors in the extreme South cannot exist"; another declared to him that the projects of the cotton-states secessionists "cannot culminate to success without the aid of the border states." If the entire slave-state group should secede, however, it was generally recognized that reconstruction would be impossible. Belmont expressed to Seward his opinion that the states could not be brought back once they had formed a Confederacy with fifteen members. Moses Grinell observed that great anxiety as to the Border existed in New York City, and that "the sentiment is strong that if the Border states withdraw, the Union *is* gone." Senator Fessenden wrote, "The secession of South Carolina, if it goes no farther, is simply ridiculous. If Mississippi, Georgia, Alabama, Florida, and Louisiana join her, still the effort will be a puny one, but if all of the Slave states are dragged into the vortex, the result will be separation." Seward himself observed cheerfully that, if the Border states did not join the Confederacy, it would fail automatically, for want of support by the states which were expected to adhere to it.[3]

3. Nathaniel P. Tallmadge to Crittenden, Jan. 7, in Crittenden MSS.; King to Nahum Capen, Jan. 21, in King, *Turning on the Light,* p. 42; W. D. Moss, Moundsville, Va., Feb. 6, to Seward, F. W. Lander, Richmond, Feb. 22, to Seward, and Moses Grinnell, Jan. 28, to Seward, in

In a third aspect, the Border states were important as the lure by which the lower South was to be drawn back into the Union. It was recognized that, after the acts of secession, South Carolina and her associates could not be won back without a certain amount of wooing. This could not be accomplished by New Englanders. But so long as some slave states remained under the old flag—especially such parent states as Virginia and Kentucky—past traditions and cultural homogeneity would tend to draw the seceding South back toward the Unionist South, and thus back toward the Union. The Border states could act as mediators in case of an adjustment; or they could lead the reaction of Southern Unionism against secession, as no Northern state could possibly do. James Barbour had all this in mind when he urged Seward to "make the V[irgini]a . . . influence the potent instrument of saving the Union. So arrange it as to secure the credit . . . to the conservative influences of this state and you at once clothe these influences with the power to recall the departing states." John A. Gilmer stressed the same view when he repeatedly told Seward that, if the Border states could be retained, the cotton states would soon be back. Charles A. Davis was thinking along related lines when, speaking of the New York financial community, he said, "We all look now to *the Border States*—the only rightful *umpires*—in adjusting this complicated question." Seward himself endorsed the same concept of the rôle of the Border states when he later urged that Sumter ought to be surrendered, because such action would hold the Border states, and that would impel the seceding states to return.[4]

Bancroft, *Seward,* II, 532–534, 539–541; Belmont to Seward, Jan. 17, in Belmont, *Letters,* pp. 46–47; Fessenden, Dec. [?], in Fessenden, *Fessenden,* I, 117; Seward to Sanford, Mar. 26, in Baker, ed., *Works of Seward,* V, 197.

4. James Barbour to Seward, Feb. 8, John A. Gilmer to Seward, Mar. 7, 8, 12, in Bancroft, *Seward,* II, 534–536, 545–548; Charles A. Davis to Crittenden, Jan. 7, in Crittenden MSS.; memorandum by Seward, Mar. 15, on the question of provisioning Sumter, in Nicolay and Hay, eds., *Works of Lincoln,* VI, 197.

Henry Adams, writing Jan. 21, in Boston *Advertiser,* Jan. 24, said,

It must also be recognized that the Border states were no less necessary for the successful prosecution of a war than for the successful avoidance of one. Later, the paramount importance of these states lay in their military value, and, if it were not for other evidence, one might suppose that Seward's leading motive was, as he let Boutwell believe, simply a concealed purpose to isolate the Gulf states before attacking them. Probably he did not ignore the fact that his policy was appropriate for war, as well as for peace. But the entire tenor of all his utterances, private as well as public, his treatment of the Confederate Commissioners, and, especially, his desire to evacuate Sumter, show that he cherished the Border, not as an essential military asset, but as a bridge over which the lower South could be brought back to the Union.

As the adherence of the Border states to the Union grew to seem increasingly vital, it also began to appear more attainable. As late as December 26, Seward had observed that "Nothing could *certainly* restrain them, but the adoption of Mr. Crittenden's compromise," but a few days later he saw hopes of holding them on more reasonable terms, and on December 29 he told Weed that the Border was growing more moderate, and could probably be held by a proposal for a convention of all states.[5] By the end of the next month, he was deeply preoccupied with efforts to confine secession to the Gulf states, and, in a letter to Lincoln, in which he scarcely mentioned any other topic, he said, "The appeals from the Union men in the border States for something of concession or compromise are very painful, since they say that without it their States must all go with the tide, and your Administration must begin with the free States meeting all Southern States in a hostile Confederacy. Chance might render the separation

"Virginia will act as mediator; will try to unite all the southern States on some ultimatum; and . . . if the price is not too outrageous, they will be back in the Union before six months are over."

5. Seward to Lincoln, Dec. 26; Seward to Weed, Dec. 29; in Seward, *Seward*, II, 485, 488.

perpetual. Disunion has been contemplated and discussed so long there that they have become frightfully familiar with it. . . . This is the dark side of the picture. Now for the brighter one. Beyond a peradventure, disunion is falling and Union rising in the popular mind. Our friends say we are safe in Maryland, and Mr. [Robert E.] Scott and others tell us that union is gaining rapidly as an element in Virginia." By this time, Seward was already engrossed in the enterprise which remained his primary concern until the inauguration—the project of stemming the secession tide in the Border states.[6]

Before he turned to this specific problem, Seward had stated his general policy on January 12, in a Senate speech which was one of the most important at that session of Congress. He always appreciated the advantage that comes of speaking infrequently, and he had not delivered a full-length address since the opening of the session. Meanwhile, formal announcement of his selection as Secretary of State had appeared, and people who had wearied of waiting for revelations from Springfield now looked to Seward for indications of the policy of the new administration. Public interest, therefore, was keen, and Seward capitalized it fully by announcing in advance that he would speak. The result was a scene quite dramatic. Three hours before Seward spoke, the Senate galleries were filled, and they later became so crowded that when a boy fainted in the crush, he was passed out over the heads of the densely packed spectators. A mob of would-be auditors jammed the corridors, invaded the cloakrooms, and overflowed into the gallery of the House. Several hundred visitors were reported to have come from Baltimore—their presence was the outward sign of an alliance (which will require further notice) between Seward and Henry Winter Davis, the political master of that city. "It seemed as though all Washington were there." In this

6. Seward to Lincoln, Jan. 27, in Nicolay and Hay, *Lincoln*, III, 365–366.

setting, Seward took the floor at one o'clock and spoke for about two hours.[7]

The remarkable speech which followed began with the declaration, by Seward, that he did not intend to engage in crimination, nor to discuss the right of secession, or of coercion. After expressing his disbelief in Congressional compromise, he then proceeded to the true thesis of his speech. This was the contention that the Union was not only a political Union, but a physical, social, economic, lingual, racial, religious, traditional Union, which could not be disintegrated by mere political action. "Our country," he observed, "remains . . . one whole well-connected and fertile region, . . . with climates and soils hardly more various than those of France or of Italy. This slight diversity quickens and amplifies manufacture and commerce. Our rivers and valleys, as improved . . . , furnish us a system of highways unequaled in the world. The different forms of labor, if slavery were not perverted to purposes of political ambition, need not constitute an element of strife in the Confederacy. . . . We are in fact, a homogeneous people, chiefly of one stock, with accessions well assimilated. We have, practically, only one language, one religion, one system of Government, and manners and customs common to all. Why, then, shall we not remain henceforth, as hitherto, one people?" This was the burden of the whole speech. Seward pointed out at length the insecurity, the dissensions, the economic stress, the loss of prestige, which would fall upon everyone if the Union should be dissolved. He dwelt lovingly on the pride with which he had seen an American man-of-war sail into a foreign harbor, and pictured the contrasting humiliation when American ships, flying diverse flags, would be contemptuously dismissed as coming "from one of the obscure republics of North America." He asserted also that the seceding Gulf states would share the full extent of the

7. Accounts of the speech by "a listener," in Baker, ed., *Works of Seward*, V, 118; by Henry Adams, letter of Jan. 13, in Boston *Advertiser*, Jan. 16; by New York *Herald*, Jan. 13 (Washington, Jan. 12).

common loss and that this was so palpable a truth that he would not trouble to argue it. Near the end of his speech, he also indicated certain points which he would concede. He admitted the wrongfulness of the Personal Liberty Laws; he agreed that the Southern states were entitled to regulate slavery for themselves, to receive back their fugitive slaves, and to expect the suppression of such incursions as the John Brown raid; he expressed himself in favor of two railroads—one Southern, and one Northern—to the Pacific; and he hastened past the territorial question with a rather feeble statement of regret that he could not support a division of the territories into two states, because constitutional obstacles prevented any arrangement for further subdivision. But, essentially, he placed no reliance upon either concession or coercion as a means of holding the Southern states. His sole purpose was to bring the South to a realization that its best interest lay with the Union, and thereby to secure its loyalty. Meanwhile, he said, he would "meet prejudice with conciliation, exaction with concession . . . and violence with the right hand of peace."[8]

The speech differed completely from his Astor House speech in tone, and agreed with it completely in point of view. Again Seward showed an extraordinary appreciation of the physical, economic, and social forces which tended to strengthen the Union—forces which most public men had failed to grasp. Like Daniel Webster's Seventh of March speech, Seward's speech of January 12 stressed the importance of physical conditions, and the relative unimportance of political measures in solving the national problems. But, like Webster, Seward found his utterances poorly received by men who were preoccupied with immediate policy, and not with ultimate truth.

In some quarters the speech was welcomed. Crittenden paid his tribute with tears, shed during the delivery of the address. Lincoln wrote, "Your recent speech is well

8. Speech, Jan. 12, in *Cong. Globe,* pp. 341–344.

received here, and, I think, is doing good all over the country." August Belmont expressed his "sincere admiration." John Bigelow reported that the speech disappointed people, but offended no one, while "it would have offended . . . many if it had satisfied the expectations . . . of any." Chase felt that it was "not so wrong as I feared . . . not so good as I hoped." But most Republicans did not qualify their damnation even with such faint praise as this. The *Tribune* compared the speech to Webster's Seventh of March Address, unaware that it complimented one because it mistook both. Sumner wrote to Samuel G. Howe, to Whittier, and to Chase, that Seward had read the speech to him in advance of delivery, and that "I protested with my whole soul, for the sake of our cause, our country, and his own good name."[9] Seward's other Republican colleagues were less severe in their condemnation, but only four of them congratulated him on the speech, and there was even an effort, later, to censure it in caucus.[10]

The most pointed criticism, however, was a remark more forthright than any of these. With brutal directness, Senator Hemphill of Texas said, "That would have been a fine address for the Fourth of July, but we are going to secede."[11] Hemphill probably did not wish to be convinced, but, in any case, he had touched the fundamental weakness of the speech. Certain states were in process of secession,

9. For Crittenden's reaction, see New York *Herald*, Jan. 13 (Washington, Jan. 12); Lincoln to Seward, Jan. 19, in Bancroft, *Seward*, II, 17; Belmont to Seward, Jan. 17, in Belmont, *Letters*, pp. 46–47; Bigelow to Preston King, Jan. 14, in Bigelow, *Restrospections*, I, 339; Chase to Julian, Jan. 16, in Clarke, *Julian*, pp. 211–212; New York *Tribune*, Feb. 9, quoted in Pierce, *Sumner*, IV, 9; Sumner to Howe, Jan. 17, and to Whittier, Feb. 5, in Pierce, *Sumner*, IV, 9, 17; Sumner to Chase, Jan. 19, in Chase MSS. For more comment by Sumner, see also, Sumner to John A. Andrew, Jan. 17, in Sumner, *Works*, V, 455, and C. F. Adams, Jr., *Autobiography*, p. 81.

10. New York *Herald*, Jan. 13 (Washington, Jan. 12), said that only Dixon, Baker, Grimes, and Anthony congratulated Seward. Grimes wrote to Seward, Jan. 12, telling him of the attempt to censure. Bancroft, *Seward*, II, 17.

11. Ralph H. Lutz, "Rudolf Schleiden and the Visit to Richmond, April 25, 1861," in American Historical Association, *Annual Report*, 1915, p. 210. In this account, Seward's speech is wrongly dated Jan. 14.

and no matter how much cosmic truth Seward's address contained, it did not contain anything to stop the process. Furthermore, the process had to be stopped, according to Seward's own view, if not in the lower South, at least in the Border.

There were not many secessionists *per se* in the Border, and the people there were strongly disposed to exalt the Union. But they believed in the institution of slavery, they sympathized with the demands of slave-owners, and, though they would not have demanded the Crittenden Compromise as the price of their adherence to the Union, they regarded the terms of the compromise as perfectly equitable, and therefore they resented its rejection by the Republicans. Even more they resented the Republican refusal to offer any other solution of the territorial question—virtually, the Republican refusal to negotiate. This feeling was probably the chief stimulus to secession in the Border states—not an insistence upon any set terms, but an insistence that the Republicans ought to manifest some consideration for the demands of the cotton states. Expressions of good will and praise of the Union they did not regard as a satisfactory equivalent. If they were not to become entirely disaffected, therefore, it behooved the Republicans to offer some counter proposal which would include a territorial adjustment.

Although Seward made no allusion to the matter in his Senate speech, he was already preparing to halt secession in the Border states by just such an offer. He concealed his connection with the matter, just as he had concealed his dealings with Stanton and Gwin, and his part in causing the congressional investigation of plots against Washington. But he was involved with Charles Francis Adams in a plan to concede New Mexico to slavery.

Adams, of course, was no puppet, and it is difficult to determine to what extent Seward influenced him, and to what extent merely agreed with him. But it is certain that they were in close co-operation. Throughout the winter, Seward visited freely at the Adams household, fraterniz-

ing with the Adams children, drying his shoes before the
Adams fire, and otherwise making himself at home.[12] In
this relationship, most people felt that Seward's rôle was
the dominant one. E. L. Pierce, voicing the opinion of the
more zealous anti-slavery element in Massachusetts, later
observed that Adams had been an "advanced" anti-slavery
man, but had made a "new departure," the key to which
was "his personal and political intimacy . . . with Mr.
Seward," with whom he had an "understanding . . . which
was more in harmony with the character of Seward than
with that of Adams."[13] Lincoln was said to have regarded
Adams as "too Sewardish" for a place in the cabinet.[14] But
C. F. Adams, Jr., confined himself to the bare statement
that, "My father and Governor Seward had . . . been
brought into close co-operation."[15] The relationship probably cannot be stated more accurately than that.

While this friendship was growing stronger, Adams had
found himself obliged to confront the territorial issue in
an acute form, because of his membership on the Committee of Thirty-three. Southern dissatisfaction had almost
wrecked that committee on December 14, when Southern
members, unappeased by the Dunn resolution, sent out
their manifesto proclaiming that "The argument is exhausted."[16] For a week following this pronouncement, the
situation remained tense, as Southern members insisted
that their "ultimatum" was the Crittenden Compromise,
especially insofar as it related to future territory. Northern members would not agree to this, and, on December
21, the committee was again on the brink of dissolution,[17]
when Henry Winter Davis introduced resolutions for the

12. Ford, ed., *Henry Adams Letters, 1858–1891*, Chapter II, is full
of proof of the intimacy between Seward and the Adams family.
13. Pierce, *Sumner*, IV, 10.
14. Henry Adams to C. F. Adams, Jr., Jan. 11, in Ford, ed., *Henry
Adams Letters, 1858–1891*, p. 78.
15. C. F. Adams, Jr., *Autobiography*, p. 73.
16. See above, p. 98.
17. Adams, "Secession Winter," in Mass. Hist. Soc., *Proc.*, XLIII,
674–675; letter of Henry Adams, Dec. 28, in Boston *Advertiser*, Jan. 1.

admission of New Mexico and Kansas as states, and for restrictions requiring that future territory should be acquired only by the consent of two-thirds of both Houses of Congress, and that the status of slavery therein should remain as at the time of acquisition.[18] Davis had been acting in close co-operation with the Republicans (he alone of non-Republican members had voted with the Republicans, on December 17, against taking up a resolution by Nelson of Tennessee, to divide the territories along the line 36° 30′[19]), and his resolutions therefore seemed likely to enjoy Republican sanction. This prospect of the organization of New Mexico as a slave state, while not satisfactory to most Southerners, was enough to prevent the impending disruption of the committee; and the Thirty-three therefore adjourned for a week, in order to give everyone time for reflection. Henry Adams later believed that Davis had saved the Committee of Thirty-three and the Border states by his action on that day.[20]

The Republicans on the House committee were at this time in much the same position as their partisans in the Committee of Thirteen. They had taken the negative attitude of refusing the Crittenden proposals, as offered by Nelson of Tennessee. They "now found themselves in the position of refusing on the one hand to accept the demands of the South, and, on the other, to make any offer of their own." This position, observed Henry Adams, was a false one, and "was intended as such by the men who offered the ultimatum. They meant to place the republican party before the country as enemies of the South. . . . It became necessary, therefore, that the republicans should do something to set themselves right before the country."[21]

One of the first Republicans to see this necessity was

18. *Journal of Committee of 33,* p. 14.
19. See above, p. 100.
20. Adams, "Secession Winter," in Mass. Hist. Soc., *Proc.,* XLIII, 674–675.
21. Letter of Henry Adams, Dec. 28, in Boston *Advertiser,* Jan. 1.

Charles Francis Adams, and he decided, as early as December 22, that he would support the Davis resolutions.[22] But before he had an opportunity to do this, and before the committee met again, the Republican members set to work to reach an agreement on the New Mexico question. "They held meetings nearly every day, and many hours each day." They arranged for Judge John S. Watts, who had resided in New Mexico for nine years, to be present at one of these meetings, and they questioned him fully on the conditions of the territory. Most of this they did independently of Seward, for their program was almost matured when he returned from his week-long visit in Albany and Auburn. At the end of their consultations, on December 26, two-thirds of them had agreed on the terms which they would offer.[23] They needed, as sponsor for these terms, an able, respected, anti-slavery Republican, and no member of the committee possessed these qualifications in as high a degree as Adams. He, therefore, at the suggestion of Thomas Corwin, was requested to take charge of the resolutions as if he were the author. He foresaw the disfavor with which Massachusetts would regard the measures, and at first declined to sponsor them. But, once convinced of their merit, he yielded to his New England conscience and consented. He did not write the resolutions himself, as he frankly acknowledged, and his detailed statement about them evades the question of authorship by saying merely that they were "carefully examined by the Republican members of the committee."[24] They were based, of course, on the Davis proposal, but

22. Henry Adams to C. F. Adams, Jr., Dec. 22, said, "C. F. A. is decided to vote for Winter Davis' proposition." Ford, ed., *Henry Adams Letters, 1858–1891*, p. 70.

23. Account of consultations in letter of Henry Adams, Dec. 23, in Boston *Advertiser*, Jan. 1; date of agreement and statement concerning Watts in Adams, "Secession Winter," in Mass. Hist. Soc., *Proc.*, XLIII, 675; statement that two-thirds of members agreed, in letter of C. F. Adams to George H. Monroe, April 8, 1861, in Rhodes, *Hist. of U. S.*, III, 267, note 6.

24. Account of circumstances of Adams' taking charge of the resolutions, in his letter to George H. Monroe, Apr. 7, 1861, in Rhodes, *Hist.*

they also contained a provision which Seward was sponsoring in the Senate—that is, a resolution to guarantee against Federal interference with slavery in the states.[25] It appears probable, therefore, that the program formulated by the Republican members of the House committee was prepared in part by that gifted author of other people's resolutions, William H. Seward.[26]

But whoever the author, Adams took the resolutions in his charge, introduced them on December 28, and secured immediate action on them on that day and the day following. The first measure to be brought to a vote was a resolution in favor of a constitutional amendment to protect slavery in the states. This passed, December 28, by a vote of 21 to 3, with 11 Republicans in favor, 2 absent, and 3 in opposition.[27] The next measure, and the more important one, provided simply for the admission of New Mexico as a state. Like Sherman's earlier proposal in the House, this resolution sought to evade the territorial question, by conferring statehood upon the region claimed for the South; unlike Sherman's resolution, it did not provide for similar treatment of other territory, and it did not allow for the creation of several states. Like the resolutions of Rice in the Senate committee, and Winter Davis in the House committee, it provided for the proposed state to occupy the New Mexico region, but unlike these, it did not seek to form any compensatory free state, either by

of U. S., III, 267, note 6. Also, Henry Adams to C. F. Adams, Jr., Dec. 26, saying that the Republican measure "will be based on Winter Davis' proposition to admit New Mexico as a state. . . . Papa will be made to sponsor the thing, being, as Corwin says, the Archbishop of anti-slavery." Ford, ed., *Henry Adams Letters, 1858–1891*, p. 72.

25. See above, p. 173.

26. Edward L. Pierce, a friend of Sumner, and well-informed on Massachusetts politics, believed it likely that Seward drew the resolutions. Pierce, *Sumner,* IV, 10. In this connection it may be significant that Henry Adams spoke of Seward as "guiding by quiet and unseen influences those who seemed to act independently." Adams, "Secession Winter," in Mass. Hist. Soc., *Proc.,* XLIII, 679.

27. *Journal of Committee of 33,* p. 19. Yeas, Adams, Campbell, Corwin, Curtis, Dunn, Howard, Humphrey, Morrill, Morse, Robinson, Windom; nays, Kellogg, Tappan, Washburne; absent, Ferry, Stratton. For statement of membership of committee, see above, p. 91.

organizing the entire territory north of 36° 30', or by admitting Kansas.[28] In effect, it would have given to slavery an even larger area than the Crittenden proposals, for the northern boundary of New Mexico Territory lay partly on the line 38° and partly on 37°, which means that it ran, on its eastern side, about 165 miles north, and, in the central and western section, some 35 miles north, of the line suggested by Crittenden. But the Adams resolution tacitly denied Southern claims to recognition for slavery in the territories, and it withheld the promise, demanded by the South, that all future territory south of 36° 30' should be open to slavery. In short, it confined itself to the bare and unqualified proposal that New Mexico should be admitted as a state. Everyone understood this to mean a slave state. This measure was put to vote, December 29, and passed, 13 to 11. Of the Republicans, 9 voted for it, 6 against.[29]

The most significant feature of the vote was not the total result, but the fact that two slave-state representatives—Winter Davis of Maryland, and Francis Bristow of Kentucky—voted in the affirmative, while others from the slave states refused to vote, or voted in opposition.[30] Henry Adams afterward claimed that this vote broke the coalition between the lower South and the Border.[31] He probably overstated the case, but it is true that it marked the beginning of a break that set cotton states and Border states on courses which did not again converge until after Fort Sumter. Literally, the South was never more divided than when Jefferson Davis became President of the Con-

28. For the Sherman, Rice, and Davis resolutions, see above, pp. 93–95, 186, 290–292.

29. *Journal of Committee of 33,* pp. 20–21. For resolution, Adams, Campbell, Corwin, Curtis, Dunn, Ferry, Howard, Humphrey, Windom; against, Kellogg, Morse, Morrill, Robinson, Tappan, Washburne; absent, Stratton.

30. *Ibid.* Hamilton of Tex., Millson of Va., Nelson of Tenn., Phelps of Mo., Whiteley of Del., voted in negative. Taylor of La., Winslow of N. C., and Houston of Ala., refrained from voting. Other Southern members were absent.

31. Adams, "Secession Winter," in Mass. Hist. Soc., *Proc.,* XLIII, 677.

federate States, and for this, the New Mexico proposal
was, in some measure, responsible.

In this sense, it was a complete success. The scheme of
Adams and Seward, as C. F. Adams, Jr., defined it later,
"was to divide the South, by conciliating the Northern
tier of Slave States, including Virginia especially; and,
holding them loyal until the tide of reaction, setting in,
should drive the seceding States into a false position from
which they would ultimately be compelled to recede."[32]
The two Republican leaders did not hope to prevent
secession in the lower South, and they did not shape their
policy to prevent it. Henry Adams, accurately mirroring
his father's thought, said, "all the cotton states may go,
and welcome, if we can keep the border ones." The Adams
resolutions, like the Davis resolutions upon which they
were based, were intended to influence the Border states.
They were "for Maryland and Tennessee and Virginia"
and not for the cotton states where "no compromise that
a republican could offer would stand a chance of acceptance"; they were directed not to the secessionists, but to
"southern whigs in the border States who appeal to the
republicans for a helping hand." Men of this class, as
Henry Adams observed, "ask some reasonable guarantee;
something, if it be only an indication of good will and
constitutional intentions, with which they may go before
their constituents and resist secession. Otherwise they say
that they are delivered up, bound hand and foot, to the
democrats, without a hope of resisting the flood that is
coming over them."[33]

Defending and explaining his father's policy in the
Boston *Advertiser*, Henry Adams repeatedly stressed the
fact that the measures were essential for saving the Border.
On January 11, he wrote: "Whether the Cotton States will
secede or not, is now not the most vital question. But the

32. C. F. Adams, Jr., *Autobiography,* p. 73.
33. Henry Adams to C. F. Adams, Jr., Dec. 26, Jan. 2, 11, in Ford, ed.,
Henry Adams Letters, 1858–1891, pp. 71, 76, 78; letters of Henry Adams,
Dec. 22, 28, in Boston *Advertiser,* Dec. 27, Jan. 1.

question which really goes deepest is, what will be the action of Virginia and Maryland? Their secession would bring about an immediate collision with all its consequences. If they do not secede, the troubles can be comparatively easily managed." Three days later he presented the situation as a dilemma, whose horns might be skillfully avoided: "The real danger is on the one side that Virginia and Maryland will go out, which will be a bad blow; or on the other, that the Crittenden compromise will pass. If the committee's plan will cut between these two and defeat both, it will be a most masterly stroke."[34]

Later, the Adams resolutions were to experience strange vicissitudes. It will be observed that in their original form they did not offer the specific text of an amendment guaranteeing slavery in the states, nor of a bill for the admission of New Mexico. They merely endorsed the principle of such an amendment and such a bill. When the specific amendment and bill were prepared therefore, the committee had to vote again. Meanwhile, Adams had struck another blow on his wedge between cotton states and Border states. To understand his maneuver, it is necessary to remember that Adams' whole policy had been to place the secessionists in a position where they would not receive sympathy from the Border. Finding, in December, that they attracted such sympathy by their claims that Republicans would not offer terms, that slavery was threatened in the states, and that they were denied an equity in the territories, he offered terms, proposed to guarantee slavery in the states, and agreed to permit slavery in the area, if not in the Territory, of New Mexico. He did this in the belief that the complaints were not sincere, and with the intention of forcing the

34. Letters of Henry Adams, Jan. 11, 14, in Boston *Advertiser,* Jan. 15, 17. The New York *Tribune,* Feb. 2 (Washington, Jan. 31), commented upon the impossibility of effecting an adjustment with the Gulf states. However, it said, "some experiment is quite possible. If any should be hit upon that would divide the Slave States and set them to quarreling among themselves, why, to that extent the plan might do some good."

secessionists to reject his measure.[35] In this purpose he had, in a sense, succeeded, for the leaders of the lower South were unwilling to accept the admission to statehood of an area which they believed to be a desert, and thereupon to waive the recognition of what they regarded as their constitutional rights. But, in addition to this, Adams wished to show that the secessionists lacked a proper sense of duty as citizens. To this end, he introduced in the committee a resolution that the peaceful acquiescence in the election of a President, legally chosen, was the "paramount duty of every good citizen." This was amended, on January 11, to read "the high and imperative duty of every good citizen," and in this form, was brought to a vote.[36]

No one chose to deny the duty of citizens as stated in the resolution, and the measures passed 22 to 0. Millson of Virginia, Bristow of Kentucky, Nelson of Tennessee, and Davis of Maryland voted in the affirmative. Four other slave-state members were absent, but seven were present and refused to vote, on the ground that the resolution did not relate to the purposes for which the committee was established.[37] Thus the slave states were utterly divided.

But at this juncture, when it appeared that Adams was just beginning to succeed in his program to separate lower South and Border, he seems to have assumed that his task ended with his demonstration that Southern members did not acknowledge their duty to recognize Lincoln as President. Accordingly, he promptly introduced another resolution proposing that since seven states would not recognize even their most evident duties, the

35. Charles Francis Adams, Jr., *Charles Francis Adams* (Boston, 1900), pp. 136–139.

36. *Journal of Committee of 33*, pp. 32–37. The expression "high and imperative" was substituted for "paramount" by a vote of 11 to 10. The negative votes were all Republican, the only Republicans voting in the affirmative being Corwin, Dunn, Kellogg, and Windom.

37. *Ibid.*, pp. 33–37. Winslow of N. C., Hawkins of Fla., Davis of Miss., Boyce of S. C., absent; Taylor of La., Phelps of Mo., Houston of Ala., Love of Ga., Rust of Ark., Hamilton of Tex., Whiteley of Del., refused to vote, and filed a statement of their reasons.

committee report itself unable to reach an agreement.[38] This resolution failed, but Adams thereupon proceeded to vote against the amendment and bill which had been drawn in pursuance of his own resolutions. They were passed over his opposition; the amendment received 20 votes, while only Adams and four other Republicans opposed it. The New Mexico bill was carried by a 14 to 9 vote, in which party and sectional lines broke completely; six Republicans voted for it, and nine, including Adams, voted against it. Of the slave-state members, six voted for the measure. Four were not present, and five, being present, refused to participate in the vote.[39]

While opinion in the committee was chaotic, the question of reporting to the House arose. The committee, by this time, had voted favorably upon the two Adams measures and certain amendments to the Fugitive Slave Law, prepared by Henry Winter Davis. So little did the members admire their handiwork, however, that only six votes could be mustered in favor of a motion to ask the concurrence of the House in the committee's measures. Of the Republicans, only Thomas Corwin voted for the motion, with four slave-state members, and a Democrat from California supporting him.[40] In default of this motion, Corwin was simply instructed to report the results at which the com-

38. Letter to Henry Adams, Jan. 11, in Boston *Advertiser,* Jan. 15.
39. *Journal of Committee of 33,* pp. 33–37.
On the proposed 13th amendment, 6 Republicans (Campbell, Corwin, Curtis, Morrill, Robinson, and Windom) voted in the affirmative, and 5 (Adams, Ferry, Kellogg, Tappan, and Washburne), in the negative. Ten Southern votes were cast in the affirmative, none in the negative.
On the New Mexico bill, the Republicans in the affirmative were Campbell, Corwin, Dunn, Howard, Humphrey, and Stratton; those in the negative were Adams, Curtis, Kellogg, Morrill, Morse, Robinson, Tappan, Washburne, and Windom. Slave-state members voting for the measure were Bristow of Ky., Davis of Md., Houston of Ala., Love of Ga., Millson of Va., and Nelson of Tenn.; those present but not voting, Hamilton of Tex., Phelps of Mo., Rust of Ark., Taylor of La., and Whiteley of Del.; those absent, Boyce of S. C., Davis of Miss., Hawkins of Fla., Winslow of N. C.
40. *Ibid.,* pp. 38–39. The four Southerners were Love of Ga., Rust of Ark., Taylor of La., and Winslow of N. C.

mittee had arrived.[41] When the measures went to the House, therefore, they went without the endorsement of the committee which reported them, and the chairman's "majority" report was accompanied by five minority reports, representing fourteen of the thirty members who were left on the committee. Bristow of Kentucky, Winter Davis of Maryland, and Millson of Virginia were the only attending slave-state members who did not file dissenting reports.[42]

Under these unfavorable auspices, the Adams measures, no longer accepted by Adams, were reported to the House, and, on January 21, became the subject of debate. Intermittent debate continued until March 1. Before the proposals were put to a vote, however, two developments of some importance took place. First, Adams changed his mind again, and returned to the support of his propositions.[43] It is not clear why he did so, for he persisted in his belief that the South did not want terms. Perhaps that is the true reason for his decision to vote for them. Second, Seward scored a distinct success by securing from Lincoln an acceptance, if not an endorsement, of the New Mexico proposal. Apparently Seward wrote to Lincoln on the subject, but it appears likely that the chief effort to win Lincoln's consent took the form of a personal mission to Springfield by William Kellogg of Illinois, a friend of Lincoln and a member of the Committee of Thirty-three. On this mission, it is fair to assume that Kellogg acted not

41. *Ibid.,* pp. 38–39.

42. *Report of the Committee of 33.* Dissenting Republicans were (1) Washburne and Tappan, opposing all compromise, (2) Adams, because "no form of adjustment will be satisfactory to the recusant states which does not incorporate into the Constitution . . . a recognition of the obligation to protect and extend slavery," and (3) Ferry. Dissenting slave-state members were (1) Taylor of La., Phelps of Mo., Rust of Ark., Whiteley of Del., and Winslow of N. C., (2) Love of Ga., and Hamilton of Tex., and (3) Nelson of Tenn. Before this time, Boyce of S. C., R. Davis of Miss., and Hawkins of Fla. had quit the committee.

43. The change was shown by the fact that Adams voted for the 13th amendment and against tabling the New Mexico bill, in the votes recorded below.

entirely for himself, but as an emissary of the Seward-Adams group. He talked with Lincoln on the same day that Corwin opened the House debate on the committee measures. The effect of Kellogg's persuasion was in part offset, when, during the visit, Lincoln received a message from Lyman Trumbull telling him not to commit himself until he received letters which Trumbull was sending. Lincoln, therefore, would tell Kellogg nothing except that he would send Seward a letter which Kellogg might see. But when Trumbull's letter arrived it did not bear on the subject, and Lincoln then wrote to Seward.[44] His tone was begrudging and reluctant. He observed that he had started not to write at all. He repeated that, on the territorial question, he was "inflexible," and would agree neither to popular sovereignty nor to a division line; but his letter concluded by conceding that he did not "care much about New Mexico, if further extension were hedged against."[45]

With the consent of Lincoln, Seward and Adams were now in position to proceed with their program as authoritative Republican policy, and to assure the Border-state representatives that they could fulfill the terms which they proposed. With these advantages, they continued to gain Border support. Representative Nelson of Tennessee declared that he had been led by Adams to take " 'an entirely different course of action.' "[46] In February, Adams confided to his son that Governor Thomas H. Hicks, Andrew Johnson, and Cassius Clay had offered to answer for the loyalty of Maryland, Tennessee, and Kentucky, respectively, on the basis of the Adams proposals; and that Rives of Virginia thought the proposals would enable the conservatives to carry the Spring elections in his state.[47]

44. Lincoln reviewed the circumstances of Kellogg's visit in a letter to Seward, Feb. 1, in Nicolay and Hay, eds., *Works of Lincoln,* VI, 102–104.

45. Lincoln to Seward, Feb. 1, in Nicolay and Hay, eds., *Works of Lincoln,* VI, 102–104.

46. C. F. Adams, Jr., *C. F. Adams,* p. 142; also see Rhodes, *Hist. of U. S.,* III, 314, note 2.

47. C. F. Adams, Jr., *Autobiography,* p. 78.

The only thing that worried Adams and Seward at this time was their uncertainty as to the policy of Lincoln.

After nearly forty days of debate and delay in the House, the Adams measures finally came to a vote on February 27 and 28, and March 1. First the House voted on the proposed Thirteenth Amendment to guarantee against Federal interference with slavery in the states. This failed, on February 27, to receive the necessary two-thirds majority, the vote being 123 for, 71 against.[48] The Republicans were distinctly responsible for this outcome, as they contributed only 37 of the affirmative votes and 68 of the negative. On the day following, however, the House adopted, by a vote of 128 to 65, a motion of Kilgore of Indiana to reconsider the measure.[49] On reconsideration, it was then approved by a vote of 133 to 65,[50] and thus the House proposed, as the Thirteenth Amendment to the Constitution, an affirmation of the right of the states to regulate slavery within their own limits. The reversal was accomplished by a change in Republican votes, but even so the passage of the amendment was accomplished over a Republican opposition of 62 votes, with only 44 in favor. The proposed Thirteenth Amendment was then transmitted to the Senate, where it was adopted by a bare two-thirds majority of 24 to 12, and recommended to the states, on March 2.[51] Again, the Republicans opposed the measure, casting only 8 votes in favor of it, and 12 against it. Every negative vote was Republican.

While the Senate was acting on the proposed amendment, the House had disposed of the New Mexico bill by tabling it on March 1. On Representative Hickman's motion to table, 115 members voted in favor, and 71 opposed.[52] The Republicans divided, 76 in favor and 26 opposed. That is to say, non-Republicans cast 39 votes to table, and 45 to save the bill. In other words, the Republi-

48. *Cong. Globe*, p. 1264.   51. *Ibid.*, p. 1403.
49. *Ibid.*, p. 1284.   52. *Ibid.*, p. 1327.
50. *Ibid.*, p. 1285.

cans again killed their own bill. This is especially worthy
of note in view of the fact that Adams later declared that
the final vote showed "slaveholders turning the scale
against the bill."[53] The excess of Republicans who voted
to table, over those who tried to save the bill, was 50; the
excess of slave-state representatives on the same question
was 2.

In this connection, it is notable that the Crittenden
Compromise was permitted to come to a vote in the last
hours of the session. Its defeat was a foregone conclusion,
but the vote was permitted as a mark of dilatory courtesy
to the people who had championed it since the beginning
of the session. In the upper house, 19 senators voted for
the Crittenden measures, and 20 voted against them. Of
these, not one Republican voted in the affirmative, but
every negative vote was Republican.[54] In the House, the
resolutions failed, 80 to 113. Again, the minority of 80
contained not one Republican, and the Republican group
constituted all but a negligible part of the vote to kill the
measure—110 of the 113 members in opposition were
Republicans.[55] Thus it was true that, between December
and March, no piece of compromise legislation ever
secured a majority of Republican votes either in Senate,
or in Committee of Thirteen, or in House, or in Committee
of Thirty-three. Once, in the Thirty-three committee,
Republicans indicated that they would vote for certain
measures, but when the measures were offered in final form
they thought better of it, and voted preponderantly in
the negative. Consequently, it remained true, there as
elsewhere, that the Republicans let the secession movement
go unchecked by any effort on their part to reassure or
conciliate the South.

On the day when the New Mexico bill was tabled in the

53. C. F. Adams to George H. Monroe, Apr. 8, 1861, in Rhodes,
Hist. of U. S., III, 267, note 6. This misstatement also appears in Henry
Adams, "Secession Winter," in Mass. Hist. Soc., *Proc.*, XLIII, 683.

54. In Senate, Mar. 2, in *Cong. Globe*, p. 1405.

55. In House, Feb. 27, in *ibid.*, p. 1261.

House, Charles Francis Adams walked home with a member of his family—probably Charles Francis, Jr.—who expressed regret that his measures had been defeated. "The reply, conveyed with unmistakable cheerfulness of tone, was, on the contrary, expressive of profound satisfaction that they were thus well out of the way, having done the work for which they were designed."[56]

In the light of Adams' original purposes, both his cheerfulness and his indifference to the fate of his bill were to be expected. He, in co-operation with Seward, had originally proposed it in order to divide the South, and to maintain the *status quo* for Lincoln. It had been a difficult objective, and at times "the conciliators and opportunists —of whom," as C. F. Adams, Jr., said, "Seward and my father were chief"[57]—had almost despaired of achieving it. But the winter had passed without an outbreak, the capital still lay between Unionist states, and secession had been confined to less than one-half of the slave states. It is understandable that Adams should have felt that the New Mexico bill had served its purpose without ever becoming the New Mexico Act.

While Adams pursued his Fabian policy in the House, Seward, as usual, followed a course which perplexed his contemporaries and has baffled historians. The only thing clear about it is that he was primarily concerned with saving the Border states, and that, to this end, he maintained a wide communication with Southern Unionists. It also appears that he held consultations of some sort with Douglas and Crittenden. He had co-operated with these two leaders in a sort of coalition once before, to defeat the Lecompton Constitution for Kansas, and it appears that, in January, he came to the very brink of a coalition with them again. The character of this relationship was carefully concealed at the time, and cannot be determined with any accuracy now. Crittenden behaved discreetly in the

56. C. F. Adams, Jr., *C. F. Adams,* p. 132–133.
57. C. F. Adams, Jr., *Autobiography,* p. 74.

matter, and revealed nothing. But Douglas, who was temperamentally brash, showed less caution.

Douglas was in position to know as much of Seward's plans as Crittenden did, for he and Crittenden were in close communion. Francis P. Blair wrote on January 2 that he had not seen Crittenden lately, but, "From what dropped from Douglas at his bowl of toddy on New Year's day, I suppose they are in *cahoot*. Probably they may make some new combination of Rice's plan about the territories at present in possession, with some scheme of advantage for the South from those in the prospective."[58] This alliance of Douglas and Crittenden, which Blair suspected, was not long in manifesting itself publicly. On January 16, the Crittenden measures were superseded before the Senate by the Clark resolutions, and Southern Unionists were consequently much depressed. But Douglas and Crittenden promptly united in a joint message to their Southern supporters urging them not to despair, as there was yet hope that a satisfactory adjustment would be reached.[59] Later, when questioned as to the basis for his hope, Douglas was evasive, and yet very confident. He asserted flatly, "I have reasons satisfactory to myself upon which to predicate . . . firm hope that the Union will be preserved." In response to demands that he specify, he refused, but observed that the Union men were holding consultations, and framing measures which it would be premature to reveal.[60]

This tantalizing statement implied strongly that Douglas and Crittenden were negotiating with someone who had the influence and inclination to commit the Republican party to compromise. All in all, no one was more able, and likely, to do this, than Seward; and Seward had been very cordial to Douglas. When Douglas gave a dinner for the

58. Francis P. Blair to Montgomery Blair, Jan. 2, 1861 [wrongly dated 1860], in Blair MSS. For "Rice's Plan," see above, p. 186.
59. Douglas mentioned, in the Senate, Jan. 31, the joint messages which he and Crittenden had sent. *Cong. Globe,* p. 668.
60. In Senate, Jan. 31, in *ibid.*, p. 669.

French minister, Seward was there, proposing a toast, "Away with all parties, all platforms of previous committals, and whatever else will stand in the way of the restoration of the American Union."[61] Could it be that Seward was in secret consultation with Crittenden and Douglas, at the same time that he was secretly engaged with Stanton and Gwin? The *Tribune* evidently got wind of some such alliance, for it reported on January 29, "We have positive information from Washington that a compromise on the basis of Mr. Crittenden's issue is sure to be carried through Congress either this week or the next, provided a *very few more Republicans* can be got to enlist in the enterprise. . . . Several gentlemen who have hitherto enjoyed the confidence of the Republican party are actively engaged in the endeavor to convert their colleagues to their new faith."[62] Scarcely a week after this, the "Public Man" recorded his expectation of such a development, because Lewis Cass had known, in January, as an "absolute certainty that Mr. Seward and Mr. Crittenden had so got their heads together as to insure a satisfactory settlement 'the very next day.' "[63]

Despite all the circumstantial evidence and the rumors current, Seward concealed his hand so skillfully that his dealings with Crittenden and Douglas almost escaped being recorded by any properly informed person. One explicit account, however, exists to confirm all the inferential evidences. Seward took John A. Gilmer of North Carolina into his confidence, when Gilmer was still being considered for a cabinet post; and Gilmer told Thomas Fitnam that, on the night of January 18, Seward and Senator James Dixon of Connecticut[64] held a long conference with Douglas and Crittenden, to come "to some

61. MSS. recollection of Justice John A. Campbell, quoted in Bancroft, *Seward*, II, 22.

62. New York *Tribune*, Jan. 29, quoted in Milton, *Eve of Conflict*, p. 534.

63. "Diary of a Public Man," Feb. 26, in *North Am. Rev.*, CXXXIX, 265.

64. For Dixon's attitude on compromise, see above, p. 129.

definite arrangement on our present national difficulties."
Fitnam informed Buchanan of this in a letter which thus
verifies the many rumors of a great non-partisan alliance.[65]
For reasons unknown, the whole scheme failed, but the
attempt shows again the diversity of Seward's connections,
the finesse of his dealings, and the extent of his exertions
to reach some amicable settlement of the sectional issue.

During and after his negotiations with Crittenden and
Douglas, Seward was also attempting to forestall hostile
action in Virginia, by maintaining an active communication with leaders of the Unionist group in that state. Late
in December he had viewed the Border situation rather
cheerfully, but during the first half of January this mood
changed to one of extreme pessimism. Governor Letcher
had called the Virginia legislature to meet in special session on January 7. It met accordingly, and precisely one
week later it passed a bill providing for a convention.
Conventions had promptly enacted ordinances of secession
in every one of the four states where they had met, and
Seward naturally feared that another secession was
foreshadowed. Henry Adams informed his brother that
"Seward is evidently very low spirited." Their father, too,
he said, showed a marked change, because of some information which was not revealed to the younger Adamses.
"Until now he has steadily believed that the border states
would not go. . . . But now I think he gives it up. His
theory is that all depends on Virginia and that Virginia
is lost. If this turns out to be the case, it increases our
difficulties very badly. It makes war inevitable; war before
the 4th of March."[66]

It is likely that Seward experienced his greatest discouragement during January. He had suddenly come to
a full recognition of the likelihood that Virginia might
secede, and of the ruin which such a secession would work

65. Thomas Fitnam to Buchanan, Jan. 25, cited in Milton, *Eve of
Conflict*, p. 534.

66. Henry Adams to C. F. Adams, Jr., Jan. 8, in Ford, ed., *Henry
Adams Letters, 1858–1891*, p. 76.

upon his policy. He had not yet foreseen any means of
averting this disaster. But Seward was temperamentally
incapable of resigning himself to fate. Consequently, he
began to seek means of communicating with the Virginians
and influencing them. The methods by which he accomplished this were hidden, and have never been revealed,
but it is known that he attained his purpose, for on January 27 he wrote to Lincoln, "Recent events have opened
access for me to Union men in Virginia and other Southern States. Among others, Mr. James Barbour of the
State of Virginia has visited me. He is a Democrat, but
the master spirit of the Union party." Already, Seward
was recovering his optimism, for "Our friends say we are
safe in Maryland, and Mr. Scott and others tell us that
union is gaining rapidly as an element in Virginia."[67]

The chief cause of Seward's more cheerful outlook was
the fact that, on January 19, the Virginia legislature had
passed a measure which was directed toward compromise
even more explicitly than the Convention Bill was directed
toward secession. This was a set of resolutions inviting all
states to send delegates to a meeting at Washington, on
February 4, for the purpose of making "an earnest effort
to adjust the present unhappy controversies, in the spirit
in which the Constitution was originally formed." In pursuance of this, there assembled at the specified time the
so-called Washington Peace Convention. The resolutions
further appointed commissioners to President Buchanan,
and to the seceding states, to request their abstention
"from any and all acts calculated to produce a collision of
arms," until the Peace Convention should have attempted
a settlement.[68]

The activities of the Peace Convention were so entirely
ineffectual that it is useless to discuss them here. Suffice

67. Seward to Lincoln, Jan. 27, in Nicolay and Hay, *Lincoln,* III, 366.
68. The Virginia resolutions appear in L. E. Chittenden, *A Report
of the Debates and Proceedings . . . of the Conference Convention . . .
held at Washington, D. C., in February, . . . 1861* (New York, 1864),
pp. 9–10.

it to say that certain Northern states sent delegates for the avowed purpose of thwarting any compromise measures, that these delegates prevented the adoption of any plan until a few days before Lincoln came to the Presidency, and that a plan was then permitted to be passed and submitted to the House of Representatives, which promptly rejected it. But in the meanwhile, the Convention was a godsend to Seward. After compromise had obviously failed in the Senate, and after the House Committee of Thirty-three had fallen into virtual anarchy, he could still insist that conciliatory measures were in progress of being formulated, and that no state ought to secede until every opportunity for compromise had been exhausted. In his protracted and difficult campaign to gain time, no other instrument served him so well as the Washington Peace Convention.

The advantage which Seward derived from the meeting of this Convention was so great that, even if there were no direct evidence, it would seem pertinent to inquire what part he had in launching the movement. It is singular that the one Virginia Unionist known to have had interviews with Seward was also the author of the Peace Convention plan.[69] By itself, this would be merely a coincidence. But along with it, one has the statement of Henry Adams, an intimate of Seward at the time, that, before the election of delegates to the Virginia Convention, "Mr. Seward had caused another Convention to be summoned at Washington."[70] Thus, the direct assertion of Adams provides the statement of fact necessary to round out the picture. Seward needed the delay which a peace convention would produce. He conferred with the Virginian who was first openly to propose such a convention. Seward's part in the matter was adroitly and deftly concealed. But to Henry Adams, with all of his family's concern for the

69. Shanks, *Secession in Virginia*, p. 253, note 26, names Barbour as the author of the Peace Convention plan.

70. Adams, "Secession Winter," in Mass. Hist. Soc., *Proc.*, XLIII, 680.

historic record, no fact was to be suppressed—and Adams declared that Seward had initiated the movement for the convention at Washington.

Though the details of this extraordinary maneuver remain unknown, other facts show that Seward devoted himself with energy to the cause of Union in Virginia. He distributed documents freely. He offered to send a messenger to communicate with the Virginia Unionists,[71] and apparently he won their confidence, for a number of them wrote to him. Among his Virginia allies were W. D. Moss, John Pendleton, Sherrard Clemens of the Wheeling district, Joseph Segar of the Tidewater region, and James and Alfred Barbour. In their letters, they advised him of their problems, urged him to prevent the passage of a "force bill" in Congress, begged him to accept the Crittenden Compromise, warned him not to suppose that the Unionism of Virginia was unconditional, and suggested that communications could be conducted secretly through the intermediation of M. M. Dent or Representative John T. Harris of Virginia.[72]

While this correspondence was in progress, Seward was much cheered by the first Unionist victory in the South. On February 4, Virginia elected the delegates to her convention. Up to that time, seven states had elected conventions, and the conventions had enacted seven ordinances of secession in the space of forty-three days. Only once had the decision been referred to the people for ratification; not once had secession been defeated in any slave state. But when Virginia voted, secession met a crushing defeat. Of the 152 delegates elected, about 122 were opposed to immediate secession, and only 30 in favor. Moreover, the Virginia electorate endorsed, by a vote of 100,536 to

71. Alfred Barbour acknowledged Seward's proposal to send a messenger, in a letter to Seward, Feb. 21, in Bancroft, *Seward,* II, 538. The messenger was apparently Frederick W. Lander. Letters from him appear in *ibid.,* II, 539–542.

72. Letters from these Virginia Unionists appear in an appendix to Bancroft, *Seward,* II, 533–539.

45,161, a provision that any act of secession must be submitted to popular vote for ratification.[73] Virginia secessionists were cast into black despair, and Virginia Unionists were jubilant. W. D. Moss wrote to Seward, "We have scarcely left a vestige of secession in Western Virginia, and very little indeed in any part of the state. . . . The Gulf Confederacy can count Virginia out of their little family arrangement."[74]

Seward and his followers were immeasurably encouraged. The day after the election, Henry Adams rushed off a letter to the *Advertiser:* "A gasp of relief went through our whole community this morning on the receipt of the news from Virginia. For more than two months the Seward republicans have been watching, hoping, praying for the signs of a break in the storm. Governor Seward's reputation as a political prophet, his influence as a statesman . . . depended and was pledged on this result. He has gone on the principle that this was only a temporary fever, and now it has reached the climax and favorably passed it."[75]

Historians have indulged in polite smiles at the self-importance which Seward exhibited during the winter of 1860–1861. His vanity at times seemed a shining mark. For instance, there was his statement that "The present Administration and the incoming one unite in devolving on me the responsibility of averting . . . disasters." Or again, "I have assumed a sort of dictatorship for defense."[76] But, upon examination, it will appear that Seward was not without cause for being complacent. In December, he had accepted the temporary leadership of his party in a time of acute crisis. He had accepted it with the stated belief that a Unionist sentiment existed in the

73. Shanks, *Secession in Virginia*, p. 153.

74. W. D. Moss, Moundsville, Va., Feb. 6, to Seward, in Bancroft, *Seward*, II, 533–534.

75. Letter of Henry Adams, Feb. 5, in Boston *Advertiser*, Feb. 8.

76. Seward to his wife, Jan. 23, to his family, Jan. 3, in Seward, *Seward*, II, 497, 491.

South, and would bring the Southern states voluntarily back to the Union, if given time to operate. But his task was the extremely delicate one of forestalling any forces which would interfere with this Unionist sentiment. Recognizing the responsibility, he had given all his energy, finesse, and resourcefulness to the problem. Fearing that the Buchanan administration would not protect the government, or that violence would be used to prevent it from passing into the hands of the Republicans, he had connived with Edwin Stanton and the House Committee of Five to stand sentinel over the government, and he had won the confidence and the military support of General Scott. Fearing that a clash of arms would be similarly fatal to reconstruction, he had acted to prevent the enactment of a "force bill" and had undertaken, through Senator Gwin, to arrange an understanding to prevent hostilities at Fort Sumter. Fearing that the secession of the Border states would likewise destroy the possibility of a Unionist reaction, he had coöperated with Charles Francis Adams to introduce in the House of Representatives a program which divided the upper South; he had conferred with Douglas and Crittenden, with the result that they continued to hold out hope of compromise; and, apparently, he had been instrumental in the calling of the Washington Peace Convention.

He had adhered to this policy, without flinching, while South Carolina, Mississippi, Florida, Alabama, Georgia, Louisiana, and Texas, in rapid order, marched into the ranks of secession. Showing no sign of dismay at these losses, he continued to insist that "The Government can be saved, if not betrayed before the Fourth of March,"[77] and that sixty days would see the crisis eased.

Then, on February 4, the tide appeared to turn. On that day, the Washington Peace Convention met, and on the same day the secessionists in Virginia received a stunning defeat in the election of delegates to their convention.

77. Frederick Seward asserts that this was a recurrent saying of his father. *Ibid.*, II, 501.

From that day forward, for more than two months, secession met with reverses as consistent as its successes had been previously, with the result that a majority of slave states refused to leave the Union. In Delaware, of course, there was no serious movement in favor of secession. In Maryland, Governor Hicks alone resisted the enormous secession pressure, and refused to call the legislature into session.[78] In Kentucky, the legislature refused to call a convention.[79] Thus three slave states were held to the Union without popular action. But in the remaining slave states of Tennessee, Arkansas, Missouri, and North Carolina, the question was submitted to the people, and in every one of these states secession was smashingly defeated. On February 9, Tennessee cast 91,803 votes for anti-secessionist candidates to her convention, and only 24,749 for secessionists, and, at the same time, dealt to the secessionists the additional blow of deciding, 68,282 to 59,449, that the convention should not meet at that time.[80] Next, on February 18, both Arkansas and Missouri voted. Arkansas authorized the meeting of a convention on March 4, but in the election of delegates, the immediate secessionists were defeated. Out of some 43,000 votes, the foes of secession triumphed by a majority of 5,699. With the control which this gave them in the convention, they defeated an ordinance of secession, on March 15, by a vote of 39 to 35, and, less than a week later, adjourned to August 19, subject to the call of the president.[81] Missouri defeated the secessionists ticket by a popular vote of 110,000 to 30,000, and elected a convention which voted 89 to 1 that there was "no adequate cause to impel Missouri to dissolve her

78. George L. P. Radcliffe, *Governor Thomas H. Hicks of Maryland and the Civil War*, pp. 21–42, in Johns Hopkins University *Studies in Historical and Political Science*, Series XIX, nos. 11–12.

79. E. Merton Coulter, *The Civil War and Readjustment in Kentucky* (Chapel Hill, 1926), pp. 30, 36–37.

80. James W. Patton, *Unionism and Reconstruction in Tennessee* (Chapel Hill, 1934), p. 12; James Walter Fertig, *The Secession and Reconstruction of Tennessee* (Chicago, 1898), p. 17.

81. David Y. Thomas, *Arkansas in War and Reconstruction* (Little Rock, 1936), pp. 56, 69–72.

relations with the Federal Union."[82] In North Carolina, on February 28, the immediate secessionists were again doubly defeated, as they elected only 42 delegates, while their opponents elected 28 conditional and 50 unconditional Unionists, and the electorate decreed, by a vote of 47,323 to 46,672, that the convention should not meet.[83]

Beginning in Virginia, and thereafter in Tennessee, Arkansas, Missouri, and North Carolina, secession was repulsed five times in 24 days, just as it had previously triumphed seven times in 43 days. When Lincoln came to the Presidency, seven slave states were out of the Union— but eight were still in. The vaunted Southern Confederacy had been held to such a limited number of states that the *Tribune* could speak of it contemptuously—and accurately —as a "heptarchy."[84]

In the light of these facts, one can understand why Seward felt that the tide had turned. One can appreciate him in the mood pictured by Henry Adams, after the vote in Virginia: "The ancient Seward is in high spirits and chuckles himself hoarse with his stories. He says it's all right. We shall keep the border states, and in three months or thereabouts, if we hold off, the Unionists and Disunionists will have their hands on each other's throats in the cotton states."[85]

In the estimation of Adams, Seward was entitled to be jubilant, for he had attained a difficult objective despite obstacles which required the supreme degree of patience and skill. "Those who saw and followed Mr. Seward during all the anxieties and cares of this long struggle," said

82. Walter H. Ryle, *Missouri, Union or Secession* (Nashville, 1931), p. 210, 220 *et seq.*

83. Joseph Carlyle Sitterson, *The Secession Movement in North Carolina* (Chapel Hill, 1939), p. 223. An older, slightly different, and less conclusive statement as to the North Carolina election appears in Henry M. Wagstaff, *State Rights and Political Parties in North Carolina, 1776–1861,* p. 135, in Johns Hopkins University *Studies in Historical and Political Science,* Series XXIV, nos. 7–8.

84. New York *Tribune,* Mar. 20.

85. Adams to C. F. Adams, Jr., Feb. 8, in Ford, ed., *Henry Adams Letters, 1858–1891,* p. 87.

Adams, would not be likely to forget his cheerfulness, his steadiness, his clear perception, his inexhaustible resourcefulness, his unfailing tact, his influence in guiding the actions of others, his power of bringing diverse connections into a vast combination, his promptness in abandoning unattainable objectives, and his pertinacity in seeking as much as was practicable. With all this "armory of weapons, he fought, during these three months of chaos, a fight which might go down to history as one of the wonders of statesmanship."[86]

When full account is taken of Seward's manifold activities during the critical winter, it becomes evident that he was not without cause for his optimism, and even his self-satisfaction. It is possible to understand why he could boast that he had whipped Senators Mason and Hunter in their home state of Virginia, and that he would carry the fight for the Union into the home states of Davis and Toombs.[87] It is even possible to share in the misguided sense of relief which caused him to write to his wife, shortly before Lincoln took office: "I am, at last, out of direct responsibility. I have brought the ship off the sands, and am ready to resign the helm into the hands of the Captain whom the people have chosen."[88]

86. Adams, "Secession Winter," in Mass. Hist. Soc., *Proc.*, XLIII, 679.
87. Language attributed to Seward by Confederate States Commissioners in a letter to Toombs, Mar. 8. Bancroft, *Seward*, II, 109.
88. Seward to his wife, Feb. 15, in Seward, *Seward*, II, 505.

CHAPTER XII

LINCOLN'S FORMULA FOR PEACE AND UNION

DESPITE the stature which Abraham Lincoln afterward assumed, he was, until he entered the White House, simply a lawyer from Springfield, Illinois—a man of great undeveloped capacities and narrowly limited background. He was far more fit to become than to be President.

This fact may seem too obvious to justify notice, and, indeed, it would be, were it not for the fact that the Lincoln legend has obscured the shortcomings of the man, and has glossed over the periods of his life during which he groped and blundered. Consequently the picture of Lincoln coming east from Springfield with his misgivings and his misconceptions, is lost. Instead, there is a picture of a man following the well-marked path of destiny to abolish slavery, to console Mrs. Bixby, to reach maximum at Gettysburg, to give his life in the cause of Union, and, finally, to belong to the ages. Writers whose minds are colored by this "knowledge of the end" are so preoccupied with justifying or discrediting Lincoln's ultimate course, that they ignore the plain evidence of his earnest efforts to avoid that course altogether. He was, in fact, reluctant to become an Emancipator—great or of other dimensions —and the conflict which immortalized him was a conflict which he had believed he could avert. In fact, when the conflict materialized, it represented a signal failure of Lincoln's policy.

To understand Lincoln's plans at the time of his inauguration, therefore, it is necessary to exclude the misleading perspective of hindsight, and to view the problem as he viewed it at the time, rather than as he later viewed it—to distinguish sharply between his intentions for dealing with it, and his later action in dealing with it. This in turn, requires a close scrutiny of every indication as to Lincoln's attitude at a time when he refused to publicize his views.

Lincoln had already given evidence that he grossly underestimated the extent of the crisis, and, perhaps, totally misconceived its nature. No one with any true perception of the public temper in the Gulf states would have said, "I am rather glad of the military preparation in the South. It will enable the people, the more readily, to suppress any uprisings there which their [the secessionists'] misrepresentations . . . may have encouraged." No one who understood the meaning of South Carolina's Ordinance of Secession would have characterized the proceedings of the South as "threats and mutterings," nor would such a person have alluded to "the danger of serious trouble" as if it were a future contingency. But Lincoln expressed these attitudes, and as winter gave place to spring, and the time approached for him to grapple with the problem, he still failed, according to two of his closest friends, to estimate the crisis properly.[1] Not only did Lamon and Herndon testify to this, but when Orville H. Browning visited in Springfield on February 9, he found that Lincoln "agreed with me that far less evil & bloodshed would result from an effort to maintain the Union and Constitution, than from disruption and the formation of two Confederacies."[2]

Whatever estimate Lincoln formed of the crisis was held privately so long as he remained in Springfield. But this ceased to be true, when, on February 11, he started on his journey to Washington. The twelve-day trip which followed was, perhaps, the most difficult and the least creditable experience in Lincoln's life. It was a period when, with little social poise, he found himself required to confront every type of social situation. Conscious of his inadequacy in this aspect, he showed himself painfully ill-at-ease. Moreover, while he did not wish to anticipate his

1. See above, p. 247.
2. Pease and Randall, eds., *O. H. Browning, Diary,* Feb. 9, I, 453.

inaugural address, he had consented to speak repeatedly at various cities along his route, and his speeches, under the circumstances, were evasive, trite, and often flippant. It was at this time that Samuel Bowles said, "Lincoln is a 'simple Susan,' and the men who fought a week at Chicago to nominate him have probably got their labor for their pains." Charles Francis Adams was only one of many who were disgusted by the spectacle of Lincoln "saying whatever comes into his head" and "perambulating the country, kissing little girls and growing whiskers!"[3]

The gravest deficiency exhibited by Lincoln on this trip, however, was not his *gaucherie* in such matters as wearing black gloves with evening dress, but his continued failure to appreciate the secession movement. Earlier, he had revealed his underestimate only to private individuals, but now, when his elevation to the Presidency was imminent, he gave public evidence, in speech after speech, that he regarded the crisis as self-liquidating.

Sometimes he took a sober view, comparing his task with that of Washington, admitting to "real anxiety," and lamenting that he, the humblest person to come to the Presidency, should face a more difficult situation than any of his predecessors.[4] But, for the most part, he consistently minimized the crisis. Speaking before the legislature of Ohio, he said, "there is nothing that really hurts anybody. We entertain different views upon political questions, but nobody is suffering anything. This is a most consoling circumstance, and from it, we may conclude that all we want is time, patience, and a reliance on . . . God." Next day, at Steubenville, Ohio, he expressed a belief that "the devotion to the Constitution is equally great on both sides

3. Bowles to H. L. Dawes, Feb. 26, in George S. Merriam, *Life and Times of Samuel Bowles* (New York, 1885), I, 317; C. F. Adams, Jr., *Autobiography,* pp. 77, 82.
4. Lincoln recognized the difficulty of his task most explicitly in speeches before the Ohio Legislature, Feb. 13; before the New York Legislature, Feb. 18; and in an address replying to Governor Curtin at Harrisburg, Pa., Feb. 22; all in Nicolay and Hay, eds., *Works of Lincoln,* VI, 121, 140, 160.

of the [Ohio] River. It is only the different understanding of that instrument that causes difficulty." Another day found him in Pittsburgh, where he observed that "there is no crisis but an artificial one." He liked this phrase well enough to repeat it the same day at Cleveland, adding, "Let it [the crisis] alone, and it will go down of itself." On February 16, the citizens of Buffalo received assurance that if they would only be calm and stand by their convictions and obligations, "the clouds now on the horizon will be dispelled." At Troy, Lincoln declared that the country did not need to be saved, for it "will save itself," and that only the institutions of the country needed protection.[5] At New York City, he told John C. Frémont personally what he had been telling the public—he firmly believed that peace would be preserved.[6] Leaving a mass of such statements as these in his wake, he finally arrived, on February 23, in Washington. There Senator Fessenden observed, a little later, that "Mr. Lincoln believed that gentleness and a conciliatory policy would prevent secession."[7]

If these utterances represent what Lincoln actually thought, they establish two vital points: he expected the Union to be saved, and he expected it to be saved without a war. That is, he, like Seward, believed in the existence of a Union sentiment in the South which would lead to voluntary reconstruction; he, like most of his contemporaries, believed that somehow a clash would be averted. He trusted that the proper policy, on his part, would secure a peaceful reunion.

While Lincoln's earlier utterances, both public and private, had given some indication of his mental attitude, no conclusive statement of his policy was available until the

5. Speeches in Nicolay and Hay, eds., *Works of Lincoln,* VI: to the Ohio Legislature, Feb. 13 (p. 122); at Steubenville, Feb. 14 (p. 123); at Pittsburgh, Feb. 15 (p. 125); at Cleveland, Feb. 15 (p. 130); at Buffalo, Feb. 16 (p. 133); at Troy, Feb. 19 (p. 143).

6. Nevins, *Frémont,* p. 471, citing Frémont MS. memoirs.

7. Fessenden, *Fessenden,* I, 126.

inaugural address of March 4.[8] For this declaration, Lincoln had prepared carefully and the country had waited anxiously. To it, the various factions responded according to their bias. Hostile secessionists, determined to see no good in the speech, interpreted it as a declaration of war.[9] Republican radicals, thinking wishfully, hoped that the Southern interpretation was correct, and since the address was not as bellicose as they had desired, they spoke approvingly of the iron hand in the velvet glove, of a policy *suaviter in modo, fortiter in re*.[10] But they knew in their hearts that a policy which would suspend Federal functions in the seceded states, as Lincoln said he would, was neither iron-handed nor *fortiter*—Andrew Jackson would never have accepted it—and though they refrained from direct attacks upon their own President, they denounced Stephen A. Douglas sharply when he defended the presidential policy.[11] Meanwhile, a level-headed North Carolina editor ignored the commentaries, studied the address itself, and concluded: "So far as coercion is concerned, Mr. Lincoln occupies the very ground occupied by Mr. Buchanan. . . . *It is not a war message.* . . . It deprecates war, and bloodshed, and it pleads for the Union. That any portion of it will be approved by the Disunionists we have no idea. If it had breathed violence and war . . . the Disunionists would have shouted for joy . . . for they would then have been sure of the attainment of . . . the permanent and final disruption of the Union."[12]

8. Nicolay and Hay, *Lincoln,* III, 327–344, contains the inaugural address, annotated to show all changes between the original draft and the finished address. This is incomparably the best text, and is the one used in the discussion below.

9. Richmond *Enquirer,* and Richmond *Dispatch,* Mar. 5, in Dumond, ed., *Southern Editorials on Secession,* pp. 474–476. The latter said, "The Inaugural Address . . . inaugurates civil war."

10. Francis P. Blair ascribes this motto to Lincoln, in a letter to Martin Van Buren, Mar. 7, in the Van Buren MSS.

11. Milton, *Eve of Conflict,* pp. 550–551.

12. Raleigh *North Carolina Standard,* Mar. 9, in Dumond, ed., *Southern Editorials on Secession,* pp. 476–479.

Partisan critics read diverse meanings, according to their partisan purposes, in Lincoln's words. To discover Lincoln's meaning, however, it is expedient to read the message in the light of his own purpose, insofar as he had revealed one. Although obscure in some respects, that purpose was clearly to facilitate a peaceful reconstruction. Essentially, this involved the same program which Seward had confronted, except that there was no longer any danger of Washington being attacked, of the new administration being obstructed from taking office, or of the Border states hastily seceding. But the problem was the same in the vital sense that Lincoln had still to uphold Federal authority, and, at the same time, to avert any clash which would produce war and thus inhibit the Southern reaction.

In strict logic this was impossible, for the very process of enforcing the Federal functions was certain to produce the sort of clash which had to be avoided. Translated into realistic terms, therefore, the circumstances required, first, that the South be reassured as to the good will, conciliatory purposes, and Constitutional scruples of the new administration; second, that a symbolic assertion of Federal authority be maintained; third, that the operation of Federal jurisdiction must be tacitly waived until it could be resumed by Southern consent. These terms for peaceable reunion were precisely the terms which Lincoln attempted to meet in his inaugural address.

The first words of the address, in fact, were intended to meet the first necessity for reunion—that is, to reassure the South. Moderates had, all winter long, demanded such a statement as Lincoln now made, giving categorical and explicit reassurance. After only two introductory sentences, he said: "Apprehension seems to exist among the people of the Southern States that by the accession of a Republican Administration their property and their peace and personal security are to be endangered. There has never been any reasonable cause for such apprehension. Indeed, the most ample evidence to the contrary has all the while existed and been open to their inspection. It is found in nearly all the published speeches of him who now addresses you. I do but quote from one of those speeches when I declare that 'I have no purpose, directly or indirectly, to interfere with the institution of slavery in the States where it exists. I believe I have no lawful right to do so, and I have no inclination to do so.' Those who nominated and elected me did so with full knowledge that I had made this and many similar declarations, and had never recanted them. And, more than this, they placed in the platform for my acceptance, and as a law to themselves and to me, the clear and emphatic resolution which I now read:

" '*Resolved*, That the maintenance inviolate of . . . the right of each State to order and control its own domestic institutions according to its own judgment exclusively, is essential to that balance of power on which the perfection and endurance of our political fabric depend, and we denounce the lawless invasion . . . of any State or Territory, no matter under what pretext, as among the gravest of crimes.'

"I now reiterate these sentiments; and, in doing so, I only press upon the public attention the most conclusive evidence of which the case is susceptible, that the property, peace, and security of no section are to be in anywise endangered by the now incoming Administration."

To validate these copious reassurances, Lincoln returned, later in his speech, to the question of Constitutional protection for slavery in the states. He alluded to the proposed Thirteenth Amendment, just passed by Congress, to guarantee slavery in the states, and added that, although he wished to speak of general policy, rather than specific measures, he would say that, holding such a guarantee to be implied in the existing Constitution, "I have no objection to its being made express and irrevocable."

Turning from the question of slavery in the states to that of fugitive slaves, he expressed an equally firm purpose to respect the provisions of the Fugitive Slave clause of the Constitution. After some discussion of this point, he then added, "I take the official oath to-day with no mental reservations. . . ." Lincoln could scarcely have used more emphatic or more unqualified language to re-assure anyone who feared an attack by him on Southern institutions.

Lincoln's first necessity had been to allay Southern fears; his second was to rally Southern Unionism by a vigorous affirmation of the national authority. This he attempted in language distinctly cogent. With firm words and careful argument he denied the right of secession: "no state upon its own mere motion, can lawfully get out of the Union." Then he pronounced the words which were, ultimately, perhaps the most weighty that he ever spoke: "I therefore consider that, in view of the Constitution and the laws, the Union is unbroken; and, to the extent of my ability I shall take care, as the Constitution itself expressly enjoins upon me, that the laws of the Union be faithfully executed in all the States. . . . I trust this will not be regarded as a menace, but only as the declared purpose of the Union that it *will* constitutionally defend and maintain itself." Continuing a little more explicitly, he added, "The power confided to me will be used to hold, occupy, and possess the property and places belonging to the Government, and to collect duties and imposts."

This fulfilled the second necessity of the peaceful reconstruction policy. In unmistakable language, Lincoln raised the banner of national authority. He did not, like Buchanan, overrefine his declaration with metaphysical distinctions between the right to coerce a state and the right to deal with individuals. He did not try to buy with compromises the adherence of secessionists to the Union. He made an appeal, not only for Union, but, as Seward did, for Unionism, on the basis of mutual advantage. He defended Union with the force of the argument that, "Physically speaking, we cannot separate. We cannot remove our respective sections from each other, nor build an impassable wall between them. A husband and wife may be divorced, and go out of the presence and beyond the reach of each other; but the different parts of our country cannot do this. They cannot but remain face to face, and intercourse, either amicable or hostile, must continue between them. Is it possible, then, to make that intercourse more advantageous or more satisfactory *after* separation than *before?* Can aliens make treaties easier than friends can make laws? Can treaties be more faithfully enforced between aliens, than laws can among friends?" At the conclusion of his address, Lincoln returned to this vital topic with one final appeal to idealistic Unionism: "I am loath to close. We are not enemies but friends. We must not be enemies. Though passion may have strained, it must not break our bonds of affection. The mystic chords of memory, stretching from every battle-field and patriot grave to every living heart and hearthstone all over this broad land, will yet swell the chorus of the Union when again touched, as surely they must be, by the better angels of our nature."

Ultimately, this high-minded appeal was perhaps the most important part of Lincoln's speech, but for the immediate problem before him, the true significance of the speech lay neither in assurance of security to the South, nor in its declaration of the Union's indestructibility, but in Lincoln's thinly veiled intimations that he would temporarily suspend the operation of the authority which he had so firmly asserted.

The suspension of Federal functions in the states, today, would operate in such multiple and far-reaching ways that it would probably jeopardize the whole social and economic structure. But in 1861, there were few ways in which the Federal government exercised a direct authority, few functions which brought it into direct contact with the people or the authorities of the states. It is probably true that all such functions fell under not more than four heads: Federal marshals and judges administered the Federal law, postal officials delivered the mails, customs officers collected duties at a limited number of Southern ports, and the army maintained forts and arsenals. These few agents of the United States were the only visible instruments of Federal power; only in them was Federal authority embodied; only by their performance of their duties did the Federal government touch the people of the South. If their posts were left vacant, or if their activities were suspended, the question of Federal authority would become an abstraction. Thereupon, the sectional *impasse* might continue indefinitely without leading to actual conflict.

It is an astonishing fact, and one which has been strangely ignored by history, that Lincoln planned, at the time of his inauguration, or soon after, to suspend every one of these four types of activity. To appreciate this, one must examine them in series.

The primary function, and the one on which Lincoln laid most stress, was the enforcement of the laws. Yet even while insisting that he would maintain the laws with full Constitutional vigor, he added the statement that, "Where hostility to the United States, in any interior locality, shall be so great and universal as to prevent competent resident citizens from holding the Federal offices, there will be no attempt to force obnoxious strangers among the people for that object. While the strict legal right may exist in the Government to enforce the exercise of these offices, the attempt to do so would be so irritating . . . that I deem it better to forego for the time the use of such offices." Lincoln made this statement in the full knowledge that there were ten states where not a single vote had been cast for him. In other words, he would enforce the laws, unless such enforcement should be unwelcome.[13] The position was not unlike that which Buchanan had assumed, and which Seward had wittily summarized to the effect that no state can secede—unless it wants to.

A less sovereign function, but a more familiar one, was

13. The Raleigh *North Carolina Standard*, Mar. 9, remarked that Lincoln "says he must execute the laws, and in the next breath he virtually omits the cotton States as Mr. Buchanan omitted South Carolina, for the simple reason that he has no officers in those States, and cannot execute them." Dumond, ed., *Southern Editorials on Secession*, p. 477.

that of delivering the mails. If Lincoln had chosen to make an issue, he might well have made it on this point, as Grover Cleveland later did, in defiance of Governor Altgeld of Illinois. But, instead, Lincoln waived the issue in one sentence: "The mails, unless repelled, will continue to be furnished in all parts of the Union."

The third group of Federal officials in the South were the customs officers. Their function presented more of a problem than that of the judicial and postal officials, for the collection of duties could not be suspended in the South without diverting a large volume of the nation's import trade to the ports where duties were not collected. Such a diversion was certain to raise a howl of protest from Northern merchants,[14] and, what was worse, it was equally certain to bring sudden prosperity to Southern ports. Such prosperity, coming soon after secession and apparently in consequence of it, would have seemed, in the eyes of Southerners, a vindication of the secession program, and would have completely inhibited a Unionist reaction in the South. Lincoln was probably mindful of all this when he declared, "The power confided to me will be used . . . to collect the duties and imposts." Was this, then, the point at which he would carry the Federal authority into the Southern states? It appeared so as he stated it, but there was still a way in which the duties might be collected without invoking the use of force within the Confederate harbors.

14. William Curtis Noyes wrote to Chase, Apr. 8, "A blockade of the ports would . . . , in my judgment, have a . . . good effect, in counteracting the apprehended evil results of the new tariff; as it would quiet the expectation that all the West and North West would import through the Confederate States. This has caused a good deal of alarm here among commercial classes and those dependent upon them, such as landlords and others." Chase MSS.

On Mar. 14, Robert Toombs, Confederate Secretary of State, wrote to Confederate Commissioners in Washington that no inducement could persuade the Confederate States to collect customs duties according to Federal rather than Confederate law. Bancroft, *Seward*, II, 120. This strongly suggests that Seward had suggested Confederate enforcement of Federal duties so that Northern commercial interests would not demand coercion for the purpose of saving their markets from the competition of Southern free ports.

This means was not openly stated by Lincoln, but it was frankly set forth in an article in the *Tribune*, shortly after the inauguration. This article remarked that some merchants "can't see how it is possible to get the revenue without blood." But the solution, it contended, was easy: "suppose such appointees [Federal collectors] are not permitted to exercise their offices. . . . What then? Why, they will report the fact to the Federal government, and forthwith they will be furnished with sufficient ships of war, from on board of which to collect the duties of the harbors or rivers of the cinq ports, which Charleston, Savannah, Mobile, New-Orleans, and Galveston, may now be appropriately called."[15] Unimportant as this proposal might seem as a newspaper suggestion, it was significant as a lucid statement of the plan which Seward proposed, and which Lincoln attempted to adopt. On March 15, Seward submitted a written suggestion that Unionism in the South might be shielded from the ruinous effects of a conflict in Southern harbors, if the collection of the revenue could be delegated to naval forces offshore.[16] The seriousness with which Lincoln received this suggestion is

15. New York *Tribune,* Mar. 9 (Baltimore, Mar. 6).

The continuation of this editorial shows how carefully the writer had considered all the problems connected with collection of duties offshore: "But what if the duties are paid to the Federal collector, and the goods are subjected to additional duties by the local collector on shore? Why, then the Federal Government will become responsible for repayment of any such exactions. But suppose the importer will not pay the Federal duties when demanded, or there is no money on board the ship, when brought to, to pay them? Why, the importer will be dealt with precisely as he would be were he in a similar situation in the harbor of New-York. But in case the goods, after paying Federal duties, are confiscated by the local collector? The Federal Government would become responsible for the loss, if it could not or did not prevent it. In other words, the importer of goods into any of the Cinq ports would be treated as a citizen of the United States, pursuing his lawful calling, and would receive every protection he now receives in the harbor of New-York; or if that is denied to him by the circumstances of the rebellion, then he will be reimbursed in all his losses and damages arising thereout."

16. Memorandum of Seward on provisioning Fort Sumter, Mar. 15, in Nicolay and Hay, eds., *Works of Lincoln,* VI, 200.

indicated by the fact that, on, March 18, he addressed notes on the subject to three of his department heads. The first, to the Secretary of the Treasury, inquired as to whether goods were coming in without paying duties, and as to the practicability of collecting duties offshore. Another, to the Secretary of the Navy, asked what naval forces could be placed at the disposal of the revenue service. The third, addressed to the Attorney General, requested an opinion as to the legal right of the executive to collect duties offshore in cases where collection in the ordinary way was impracticable.[17]

As matters later developed, offshore collection of duties was not attempted—but collection of duties at the customs houses was not attempted either. When war came, Lincoln's administration was not enforcing the revenue laws in the South, and instead of planning measures to compel the South to submit to them, Lincoln was working upon a formula to enforce them without compelling specific Southern submission.

Assuming that the revenue problem should be eliminated, the remaining aspect of Federal authority was that which related to Federal forts and arsenals. Lincoln's attitude toward this problem shows how completely he had abandoned a policy of force. Nearly all Federal military property had been seized by secessionists, as their states went out of the Union, and Lincoln could have found no better issue on which to assert Federal authority than in the attempt to repossess this government property. He had, at one time, intended to force this issue. In December, he had sent a message to Winfield Scott, asking him to be ready to retake the forts, and, at the same time, he had contemplated making a public announcement that the forts would be retaken when he came to office.[18] He had withheld

17. Letters of Lincoln, Mar. 18, to Secretaries Chase and Welles, and Attorney General Bates, in *ibid.*, VI, 224–225.
18. Lincoln's message to Scott was sent in a letter to E. B. Washburne, Dec. 21, in *ibid.*, VI, 84. His proposed public announcement was mentioned in a letter to Trumbull, Dec. 24, in Tracy, ed., *Uncollected Lincoln Letters,* p. 173.

the statement then, but he included it in the original draft of his inaugural address: "All the power at my disposal will be used to reclaim the public property and places which have fallen; to hold, occupy, and possess these and all other property and places belonging to the government."[19] Had Lincoln persisted in this vigorous language, it might appear that on this point he intended to make his test of strength with the secessionists. But, before the inauguration, he consulted his associates, and when they objected to this passage, he modified it. A prolix substitute, suggested by Seward, did not appeal to Lincoln, but Orville H. Browning proposed a neater change which altered the wording slightly, and the meaning greatly. Lincoln accepted this, and, in its final form, his message said: "The power confided to me will be used to hold, occupy, and possess the property and places belonging to the Government." In this statement, he abandoned his clear-cut notice that he would "reclaim the public property." Time was soon to show that he had abandoned the purpose, as well as the notice.

Interpreted in practical terms, the promise to "hold, occupy, and possess," meant only that the Lincoln government would retain control of the two offshore forts of Pickens, at Pensacola, and Sumter, at Charleston. All other property had already passed into secessionist hands. Both of these forts, it appeared, could be held as symbols of national authority—and as such they would be highly important, giving a visible, physical embodiment to Lincoln's claims of an unbroken Union. Yet both could be retained, it seemed, without assuming the initiative, or inviting a clash. Pickens had been retained under the terms of a formal truce which had applied ever since January, and as for Fort Sumter, the War Department and the public both supposed that Major Anderson could maintain himself there without supplies or reinforcements for an indefinite time.

19. The original text and the history of the changes in this passage are given in Nicolay and Hay, *Lincoln,* III, 333, note 12.

This, then, was the much vaunted "firm" policy of Lincoln. He would assert the Federal authority vigorously —but he would not exercise it. He would enforce the laws —where an enforcement mechanism existed. He would deliver the mails—unless repelled. He would collect the duties —offshore. He would hold the forts—at least the ones which Buchanan had held, and which seemed capable of holding themselves.

It was a superb pattern for reconstruction, one which seemed to eliminate every possibility of a clash. The rival sections were segregated by a sanitary cordon of neutral states which would prevent the possibility of any border incident causing an outbreak. Behind this barrier, the operation of Federal force would be, in effect, suspended so far as seemed necessary to give Unionism full and free scope. With every point of contact carefully muffled, friction might be avoided indefinitely. Meanwhile the abdication of Federal authority would be concealed and Union sentiment would be rallied by the firm language of the President, and by the retention of Fort Sumter, which had come to have enormous emotional significance as a symbol of the national authority.

Regarded in this way, it appears that Lincoln's policy was positive, detailed, and explicit. There were some indications that it was, for a time, even recognized as such, and that Republican editors attempted to write in support of the policy which their President had announced. Without claiming to interpret administration policy, both the New York *Times* and the *Tribune* carried editorials which echoed Lincoln's purposes, and cogently defended his policy, without attributing it to him. Two of these editorials are especially to the point. One, which appeared in the *Times* of March 21, began, "The true policy of the government is unquestionably that of *masterly inactivity*," and continued, "The object to be aimed at is, the conversion of the Southern people from their Secessionism. The appeal of the Government must be to the minds of the people,—to their judgment, their political sagacity, their common sense. Force, as a means of restoring the Union, or of permanently preserving it, is out of the question. It has its place in our system of Government as in every other. It may and must be used to repel aggression,—to hold public property and to enforce obedience to the laws, in every case where temporary disobedience would not be a less evil than the attempt to compel assent: and of this the Government itself must be the judge. But no war,—no force can ever restore the Union. *That* work must be done by other means. The people of the South must *come* back, —not be driven back: and they will do it whenever they are convinced that their safety will permit, and that their interests require, it. It must be the aim of the Government to *convince them of this fact*,—and to avoid everything which will change the issue and prevent the people from exercising their calm judgment upon the subject. It must not dissolve the Union, nor recognize its dissolution—nor permit any of the bonds of Union which still remain to be severed. Let it hold its forts, its arsenals, and all its public property —not menacingly, but as a matter of right and of duty,— and let it make no attack, and repel none for any other purpose than strict defence and self-preservation.

"This, in our judgment, is the policy by which the Union may be preserved, and must be, if it is preserved at all."

Less than a week after the appearance of this editorial in the *Times*, the *Tribune* also urged the importance of "masterly inactivity." It began by asserting that there were but three possible ways in which to meet the secession movement: "1. By prompt, resolute, unflinching resistance. . . . 2. By complete acquiescence in . . . Secession. . . . 3. By a Fabian policy, which concedes nothing, yet employs no force in support of resisted Federal authority, hoping to wear out the insurgent spirit and in due time reestablish the authority of the Union throughout the revolted or seceded States, by virtue of the returning sanity and loyalty of their own people.

"We do not assume," said the *Tribune*, "that this last is the wisest policy, nor yet that it has been resolved on by the new Administration; we propose simply to set forth the grounds on which it is commended and justified.

"This Government, it is said, is based not on force but on reason; not on bayonets and battalions, but on good will and general consent. . . . To war on the Seceders is to give to their yet vapory institutions the strong cement of blood—is to baptize their nationality in the mingled life-blood of friends and foes. But let them severely alone —allow them to wear out the military ardor of their adherents in fruitless drilling and marches, and to exhaust the patience of their fellow-citizens by the amount and frequency of their pecuniary exactions—and the fabric of their power will melt away like fog in the beams of a morning sun. Only give them rope, and they will speedily fulfill their destiny—the People, even of South Carolina, rejecting their sway as intolerable, and returning to the mild and paternal guardianship of the Union.

"In behalf of this policy, it is urged that the Secessionists are a minority even in the seceded States; that they have grasped power by usurpation and retain it by terrorism; that they never dare submit the question of Union or Disunion fairly and squarely to the people, and always shun a popular vote when they can. In view of these facts, the Unionists of the South urge that the Government shall carry forebearance to the utmost, in the hope that the Nullifiers will soon be overwhelmed by the public sentiment of their own section, and driven with ignominy from power."[20]

As Lincoln conceived it at the time when he assumed the Presidency, and as many of his followers conceived it during the brief remaining span of peace, the preservation of the Union was to be achieved by forbearance, and not by

20. New York *Tribune*, Mar. 27. As a forerunner of this editorial, see the Washington dispatch, Jan. 30, signed J. S. P[ike]., in the *Tribune* of Feb. 1. This dispatch declared, "Their [the secessionists'] whole scheme is likely to prove a total failure if nothing is done to help them out. . . . A 'masterly inactivity,' accompanied with firmness and determination, is the surest policy to set them all by the ears in a short time."

force; the term "reconstruction" was used without any taint of its later connotations. But in a very brief time, this concept was rendered obsolete. Within five weeks, confusion and misunderstanding as to Lincoln's policy became evident.[21] During and after the war, the short-lived prevalence of this policy was almost wholly forgotten.

It was forgotten partly because of sectional violence. The Northern tradition has enshrined Lincoln for striking fearlessly at disunion and slavery. The Confederate tradition has damned him for destroying the old state-rights system. Some have lauded and some have stigmatized him for enforcing the national authority, but few have paused to note how extremely reluctant he was to enforce this authority or to accomplish these ends.

The policy is forgotten, also, because the Unionism which existed in the South, and upon which Lincoln relied, was soon covered and obliterated by the Confederate gray. Without that Unionism, and without a recognition of it, Lincoln's plan is incomprehensible. When the previous existence of Southern Unionism was forgotten by loyal Confederates and angry Northerners, the existence of a plan based upon an appeal to Southern Unionism was forgotten also.

Finally, Lincoln's plan is forgotten because his policy was stillborn. His whole plan was built upon the assumption that Sumter could be passively retained as a symbol of the vitality of the Union. On the morning after he delivered the inaugural address, Lincoln learned that he had based it on a false premise. Unexpected word reached him from Major Anderson that the fort must fall in a few weeks unless supplies were thrown in.

21. Seward's memorandum to Lincoln, Apr. 1, in Nicolay and Hay, eds., *Works of Lincoln,* VI, 234, said that the government had declared no policy—this despite the fact that Seward had personally shared in the revision of the inaugural address. Lincoln wrote to a committee from the Virginia convention, on Apr. 13 (in *ibid.,* VI, 243): "Having, at the beginning of my official term, expressed my intended policy as plainly as I was able, it is with deep regret and some mortification I now learn that there is a great and injurious uncertainty in the public mind as to what that policy is, and what course I intend to pursue."

Immediately he was confronted with the dilemma that he must sacrifice that vital symbol, or abandon his plan of passivity. His efforts to escape this dilemma constitute the final episode in the attempt to preserve a voluntary Union.

NOTE ON MAJOR ROBERT ANDERSON'S LETTER DELIVERED TO LINCOLN ON MARCH 5

Anderson's important letter of February 28, which was received in the last hours of the Buchanan administration and shown to Lincoln on March 5, is missing, and has never been used by historians. Its absence was noted in the *Official Records*, Series I, Vol. I, p. 191, note; and a search, made for the author in the summer of 1941, in the National Archives, yielded no record of it. The letter may be in the Lincoln manuscripts (closed until 1947) in the Library of Congress.

A recent volume, *Lincoln Takes Command* (Chapel Hill, 1941), by John Shipley Tilley, questions whether any such letter was ever sent, and suggests that the whole story of the starving garrison may have been fabricated to afford a pretext for an aggressive policy. This argument contains much special pleading, and it rests too much upon a demonstration of errors in other historical accounts, and not enough upon actual evaluation of the sources. Essentially, however, it is based upon two major arguments:

(I) That there is no good first-hand evidence that Anderson ever sent any such letter. This contention is invalidated by several important sources: (1) President Buchanan made a memorandum of the cabinet meeting of March 4, in which he spoke of Holt announcing that he had "received extraordinary dispatches from Major Anderson saying that without a force of some twenty or thirty thousand men to capture the batteries which had been erected, he could not maintain himself at Fort Sumter." Other memoranda by Buchanan showed that these dispatches were transmitted by Secretary of War Holt to Lincoln, on March 5. The substance of these memoranda was repeated in Buchanan's *Mr. Buchanan's Administration on the Eve of the Rebellion*. All in Moore, ed., *Works of Buchanan*, XI, 156; XII, 190–191. (2) Joseph Holt wrote to Lincoln on March 5, enclosing Anderson's dispatches "which are of a most important and unexpected character" inasmuch as Anderson had been requested to report "whenever, in his judgment, additional supplies or re-enforcements were necessary. . . . So long, therefore, as he remained silent upon this point, the government felt that there was no ground for apprehension." Moore, ed., *Works of Buchanan,* XI, 191–193. (3) Gideon Welles declared in his diary that on March 6 he was present at a conference with Holt, General Scott, and others, at which Scott declared that the meeting was called especially because of "certain intelligence of a distressing character from Major Anderson at Fort Sumter, stating that his supplies were almost exhausted, that he could get no provisions in Charleston, and that he, with his small command would be wholly destitute in about six weeks." Morse, ed., *Welles Diary,* I, 4. Tilley mentions this but fails to note the highly significant point that Holt was present when Scott made these assertions, that Holt possessed an independent knowledge of the contents of the Anderson dispatch, and that, even if Lincoln could have deceived Scott, he could not possibly have deceived Holt. Nor did Holt have any cause for collusion with Lincoln in such a fantastic distortion of the contents of a War Department communication. (4) Edward Bates, in his diary for March 9, noted that, at a cabinet meeting, "I was astonished to be informed that Fort Sumter . . . must be evacuated, and that General Scott, Gen[era]l Totten, and Major Anderson concur in opinion, that, as the place has but 28 days [*sic*] provision, it must be relieved, if at all, in that time." Beale, ed., *Bates Diary,* p. 177. (5) Lincoln, himself, in his message to Congress, July 4, 1861, declared that, on March 5, a letter from Major Anderson, Feb. 28, had been handed to him; and that this letter expressed the opinion that "reinforcements could not be thrown into the fort within the time for his relief, rendered necessary by the limited supply of provisions. . . ." Nicolay and Hay, eds., *Works of Lincoln,* VI, 310. (6) The testimony of John G. Nicolay, given in his own book, *The Outbreak of the Rebellion* (New York, 1882), p. 50, and in Nicolay and Hay, *Lincoln,* III, 325, to the effect that Anderson reported a food shortage at Sumter, may be regarded as a primary source, since Nicolay was Lincoln's private secretary.

(II) That Anderson could not have sent such a message, because it was inconsistent with all his earlier reports that there was no shortage of supplies. Undeniably, the inconsistency appeared, strongly enough to astonish the heads of the War Department. Instead, however, of denying that so great a reversal could have taken place, it may be more pertinent to inquire why Anderson reversed himself. Without attempting to make a complete answer to this query, it seems significant to note the assertions current at the time that Anderson had deliberately refrained from asking for supplies which he knew to be necessary. New York *Tribune,* Mar. 13 (Charleston, Mar. 9) and 14 (Washington, Mar. 9). This does not necessarily imply a treasonable intent to betray the fort to the Confederates, but only an unwillingness to call on the government to send supplies and thus, as Anderson knew, precipitate war, while there was still hope of peace. When he did, at last, give notice of his impending food shortage, it was with the implication that he ought to be evacuated (still preserving peace) rather than that supplies ought to be sent. Until the time of the firing, Anderson consistently discouraged all plans to relieve him.

XIII

THE LAST PHASE OF PEACEABLE RECONSTRUCTION

WHEN Lincoln came to the Presidency, he had evolved a policy which provided against the outbreak of war through any existing contingency. But no sooner had he been inaugurated than the contingencies were altered. Anderson's unexpected notice, requiring either the evacuation of Sumter or the active provisioning of that fort, ruined Lincoln's policy of passive nationalism. During the next six weeks, the administration sought desperately to modify the inaugural formula in some way, so that it might still save the Union without civil war.

For nearly a month, evacuation of the fort was regarded almost as a foregone conclusion. Seward assumed this with such certainty that he offered an unauthorized promise of evacuation as a means of preventing the Confederate Commissioners at Washington from precipitating a crisis. Meanwhile, the administration considered various measures designed to show the vitality of the national organism, and thus to offset the effect of evacuation. First, Lincoln and Seward together sought to inspire a Unionist demonstration in Texas. Even before this, Lincoln had contemplated a trade, by which he would abandon the fort in return for a promise of adherence to the Union by the Virginia Convention; and as prospects of holding the fort grew faint, the advantage of trading it away, rather than giving it away, became increasingly evident. Meanwhile, plans were made to transfer attention to Fort Pickens as a substitute symbol of national authority. But the developments at Pickens prevented it from being used as an equivalent for Sumter, whereupon Lincoln took the momentous decision to send supplies to the fort at Charleston. He sought still to keep the peace by promising not to reinforce the fort, if the food supplies were not resisted. Seward viewed this expedient with justified pessimism, and hastily organized an expedition to Pickens in the hope that it might still become the symbol of national authority. When this failed, Seward desperately proposed a foreign war as the only remaining device for escaping a domestic conflict.

The problem of Sumter confronted Lincoln at a very difficult time. Inexperienced, and beset by office-seekers as he was, he faced his hardest problem before he had even learned which of his officials were reliable. One of his first questions was to inquire of Holt whether Anderson could be trusted.[1] Yet the situation would admit of no delay, and the new President turned his attention to the problem of Sumter very promptly. As early as March 6, a conference was held with Joseph Holt, General Scott, Brigadier General Totten, Gideon Welles, and others in attendance. Lincoln did not attend this meeting, but on the day following, substantially the same conferees met with the President at the White House.[2] A number of cabinet discussions were held, and after these preliminary consultations Lincoln moved toward a decision. On March 9, he submitted to General Scott questions as to the length of time for which Anderson could maintain himself, and the capacity of the army to relieve him.[3] Scott responded on March 12 with a detailed opinion that relief could only be accomplished by a force larger than could be raised, and that the fort ought to be abandoned.[4] The naval authorities, and particularly Captain Gustavus V. Fox, brother-in-law of Postmaster General Montgomery Blair, had already ex-

1. Crawford, *Story of Sumter*, p. 285.
2. Morse, ed., *Welles Diary*, I, 3–6.
3. Lincoln to Scott, Mar. 9 cited in Nicolay and Hay, *Lincoln*, III, 379.
4. Scott to Lincoln, Mar. 11, 12, quoted in part in *ibid.*, III, 381, and in *Official Records*, Ser. I, Vol. I, p. 197.

pressed a contrary opinion.[5] Therefore, the military possibilities were still obscure when, on March 15, Lincoln
submitted to his cabinet a question as to the wisdom of provisioning Sumter, assuming that it could be accomplished.[6]

The answers were preponderantly in favor of evacuation. Only Blair advocated sending provisions without reference to consequences. Chase also favored provisioning,
but he indicated his belief that supplies could be furnished
without causing war, and that he would not favor the
measure if it entailed war. All other members of the cabinet favored evacuation. Welles predicted that a relief expedition would cause war, and "I am not prepared to advise a course that will provoke hostilities." Caleb Smith
also predicted that war would ensue, and preferred that,
if it were coming, the South should cause it by resisting
law officers rather than military forces. Simon Cameron
opposed provisioning because it "would initiate a bloody
and protracted conflict." Bates, likewise, thought that
such action was sure to lead to war, which he deprecated
because it would prevent the peaceful reconstruction of
the Union, for which he still hoped. Seward wrote an extended answer, in which he set forth, once more, his belief
in the "profound and permanent" Union sentiment in the
South, which would cause the people there "to reverse
upon due deliberation, all the . . . acts . . . by which
they were hastily . . . committed to disunion." He also
pointed out the extreme forbearance which had been
necessary in order to hold Virginia, Maryland, Kentucky,
North Carolina, Tennessee, Missouri, and Arkansas to
the Union, and argued that continued forbearance would
be required in order to keep them. An expedition, he said,
would gain no military advantage, would lose the Border
states, and would precipitate war. He was opposed to it.[7]

5. Beale, ed., *Bates Diary*, Mar. 9, p. 177; Fox, memorandum, Feb. 6,
and letter to Blair, Feb. 23, in *Official Records*, Ser. I, Vol. I, pp. 203–204.

6. Nicolay and Hay, *Lincoln*, III, 385.

7. These opinions, dated Mar. 15 and 16, except in the case of Blair,
undated, appear in Nicolay and Hay, eds., *Works of Lincoln*, VI, 192–
220.

These opinions were submitted to Lincoln on March 15 and 16, and it is safe to say that he tentatively adopted the view which they expressed. If he had been required to make a final decision on the Sumter question at that time or for two weeks thereafter, he would almost certainly have decided in favor of evacuation. It was generally supposed that he had already made the painful decision, or would inevitably do so when it could be put off no longer. According to Welles, the President "appeared to acquiesce," and Blair was so convinced of the finality of the decision that he wrote out his resignation.[8] Stephen A. Douglas and Lyman Trumbull both understood that Lincoln had accepted the opinion of his cabinet, and that there was a decision to evacuate the fort.[9] General Scott, also, apparently supposed that the evacuation of the fort had been determined upon.[10]

On March 19, however, Lincoln took a step which should have served as conclusive warning that he had not fully made up his mind. He sent a request to Scott, through the Secretary of War, that some suitable person be sent to Charleston to secure accurate information as to Anderson's position. Scott appointed Gustavus Fox for this mission. Fox left on the same day on which Lincoln made the request, went to Charleston, and saw Anderson, who told him that he could hold out until April 15, and that he did not consider plans of reinforcement feasible.[11]

Before Fox could return to Washington, however, an-

8. Morse, ed., *Welles Diary*, I, 9, 13.

9. Orville H. Browning, Apr. 26, wrote, "Douglass [*sic*] and Trumbull both told me that it had been determined upon in Cabinet to evacuate Fort Sumter, but that Lincoln would not issue the order." As this statement continues, it indicates that Douglas received his information from the Confederate Commissioner, John Forsyth. Pease and Randall, eds., *O. H. Browning Diary*, I, 466. "Public Man," however, declared that Douglas claimed to have his information directly from Lincoln. "Diary of a Public Man," Mar. 11, in *North Am. Rev.*, CXXIX, 493.

10. Montgomery Blair to Samuel W. Crawford, May 6, 1882, in Crawford, *Story of Sumter*, p. 365.

11. For selection of Fox by Scott, see *Official Records*, Ser. I, Vol. I, pp. 208-209. For his mission, see Crawford, *Story of Sumter*, pp. 369-373.

other and a more curious mission had been sent after him. As it happened, there was present in Washington a friend of Lincoln's named S. A. Hurlbut, a citizen of Illinois, but a native of Charleston. Lincoln, it appears, sent for him on March 21 and asked him to go to Charleston and ascertain whether there was actually a strong Unionist party there. Hurlbut undertook the assignment, went to Charleston, and talked with many people, including James Louis Petigru, his former law preceptor and the most eminent Unionist in the state. From this investigation, Hurlbut concluded that Unionism was virtually extinct in Carolina.[12] Thus, his mission was most productive. But the curious feature of his trip is that he was accompanied by Lincoln's muscular and bibulous young friend, Ward Lamon. What conceivable service Lamon could have rendered is difficult to imagine. But what he did do, on all sides, was to leave the impression that the evacuation of Sumter was imminent. He sought an interview with Governor Pickens, and informed him that he had come to arrange for the removal of the garrison. With the greatest air of authority, he even proceeded to discuss the type of vessel which should be used and the details of evacuation. As if this were not enough, he wrote to the Governor shortly after his departure, saying that he would soon return to arrange for the removal.[13]

12. Nicolay and Hay, *Lincoln,* III, 390–392, including a report of Hurlbut to Lincoln, Mar. 27.

13. Rhodes, *Hist. of U. S.,* III, 333, citing letter of Pickens, Aug. 3, in Charleston *Courier,* Aug. 6; Crawford, *Story of Sumter,* pp. 373–374, citing Pickens' message, Nov., 1861. No conclusive explanation has ever been offered, either for the sending of Lamon to Charleston, or for his conduct after he got there. It may be that he was sent to provide some degree of protection for Hurlbut. It may be that, as a native Virginian with friends in Charleston, he was expected, like Hurlbut, to investigate the degree of Unionism in the South. Seward may have had some part in sending him, for he wrote to Seward from Charleston, Mar. 25. Bancroft, *Seward,* II, 107.

Even more difficult to explain is Lamon's conduct after he arrived in Charleston. Conceivably he was the agent in a sinister design to mislead the Carolinians, but more probably his impulsiveness and his vanity led him to assume the role of spokesman for the policy which he believed the

On the face of it, Lincoln's desire for information on conditions at Charleston would suggest that he was still undecided as to Sumter, but Lamon's dogmatic promises of evacuation, coupled with the general expectation in Washington, led to a widespread and unqualified belief that the question was settled. An Associated Press dispatch of March 19 announced that evacuation had been ordered for the next day.[14] The *Tribune's* Charleston correspondent reported that "the authenticated report" that the fort would be abandoned "affords inexpressible relief to hundreds of families . . . that had husbands and brothers in the rebel ranks." [15] Joseph Holt and Edwin Stanton, in letters to Buchanan, assured him of the same decision. From New York, John A. Dix wrote of the bad effects of "the intelligence that Fort .Sumter is to be abandoned." But the stock exchange regarded it as good news, and securities rose.[16]

The complete credence with which the public accepted these reports is shown by a tendency to regard the evacuation almost as an accomplished fact. Among the correspondents of Chase, for instance, one wrote, "The news received yesterday was anything but pleasant. The surrender of the forts will give great dissatisfaction." Another said, "You . . . have no idea of the despondency and discouragement of the Republicans . . . in this part of the country." On April 1, the Republicans lost a state election in Ohio, and they were prompt to attribute this defeat to the situation at Sumter. One of them wrote, "Ohio yesterday spoke in thunder tones against the surrendering of Fort Sumpter [*sic*]. . . . It is to us a Water-

administration had adopted. In this connection, it may be that Seward, in his anxiety to forestall an attack upon Sumter, encouraged Lamon to tell the Carolina leaders that it would be evacuated.

14. New York *Tribune,* Mar. 20 (Washington, Mar. 19, Associated Press).

15. *Ibid.,* Mar. 16 (Charleston, Mar. 12).

16. Buchanan received repeated assurances from Stanton (Mar. 12, 14, 16, Apr. 3), Holt (Mar. 14, 20), and Dix (Mar. 14, 28), that Sumter would be evacuated. All in Curtis, *Buchanan,* II, 531–538. Also see citations in Rhodes, *Hist. of U. S.,* III, 332–333.

loo defeat, and all know that the supposed evacuation
. . . is what did it." Similarly, Rutherford B. Hayes declared, "Yes, giving up Fort Sumter is vexing. It hurts
our little election, too." [17]

It is clearly evident that a general understanding existed that Major Anderson was to be withdrawn. It is also
evident that Lincoln shared in this understanding, for he
told Francis P. Blair, Sr., that it had not yet been fully
decided, but that the cabinet was almost a unit in favor
of it and "that he thought such would be the result." [18]
It is sometimes said that actual orders of evacuation were
drawn up and signed.[19] But probably there was never
more than an informal understanding, and, to the cabinet
members, who did not yet know that Lincoln was capable
of overruling their opinion, nothing more seemed necessary. Seward certainly entertained no doubt as to the
outcome, and his presumption led him into what was probably the least creditable episode of his career.

It was the misfortune of the new administration, at the
same time when it was vexed by the Sumter question, to be
troubled also by demands, presented by Confederate commissioners, for recognition of the Davis government. Two
of the commissioners, Martin J. Crawford, and John Forsyth, were in Washington by March 8, and were later
joined by A. B. Roman. They perceived that the Lincoln
government was eager for peace, and, accordingly, they

17. Letters to Chase from A. Sanders Piatt, Mar. 12; J. H. Jordan,
Mar. 27; J. W. and J. B. Antram, Apr. 2; in Chase MSS. Hayes to S.
Birchard, Mar. 17, in Williams, ed., *Diary and Letters of Hayes,* II, 6.

18. Blair gave this account to Crawford. Crawford, *Story of Sumter,*
p. 364.

19. For full evidence that Lincoln contemplated abandoning the fort,
see Wilmer L. Hall, "Lincoln's Interview with John B. Baldwin," in *South
Atlantic Quarterly* (1914), XIII, 260–269. Its most striking citations
are to an article in the Richmond *Examiner,* Aug. 8, 1861, containing the
text of a statement which it is claimed that Lincoln once approved in
proof, justifying the necessity of evacuation; and an unverified statement by R. R. Howison, "History of the War," in *Southern Literary
Messenger,* XXXIX, 404, that Lincoln once signed an order for evacuation.

determined to press for recognition.[20] Since the ordinary channels of diplomatic intercourse were closed to them, they enlisted Seward's friend, Senator Gwin, as an intermediary. Gwin was peculiarly well fitted for this purpose, inasmuch as he was known to be a Southern sympathizer, and yet he had served Seward in matters of great confidence: he had aided him in trying to induce the Buchanan administration to come to an understanding with the Carolinians after Anderson's removal from Moultrie; he had also, at Seward's instance, told Lincoln of the extreme fragility of Unionism in the Border states; he had rendered Seward an even more signal service by writing twice to Jefferson Davis to assure him that the Republican administration would seek peace and an amicable settlement of issues.[21] With these qualifications, Gwin was brought into the negotiations very early, and it may even be that he was first employed by Seward to extend assurances of good-will to the commissioners, while withholding recognition. If so, however, the effort failed, and Gwin next appeared on behalf of the Confederates. Acting for them, he conveyed to Seward the suggestion that if they were not received, Sumter would be attacked.[22] Shortly after this, he applied for an interview with Seward, at which he apparently intended to ask that the commissioners be re-

20. Letter of commissioners to Secretary Toombs, Mar. 8, in Bancroft, *Seward,* II, 110.

21. Gwin, "Gwin and Seward," in *Overland Monthly,* 2nd series, XVIII, 467–469, recounts these services. For the effort to influence Buchanan, see above, p. 269. The letter to Davis is confirmed by an undated memorandum, no. 1, of Sam Ward to Seward, in which he (Ward) tells of hearing Browne, of the Washington *Constitution,* say that Jefferson Davis had shown him (Browne), the letter from Gwin. Bancroft, *Seward,* II, 543–545. Gwin also told Crawford of the letter to Davis. Crawford, *Story of Sumter,* p. 320.

22. Undated memorandum, no. 2, of Sam Ward, to Seward, declared that if the commissioners were refused, Davis could not prevent an attack on the forts. Bancroft, *Seward,* II, 543–545. A letter of the commissioners to Toombs, Mar. 8, in *ibid.,* II, 109–110, shows that the commissioners arranged for Gwin to tell Seward that they would precipitate the Sumter issue at once, unless Seward gave them certain assurances.

ceived informally. But when he called at Seward's quarters the next day, he was informed that the Secretary was ill and could not see him. Thereupon he withdrew from the negotiations, either because he disbelieved Seward's illness, or because he was leaving Washington for New York.[23]

When Gwin withdrew from the scene, Senator Robert M. T. Hunter of Virginia was enlisted in his place, and, on March 11, he called on Seward and requested that he grant an informal interview to the commissioners. Seward was obviously troubled by this request, and he sought refuge in the plea that he must refer the matter to Lincoln. On the following day, when Hunter came for an answer, Seward handed him a written statement: "It will not be in my power to receive the gentlemen of whom we conversed yesterday. . . . This decision proceeds solely on public grounds, and not from any want of personal respect." Thus the prospect of negotiations appeared to be blasted, and the commissioners therefore took the formal step of filing at the State Department a request for recognition. Seward put off making a reply, for which they called on March 14 and again on March 15, but it was evident that he must soon reject their request, and thus

23. The story of Gwin's connection with this affair is much confused, because he was superseded in the midst of the negotiations by R. M. T. Hunter. The confusion was intensified when Seward, in a paper refusing the demands for recognition, spoke of the intermediation of "A distinguished senator." This ambiguity has led some historians to ignore Gwin, and assume that Hunter was the only intermediary. Rhodes, *Hist. of U. S.,* III, 328; Crawford, *Story of Sumter,* p. 322. Gwin, on the other hand, appears to have assumed that he was the "distinguished senator," and to have altered his chronology to fit this assumption. Gwin, "Gwin and Seward," in *Overland Monthly,* 2nd series, XVIII.

The point at which Gwin dropped out and Hunter came in is indicated by a letter of the commissioners to Toombs, Mar. 12. This speaks of Seward's illness (which Gwin had encountered) and remarks that he returned to his office Mar. 11, whereupon they decided to send their memorandum. But, "The gentleman who was to carry it had . . . left the city; and feeling unwilling to lose time in waiting for him, we availed ourselves of the kind consent of Senator Hunter, of Virginia, to see Mr. Seward." Bancroft, *Seward,* II, 111. Gwin gave his dissatisfaction with Seward's "illness," and not his departure from Washington, as the cause of his withdrawal. Gwin, "Gwin and Seward," p. 469.

incur the possibility that they would execute their threat against Sumter.[24]

Seward was, of course, uneasy at this prospect, but at the very moment when it seemed that every possibility of an understanding had failed, a new channel of communication opened. Justice Samuel Nelson of the Supreme Court called on Seward to discuss certain constitutional problems of enforcing the law in the Southern states. During their conversation, Seward told Nelson of the commissioners' demands, and of the irritation which he anticipated would result from his refusal. Nelson requested that his colleague, Justice John A. Campbell of Alabama, might be brought into this phase of the conversation. Consequently, the discussion was renewed with both justices present, and both pressing for a recognition of the commissioners. In response to their urging, Seward exclaimed, "I wish I could do it. See Montgomery Blair, see Mr. Bates, see Mr. Lincoln himself. I wish you would. They are all Southern men. Convince them. No, there is not a member of the cabinet who would consent to it. If Jefferson Davis had known the state of things here, he would not have sent those commissioners. The evacuation of Sumter is as much as the administration can bear."

Campbell instantly recognized that Seward's rejoinder offered a basis of escape from the *impasse:* if Seward would pledge the evacuation of Sumter, the Confederates ought to suspend their claims for recognition. He offered to suggest this in a letter to Jefferson Davis, and received Seward's consent. "And what shall I say to him?" asked Campbell. "You may say to him," answered Seward, "that before that letter reaches him—how far is it to Montgomery?" "Three days," replied Campbell. "You may say to him that before that letter reaches him, the telegraph will have informed him that Sumter will have been evacuated."

This was the assurance which Campbell needed. He sent

24. All this is evident from the letters of the commissioners to Toombs, Mar. 12, 22, in Bancroft, *Seward,* II, 111–113, and Mar. 12 (second letter) in Nicolay and Hay, *Lincoln,* III, 401–403.

it to Davis at once, and then, on the same day, called on Commissioner Crawford, urged him not to press for recognition, and insisted that the government ought not to be embarrassed by other demands at a time when it was preparing, as he knew, to evacuate Sumter. Crawford demanded to know his authority, and Campbell scrupulously replied that he would not name an authority, but would be responsible for the statement personally. Crawford, however, readily guessed that Campbell had the word of Seward, and he agreed not to call for the answer to his request for recognition if Campbell would give him a written statement of his personal assurance that the fort would be evacuated. Campbell complied, writing a note which expressed his "perfect confidence in the fact that Fort Sumter will be evacuated in the next five days," and asked for a ten day delay on the part of the Confederates. The note was approved by Justice Nelson, and a copy was sent to Seward.

After Seward received the note, he could no longer misunderstand that his statement had been regarded as a pledge. If he was unwarranted in making a pledge—as it appears that he was—he should have corrected the matter then. If he was authorized by Lincoln to offer a pledge—as he almost certainly was not—he should have resigned when the pledge was repudiated. But in a spirit of gambling opportunism, Seward let the pledge stand, in the hope that he could fulfill it.

From the day of this pledge, Seward was constantly pressed for the execution of his promise. After waiting five days, the commissioners learned from Charleston that no preparations for evacuation were evident. When they transmitted this information to Campbell, he, with Justice Nelson, called on Seward and received new assurances. With renewed confidence, Campbell, on March 21, gave the commissioners a second note, stating his faith that Sumter would be evacuated, and promising a further statement after an interview with Seward next day. In accordance with this promise, Campbell talked again with

Seward, found him "buoyant and sanguine," and thereupon supplied the commissioners with a third note (March 22), in which he said, "I have still unabated confidence that Fort Sumter will be evacuated." Justice Nelson again appeared as a sort of co-guarantor, but he seems to have had less elastic confidence than Campbell, and he withdrew from the negotiations at this time.

On this precarious basis, the status remained unchanged[25] until the impatient authorities of South Carolina caused the commissioners to press for action. Governor Pickens, after five days of waiting, sent the commissioners telegraphic information (March 30) of Lamon's promise (March 25), that Sumter would be abandoned. The commissioners thereupon sent Campbell to Seward with Pickens' telegram. Seward promised to make an answer to it on April 1. As is now known, Seward made his supreme effort to get control of the administration on that day. Perhaps the vigor of the effort resulted partly from his anxiety to fulfill his pledge. But, in any event, when Campbell called again, Seward wrote in his presence, and handed to him, a statement that "the President may desire to supply Fort Sumter, but will not undertake to do so without first giving notice to Governor Pickens." [26]

Campbell saw at once that this was an effort to shift ground: a promise to evacuate differed vastly from a promise to give notice before reinforcing. He demanded

25. On March 23, Seward, in a conversation with the Russian minister, Baron Stoeckl, expressed the hope that the Confederate States would return to the Union voluntarily, but said that if they should not, he believed they ought to be allowed to go in peace. He then expressed a desire to meet the Confederate commissioner, A. B. Roman, at the Russian legation. Baron Stoeckl offered to arrange such a meeting at tea on March 25, and Seward agreed. Roman accepted an invitation and the meeting was all arranged, when Seward sent his regrets, declaring later that he could not risk the possible publicity. This episode is substantiated by letters of Roman to Toombs, Mar. 25, and of the commissioners to Toombs, Mar. 26, cited in Bancroft, *Seward*, II, 117.

26. At the same interview, Seward withdrew this statement, and substituted, as an equivalent, "I am satisfied the government will not undertake to supply Fort Sumter without giving notice to Governor Pickens."

an explanation, and one can imagine that Seward's glibness was fiercely tried. But he rose to the occasion. He
argued that the decision to evacuate had been reached in
cabinet, and that there was no reason to expect that it
would be reversed. As for Lamon, he had been sent simply
to enable the government to claim that the matter had
been fully investigated. As for the delay, the administration was forced to wait until after the elections in Connecticut and Rhode Island. And as for his earlier promises,
their import remained unaffected.

Seward succeeded in persuading Campbell that evacuation would take place, but one fact, already suspected,
was now established: the President had either authorized
no pledge, or had repudiated his authorization. The erst-
while promise now became a probability. The probability,
however, was strong, and the commissioners chose to accept
it. Therefore, they still did not call for the answer to their
demand for recognition, though they knew that it had
long been ready. But while they waited, they watched
closely for any sign of a change in policy. In the first days
of April they began to detect evidences of military preparation, and, in the light of these developments, they could
not share in Campbell's belief that the government dared
not deceive him. Consequently, they called upon the Justice to explain why his pledge had not been fulfilled. He,
in turn, demanded an explanation from Seward, and, in
response, received on April 8 an undated, unsigned statement, "Faith as to Sumter fully kept; wait and see."

So far as "faith" consisted in giving notice before sending supplies to Sumter, it was indeed "fully kept," for
such notice had already been sent to Governor Pickens. So
far as it consisted in fulfilling Seward's assurance that
Sumter would be evacuated, it was, of course, not kept.
Nor is it true, as it is sometimes speciously argued, that
Seward did not understand that his statement was interpreted as a pledge. Three times he was required to make
his affirmation, in the presence of two justices of the Supreme Court, and three times he received copies of written

memoranda showing that the justices had accepted responsibility for the validity of his statement. One can only conclude that Seward's optimism—or his desperation—caused him to assume an entirely false position. The fact that the commissioners suspected it to be false, and understood the true struggle taking place in the administration, does not alter the essential fact. Nor is it altered by the consideration that the commissioners were more willing to delay than they appeared to be.

The commissioners found Seward's last reply unsatisfactory. Consequently, on the same day (April 8) that it was given, they at last called for the reply to their demand for recognition. This document, ready since March 15, was handed to them at once. Thus, after many delays, the "negotiations" with the commissioners finally broke down. But, at a heavy cost to his personal credit, Seward had prevented for four full weeks the precipitation of a diplomatic crisis which might have had immediate military repercussions.[27]

While Seward was temporizing with the commissioners, or the commissioners were temporizing with Seward, as the case may be, Lincoln and Seward together were engaged in a project which has been entirely ignored, except in Texas history; yet it was one of the most revealing of all their activities, insofar as it gave concrete proof of their belief in Southern Unionism.

When Lincoln became President, all the states of the lower South had seceded, and in all except one of these

27. The whole story of the intermediation of Justice Campbell, and of relations between the State Department and the commissioners, from Mar. 15 to Apr. 8, is fully set forth in the MS. correspondence of the Confederate Commissioners with Toombs, and in certain writings of Justice Campbell: letters to Seward, Mar. 15, 16, Apr. 7, 13; letter to Jefferson Davis, Apr. 3; a manuscript entitled "Facts of History"; and a paper prepared for the Southern Historical Society, Dec. 20, 1873. My account is based on the quotations and paraphrases of these manuscripts in Nicolay and Hay, *Lincoln*, III, 396–414; Bancroft, *Seward*, II, 113, and 130–131, 140–141; and, especially, Crawford, *Story of Sumter*, pp. 325–345. The last gives the text of all of Campbell's memoranda to the commissioners.

states, the governor and legislature had hastened the process. In Texas, however, Governor Sam Houston had resolutely refused to call a meeting of the legislature, thus compelling the secessionists to resort to extra-legal, though democratic, action. Thus, Houston appeared to be the outstanding exemplar of Unionism in the South, and Seward and Lincoln, therefore, hit upon the project of offering support to him in an effort to rally Southern Unionists. It is said that, even before the inauguration, Lincoln had sent one George D. Giddings to the Texas Governor, with an offer to send Federal troops to the Texas coast after March 4, to sustain Houston in a stand for the Union.[28] But whether such a messenger was sent at that time or not, it is certain that Lincoln and Seward sent F. W. Lander, who had previously acted as Seward's agent in Virginia,[29] as a confidential messenger to Houston, and that he was in Austin on March 29. He was evidently instructed to offer Houston the support of United States troops then on the Texas coast. Meanwhile, in order that the troops should be available, General Scott sent orders, on March 19, to their commander, Colonel Carlos A. Waite, countermanding previous orders, as late as March 12, for the embarkation of the troops, and instructing him to fortify and hold Indianola, Texas, and to support Houston or other state authorities in defense of the Federal government. The order continued, "You will communicate as freely as practicable with General Houston or other leaders of the Union party, and comply with his wishes or suggestions, if practicable." [30]

28. Marquis James, *The Raven, A Biography of Sam Houston* (New York, 1929), p. 410, is the only authority for the mission of Giddings. He cites a letter of Temple Houston Morrow to him. However, he entirely ignores the Lander mission (discussed immediately below), and since it is unlikely that there was more than one mission, it would seem that James is misinformed as to the time of that mission, and that, perhaps, Lander concealed his identity under the name of Giddings.

29. See above, p. 309, note 71.

30. Lander's presence in Texas is shown by his letter to Waite, Mar. 29, in *Official Records*, Ser. I, Vol. I, pp. 551–552. His mission is shown by his statement, in the letter, that Scott's orders to Waite relate to it. Scott's orders to Waite, Mar. 19, and the superseded orders of Mar. 12, are in *ibid.*, 598–599.

The whole scheme failed when Houston refused the proffered aid. He called a meeting of his associates, laid Lincoln's offer before them, and, proceeding as if in a war council, took the opinion of each man, beginning with the youngest. All but one of them advised against any such alliance. Houston heard them, one by one, and, at the conclusion, told them that he had asked their advice, and would take it, but that, if he were a younger man, he would not hesitate to accept Lincoln's offer.[31]

Thereupon, on March 29, he wrote to Colonel Waite, mentioned Lincoln's offer of assistance, and said, "Allow me most respectfully to decline any such assistance of the United States Government, and to most earnestly protest against the concentration of troops or fortifications in Texas, and request that you remove all such troops out of this State at the earliest day practicable." [32] In the light of this communication, Colonel Waite decided that his latest orders from Scott were no longer binding.[33] He therefore proceeded to embark his troops.

Thus the Houston episode, like other efforts to implement the Unionism of the South, ended in failure. But the offer to furnish troops and the command to Waite to place his forces at Houston's disposal, are signal proofs that the administration looked to Southern Unionism with a hope and faith which was genuine and not pretended.[34] No

31. Accounts of this council, based on verbal narrations by participants, and similar except in detail, are: Charles A. Culberson, "General Sam Houston and Secession," in *Scribner's Magazine*, XXIX (1906), 586–587; and A. W. Terrell, "Recollections of General Sam Houston," in *Southwestern Historical Quarterly*, XVI (1912), 134–135. James, *Raven*, p. 410, has an account based on these, but varying in detail, presumably because of facts which he had from Temple Houston Morrow.

32. Houston to Waite, Mar. 29, in *Official Records*, Ser. I, Vol. I, p. 551.

33. Waite to Assistant Adjutant General, Apr. 1, in *ibid.*, Ser. I, Vol. I, pp. 550–551.

34. Unfortunately, there is no way of knowing whether the following newspaper dispatches were inspired by the administration:

"Letters received in town from Texas bring the tidings that Gen. Houston is in full revolt against the rebels, and that he intends to call on the President for succor to put down the insurrection against the State authorities. If this be so, it will be well. Such a demand could not be evaded by the administration, and could be promptly responded to

stronger proof exists that their appeal to such Unionism was made in earnest, and not, as is frequently asserted, for effect.[35]

In the Texas venture, the administration had everything to gain, and nothing to lose. Inasmuch as the offer to Houston did not involve any sacrifice of other objectives, it did not indicate what concessions Lincoln would make in his effort to invoke Southern Unionism. But other developments had already demonstrated that he was willing to pay a high price for an affirmative demonstration of Unionist spirit in the South. The fact is not generally known, but there can be little doubt that, even before the inauguration, Lincoln offered to abandon Fort Sumter if the Virginia Unionists would adjourn the state convention at Richmond.

without compromitting its peace policy. But I fear that the news is too good to be true." New York *Tribune,* Mar. 20 (Baltimore, Mar. 18).

"Private information received here from Texas gives reliable assurance that Gov. Houston intends to resist the conspirators who aim at the possession of State power by deposing him from the Executive chair in order to carry out their designs of Disunion. . . . This . . . may involve a collision in Texas, and, if the Governor formally calls upon the President for aid in suppressing rebellion, or the proper execution of the laws, he cannot refuse to furnish it. Some such requisition is expected, unless affairs should assume an unexpected phase in that region." *Ibid.,* Mar. 21 (Washington, Mar. 20).

35. Lord Lyons, British Ambassador, wrote to Lord John Russell, Mar. 26, that Seward had told him, on Mar. 20, of his hope for a counter-revolution in the South, "that he hoped and believed that it would begin in the most distant state Texas where indeed, he saw symptoms of it already." Lord Newton, *Lord Lyons, A Record of British Diplomacy* (New York, 1913), I, 31.

William H. Russell wrote to John Bigelow, about Apr. 14, saying that if the military preparations then on foot were intended for war, "it means that the Gov[ernmen]t has a good understanding with Mexico and with Mr. Houston." Bigelow, *Retrospections,* I, 347.

John Bigelow met Thurlow Weed on a train trip during March, and they had a long talk. Weed told Bigelow of Lander's mission, and said that Representative Andrew J. Hamilton of Texas had furnished Lander with letters to Houston. Bigelow's account of the conversation shows that Weed was thoroughly conversant with every aspect of the Texas project, which had probably been revealed to him by Seward. *Ibid.,* I, 339.

When Lincoln reached the capital late in February, the Washington Peace Convention was still in session there. A group of the delegates, including William C. Rives and George Summers of Virginia, Alexander W. Doniphan of Missouri, and James Guthrie and C. S. Morehead of Kentucky,[36] had an interview with Lincoln; and Morehead sent an account of the interview to Crittenden less than a year later. According to this account, Morehead urged Lincoln to evacuate Sumter, arguing that such an act would save the eight slaveholding states then in the Union, and that the others would be drawn back "by the mere force of gravitation." Rives pressed the same point and "Mr. Lincoln said he would withdraw the troops if Virginia would stay in the Union. I took occasion to write down the entire conversation soon after it occurred." [37]

Taken by itself, this story would be open to the doubt which clouds much of the Lincoln apocrypha. But in this case the story is confirmed by the highest authority—that of Lincoln himself. In the October following, Lincoln, John Hay, and perhaps some others, were at Seward's one evening, when Lincoln alluded to the events of the previous spring. Hay, recording the gist of it in his diary, said Lincoln "spoke of a committee of Southern pseudo-Unionists coming to him before Inauguration for guaranties [sic], etc. [This exactly fits Morehead's group of Border Unionists]. He promised to evacuate Sumter if they would break up their convention, without any row or nonsense. They demurred. Subsequently he renewed [the]

36. This list of persons present is given by Morehead (see note below). Another list appeared in the New York *Tribune,* Feb. 28 (Washington, Feb. 27): "Last night, ex-Senator Bell of Tennessee, Judge Douglas, Mr. Guthrie, Mr. Rives, Governor Hicks, and others, urgently appealed to Mr. Lincoln to interpose for a settlement. Their interview continued several hours."

37. C. S. Morehead to Crittenden, Feb. 23, 1862, in Coleman, *Crittenden,* II, 336-338. Also see a longer account by Morehead, in a speech at Liverpool, Ohio, Oct. 9, 1862, published in the Liverpool *Mercury,* Oct. 13, 1862, and republished in David R. Barbee and Milledge L. Bonham, Jr., eds., "Fort Sumter Again," in *Mississippi Valley Historical Review,* XXVIII (1941), 63-73.

proposition to [George W.] Summers, but without any result. The President was most anxious to avoid bloodshed." [38]

This furnishes the plainest conceivable evidence that, in February, Lincoln offered to evacuate Fort Sumter on a contingency—offered to abandon his symbol of nationalism, if the leading slave state would accept the essence of it—offered to waive the formal authority of the Union if he could thereby win voluntary acceptance of it in Virginia.

It is regrettable that history has largely ignored this offer of February, while controversy has raged over a question as to whether an identical offer was made by Lincoln after the inauguration. According to Lincoln's statement to Hay, the offer was renewed, for he speaks of repeating it to Summers. John Minor Botts also asserted that the proposal was made again, to a group consisting of F. H. Pierpont, later Governor of West Virginia, Representative John S. Millson, "Dr. Stone of Washington," Garrett Davis of Kentucky, Robert A. Gray, Campbell Tarr of Wheeling, and three other gentlemen. Botts also declared that he had letters to verify this astonishing statement, but he significantly omitted these documents from his book. [39]

None of these later offers, therefore, has ever been corroborated, and attention has centered exclusively upon an interview between Lincoln and John B. Baldwin of the Virginia Convention on April 4.

At the time of this interview, the Virginia Convention had been in session for seven weeks. [40] The election of this body had marked a defeat for the secessionists, and Seward and Lincoln had therefore expected the convention to

38. Diary of Hay, Oct. 22, 1861, in Tyler Dennett, ed., *Lincoln and the Civil War in the Diaries and Letters of John Hay* (New York, 1939), p. 30. This item was previously published, with Summers' name deleted, in Clara S. Hay, ed., *Letters of John Hay and Extracts from his Diary* (privately printed, 1908), I, 47.

39. Botts, *Great Rebellion,* pp. 200–201, note.

40. Convened Feb. 13.

repudiate secession and adjourn promptly. But, instead, with that peculiar blend of emotional devotion to the Union as a voluntary association, and intellectual adherence to the doctrine of secession, the convention continued to sit, in order that it might act if coercion were attempted. In such an event, it resolved that Virginia would go with the South. Unionism thus failed of a complete triumph. To stimulate the waning Union cause, Seward began to distribute more of his assurances that Sumter would be evacuated. He communicated these reports, apparently, through several channels. According to "Public Man," Seward sent an agent to Richmond on March 6, with "positive assurances" that the garrison would be withdrawn from Sumter.[41] This agent may have been F. W. Lander, who was sent to Texas soon afterward. Also, Seward persuaded J. C. Welling, an editor of the *National Intelligencer*, to write to George W. Summers, leader of the Unionists in the Virginia Convention, to assure him that the fort would be abandoned. Welling sent this message before March 19, and Summers replied that it had "acted like a charm—it gave us great strength," but that reënforcement of the garrison would "ruin us." [42]

As time passed, and the hope of evacuation was not realized, the Unionist majority in the convention found increasing difficulty in holding its ranks firm. By the first of April this weakness had reached an advanced stage,[43] and meanwhile Lincoln had reacted vigorously against evacuation—so vigorously, in fact, that he had ordered an expedition prepared in case he should decide to relieve the fort.[44] Both the weakness of the Virginians and the vigor of Lincoln's policy seemed unfortunate from Seward's viewpoint, and it is altogether probable that he urged Lincoln to renew the offer of evacuation of the fort

41. "Diary of a Public Man," Mar. 6, 9, in *North Am. Rev.*, CXXIX, 487, 490.

42. James C. Welling, "The Proposed Evacuation of Fort Sumter," in *The Nation*, XXIX (1879), 383–384.

43. Shanks, *Secession in Virginia*, pp. 182–190.

44. See below, pp. 361–362.

in return for the adjournment of the convention. Thus Seward might simultaneously rid himself of the troublesome Sumter question, bolster the Virginia Unionists, and redeem his pledges, which were depreciating rapidly. Somehow, he seems to have persuaded Lincoln.[45]

It is significant that, when Lincoln decided to communicate with the Virginia Unionists, Seward made all the arrangements. On April 3, acting on the recommendation of Robert Chew of the State Department, he sent for Allan Magruder, a Virginian resident in Washington, and, after a preliminary conversation, took him to Lincoln. The President asked Magruder to carry to Summers, in Richmond, a request that he come to Washington for an interview on urgent and important matters. Magruder suggested that a time limit would be desirable, and that, since Summers might be unable to leave the convention, it would be well to state whether any other person could be accepted in his stead. To these suggestions, Lincoln replied, according to Magruder, that if Summers could not come, he should send some reliable Unionist in the convention, to arrive not later than April 6. That night Magruder went to Richmond and found, as he had anticipated, that Summers could not leave. But the Unionist leader delegated Colonel John B. Baldwin, a member of his group in the convention, to go in his place. Magruder and Baldwin proceeded at once to Washington, and on April 4 Seward took Baldwin to Lincoln for an interview at which only the two were present.[46]

The interview has long been a source of controversy. Baldwin afterward asserted that Lincoln made no offer of any sort, but repeated over and over the cryptic assertion, "I am afraid you have come too late." John Minor Botts, on the other hand, talked with Lincoln during the

45. Seward's interest in the matter is inferred from the eagerness with which he facilitated the attempted arrangements.

46. Allan B. Magruder's part in this affair is undisputed, and is fully set forth in his article, "A Piece of Secret History: President Lincoln and the Virginia Convention of 1861," in *Atlantic Monthly*, XXXV (1875), 438-445.

following week, and claimed his authority for a counter-assertion that the Virginian had kept Lincoln waiting a week instead of coming the next day, and that the orders to relieve Sumter had been issued in the *interim*, but that Lincoln nevertheless offered to recall the expedition, if the Virginia Unionists would adjourn the convention. Baldwin, however, according to Botts, rejected the proposal rudely, and later tried to suppress all knowledge that it had been made. Botts also accused Baldwin of admitting the suppression to him and to his friend John F. Lewis, whom he called as witness.[47]

The problem is of such a nature that absolute proof of either narrative is impossible. Botts' statement is full of demonstrable errors of fact as to the date of the interview, the time at which the relief expedition sailed, and the course of events in the Virginia Convention at that time.[48] In fact, Botts was chronically addicted to error, and in the question of credibility between him and Baldwin, one must tentatively conclude that Lincoln withheld the offer which he had, doubtless, planned to make.

Because of its controversial aspects, the Baldwin interview has received undue attention. For evidence exists, independently of this question, that Lincoln had offered, before inauguration, to abandon the fort for an equivalent; and if a solution of the Baldwin-Botts controversy were possible, it would prove only that Lincoln did, or did not, renew his previous offer. The important point is that he relied so strongly upon Unionism in the South that he seriously considered sacrificing Fort Sumter to encourage

47. The testimony of this dispute appears in several places. Baldwin set forth his story in a pamphlet, "Interview between President Lincoln and John B. Baldwin, April 4, 1861" (Staunton, Va., 1866). This was corroborated indirectly by Magruder's narrative, cited in the preceding note. Botts stated his case in his book, *The Great Rebellion*, pp. 194–202, including corroborative letters from John F. Lewis. The Joint Committee on Reconstruction questioned Lewis, Baldwin, and Botts, and their testimony appears in *Report of the Joint Committee on Reconstruction*, 39th Cong., 1st sess., part II, pp. 71, 102–106, 114–119.

48. Shanks, *Secession in Virginia*, pp. 193–194, shows these errors succinctly.

it. He offered once, and intended to offer again, to lay heavy stakes upon his faith in Southern Unionism.

The supposed necessity of evacuating Sumter was the formative factor of all administration policy during March. It was this which led Seward to make his incautious pledges to Campbell. It was probably the desire to start the Unionist reaction before this necessity materialized which prompted Lincoln to offer aid to Houston. If he repeated to the Virginians his earlier offer to give up Sumter in return for an adjournment of their convention, he did this partly in the effort to salvage something from an inescapable loss. At the same time, the search for some form of compensation gave vast importance to Fort Pickens, at Pensacola. Pickens and Sumter were the only possessions which the Federal government retained within sight of the Confederate mainland, and as the abandonment of Sumter drew near, circumstances pointed to Pickens as the only remaining visible sign that the authority of the United States still extended into the lower South. As matters developed, therefore, Pickens began to assume some of the symbolic importance which had formerly pertained to Sumter. One of Chase's friends wrote to him, "The evacuation of Fort Sumter is a bitter pill: it is all we can do to bear up against it; . . . But the evacuation of Fort Pickens,—my God! . . . it would *utterly demoralize the Government!*" Another assured him, "Our people may possibly tolerate the evacuation of Fort Sumter as a 'Military necessity,' But no necessity ever can exist which will enable this administration to survive the humiliation and disgrace of surrendering Pickens." [49] That Lincoln himself viewed the situation in this way, appears from a later message to Congress. Reviewing the situation as of March, 1861, he explained that an abandonment of Sumter, without any action to offset it, would have been "ruinous," discouraging the Unionists, emboldening their ad-

49. J. H. Jordan to Chase, Mar. 27; W. H. West to Chase, Mar. 26; in Chase MSS.

versaries, and leading to "national destruction consummated." But there was still time to offset it: "Starvation was not yet upon the garrison, and ere it would be reached, Fort Pickens might be reinforced. This last would be a clear indication of policy and would better enable the country to accept the evacuation of Fort Sumter as a military necessity." [50]

Proceeding on this theory, Lincoln had tentatively acquiesced in the "military necessity," and had promptly issued orders for a firm policy at Pickens. At that fort, a curious situation existed. A company of troops had been sent to Pensacola Harbor on board the U.S.S. *Brooklyn*, in January, but, under a "truce" made by Buchanan, they had been ordered to remain on board ship, and not to reinforce the fort. There they remained when Lincoln took office. Thus it appeared that reinforcement would be easy, and, on March 11, Lincoln sent a written order to the War Department for the movement of the troops into the Florida fort.[51] Accordingly, General Scott dispatched the *Mohawk* on March 12 with orders to Captain Vogdes, on shipboard in Pensacola Harbor, to land his company as a garrison for Pickens.[52] When this order should be executed, the focus of attention might then be turned away from Sumter.

While Lincoln awaited this development he must have pondered the abandonment of Sumter with strong misgivings. The anticipated withdrawal from the fort had already caused bitter comment. Chase's correspondents, for instance, denounced evacuation hotly: it was "submission to a band of traitors"; it would give Lincoln "a blacker and more infamous name" than Buchanan's; it would prepare the Republicans to sing their own requiem. One writer warned that six weeks more of vacillation would

50. Message of Lincoln to Congress, July 4, 1861, in Nicolay and Hay, eds., *Works of Lincoln,* VI, 301.

51. Nicolay and Hay, *Lincoln,* III, 393, citing M. C. Meigs' diary, Mar. 31.

52. Orders of Scott to Captain Vogdes, Mar. 12, in *Official Records,* Ser. I, Vol. I, p. 360.

leave but two opinions of Lincoln: "The South will proclaim him a Damned fool, and the North a damned Rascal. Sir let no false delicacy keep you from letting Mr. Lincoln peruse this." [53]

These views were representative of prevalent Republican opinion. Lyman Trumbull served his party better than his friend, the President, when he introduced into the Senate, on March 28, resolutions that "it is the duty of the President to use all the means in his power to hold and protect the public property of the United States." [54] Lincoln must have winced under that resolution. He must have felt rebuked again when the Ohio elections went against the Republicans. He knew, as John A. Dix knew, that "the disappointment [resulting from the relinquishing of Sumter] will be very great, and it will go far to turn the current against the new administration." [55] Accordingly, he must have been keenly responsive when Francis P. Blair, Sr., came to him with vigorous protests against evacuation. It is unlikely that these protests caused him to change his mind, as was afterward claimed, but they may well have influenced him.[56] Moreover, the tenderness which Lincoln felt under the jibes of his critics must have been rendered all the more acute by the fact that, in his heart, he shared their distaste for the policy which he was pursuing. Against the pressure of criticism, he was sustained only by the conviction that he could still make a stand at Pickens, and that he was acting under a military necessity, as certified by General Scott.

But on March 28 he was rudely deprived of a part of this assurance. On that day Scott sent him a message ad-

53. Letters to Chase in order quoted, from A. Sanders Piatt, Mar. 12; T. J. Young, Mar. 12; William D. Bickhorn, Apr. 2; H. Abram, Mar. 25; in Chase MSS.

54. Resolutions in *Cong. Globe,* 36th Cong., 2nd sess., p. 1519.

55. Dix to Buchanan, Mar. 14, in Curtis, *Buchanan,* II, 533.

56. Morse, ed., *Welles Diary,* I, 13–14, asserts that Blair's protests caused Lincoln to decide in favor of holding Sumter. Francis P. Blair, Jr., described these protests, but did not claim they were decisive, in a statement to S. W. Crawford. Crawford, *Story of Sumter,* p. 364.

vising the abandonment of both forts. The General's memorandum clearly betrayed a political rather than a military motivation, for it said: "It is doubtful . . . according to recent information from the South, whether the voluntary evacuation of Fort Sumter alone would have a decisive effect upon the States now wavering between adherence to the Union and secession. It is known, indeed, that it would be charged to *necessity*, and the holding of Fort Pickens would be adduced in support of that view. Our Southern friends, however, are clear that the evacuation of both the forts would instantly soothe and give confidence to the eight remaining slave-holding states, and render their cordial adherence to the Union perpetual." [57]

This was probably Lincoln's first great disillusionment as President. He had accepted Scott as a military hero, and Scott's opinion as military gospel. Now Scott abandoned the sphere of his preëminence to offer an unsolicited and inexpert opinion based on political surmise. That night, as the guests left Lincoln's first state dinner, he invited his cabinet members to remain, and informed them, "with evident emotion," of Scott's new recommendation. For a moment they absorbed this news in silence, and then Montgomery Blair burst into denunciation of Scott's political generalship.[58] No one could deny the justice of Blair's criticism. Next day, Lincoln polled his cabinet again, and found that only Seward and Caleb Smith still favored evacuation.[59] It is doubtful, however, that this poll contributed much to Lincoln's decision. Scott's message had taught him that he must act for himself, and, on March 29, he ordered an expedition prepared for the

57. Memorandum of Scott, Mar. 28, in *Official Records,* Ser. I, Vol. I, pp. 200–201.

58. The scene on the night of Mar. 28 is described by Blair in a letter to Welles, May 17, 1873, cited by Welles, *Lincoln and Seward* (New York, 1874), p. 65; and in a letter of Blair to Crawford, May 6, 1882, in Crawford, *Story of Sumter,* p. 365.

59. The opinions of cabinet members, Mar. 29, are given in Nicolay and Hay, eds., *Works of Lincoln,* VI, 227–231.

relief of Sumter,[60] to be "used or not, according to circumstances." [61] If Lincoln had decided on the evacuation
of Sumter, he now withdrew that decision, and prepared
for any course which might be indicated.

At some time soon after this, Lincoln determined to
send to Anderson the expedition which he had prepared.
The precise time of the decision cannot be fixed, but, according to John B. Baldwin, Lincoln told him, on the
afternoon of April 4, that he had "come too late" for a
proposal which Lincoln intended, on the previous day, to
make. It was also on April 4 that Lincoln sent Anderson
a message that "the expedition will go forward." [62]

Even at this time, however, no irrevocable step had been
taken. The expedition had not sailed; Governor Pickens
had not been informed that provisions would be sent; and,
if news of a successful occupation of Fort Pickens had
arrived, the Sumter expedition could have been counter-
manded. Ever since March 11, Lincoln had waited for
just such news. But Scott had sent the orders to Pickens
by sea, and they were slow to arrive. Consequently, it was
not until April 6 that a reply came from Pensacola Harbor. On that day, at last, the news of an ironic failure
arrived. The orders of the War Department had been
delivered, but Captain Adams, commanding the ship on
which the troops were waiting,[63] was not subject to Army
orders. He was still under Navy Department instructions
to respect Buchanan's truce. Consequently, he had refused,
without further orders, to render the aid essential for
throwing the troops into Fort Pickens.[64] Captain Vogdes

60. Lincoln's order, Mar. 29, in *Official Records of the Union and Confederate Navies in the War of the Rebellion* (Washington, 1894–1922),
Ser. I, Vol. IV, p. 227. Cited hereafter as *Official Records, Navy.*

61. Lincoln, message to Congress, July 4, 1861, in Nicolay and Hay,
eds., *Works of Lincoln,* VI, 302.

62. For the Baldwin interview, see above, p. 354 ff.; for the text of Lincoln's message to Anderson, Apr. 4, Nicolay and Hay, *Lincoln,* IV, 27.

63. The troops had been transferred from the *Brooklyn* to the *Sabine*
on Mar. 22.

64. Letter of Captain I. Vogdes to Captain Henry A. Adams, Apr. 1,
requesting co-operation of Navy in executing War Department orders to

and his company, therefore, were still on board ship, and would necessarily be there when Anderson's supplies were exhausted. This meant plainly that Lincoln could not display at Pickens that "clear indication of policy" which would "better enable the country to accept the evacuation of Fort Sumter as a military necessity." Accordingly, the President took the decisive step. On the same day when the news from Fort Pickens arrived, he fulfilled his pledge, given through Seward, and informed Governor Pickens that provisions would be sent to Fort Sumter and thrown in by force if necessary.[65] If the Republicans had an hour of decision, this was it.

While Lincoln did not decide until April 4 to hold Sumter, and did not act on his decision until two days later, the turning point of his policy really came on March 29 when he perceived that Scott's military advice was colored by his political wishes. This realization caused him, for the first time, to ignore Scott's opinion and order the Sumter expedition prepared.

This sudden turn of events pointed directly toward war. It jeopardized the period of delay for which Seward had played so skillfully, and it threatened to nullify all his efforts. As circumstances closed in upon the Secretary of State, he made two last desperate attempts to alter the course of the administration and ward off the imminent crisis.

In this frantic rear-guard action, Seward first endeavored, in every way possible, to shift Federal action from Fort Sumter to Fort Pickens. While the prospect of evacuation of Sumter remained strong, Seward had evinced little concern for Fort Pickens. But when Lincoln

move troops into Fort Pickens, and letter of Adams to Navy Department, Apr. 1, explaining his refusal to comply, and requesting further orders, in *Official Records, Navy,* Ser. I, Vol. IV, pp. 109–110. Date of receipt of Adams' letter in Lincoln's message to Congress, July 4, in Nicolay and Hay, eds., *Works of Lincoln,* VI, 302.

65. Lincoln, instructions to R. S. Chew, Apr. 6, to notify Pickens, in Nicolay and Hay, eds., *Works of Lincoln,* VI, 241.

resolved on a show of firmness at Sumter, Seward sought strenuously to divert the action to the Florida fort. This took place before news arrived in Washington that the orders of March 12 for the reinforcement of Pickens had not been executed.

Seward first advocated his new policy on March 29 when Lincoln polled the cabinet on the question of evacuating Sumter. As on the earlier poll, Seward advocated withdrawal, but he coupled this advice with a proposal that Pensacola Harbor and the Texas coast be defended, even at the cost of war.[66] This was pure opportunism, for it is altogether likely that Seward had approved of General Scott's recommendation that Pickens be abandoned. But if Lincoln insisted upon firmness, Seward preferred it anywhere rather than at Sumter.

In vigorous pursuance of his new policy, Seward hastened to work out plans for an expedition to Pickens. On the same day that Lincoln ordered the preparation of the Sumter expedition, Seward sent for Captain Montgomery C. Meigs, and carried him to Lincoln for an interview. Meigs knew the Pickens situation well, and he spoke very convincingly of the ease with which an expedition could reinforce Pickens. The chief danger lay in the possibility that the Confederates would learn of the project and reduce the fort before aid could arrive. Therefore the major requirement of the expedition was secrecy.

Lincoln proved thoroughly receptive to the proposal. He acquiesced so readily, in fact, that, on the following morning, Seward was enabled to carry orders from Lincoln to General Scott for the preparation of an expedition to relieve Fort Pickens. Scott raised certain technical objections, but these were overruled. On March 31, Lincoln reviewed the plan again, and Scott was induced to approve it, with slight alterations.

On April 1, the project was again submitted to Lincoln for his final approval. In outline it called for troops to be

sent to Pickens by transport and to be thrown into the
fort. This operation required naval co-operation, which
was to be furnished by Lieutenant David D. Porter, who
was placed, by special and secret order, in command of a
vessel of his own choosing, the *Powhatan*. Lincoln adopted
the plan in this form and signed the necessary orders,
which had been drawn up by Seward. The expedition was
prepared accordingly, and Porter sailed with the *Powhatan* on April 6. On April 16 and 17, the reinforcements
arrived off Pensacola, and the troops were thrown into
the fort without the naval aid which had been thought
necessary.[67]

However the Sumter expedition had already sailed, and
the Confederates, in response to it, had already attacked
the fort. As a device to forestall the crisis at Charleston,
the Pickens expedition was, therefore, a failure. Had it
moved ten days earlier, it might have so bolstered the
prestige of the administration that the evacuation of
Sumter could have been afforded.

The story of Seward's effort to substitute Pickens for
Sumter as the point of focus for Unionism might end
here, were it not for the extremely curious events connected with the *Powhatan*. For Porter was not alone in
recognizing the availability of that vessel. Gideon Welles,
one must recall, was simultaneously fitting out the Sumter
expedition, and for this project he ordered the *Powhatan*
put in readiness.[68] He had no reason, of course, to suspect
that any naval orders were being issued without his knowl-

67. Letter of Meigs, in Seward, *Seward*, II, 538–540; brief account,
citing Meigs' diary and certain orders, in Nicolay and Hay, *Lincoln*, IV,
4–7; Morse, ed., *Welles Diary*, I, 25–32. The best account of this affair is
in Crawford, *Story of Sumter*, pp. 407–416. This narrative teems with
documents and contains certain undocumented statements which were
probably based on the record kept by Meigs in his diary. *Official Records,
Navy*, Ser. I, Vol. IV, pp. 107–109, shows orders by Scott, Apr. 1, for
reinforcement by the army, and a series of five special orders by Lincoln,
Apr. 1, to make the *Powhatan* available, to place Porter in command,
and to secure the compliance of Army and Navy officials.
68. Order of Welles to Brooklyn Navy Yard, Apr. 1, in *Official Records, Navy*, Ser. I, Vol. IV, p. 235.

edge. Thus, because of Lincoln's secret orders by which the Secretary of State administered important naval affairs, two expeditions were planned, in both of which the *Powhatan* had a key position. The result was a great deal of rather ludicrous confusion: the officials of the Brooklyn Navy Yard were torn between their conflicting orders from President and Secretary; yet they dared not tell the Navy Secretary of Lincoln's orders, for they were not sure that the President had not purposely concealed his action from Welles. Shortly after the *Powhatan* sailed, Lincoln learned of Welles' need for it, and told Seward to recall the ship;[69] Seward, accordingly, wrote to Porter a message which was delivered to him at sea by a fast tug. This said, "Deliver up the *Powhatan* to Captain Mercer. W. H. Seward";[70] but Porter, recognizing no responsibility to the Secretary of State, ignored the order and continued on his voyage to Pensacola.[71] Thus, when the Sumter expedition sailed, her flagship was on the way to Florida.

Gideon Welles, thoroughly angry at the ruin of his expedition, the disrespect shown by ignoring him in matters which concerned his own department, and the meddling of Seward, was not content to see in this episode, as an objective historian has seen, merely "administrative looseness . . . struggle for authority . . . interference . . . confusion . . . and inefficiency (some might say audacity)." [72] Instead, he regarded it as a deliberate plan on the part of the Secretary of State to prevent the relief of Sumter. Welles specifically charged Seward with being "aware" that "the *Powhatan* was the flagship . . . of the Sumter expedition." [73]

The claims of Welles were entirely circumstantial. Be-

69. Morse, ed., *Welles Diary*, I, 23–25.
70. For Seward's message, and reports concerning tug overtaking Porter, see *Official Records, Navy*, Ser. I, Vol. IV, 112, 239.
71. For Porter's message, refusing to return, see *ibid.*, Ser. I, Vol. IV, p. 112.
72. Randall, *Civil War and Reconstruction*, p. 239, note 9.
73. Morse, ed., *Welles Diary*, I, 24.

cause Seward was known to favor the evacuation of Sumter, Welles regarded it as especially sinister that Seward had acted secretly, and that Lincoln had signed, without scrutinizing them, the orders, prepared by Seward, for the expedition.[74] But while Welles' indignation is understandable, his accusations do not seem justified. Secrecy was undeniably necessary for the expedition, and while Welles was entitled to complain of a degree of concealment which excluded him from the transaction, he could not have denied that it was necessary to act without the knowledge of the Navy Department personnel, for he did not, at this time, trust his own subordinates.[75] As for the suggestion that Lincoln had not read the orders, this claim may have been invented by Lincoln to placate Welles, and even if it is true, it can hardly be charged against Seward. Certainly, Lincoln had approved the plan in all essentials, and if, as Welles admits, Lincoln did not realize that the *Powhatan* was intended for the Sumter expedition,[76] there is no reason to suppose that Seward would have realized it, especially since the orders of Welles, like those of Seward, were confidential. Moreover, it is by no means certain that Welles' plans for the use of the *Powhatan* had been formulated at the time when Seward formed his design to use the vessel.[77] Insofar as Seward was involved, the affair only shows that he was so intent on the Pickens expedition as to be utterly oblivious to other considerations.

One may disbelieve that, even in this moment of desperate gambling, Seward did anything so crafty and unscrupulous as deliberately to wreck an expedition ap-

74. *Ibid.,* I, 17–18.   75. *Ibid.,* I, 5.
76. *Ibid.,* I, 24.
77. When Lincoln issued orders, on Mar. 29, for the Sumter expedition, these orders called for the use of the *Pawnee,* the *Pocahontas,* and the *Harriet Lane.* On Apr. 1, Welles ordered the *Powhatan* prepared for service also, and, on the same day, Lincoln signed the order placing the *Powhatan* at Porter's command. *Official Records, Navy,* Ser. I, Vol. IV, pp. 108, 227–228, 229.

proved by his own administration. But he was undeniably desperate. He appears to have become progressively more rash and less sensitive to the fitness of things as the crisis deepened around him. His unwarranted pledges to the Confederate Commissioners, through Justice Campbell, for instance, crossed the line, which he had skirted all winter, between deviousness and deceitfulness. And, as April 1 came, he made one wild plunge which argued a temporary loss of the coolness and poise which had stood him in such good stead up to that time.

On the day stated, he submitted to Lincoln that curious document entitled, "Some thoughts for the President's consideration." But the thoughts which were suggested must have been very different from those intended by Seward. He suggested that the administration was without a policy and that one should be adopted—both domestic and foreign. As for the domestic problem, he would "CHANGE THE QUESTION BEFORE THE PUBLIC FROM ONE UPON SLAVERY, OR ABOUT SLAVERY, for a question upon UNION OR DISUNION." The Sumter question, he continued, "though not in fact a slavery or a party question, is so regarded." He favored abandoning Sumter, therefore, and, "For the rest, I would simultaneously defend and reenforce all the ports [forts] in the gulf." "This," he asserted, as if it were self-evident, "will raise distinctly the question of union or disunion." Then, almost incoherently, he added, "I would maintain every fort and possession in the South."

Thus far, Seward's program was nothing but a rather inferior repetition of ideas which he had expressed before. But when he turned to foreign policy, he advanced proposals which must have disappointed Lincoln as keenly as General Scott's political essay of three days before. With implicit reference to recent Spanish and French aggressions in San Domingo, Seward said, "I would demand explanations from Spain and France, categorically at once. . . .

"And if satisfactory explanations are not received from Spain and France,

"Would convene Congress and declare war against them.

"But whatever policy we adopt, there must be an energetic prosecution of it. . . .

"Either the President must do it himself, and be all the while active in it, or

"Devolve it on some member of his cabinet. Once adopted, debates on it must end, and all agree and abide.

"It is not in my especial province;

"But I neither seek to evade nor to assume responsibility."[78]

All too evidently, Seward was at the end of his tether, and his proposals were not significant except insofar as they indicate the exhaustion of Seward's hope, and the deterioration of his policy. However, it should not be supposed that these fantastic proposals represented an entirely new departure in Seward's thought. Certainly his readiness to direct the new administration had been expressed before, though never so frankly. As regards foreign policy, Seward had long been pondering the effect of a foreign war as the catalytic agent for reunion of North and South. At his appearance before the New England Society, in December, he had asserted that, if there were an invasion by "Louis Napoleon, or the Prince of Wales, or his mother, or the Emperor of Austria, all the hills of South Carolina would pour forth their population for the rescue of New York." [79] He did not, at that time, go so far as to express the hope that some of these crowned heads would intervene to stimulate the loyalty of Carolinians, but a month later he is said to have expressed to Rudolf Schleiden, minister of the Republic of Bremen, the conviction that "If the Lord would only give the United States

78. Seward's memorandum to Lincoln, Apr. 1, in Nicolay and Hay, eds., *Works of Lincoln,* VI, 234–236.

79. See above, p. 242.

an excuse for a war with England, France, or Spain, that would be the best means of reestablishing internal peace."[80] A little later, according to Schleiden, Seward expressed regret that there was no foreign complication which offered an excuse for embroilment.[81] It was Seward's nature, however, to spend no time repining, but to strive to create the situation which he desired. Accordingly, it appears that he comported himself in quite a bellicose manner. At a dinner at the British Embassy, on March 25, the ambassador, Lord Lyons, observed that "Mr. Seward . . . went off into a defiance of Foreign Nations, in a style of braggadocio which was formerly not uncommon with him, but which I had not heard before from him since he had been in office. Finding he was getting more and more violent and noisy, and saying things which it would be more convenient for me not to have heard, I took a natural opportunity of turning, as host, to speak to some of the ladies. . . ."[82] Lyons had already had occasion, in January, to observe that Seward regarded the relations between the United States and Great Britain as "good material to make political capital of." He had also shrewdly anticipated, at the same time, that the Republican administration would feel a "temptation . . . to endeavour to divert the public excitement to a foreign quarrel."[83]

Seward's proposal for a foreign war was, then, not an aberrant impulse. But it was a wild one, nevertheless. It was Seward's last writhing paroxysm in the struggle against circumstance. At the beginning of that struggle he had shown resourcefulness, poise, and technical skill.

80. Lutz, "Schleiden and the Visit to Richmond," in Am. Hist. Assn., *Report,* 1915, p. 210.   81. *Ibid.*

82. Lyons to Lord John Russell, Mar. 26, in Newton, *Lord Lyons,* I, 33.

83. Lyons to Lord John Russell, Jan. 7, in *ibid.,* I, 30.

Russell, *My Diary,* Apr. 4, I, 60, speaks of the strong language which Seward had used toward foreign governments. "Was it consciousness of the strength of a great people, who would be united by the first apprehension of foreign interference, or was it the peculiar emptiness of a bombast which is called Buncombe? In all sincerity, I think Mr. Seward meant it as it was written."

But as it approached the end, he had passed from cool daring to mere blind gambling. His former shrewd opportunism had descended to slap-dash improvisation, and what had once been bold imagination was now baseless phantasy. All in all, it was a pitiful end for a policy which had once halted the tide of secession.

While Seward plunged recklessly, mismanaging his own policies and those of Secretary Welles also, Lincoln pinned his hope for peace on a less spectacular and more practicable expedient. It had been his original purpose to hold Sumter without changing the status there. Anderson's necessity had frustrated this purpose, and he had sought some device by which he might abandon the fort without abandoning his policy. But as these efforts failed, he reverted, in effect, to his original policy. He would not disturb the status of Sumter, but, in order merely to preserve that status, he would send to the garrison such foodstuffs as were necessary to prevent it from being starved out.

Lincoln stated this policy flatly in his message, sent in conformity with Seward's pledge to Campbell that no expedition would go to Sumter without notice. The messenger was instructed to say to Governor Pickens: "I am directed by the President of the United States to notify you to expect an attempt will be made to supply Fort Sumter with provisions only; and that, if such attempt be not resisted, no effort to throw in men, arms, or ammunition will be made without further notice, or in case of an attack upon the fort." [84] In conformity with this promise, the officers of the Sumter expedition were ordered to confine themselves strictly to supplying the fort, unless resisted.[85]

84. Instructions of Lincoln to R. S. Chew, Apr. 6, in Nicolay and Hay, *Lincoln,* IV, 34.

85. Instructions of the War Department to G. V. Fox, Apr. 4, and of the Navy Department, to Captain Samuel Mercer, Apr. 5 ("The primary object of the expedition is to provision Fort Sumter. . . . Should the authorities at Charleston permit the fort to be supplied, no further particular service will be required of the force under your command."). *Official Records, Navy,* Ser. I, Vol. IV, pp. 232–235.

The Confederates, of course, regarded Federal control of a fort in a Confederate harbor as intolerable, which, from their standpoint, it certainly was. On their theory, the presence of the Federal force constituted an aggression, which justified them in launching an assault. Nevertheless, it is evident that the initiative in beginning active hostilities lay with them. This action, which necessarily assumed an aggressive form, inasmuch as Sumter's garrison received the attack on the defensive, appeared even more aggressive when it was pictured as an action, not to prevent reinforcement of the garrison, but to forestall the sending of food into the fort. This aspect of the Confederate operations against Sumter later served the Federal forces as a basis for claiming that the Confederacy began the war on the Union. Thus, the bombardment of Sumter gave an important advantage to Lincoln. One eminent Southern historian has argued that this advantage was not fortuitous, but was sought and gained by skillful maneuver,[86] deliberately intended to cause the South to initiate hostilities. This argument is constructed, for the most part, upon a demonstration that, if Lincoln expected war to begin, he might well have wished it to begin in this way, and upon a later statement by Orville H. Browning, who enjoyed a shade too much hindsight.

On July 3, 1861, Browning had an interview with Lincoln, who was his old friend. The conversation turned to the events leading to the outbreak of war, and Lincoln spoke freely of the troubles which he had experienced. Browning made a record of the conversation in his diary, and, according to that diary, Lincoln "himself conceived the idea, and proposed sending supplies, without an attempt to reinforce[,] giving notice of the fact to Gov[ernor] Pickins [sic] of S[outh] C[arolina]. The plan succeeded. They attacked Sumter—it fell, and thus, did more service than it otherwise could." [87]

86. Charles W. Ramsdell, "Lincoln and Fort Sumter," in *Jour. Southern Hist.*, III, 259–288.
87. Pease and Randall, eds., *O. H. Browning, Diary*, I, 476.

One wonders, of course, how correctly Browning understood Lincoln, how much interpretation he supplied, how
far he distorted his information in order to conceal from
himself the fact that his chief had adopted a policy which
failed and had become involved in a war which he sought
to avert. But despite all doubts, the Browning statement
is important, and might be convincing if it did not accord
so ill with all the circumstances.

Two unquestioned facts about the Sumter expedition
suggest that it was not a device for initiating war under
favorable terms. First, the notice to Governor Pickens,
with its potentialities for spurring him to aggressive action, was not planned by Lincoln himself, but was sent to
honor a pledge which had been almost wrung from Lincoln by Seward, in an effort to avert that very aggression
which Lincoln is supposed to have desired. Seward, in
turn, was, of all persons, least desirous of war; in fact, he
clung to his objective after hope was gone, and even sent
another peace agent to Richmond after the firing on
Sumter.[88] A vital part of the "plan" by which Lincoln
"goaded" the South to strike first was, therefore, not his
own contribution. Second, the expedition was withheld
until the fort was almost starved out, and it was withheld
because Lincoln still hoped that he could transfer the
issue of Union to Fort Pickens before the Sumter question
reached a crisis. Even beyond the point of safety, Lincoln
had delayed, hoping that a display of Federal authority
elsewhere would enable him to evacuate Fort Sumter.

If the assumption be made that Lincoln accepted the
necessity of war, it is easy to construct an argument to
show that his policy tended to initiate the war in a way
favorable to him: a Confederate attack to prevent food
from going to Sumter would constitute an offensive act;
therefore Lincoln, wishing to force the South to take the
offensive, sent food to Sumter. But assuming that Lincoln wanted to avert war, as other events indicate, it will

88. Lutz, "Schleiden and the Visit to Richmond," in Am. Hist. Assn.,
Report, 1915, pp. 209–216.

then appear that his policy offered maximum possibilities of avoiding conflict: a Confederate attack to prevent food from going to Sumter would constitute an offensive act; therefore Lincoln, wishing to save Sumter without a fight, sought to hold it by a policy so purely defensive that the South would hesitate to make an issue of it.[89] The fact that Lincoln's policy resulted in war does not necessarily mean that it was a war policy.

In the light of all the circumstances, it appears that the war which followed the bombardment of Sumter was, perhaps, the result of Republican misconceptions, but was certainly not the result of a deliberate war policy. Whether, in the language of Talleyrand, this misconception was a blunder worse than the crime of purposely provoking a war, is not a question for dogmatic answer. But at least, the two issues should not be confused.

From first to last, Republican policy was consistent. At the outset, party leaders jeered at the threat that the Southern states would secede. Later, when the threat was put into effect, they modified their previous incredulity only so far as to admit that Southern Unionism was temporarily overpowered, but they still insisted that delay

89. Proceeding from the hypothesis that Lincoln wished to induce the South to strike, Professor Ramsdell has said that the notice to Governor Pickens "carried a threat that force would be used if the provisions were not allowed to be brought in. It was a direct challenge." (Ramsdell, "Lincoln and Fort Sumter," in *Jour. Southern Hist.*, III, 280.) If one accepts the hypothesis, the validity of this statement clearly follows. But if one assumes a different hypothesis, that Lincoln wanted peace, it is then equally valid to say that the notice to Governor Pickens carried a promise that force would not be used, if provisions were allowed to be brought in. Conclusions based on alternative assumptions, therefore, prove nothing except that Lincoln's notice to Governor Pickens promised to be advantageous to him, no matter what happened. As Professor J. G. Randall effectively states it, "To say that Lincoln meant that the first shot would be fired by the other side *if a first shot was fired,* is by no means the equivalent of saying that he deliberately maneuvered to have the shot fired. This distinction is fundamental." (Randall, "When War Came in 1861," in *Abraham Lincoln Quarterly,* I [1940], 41. See entire discussion, pp. 23–42.)

and avoidance of friction would create a condition under which Unionists in the South could regain the ascendancy, and restore their states to the Union. Because of this belief, and not because of any choice of the alternative of war, Republican leaders refused to deal with any of the essential issues involved in the crisis, refused to make concessions on the vital territorial question, and confined their activities to a policy of maintaining the government's position and avoiding all causes of friction until the Southern reaction should set in.

Tactically, the policy was executed with great skill. Strategically, it was defective in that it overestimated the extent of Southern Unionism in some measure, and misconceived the character of Southern Unionism entirely. Therefore, it failed. But, to the end, the faith of Lincoln and Seward in the basic Unionism of the South was never entirely shattered. When Lincoln appealed to Congress on July 4, 1861, for the powers which would enable him to wage a titanic war to compel adherence to the Union, he still insisted that there was much loyalty to the United States within the Confederacy. Toward the end of his message he declared, "It may well be questioned whether there is today a majority of the legally qualified voters of any State, except perhaps South Carolina, in favor of disunion. There is much reason to believe that the Union men are the majority in many, if not in every one, of the so-called seceded States." [90]

In the months that followed, Lincoln exhibited great forbearance and charity toward the South. That he did so may not be entirely a consequence of his personal magnanimity. It may also have derived from a conviction that, if the matter had been handled differently—if, indeed, he had handled the matter differently—the conflict might have been averted. For he still continued to make affirmation of his faith in the policy that had failed, even when he accepted the alternative of war.

90. Message to Congress, July 4, 1861, in Nicolay and Hay, eds., *Works of Lincoln*, VI, 319.

BIBLIOGRAPHICAL NOTE

In such a study as this one, limited to a brief interval of time and concerned with matters which have been the subject of repeated narration, the success of the investigation depends less upon the exploitation of unused sources, than upon the close and critical scrutiny, dissection, and comparison of the sources already known. Over a long period of time, a vast body of source material has become available. Much of it, although relevant, has never been used to illuminate the question of Republican policy on matters which were probably the most important in the history of the party. My purpose has been to utilize this material in an intensive study of the viewpoint, intentions, and activities of Lincoln and the Republican leaders in the crisis preceding the Civil War. For this purpose, information has been drawn from extremely varied sources, which are indicated by footnotes in the text. Instead of providing a catalog of all of these items, this bibliography is confined to a discussion of the more valuable sources.

MANUSCRIPTS

The unpublished materials which I have used are chiefly the Pierce, Breckinridge, Van Buren, Crittenden, Trumbull, Blair, and Chase MSS. in the Library of Congress. It will be observed that, of these collections, only the last three embody matter which is subjectively Republican. However, it is frequently true that the shrewdest comments on Republican maneuvers were made by those outside of the party ranks.

Also, it has been impossible to evaluate any Republican attitude or measure without constant reference to the general conditions with which Lincoln and Seward were attempting to deal. Inasmuch as their policy was based upon a belief that the Unionism of the South would cause the internal collapse of secession, it has been especially necessary to examine this belief in the light of actual conditions in the South. The necessity of distinguishing between things as they seemed to Lincoln, things as they were, and things as they later appeared by hindsight, has required the scrutiny of many sources that were not directly pertinent to the program of Lincoln and the Republicans.

Of the manuscripts used, the Breckinridge papers were, perhaps, least fruitful, for they contain no material representing John C. Breckinridge during the secession crisis. However, Rev. Robert J. Breckinridge was an active protagonist of measures of adjustment between North and South, and the numerous letters to him are of some value. The correspondence of Franklin Pierce for this period is not voluminous, but it gives a very good insight into the viewpoint of Northern Democratic sympathizers with the South—if not with secession. The Van Buren MSS. also are very limited in the quantity of relevant material, but the quality is good, for there is a heavy representation of letters from the Blairs, and Van Buren's own comments show striking astuteness.

The Crittenden collection far overshadows any of these others. Because of Crittenden's leadership of the compromise movement, his correspondence swelled to unusual dimensions and embraced a body of men widely distributed and of a high average of distinction. While few of the writers were men of national reputation, they were figures of local prominence, and, often, of political sagacity. An unusually high percentage of them are listed in standard biographical dictionaries. Their comments are important in showing the position of the moderates in general, and especially the attitude of the Border states, which Republican leaders never understood.

The Blair papers include many letters between members of the family. These show the characteristic Blair fondness for drastic action (in this case, against the secessionists), but they are less truly representative of radical opinion than the Chase and Trumbull correspondence. Both of these collections are debased in quality by the copiousness of appeals from officeseekers. Omitting these, there is an excellent body of letters from Republican radicals, both major and minor. No source shows better than these the nature of the partisanship which Lincoln and Seward always confronted on their left wing.

There are other manuscript materials which, for one reason or another, have not been consulted. The Lincoln collection, in the Library of Congress, remains closed until 1947, and impatient scholars must wait until then to know whether Nicolay and Hay, who had access to the 12,000 items of that collection, skimmed the cream from it. It is known that this collection contains scarcely any unpublished letters by Lincoln himself, but it is believed that many revealing letters *to* Lincoln may be exposed. Anyone who has used Nicolay and Hay's edition of Lincoln's works will appreciate the value which would lie in a knowledge of the letters to which he was replying. Next to the Lincoln papers, the papers of William H. Seward, in the possession of his descendants, are probably most valuable for the purposes of this study. They have been so freely used by Frederick Seward and by Bancroft, in their lives of Seward, that it seemed unnecessary to seek access to them, especially since Bancroft published the full text of a group of particularly pertinent letters in his appendix. Charles Francis Adams was less important personally than some other leaders, but, because of his intimate association with Seward during the winter of 1860–1861, and because of his family's penchant for making and keeping written records, his diary and letters would probably be more useful than any other undisclosed source. They are deposited in the Massachusetts Historical Society Library, but like the Lincoln collection, they are not at present accessible.

NEWSPAPERS

By 1860, American journalism had begun to make free use of the telegraphic dispatch and the special correspondent. Political speeches, meetings, letters, or even rumors, received detailed attention. Because of these features, newspaper files are an invaluable source for the developments of the secession crisis. Editorial bias was strong, but was not concealed, and therefore can easily be discounted.

To see themselves as others saw them, Lincoln and the Republicans had only to read the New York *Herald*. James Gordon Bennett's paper was violently and unscrupulously Democratic, but it possessed an unsurpassed news coverage. Files of the *Herald* have been drawn upon freely in this study. In contrast to the *Herald*, Horace Greeley's New York *Tribune* was the oracle of the anti-slavery and anti-compromise Republicans, and it, too, was alert for news. More moderate Republicanism found expression in the New York *Times*, under the editorship of Henry J. Raymond. The most conservative phase of Republican thought was expressed by the Albany *Evening Journal*, which was the personal instrument of Thurlow Weed. These journals have been utilized for both their news and their editorials. In addition, the Boston *Advertiser* has been used in a more special sense, for a series of letters which Henry Adams contributed to it. Other newspapers have been used occasionally, as indicated in the footnotes. For a varied range of editorial opinion, there are copious selections of editorials in book form, by Dumond and by Perkins. These are discussed immediately below.

GENERAL SOURCE COLLECTIONS

Among the best of reprinted sources are the one-volume collection of *Southern Editorials on Secession* (New York, 1931), edited by Dwight L. Dumond, and its more recent and more extensive counterpart, *Northern Editorials on Secession* (New York, 1942), in two volumes edited by Howard C. Perkins. Together, these two works contain 678 editorials from 218 newspapers. Perkins' work came off the press shortly before this book went on, and it could not be utilized as fully as Dumond's. However, Dr. Perkins had previously allowed me to consult his manuscript thesis on "The Northern Press On Approaching Civil War" (Yale), and this opportunity compensated in a measure for the fact that I was not able to draw upon his selected editorials.

Except for newspapers, probably no source offers such a wide range of viewpoints and material of such uneven value as the *Congressional Globe*. Every shade of opinion found its expression —sometimes its definitive expression—on the floor of the Senate or the House. Often, a roll-call vote provided the best available index of Republican sentiment upon a question. At times, the action of Congress was the manifestation of party policy. For these reasons, the *Globe* is indispensable. In a lesser degree, the *Journals* of the select committees of Thirteen, in the Senate, and of Thirty-three, in the House, are also important, though they contain no report of the debates in committee. As a supplement to the proceedings in Congress, the record of the Washington Peace Convention is also pertinent. L. E. Chittenden, a member of this body, published its proceedings, with a full transcript of debates, in *A Report of the Debates and Proceedings in the Secret Sessions of the Conference Convention . . . Held at Washington, D. C. in February, A.D. 1861* (New York, 1864).

Before passing to works of more limited scope, the greatest of all Civil War source collections should be mentioned. This is

the 128-volume compilation entitled *The War of the Rebellion
. . . Official Records of the Union and Confederate Armies* (Washington, 1880–1901). The documents included are, of course, primarily military, but the first volume is essential for the history of the situation at Fort Sumter and Fort Pickens, and unexpected bits of relevant material occur in the later volumes. The companion series of *Official Records of the Union and Confederate Navies in the War of the Rebellion* (26 vols., Washington, 1894–1922), is also important.

BIOGRAPHIES, MEMOIRS, DIARIES, LETTERS, COLLECTED WORKS

In discussing the literature relating to individual participants in the events of the secession crisis, it is impossible to establish a rigid distinction between source materials and secondary treatments. For instance, Baker's *Works of Seward* is clearly a collection of sources. Frederick W. Seward's *Seward at Washington*, on the other hand, has the form of a secondary biography. Yet, in it, the narrative is little more than a thread, upon which Seward's letters are strung like beads. Even when the narrative predominates, it is the record made by a man who lived in intimate personal association with Seward. In this study, I have taken care to rely solely upon source material, whatever its context, and therefore no sweeping distinction will be attempted between volumes where source material alone appears, and those where source material is mingled with other matter which has not been used.

Because of their position as Lincoln's secretaries, and later, as his official biographers, John G. Nicolay and John Hay enjoyed an intimate personal knowledge of Lincoln, and a virtual monopoly upon the use of his papers. These papers, together with other documents, were used freely in the preparation of their ten-volume biography, entitled *Abraham Lincoln, A History* (New York, 1890). Although partisan and adulatory in tone, this work was of great value because of the source materials which it incorporated. As a complement to their biographical history, Nicolay and Hay also edited the *Works of Abraham Lincoln*. This collection has been through several editions, of which the Thomas-Tandy edition (12 vols., New York, 1905) is perhaps the best. These two sets of volumes remain the cornerstone for all research on Lincoln.

Fortunately, others who knew Lincoln viewed him less reverently than did his secretaries. One such figure was his law partner, William H. Herndon, who, with Jesse W. Weik, wrote the classic *History and Personal Recollections of Abraham Lincoln* (Chicago, 1888). Another intimate of Lincoln was Ward Hill Lamon, who secured the collaboration of Chauncey F. Black as a silent partner in writing his *Life of Abraham Lincoln: From his Birth to his Inauguration as President* (Boston, 1872). Both of these works contain brief but valuable information on Lincoln during the winter before the war. Other reminiscent accounts, which do not deal with this period, need not be mentioned here, but two recent publications are pertinent. These are *Lincoln and the Civil War in the Diaries and Letters of John Hay* (New York, 1939), edited by Tyler Dennett, and *Lincoln on the Eve of '61* (New York, 1941), edited by Harold G. and Oswald Garrison Villard. The latter consists of a selection from the dispatches which Henry Villard wrote from Springfield to the New York *Herald* during the period when Lincoln was President-elect. For research purposes, reliance should be placed not upon these interesting selections, but upon the entire body of dispatches which appear in the *Herald*.

Among the scores of later writers on Lincoln, the general biographers have dealt superficially with the period when he was President-elect, and the specialists have not concerned themselves with his policy toward the secessionists. Even in so full and ably written an account as Carl Sandburg's *Abraham Lincoln, The War Years* (4 vols., New York, 1939), the emphasis is placed upon a narration of events, rather than upon the analysis of what Lincoln was attempting to do during this period.

Lincoln's own writings, as collected by Nicolay and Hay, have been supplemented by Paul M. Angle's *New Letters and Papers of Lincoln* (Boston, 1930), by Gilbert A. Tracy's *Uncollected Letters of Abraham Lincoln* (Boston, 1917), by Emanuel Hertz' *Abraham Lincoln, A New Portrait* (2 vols., New York, 1931), by the appendix to Ida Tarbell's *Life of Abraham Lincoln* (2 vols., New York, 1899), and by *Lincoln Letters Hitherto Unpublished, in the Library of Brown University and Other Providence Libraries* (Providence, 1927). The letters compiled by Tracy were of especial value for this study. For a critical discussion of the Lincoln bibliography, see J. G. Randall, "Has the Lincoln Theme Been Exhausted," in *American Historical Review*, XLI (1936), 270–294.

The only person of influence comparable to Lincoln's was William H. Seward. He, too, is the subject of several useful works. These include: George E. Baker, *The Works of William H. Seward* (5 vols., Boston, 1853–1884), containing nearly all of his speeches and other formal pronouncements; Frederick W. Seward's memoir, entitled *Seward at Washington* (2 vols., New York, 1891)—a work which has been much neglected by scholars who could have used effectively the copious extracts from Seward's personal letters; and Frederic Bancroft's able, thorough *Life of William H. Seward* (2 vols., New York, 1900). Seward and Weed were so intimate that works on the two men are reciprocally indispensable. Thus, along with the works on Seward, Weed's *Autobiography* (Boston, 1883), edited by his daughter, Harriet A. Weed, and the *Memoir* (Boston, 1884) of him by his grandson, Thurlow Weed Barnes, require to be mentioned. The latter contains many letters.

Next to the works on Lincoln and Seward, I have relied most heavily on a number of accounts of the activity of Charles Francis Adams, written by his sons, Henry and Charles Francis, Jr. In lieu of his own papers, these are excellent substitutes, for the young men were well informed on their father's extremely significant alliance with Seward. In addition to Henry Adams' letters in the Boston *Advertiser*, there is also a series of intimate letters to Charles Francis, Jr., in Worthington C. Ford's edition of the *Letters of Henry Adams (1858–1891)* (Boston, 1930); there is a narrative entitled, "The Secession Winter, 1860–61," written soon after the crisis, but not published in the Massachusetts Historical Society *Proceedings*, Vol. XLIII, until 1910. By Charles Francis, Jr., there is his own ably written and extremely incisive *Charles Francis Adams, 1835–1915, An Autobiography* (Boston, 1916), and his less finished life of his father, ambiguously entitled *Charles Francis Adams* (Boston, 1900).

These important works are accompanied by valuable books on many other leaders of the Republican party. On the right wing of the party, Edward Bates is represented by his own *Diary*, fully edited by Howard Beale for the American Historical Association, *Report*, 1930. *The Diary of Gideon Welles* (3 vols., Boston, 1911), edited by John T. Morse, Jr., is more elaborate, but the text for the period prior to August, 1861, is not a true diary. It was written several years later, but is nevertheless an important source. The papers of Hamilton Fish bulk too large for publication, but have been used effectively in Allan

Nevins' *Hamilton Fish* (New York, 1936). Hannibal Hamlin is commemorated in a *Life and Times* (Cambridge, 1899), by Charles E. Hamlin. Orville H. Browning is represented by an unusually full *Diary*, which has been published under the editorship of Theodore C. Pease and J. G. Randall, in the Illinois Historical Collections, Vols. XX, XXII (1927–1933). Francis Fessenden contributed a *Life and Public Services of William Pitt Fessenden* (2 vols., Boston, 1907). These works give rather complete insight into the attitude of the Republican moderates, and those who tended to be moderate.

Of course, no arbitrary line can be drawn between Republican moderates and radicals, but it seems valid to say that the radical position finds expression in John Bigelow's *Retrospections of an Active Life* (5 vols., New York, 1909–1913). This is less because of Bigelow's own attitude than because of the many letters from Preston King, which Bigelow published in his work. The *Life of Lyman Trumbull* (Boston, 1913), by Horace White, and the *Life of James W. Grimes* (New York, 1876), by William Salter, present the careers of two senators who were inclined to be radical. O. J. Hollister's *Life of Schuyler Colfax* (New York, 1886), portrays one of the leaders of the radical group in the House of Representatives. There are a number of books on Salmon P. Chase, but the secession months receive scant treatment in all of them.

The attitude of the extreme radicals is well displayed in William Ernest Smith's study of *The Blair Family in Politics* (2 vols., New York, 1933), and in Grace Julian Clarke's *George W. Julian* (Indianapolis, 1923)—again, with letters. It is set forth even more fully in two works on Charles Sumner, one the long and fully documented *Memoir and Letters of Charles Sumner* (4 vols., Boston, 1877–1893), by E. L. Pierce; the other, a brief but extremely searching paper by Laura A. White, entitled "Charles Sumner and the Crisis of 1861," in *Essays in Honor of William E. Dodd* (Chicago, 1936), edited by Avery Craven.

Altogether, these works furnish material for a complete elaboration of all aspects of Republican thought. But it is often true that the observations and activities of individuals outside of the Republican ranks must be taken into account before the position of the party can be properly understood. This outside view is shown with especial effectiveness in Mrs. Chapman Coleman, *Life of John J. Crittenden* (2 vols., Philadelphia, 1871), which bristles with selections from the Crittenden correspondence. A similar insight into "Union-saving" activities is furnished by the privately printed *Letters, Speeches, and Addresses of August Belmont* (1890). The varied aspects of Democratic statesmanship appear, for the Southern Democrats, in Ulrich B. Phillips' *Life of Robert Toombs* (New York, 1913), and in his edition of *The Correspondence of Robert Toombs, Alexander H. Stephens, and Howell Cobb*, in the American Historical Association *Report* for 1911. Additional insight into southern attitudes may be gained from Percy Scott Flippen, *Herschel V. Johnson of Georgia, State Rights Unionist* (privately printed, 1931). The voluminous writings by and about Jefferson Davis and Alexander H. Stephens are more concerned with the right of secession than with the reason for it, and are, therefore, of little value for this study. The importance, within the Confederacy, of schemes to reconstruct the Union, is vividly shown in Laura A. White's *Robert Barnwell Rhett, Father of Secession* (New York, 1931), and in "The Correspondence of Thomas Reade Rootes Cobb, 1860–1862," in Southern Historical Association *Publications*, XI (1907).

For the northern Democrats, there is a paucity of good material, except on James Buchanan. John Bassett Moore's edition of *The Works of James Buchanan* (12 vols., Philadelphia, 1908–1911), contains many letters, and also the text of Buchanan's own *Mr. Buchanan's Administration on the Eve of the Rebellion*. Buchanan's Postmaster General, Horatio King, wrote a defense of his chief under the title, *Turning on the Light: A Dispassionate Survey of President Buchanan's Administration from 1860 to its Close* (Philadelphia, 1895). It is valuable chiefly for documents which it contains. George T. Curtis' *Life of James Buchanan* (2 vols., New York, 1883), also contains material on the secession crisis. Buchanan's only modern advocate has been Philip Auchampaugh, whose *James Buchanan and his Cabinet on the Eve of Secession* (privately printed, 1926) deserves notice.

The only important life of Stephen A. Douglas is that by George Fort Milton. Entitled *The Eve of Conflict: Stephen A. Douglas and the Needless War* (Boston, 1934), this volume is based upon a large collection of papers previously unused. Although sometimes factually inaccurate, it is the best study of the Northern Democracy. Also by George Fort Milton is a paper on "Stephen A. Douglas' Efforts for Peace," in the *Journal of Southern History*, I (1935), 261–275.

Further material on the Northern Democrats may be garnered from the contemporary reminiscences of S. S. Cox, entitled *Three Decades of Federal Legislation* (Providence, 1885), and from the incisive biography of *Jeremiah Sullivan Black* (Philadelphia, 1934), by William N. Brigance.

Two other diaries should be mentioned, though their authors defy classification. One of these, *My Diary, North and South* (2 vols., London, 1863), by William H. Russell, shows the reactions of an experienced Englishman to Lincoln, Seward, and others whom he met personally. The other was by the anonymous "Public Man," whose existence historians have doubted, and whose lively passages they have quoted ever since "The Diary of a Public Man" appeared in the *North American Review*, Vol. CXXIX, in 1879.

SECONDARY MATERIALS: GENERAL ACCOUNTS AND MONOGRAPHIC STUDIES

In the chapters of this book, I have refrained from discussing the background of sectional antagonism that preceded secession. I have attempted no verdict as to the repressibility of the conflict, nor as to the greater issues that were involved in it. But it may not be amiss to indicate a number of papers which have dealt most effectively with these inexhaustible topics. Four such papers of major importance have appeared in the *Journal of Southern History*. These are, "The Coming of the War between the States," II (1936), 303–322, by Avery Craven; "The Changing Interpretation of the Civil War," III (1937), 3–27, by Charles W. Ramsdell; "The Civil War Restudied," VI (1940), 439–457, by J. G. Randall; and "The Fundamental Cause of the Civil War: Egocentric Sectionalism," VII (1941), 3–18, by Frank L. Owsley. In "The Nationalistic Tradition of the Civil War," *South Atlantic Quarterly*, XXII (1933), 294–305, Richard H. Shryock discussed the cost and the value of preserving the Union, but he wrote before the struggle with totalitarianism had demonstrated the full importance of union for the American people. Arthur C. Cole and J. G. de Roulhac Hamilton presented negative and affirmative responses to the question, "Lincoln's Election an Immediate Menace to Slavery in the States?" in the *American Historical Review*, XXXVI (1931), 740–767, and XXXVII (1932), 700–711. J. G. Randall deals more directly with the immediate preliminaries of the conflict in "When War Came in 1861," *Abraham Lincoln Quarterly*, I (1940), 3–42. Short interpretative volumes are *The Course of the South to Secession* (New York, 1939), by Ulrich B. Phillips, and *Antislavery Origins of the Civil War in the United States* (Ann Arbor, 1939), by Dwight L. Dumond. These books and papers subject many historical stereotypes to reexamination; they offer fruitful and unfamiliar interpretations; and, collectively, they provide an excellent introduction to the history of the sectional crisis.

Of the dozens of factual narratives which relate the events of the secession winter, probably no brief account is as satisfactory as that of J. G. Randall in *The Civil War and Reconstruction* (New York, 1927). Despite the passage of years and the opening of new sources, James Ford Rhodes' *History of the United States from the Compromise of 1850* (New York, 1893–1906) still contains one of the fullest and best treatments of the critical months preceding the war. Another general item of especial value is Arthur C. Cole, *The Irrepressible Conflict, 1850–1865* (New York, 1934). Although concerned primarily with social history, Professor Cole's study contains able summaries of several topics which are pertinent to this volume.

In the field of monographic studies, the history of secession has received much more satisfactory treatment than either the compromise movement or the policies of Northern groups. The best general account of secession is Dwight L. Dumond's study, which bears the inclusive title, *The Secession Movement, 1860–1861* (New York, 1931), although it is confined to the secession of the lower South. The upper South, however, is well represented by two able monographs on secession in individual states: Henry T. Shanks' *The Secession Movement in Virginia, 1842–1861* (Richmond, 1934), and Joseph Carlyle Sitterson, *The Secession Movement in North Carolina* (Chapel Hill, 1939). A number of other accounts deal with secession in various states. Perhaps the best of these are P. L. Rainwater, *Mississippi, Storm Center of Secession, 1856–1861* (Baton Rouge, 1938), and Clarence P. Denman, *The Secession Movement in Alabama* (Montgomery, 1933). Others are indicated in footnotes for chapters VIII and XI. In attempting to estimate the practicability of Lincoln's plan to appeal to the Unionism of the South, Lillian A. Kibler, "Unionist Sentiment in South Carolina in 1860," in *Journal of Southern History*, IV (1938), 346–366, is especially significant.

On the history of Fort Sumter, the most valuable work is Samuel W. Crawford's *The Genesis of the Civil War, The Story of Sumter* (New York, 1887). Because of his presence at Sumter and his generous inclusion of documents, Crawford's account is a source, as well as a secondary narrative. A recent volume, *Lincoln Takes Command* (Chapel Hill, 1941), by John Shipley Tilley, presents an extreme pro-Southern version of the events at Forts Pickens and Sumter. This account suffers from the fact that the author writes of the events at Charleston and Pensacola without reference to the situation in Washington. He ignores, for instance, the divergence of views between Lincoln and Seward, and their common anxiety to shift the focus of attention away from Fort Sumter. For further comment see the note to Chapter XII. A more restrained statement of the case against Lincoln appears in "Lincoln and Fort Sumter," in *Journal of Southern History*, III (1937), 259–288, by Charles W. Ramsdell.

On the compromise movement, there are two monographs: *The Peaceable Americans of 1860–1861*, in Columbia University *Studies in History, Economics, and Public Law*, Vol. XCVI, No. 3, by Mary Scrugham; and *Immediate Pre-Civil War Compromise Efforts*, in George Peabody College for Teachers, *Contributions to Education*, No. 131 (1934), by Gilbert Graffenreid Glover. The former of these offers valuable comments on certain aspects of the compromise movement, without providing adequate treatment of the movement as a whole. The latter contains little that cannot be found in other secondary works, and it lacks essential background—for instance, it fails to distinguish between Republicans and abolitionists. Various aspects of the compromise movement are treated in "The Final Efforts at Compromise, 1860–61," in *Political Science Quarterly*, VI (1891), 401–423, by Frederic Bancroft; in "The Possibilities of Compromise in the Senate Committee of Thirteen and the Responsibility for Failure," in *Journal of Negro History*, XVII (1932), 437–465, by Clinton E. Knox; and in "The Responsibility for the Failure of Compromise in 1860," in *Historical Outlook*, XIV (1923), 85–93, by W. E. Tilberg.

Throughout the secession crisis, Lincoln, Seward, and other Republican leaders were subjected to heavy pressure from commercial interests which desired a conciliatory policy, and from the radical Republicans who advocated a coercive program. Two recent studies tell, for the first time, the story of these pressure groups. Philip S. Foner's *Business & Slavery: The New York Merchants & the Irrepressible Conflict* (Chapel Hill, 1941), contains chapters on the exertions of capitalistic interests in behalf of compromise. T. Harry Williams' *Lincoln and the Radicals* (Madison, 1941), begins with the outbreak of war, and therefore omits the story of radical opposition to compromise. Although not directly pertinent to this study, it shows the ultimate development of that antagonism between moderate and radical Republicans which impinged upon Lincoln's policy from the day of his election.

INDEX

Corwin, Thomas, 292, 300; political background of, 21; on negrophiles, 37n; member, committee of 33, 91; resolution and speech in committee of 33, 99; intermediary between Lincoln and Gilmer, 144; corresponds with Lincoln, 156

Cox, S. S., on Republican trend toward compromise, 179

Craft, Addison, belief in voluntary reconstruction, 227

Crawford, Martin J., Confederate States Commissioner, 342; negotiations with Campbell, 346

Crittenden, John J., coalition with Seward and Douglas, 26–27; proposed by Blairs for Republican nomination, 32n; feared by Kentucky Republicans, 37; career of, 102; character of, 102; compromise plans attributed to, 103–104; leads compromise movement, 111; and Douglas, 103; methods in Senate, 104; introduces compromise resolutions, 105; member, committee of 13, 111; supported by capitalists, 120; suggested for cabinet, 148; on support of compromise, by Republicans, 192, by North, 195; on attitude of Southerners toward compromise, 204n, 205; on Republican incredulity of secession, 235; reaction to Seward's speech of Jan. 12, 287; alliance with Seward and Douglas, 303–306
See also Crittenden Compromise

Crittenden Compromise, introduced, 105; terms of, 105–108, discussed, 108–110; Lincoln disapproves of, 145; reasons for Lincoln's disapproval of, 219; defeated in committee of 13, 171–172; causes for defeat of, in committee of 13, 181–184; consideration of, defeated in Senate, 184; responsibility of South in defeat of, 204–207; supported by petitions and mass meetings, 198–199; attitude of South toward, 200–207; support of, by Republicans, 191–192; support of, by North, 195–200; Republican fear of slavery expan-

sion under, 222–223; encourages Southern filibustering, 219–220; vote on, in House, 302, in Senate, 302

Croswell, Edwin, supports Crittenden, 120

Cuba, attempts to annex, 220–221

Curry, Jabez L. M., threatens secession in campaign of 1860, 4

Curtis, George William, prevented from speaking, 199

Curtis, Samuel R., conciliatory speech of, in committee of 33, 99; favors compromise, 126

Customs duties, Lincoln's policy on collection of, 325–327

Dakota territory, organized without slavery restriction, 277–278

Dana, Charles A., connects Seward with Weed's compromise plan, 84

Davis, Charles Augustus, on commercial crisis of 1861, 119; supports Crittenden, 120; belief in voluntary reconstruction, 236; on need for retaining Border, 283

Davis, David, suggests Southerners for cabinet, 152

Davis, Garrett, belief in voluntary reconstruction, 227; interview with Lincoln, 354

Davis, Henry Winter, 299; rivalry with Blairs, 38; W. C. Snethen on, 38; alliance with Seward, 285
   In committee of 33, member, 91; resolutions on fugitive slave issue, 100; resolutions on New Mexico and Kansas, 290–292; alliance with Republican members, 291; vote on resolutions, 294

Davis, Jefferson, threatens secession in campaign of 1860, 4; belief in voluntary reconstruction, 227
   In committee of 13, member, 110; action on Crittenden resolutions, 171, 172; responsibility in defeat of compromise, 204–207
   As Confederate president, policy of voluntary reconstruction, 230–232; policy criticized, 231–232; assured of Republican goodwill, 343;

THE YALE PAPERBOUNDS

YALE WESTERN AMERICANA PAPERBOUNDS